Brimming with creative inspiration, how-to projects, and useful information to enrich your everyday life, Quarto Knows is a favorite destination for those pursuing their interests and passions. Visit our site and dig deeper with our books into your area of interest: Quarto Creates, Quarto Cooks, Quarto Homes, Quarto Lives, Quarto Drives, Quarto Explores, Quarto Gifts, or Quarto Kids.

First Published in 2021 by Motorbooks, an imprint of The Quarto Group, 100 Cummings Center, Suite 265-D, Beverly, MA 01915, USA.
T (978) 282-9590 F (978) 283-2742 QuartoKnows.com

Motorbooks titles are also available at discount for retail, wholesale, promotional, and bulk purchase. For details, contact the Special Sales Manager by email at specialsales@quarto.com or by mail at The Quarto Group, Attn: Special Sales Manager, 100 Cummings Center, Suite 265-D, Beverly, MA 01915, USA.

25 24 23 22 21   1 2 3 4 5

ISBN: 978-0-7603-6905-0

Digital edition published in 2021
eISBN: 978-0-7603-6906-7

Library of Congress Cataloging-in-Publication Data

Names: Smale, Glen, author.
Title: Porsche at Le Mans : 70 years / Glen Smale.
Description: Beverly, MA : Motorbooks, 2021. | Includes index.
Identifiers: LCCN 2021004675 (print) | LCCN 2021004676 (ebook) | ISBN 9780760369050 (hardcover) | ISBN 9780760369067 (ebook)
Subjects: LCSH: 24 Heures du Mans (Automobile race)--History--Pictorial works. | Porsche automobiles--Pictorial works.
Classification: LCC GV1034.48.L4 S63 2021 (print) | LCC GV1034.48.L4 (ebook) | DDC 796.720944/17--dc23
LC record available at https://lccn.loc.gov/2021004675
LC ebook record available at https://lccn.loc.gov/2021004676

Acquiring Editor: Dennis Pernu
Design and page layout: Evelin Kasikov

Printed in China

Front dustjacket: *John Brooks*
Front cover: *Corporate Archives Porsche AG*
Front endpapers: *Fred Ihrt/LightRocket via Getty Images*
Rear endpapers: *Dean Treml/Red Bull via Getty Images*
Rear cover: *Corporate Archives Porsche AG*
Rear dustjacket: *Corporate Archives Porsche AG*
Half Title: *Corporate Archives Porsche AG*

PORSCHE AT LE MANS

70 YEARS

GLEN SMALE

motorbooks

Contents

CHAPTER 1

1950s

Edgar Barth leaps into the No. 34 Porsche 718 RSK (chassis 006) driven by him and Wolfgang Seidel in 1959. It is hard to imagine the same level of athleticism at the start of a top-level race like this today, although the ACO did reintroduce a symbolic reenactment of this sprint for the 2010 race. The No. 34 car (Sports 1500 class) retired on lap 168 with gearbox problems. *Corporate Archives Porsche AG*

Testing the Waters

With the end of the World War II, a great weight had been lifted from people's lives and a new decade beckoned with fresh possibilities. The late 1940s and early 1950s saw many changes in the automobile industry, with many new manufacturers springing up across western Europe and Great Britain, since engineering innovations and solutions that had been developed during the war years were now applied to the production of materials and products.

One company that had its roots in prewar Germany, *Dr. Ing. h.c. F. Porsche GmbH Konstruktion und Beratung für Motoren- und Fahrzeugbau* (Dr. Ing. h.c. F. Porsche GmbH Construction and Consultancy for Engines and Vehicles) was established in Stuttgart on April 25, 1931. To meet the demand for design and engineering, a new manufacturing plant was built in the Zuffenhausen district of Stuttgart in 1938 by Dr. Ferdinand Porsche, where the forerunner of the Volkswagen Type 1 (known to all as the Beetle) was first produced in June of that year.

As air raids over Stuttgart increased in intensity during the early 1940s, it became increasingly difficult for the company to continue its activities there, and Porsche was forced to relocate its operations to the town of Gmünd in the Austrian province of Carinthia in the autumn of 1944. It was here that the production of the first Type 356/2 coupes and cabriolets began in the second half of 1948.

Designed and constructed by Erwin Komenda, the company's director of body development, both the prototype 356 No. 1 (registration K45-286) and the Type 356/2 featured advanced, streamlined aluminum bodies. Unlike the first midengine prototype (356 No. 1), which was formed around a tubular steel framework, the Type 356/2 was based on a VW platform, with its engine fitted behind the rear axle to provide greater luggage space behind the front seats and to offer better traction in muddy and snowy conditions.

Following the cessation of hostilities in 1945, Porsche sought to return to Stuttgart, where a better industrial infrastructure favored the manufacture of automobiles. The company's former plant in Zuffenhausen was being used by the Americans and was therefore unavailable, so Ferry Porsche rented 600 square meter production hall from Karosseriewerke Reutter & Co. GmbH, a coachbuilder in Stuttgart-Zuffenhausen. This temporary inconvenience worked out well for the company, with Reutter commissioned to build the first consignment of five hundred Porsche car bodies. The Stuttgart coachbuilder had no experience in welding light alloy, which forced the company to switch to steel, offering the dual advantage of being cheaper and in greater supply than aluminum; it also gave the bodies increased rigidity.

Before there had been sufficient time for the factory to realize the true motorsports potential of the 356, several privateers began experimenting with the sports cars by modifying and further streamlining the bodies of their Porsches. As a result, Porsche's relationship with a number of privateer racers who had seen the race potential of the 356—namely Porsche distributor Walter Glöckler and Heinrich Sauter—began to bear fruit after recording some positive performances.

The decade of the 1950s was certainly one of the most experimental periods in motorsports: aerodynamics and airflow influenced race car design more than it had at any time in the past. In 1950, the Cunningham-entered Cadillac *Le Monstre* took this relatively new science to the extreme, but, with its classic design, the graceful Jaguar XK120 of 1951 epitomized the style of sports racing cars to come, replacing the traditional cycle-winged and upright racers of the 1940s with more streamlined, smoother bodies that offered less wind resistance.

1951

June 23–24

The first running of the twenty-four-hour endurance race at Le Mans after World War II took place in 1949. When Le Mans race organizer Charles Faroux met with Dr. Porsche and son, Ferry Porsche Jr., at the Paris Motor Show in 1950, Faroux was able to persuade them to consider entering a pair of 356s in the following year's event. Despite his poor state of health, the senior Porsche could clearly see the benefit that such international exposure would bring the fledgling company.

French Porsche importer Auguste Veuillet needed little convincing, and he wasted no time signing up fellow French driver Edmond Mouche to partner with him in the race. Fortunately, Porsche still had several unsold aluminum-bodied Gmünd coupes following the introduction of the steel-bodied production 356 built by Reutter in Zuffenhausen. Three of these were modified for racing during 1950 and 1951. Following extensive body modifications, they were renamed 356 SL, which stood for *Super Leicht*, "super light."

For Porsche, though, running a factory team at Le Mans signaled the start of their long-term plans—ultimate success in the 24 Hours of Le Mans—which was a goal that they took very seriously. There was little money for any additional promotional campaign, so a strong finish for the Stuttgart team was vital to justify the expense.

Right from the start, things went disastrously wrong for Porsche. During prerace testing, one vehicle in the two-car team was totally written off, while the other car was also badly damaged. Porsche still considered it worth preparing the third car for the event, though: this was piloted by the French duo of Auguste Veuillet and Edmond Mouche. The two French drivers piloted the remaining 356/2 Gmünd coupe to an impressive twentieth place overall at the company's debut at Le Mans.

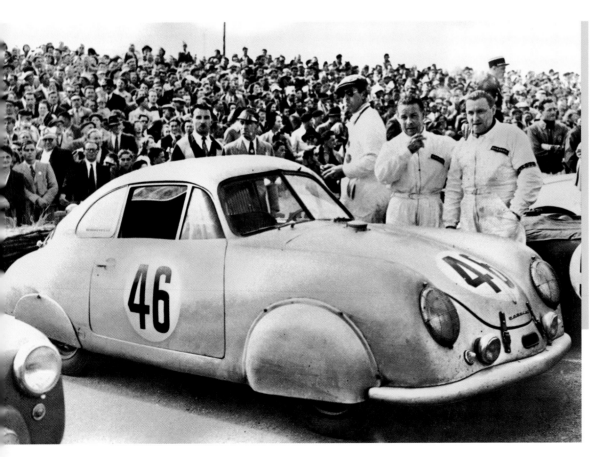

In its standard Volkswagen form, the Porsche-designed flat four engine displaced 1,131cc, but in the 356 SL this was reduced to 1,086cc to make the young sports car eligible for the highly competitive 751–1,100cc racing class. Equipped with a special Fuhrmann-designed cam, high-compression heads, and twin carburetors, the 356 SL developed 40 horsepower, which propelled the lightweight coupe to a top speed of around 100 miles per hour (160 kilometers per hour). Improved airflow over the car was achieved thanks to the narrow, streamlined shape of the aluminum body (narrower than the steel-bodied production 356) and special wheel covers. *Corporate Archives Porsche AG*

French drivers Auguste Veuillet and Edmond Mouche piloted the 356/2 Gmünd coupe to an impressive twentieth place overall in the company's first outing in the 24 Hours of Le Mans. The factory mechanics had little to do on the car during the race, as the 356 performed faultlessly throughout the event. *Corporate Archives Porsche AG*

The Porsche 356 SL, also known as the Gmünd coupe, used many standard Volkswagen-derived parts in the engine and suspension, which helped improve the car's reliability. With the engine located behind the rear axle, the wheelbase could be considerably shortened, thus aiding the car's maneuverability. *Corporate Archives Porsche AG*

The Veuillet/Mouche Gmünd coupe came home in twentieth place overall and, most importantly, first in the highly competitive 1,100cc class. *Corporate Archives Porsche AG*

1951 Race Results

Pos.	Car/Model	No.	Driver(s)	Entered	Class	Cl. Pos.	Laps	Reason
20	356 SL	46	Auguste Veuillet (FR)/Edmond Mouche (FR)	Porsche	751-1100	1	210	
DNS	356 SL	47	Rudolph Sauerwein (DE)/Robert Brunet (FR)	Porsche	751-1100			Accident in practice

1952

June 14–15

Encouraged by their showing at the previous year's event, Porsche once again prepared three Gmünd coupes and entered them all in the 1952 race. Little was changed on the cars from the previous year, but Ferry Porsche and his engineers were only too aware that they were racing what was essentially a road-going sports car that possessed impressive, but limited, competition potential. The company was not complaining about the bankable reputation that the 356 was drumming up, though, which resulted in a healthy sales trend for the young company.

For 1950, Glöckler and his mechanic, Hermann Ramelow, had conceived of constructing an altogether new race car. Basing their project on a shortened VW platform, they turned the engine/gearbox around so that the engine sat in the midposition, just as Ferry had done with the company's original 1948 roadster. From such simple beginnings Glöckler had eventually developed a succession of race cars that inspired Porsche to create the 550 Spyder.

To date, Porsche had shown little appetite for building dedicated race cars, but the efforts of a couple of committed private racers soon showed that the sports cars from Stuttgart possessed excellent potential. The results achieved by the likes of Walter Glöckler and Heinrich Sauter caused Porsche to sit up and take notice. Glöckler in particular demonstrated an unusual flair and an understanding of the value of good aerodynamic body design and lightweight chassis construction; it wasn't long before Porsche started to learn from this talented privateer driver.

Showing the potential for success, and following their class win at Le Mans the previous year, Ferry Porsche gave the go-ahead in 1952 for the design and construction of a new, higher-performance engine (Type 547) and a suitable race car into which such an engine could be fitted. Ernst Fuhrmann received the engine project, while the design for a new racer was given to Erwin Komenda (Type 550). Both projects fell under the watchful eye of Karl Rabe.

The 1952 results were almost a repeat of the previous year: three 356 SLs were entered in the race, but just a single Porsche crossed the finish line. This time, though, that vehicle was the No. 50 Porsche 356 driven by Auguste Veuillet/Edmond Mouche, which finished higher up the overall leaderboard in eleventh place out of 44 starters.

Caught together before the 1952 Le Mans race. *From left*: Wilhelm Hild (race engineer), Hans Klauser (head of customer services), Edmond Mouche (driver), Ferry Porsche, Auguste Veuillet (French Porsche importer and driver), Eberhard Storz (Porsche mechanic), Hermann Briem (senior foreman in charge of engine and chassis developments), and Rolf Wütherich. *Corporate Archives Porsche AG*

BARON HUSCHKE
VON HANSTEIN

Thanks to a number of early successes with the 356, several privateer racers began to take notice of the newcomer from Stuttgart-Zuffenhausen, which resulted in certain performance and body modifications being made to those privately entered cars. Further strong results followed, and Porsche found itself without full, direct control over the cars in private hands. This meant that any good publicity that came from successes couldn't be used by the company to full advantage.

Race victories alone could not maintain public interest indefinitely, so the company needed a coordinated effort to maximize media coverage generated by its motorsports activities. The solution arrived in the form of Baron Huschke von Hanstein, who joined the company in 1952. Von Hanstein proceeded to revolutionize the way Porsche handled its publicity.

With his aristocratic background, von Hanstein was well connected in international circles and among the social elite of the day. Many of Porsche's racing customers came from privileged families, and the Baron was the right figure to satisfy their racing demands.

In his dual role as racing director and public relations director, von Hanstein had the knowledge to seek out new and exciting race venues for the company to exploit its products. And, as a natural publicist, he was able to work the media with ease. Porsche could race in new territories, even in locations where they were not officially represented at that time, so von Hanstein applied his effervescent and persuasive personality to ensure that Porsche attracted all the right kind of attention in the media.

With Porsche's hunger and determination for success—coupled with Ferry Porsche's management style, which encouraged his engineers to constantly explore new innovations—von Hanstein found himself in an environment that perfectly suited his bubbly character. This situation allowed

the PR supremo to begin planning a combined motorsports program and publicity campaign that brought much-needed organization in this area and laid the foundation for a successful future in competition.

As an accomplished racing driver himself, von Hanstein knew the value of good media relations as part of a calculated program of publicity and motorsports development.

This well-known image of Baron Huschke and his boss, Ferry Porsche, taken at the 1953 Le Mans perfectly illustrates the strength of the relationship that had developed between the two men. Also notable is Ferry Porsche's commitment to motorsports, so typical of a company owner during this period. *Corporate Archives Porsche AG*

The Porsche team and drivers posing for the camera before the start of the 1952 race. *From left:* Huschke von Hanstein, Auguste Veuillet, Auguste Lachaize, Eugène Martin, Edmond Mouche, and Petermax Müller. *Corporate Archives Porsche AG*

In 1952, the No. 51 Porsche 356 SL, driven by von Hanstein/ Müller, dropped out with gearbox problems in the sixth hour, while the French pairing of Auguste Lachaize/ Eugène Martin in the similar No. 47 car also failed to finish due to an accident in the nineteenth hour. *Corporate Archives Porsche AG*

1952 Race Results

Pos.	Car/Model	No.	Driver(s)	Entered	Class	Cl. Pos.	Laps	Reason
11	356 SL	50	Auguste Veuillet (FR)/Edmond Mouche (FR)	Porsche	751-1100	1	220	
DNF	356 SL	47	Auguste Lachaize (FR)/Eugène Martin (FR)	Porsche	751-1100		19th hour	Accident
DNF	356 SL	51	Huschke von Hanstein (DE)/Petermax Müller (DE)	Porsche	751-1100		6th hour	Gearbox

1953

June 13–14

Porsche's third visit to Le Mans included a combination of both old and new cars. Making up the party of four cars were two 356 SL stalwarts accompanied by two examples of Porsche's latest weapon, the new 550, which was the company's first purpose-built race car.

It had become clear to Porsche and his engineers that the 356 engine had great potential for further development, but what was needed was a dedicated race car into which such an improved engine could be fitted, and where it could be further refined for competition purposes. Inspiration for the 550 series racers came from work done and successes achieved by several of Porsche's privateer drivers, most notably Walter Glöckler, who had developed the 356 concept into an effective single-seater racer.

In developing the 550, Porsche adopted much of what Glöckler had already designed and implemented in his cars, so the new factory racer featured the same simple ladder frame used by Glöckler, but with a lighter, more streamlined body than the 356. The larger 1,488cc factory-tuned engine, which now developed a healthy 98 horsepower and sat ahead of the rear axle in what was an advanced midengine layout, could propel the 550 racer to 124 miles per hour (200 kilometers per hour). Although the 550 made its debut at Le Mans in 1953, the new racer was first shown to the public at the Paris Motor Show in October of that year.

Lined up in front of Werk 2, two Porsche 356 SLs and two 550 coupes stand ready for action ahead of the 1953 24 Hours of Le Mans. *Corporate Archives Porsche AG*

With the hour of reckoning near, the No. 49 Porsche 356 SL of Auguste Veuillet and Petermax Müller lines up alongside the similar but larger-engined No. 46 car of Gustave Olivier and Eugène Martin, while the two 550s can be seen in the background. *Corporate Archives Porsche AG*

Prior to the start, the No. 44 Porsche 550 coupe (550-01) attracts attention in the pits. This car, driven by Hans Herrmann and Helmut Glöckler, finished sixteenth overall and second in class behind the No. 45 car of similar spec. Many drivers found the coupe version of the 550 claustrophobic in long races, but Porsche found the car to be more streamlined, which was important for top speeds on the long Mulsanne Straight. *Corporate Archives Porsche AG*

Early in the race, the No. 44 (550-01) Glöckler/Herrmann car leads the No. 45 (550-02) car of Richard von Frankenberg/ Paul Frère. These two cars can be regarded as the forefathers of the later Porsche Spyder racers; their bodies differed significantly from the cars to come, and they were never meant to be fitted with the Fuhrmann four-cam engine, which only became available the following year. *Corporate Archives Porsche AG*

FAST AND LIGHTWEIGHT

With the company only five years old, Porsche had already built up a reputation for producing lightweight, state-of-the-art race cars. Often referred to as "giant killers," the cars from Stuttgart frequently beat larger-engined and more established competitors.

It had always been Ferry Porsche's aim to produce light, nimble, and fast cars that did not rely on brute power to beat the opposition. Advanced aerodynamics ensured that streamlined bodies allowed Porsche sports cars to achieve high top speeds and to out-corner many larger cars.

By comparison, the 1953 Le Mans–winning Jaguar C-Type featured a 3.4-liter straight six engine, which developed 200 horsepower and weighing 2,127 pounds (965 kilograms), while the Cunningham C5-R was powered by a Chrysler 5.4-liter V-8 engine, developing 310 horsepower and tipping the scales at a whopping 5,200 pounds (2,359 kilograms). The Jaguars and Cunninghams filled the first four places

at Le Mans that year and, along with the Ferrari 340 MM, which finished in fifth, all followed the traditional front-engine rear-wheel-drive layout.

Porsche engineer and factory driver Jürgen Barth recalls, "It already started with the first 356. If you have a light car, you don't need so much power and you don't need so much fuel. At the time, it was also an important point in the Porsche racing philosophy, that we needed to build cars that did not use so much fuel in order to experiment with new techniques. But the main thing was the fuel consumption, and fuel consumption goes hand-in-hand with good aerodynamics in a light car."

Placing the engine in the rear of the car (as in the 356) had long been the intention of Ferry Porsche, giving the car better traction at the rear wheels and enabling the front of the car to be lower, thereby improving aerodynamics. Locating more weight over the rear axle gave the 356 better acceleration out of corners, but when the 550 was created, the midengine layout was achieved by once

again reversing the engine/gearbox orientation so that the engine sat ahead of the rear axle. Professor Porsche had already established better overall weight distribution with his design of the mighty Auto Unions in the 1930s and the Type 360 Cisitalia of 1947.

The three Porsche 356/2 Gmünd coupes that were considered for the 1953 Le Mans. One of the three cars (*background*) had an elevated roof due to a regulation change for the 1952 Monte Carlo. Only two 356s were taken to Le Mans that year. *Corporate Archives Porsche AG*

The No. 45 car of Richard von Frankenberg and Paul Frère receives some attention in the pits during the 1953 race. Attending to the car at the rear, in a white coat, is master mechanic (Obermeister) Eberhard Storz. Together with Bruno Trostmann, the well-liked and highly professional Storz was responsible for the installation and testing of the famous Fuhrmann engine. He was killed while testing a car for Louise Piëch in the 1970s. The car pictured here finished fifteenth, the highest placing Porsche in the 1953 Le Mans race. *Corporate Archives Porsche AG*

1953 Race Results

Pos.	Car/Model	No.	Driver(s)	Entered	Class	Cl. Pos.	Laps	Reason
15	550 Coupe (550-02)	45	Richard von Frankenberg (DE)/Paul Frére (BE)	Porsche	Sports 1500	1	247	
16	550 Coupe (550-01)	44	Helmut Glöckler (DE)/Hans Herrmann (DE)	Porsche	Sports 1500	2	247	
DNF	356 SL	49	Auguste Veuillet (FR)/Petermax Müller (DE)	Porsche	Sports 1100		147	Engine
DNF	356	46	Gustave Olivier (FR)/Eugène Martin (FR)	Gustave Olivier	Sports 1500		115	Engine

1954

June 12–13

In 1953 the new 550 (chassis 550-01 and 550-02) had raced with a 1,500cc pushrod version of the basic VW-derived engine as used also (although with smaller displacement) in the 356. Porsche engineer Ernst Fuhrmann had been working on a high-performance version of this engine, and late in 1953 Hans Herrmann had tested a 550 Spyder equipped with this latest engine during practice for a supporting race at the German Grand Prix at the Nürburgring. But for the race, Herrmann, feeling it would be more reliable than the new, higher-performing engine, chose to go with the earlier pushrod-engined 550. This was a

somewhat unflattering start to a racing career that would see different versions of this potent Fuhrmann four-cam engine powering Porsche sports and race cars well into the 1960s.

Porsche's entry for the 1954 Le Mans event, however, saw no less than three of the new 110 horsepower, 1,498cc four-cam engined 550s on the starting grid and one lone 1,100cc 550 driven by Zora Arkus-Duntov, the "father" of GM's Chevy Corvette. Once again, the big Jaguars, Ferraris, and Cunninghams dominated the top spots, but the little Porsches put in a gallant performance, taking two class honors.

Leading the Porsche contingent on a media parade lap ahead of the 1954 Le Mans is the No. 40 Porsche 550 of Glöckler/von Frankenberg (chassis 550-10) 1,498cc Spyder followed by the similarly spec'd No. 39 car of Johnny Claes/Pierre Stasse (chassis 550-12), with the No. 41 car of Herrmann/Polensky (chassis 550-11) just behind. At the rear is the No. 47 550 driven by Zora Arkus-Duntov/Gustave Olivier (chassis 550-13), the class-winning 1,098cc car. *Corporate Archives Porsche AG*

PORSCHE TYPE 547
A Brief History of This Famous Engine

A month before the Le Mans race of 1954, a four-cam Fuhrmann-engined 550 Spyder made its international debut in an endurance race at that year's Mille Miglia. In the now famous incident in which Hans Herrmann/Herbert Linge shot under a closing railway barrier, the 550 Spyder came home in a commendable sixth place overall. There followed the Le Mans in June, covered in this chapter, before Porsche installed a 547 four-cam Le Mans–type engine in one of the old Gmünd coupes for the Liège–Rome–Liège rally in August 1954, which Polensky promptly won.

In September of that year, the Fuhrmann engine came into its own when Hans Herrmann brought the Fletcher Aviation/Telefunken–sponsored 550 Spyder home in third place overall in the final Carrera Panamericana road race in Mexico, having been beaten to the line by two Ferraris. Although this wasn't an overall victory, their third place must have felt like a win to the team against such stiff opposition and in such a harsh environment. It was this achievement that gave the 547 four-cam Fuhrmann engine its Carrera moniker, a name that has stuck with the company to this day.

The potent four-cam engine had to be driven hard in order to exploit the unit's power, a challenge that many Porsche drivers recognized. Where the old pushrod engine driver would be conscious of the engine's upper rev limit, the Fuhrmann engine had a narrow power band, between 6,000–7,000 rpm, and one had to literally drive the car "on the tacho" to maximize its performance.

Final preparations are carried out in the pits just before the start of the 1954 Le Mans. Five Porsche 550 Spyders are lined up, *from left to right*: No. 47 car of Zora Arkus-Duntov/Gustave Olivier and the No. 41 road-registered car perhaps used for testing, followed by three cars parked in order of the board above the pit garage, Nos. 39, 40, and 41. *Corporate Archives Porsche AG*

Still bunched up on the first lap, the No. 40 1,498cc 550 Spyder of Helmut Glöckler/ Richard von Frankenberg (chassis 550-10) leads through the corner at the end of the Mulsanne Straight. Unfortunately, this car went out with engine trouble after just four laps. *Corporate Archives Porsche AG*

The somewhat battle-scarred No. 39 Porsche 550 of Belgian duo Johnny Claes/Pierre Stasse leads the 1,098cc No. 47 Spyder of Zora Arkus-Duntov/Gustave Olivier. Both cars were class winners, with the larger 1,498cc No. 39 car finishing a credible twelfth overall and No. 47 crossing the line in an impressive fourteenth place. *Corporate Archives Porsche AG*

The No. 39 550 Spyder of Claes/Stasse was Porsche's top finisher in 1954: twelfth overall and first in the 1,500cc class. *Corporate Archives Porsche AG*

1954 Race Results

Pos.	Car/Model	No.	Driver(s)	Entered	Class	Cl. Pos.	Laps	Reason
12	550/1500 RS Spyder (0012)	39	Johnny Claes (BE)/Pierre Stasse (BE)	Porsche	Sports 1500	1	228	
14	550/1100 Spyder (0013)	47	Zora Arkus-Duntov (US)/Gustave Olivier (FR)	Porsche	Sports 1100	1	216	
DNF	550/1500 RS Spyder (0011)	41	Hans Herrmann (DE)/Helmut Polensky (DE)	Porsche	Sports 1500		148	Engine
DNF	550/1500 RS Spyder (0010)	40	Helmut Glöckler (DE)/Richard von Frankenberg (DE)	Porsche	Sports 1500		4	Engine

1955

June 11–12

The 1955 race will forever be remembered in motor racing as the blackest year in the history of the sport. The facts surrounding the collision between the Mercedes-Benz 300 SLR of Pierre "Levegh" Bouillin and Lance Macklin's Austin-Healey have been examined over and over, the causes debated and scrutinized by race historians ever since, but the outcome remains as sad today as it was that fateful Saturday in 1955. The driver of the Mercedes-Benz was killed instantly, which in those days was not unexpected in the sport, but the death of over eighty spectators sent the world of motorsports into a nearly irrecoverable nosedive. From the disaster came some consolation: the event resulted in a timely reexamination of driver, track, and crowd safety from which the sport has benefited immeasurably.

As a result of the horrific accident, Mercedes-Benz withdrew from the event that day, which elevated Jaguar and Aston Martin to the top of the leaderboard, taking with them three Porsche 550/1500RS Spyders. In just their fifth appearance at Le Mans, Porsche was competing with the major players, filling not only the fourth spot, but the fifth and sixth places too. There was to be great joy mixed with great sadness in Stuttgart that evening.

This sudden exposure to success meant that the Zuffenhausen engineers' cars were indeed ready to take on major competition. With just a little more effort, they could be challenging for a place on the podium. That accolade, however, was still several frustrating years away.

The No. 66 Porsche 550 Spyder of Olivier Gendebien/ Wolfgang Seidel leads the pack in the opening stages of the 1955 Le Mans. *Corporate Archives Porsche AG*

Helmut Polensky/Richard von Frankenberg put in a fine performance in the four-cam Fuhrmann-engined 550/1500RS Spyder, eventually finishing in a remarkable fourth place. *Corporate Archives Porsche AG*

Porsche No. 49, driven by Zora Arkus-Duntov/Auguste Veuillet, finished thirteenth overall and first in the 751–1,100cc class. Despite working on the Corvette program for General Motors, Duntov enjoyed a favorable relationship with Porsche, having once applied for a job with the Stuttgart firm years earlier. Perhaps his buccaneer management style had counted against a possible career at the conservative German establishment, but that didn't stop the development of a fruitful relationship that saw him driving Porsches more than just this once—a situation that didn't always go down well with his Detroit bosses. *Corporate Archives Porsche AG*

The No. 38 1,498cc Spyder of Walter Ringgenberg/Hans-Jörg Gilomen failed to finish, dropping out on lap 65 with engine trouble. *Corporate Archives Porsche AG*

Entered by Gustave Olivier, the No. 65 Porsche 550 Spyder, driven by Olivier himself and Josef Jeser, would finish second in the Sports 1100 class and eighteenth overall. *Corporate Archives Porsche AG*

The No. 66 Porsche 550 Spyder of Olivier Gendebien/Wolfgang Seidel entered by Équipe Nationale Belge would eventually finish in a credible fifth overall and second in the Sports 1500 class. *Corporate Archives Porsche AG*

1955 Race Results

Pos.	Car/Model	No.	Driver(s)	Entered	Class	Cl. Pos.	Laps	Reason
4	550 RS Spyder (0046)	37	Helmut Polensky (DE)/Richard von Frankenberg (DE)	Porsche	Sports 1500	1	284	
5	550 RS Spyder (0015)	66	Olivier Gendebien (BE)/Wolfgang Seidel (DE)	Équipe Nationale Belge	Sports 1500	2	276	
6	550 RS Spyder (0047)	62	Helmut Glöckler (DE)/Jaroslav Juhan (CZ)	Porsche	Sports 1500	3	273	
13	550 Spyder (0048)	49	Zora Arkus-Duntov (US)/Auguste Veuillet (FR)	Porsche	Sports 1100	1	245	
18	550 Spyder (0016)	65	Gustave Olivier (FR)/Josef Jeser (DE)	Gustave Olivier	Sports 1100	2	234	
DNF	550 RS Spyder (0031)	38	Walter Ringgenberg (CH)/Hans-Jörg Gilomen (CH)	Walter Ringgenberg	Sports 1500		65	Engine

1956

July 28–29

Owing to the horrendous accident at Le Mans the previous year, the Automobile Club de l'Ouest (ACO) pushed out the date for the 1956 race by about six weeks to give construction teams sufficient time to complete the new grandstands and public protection facilities ahead of the 1956 event.

By the end of 1955, the East German manufacturer, Eisenach EMW (previously a BMW plant located in the Russian zone of East Germany after the war), and Maserati with their 150S, began to make inroads into Porsche's domain in the sport with smaller, more compact, and lighter race cars.

In response to these advances, the second half of the decade saw Porsche introduce their new higher-performing 550A/1500RS Spyder, which featured a stiffer but lighter tubular frame instead of the flat-section frame (down from 1,301 pounds [590 kilograms] to 1,213 pounds [550 kilograms]). With engine output up from 110 horsepower to 135 horsepower, the 550A's top speed jumped from 136 miles per hour (220 kilometers per hour) to a more-than-useful 158 miles per hour (254 kilometers per hour) thanks also to a new five-speed gearbox. The hike in power came courtesy of the increased compression ratio from 9.5:1 to 9.8:1 and the switch from Solex to Weber carburetors.

A more advanced multilink rear suspension with a lower pivot point replaced the old-fashioned swing axles, and larger dual-circuit drum brakes improved stopping power, while the lower, more streamlined aluminum bodywork (5.3 inches/135 millimeters lower than the 1955 model) featured sharklike gills on the flanks just behind the doors, offering improved engine cooling.

The ACO authorities had introduced new regulations that included heightened windscreens. Held a month later than usual, the race was certainly one of the wettest, and the raised windscreens posed some problems with spray and visibility.

Porsche introduced the 356 A 1500 GS Carrera in the 1956 model year, a road car fitted with the four-cam Fuhrmann engine. The arrival of the name's official use had been somewhat circuitous. For some time Porsche mechanics had applied it unofficially to the four-cam engine used in the 550 that raced in the Carrera Panamericana race in Mexico, where the car had finished a credible third; it was easier for them to refer to the engine in this way, and the name stuck. Eventually picked up by the marketing department, when it was suggested that they should give the name to the new high-performance 356 A fitted with the same Fuhrmann engine, the 1956 model saw the first official use of the name "Carrera." This move gave the 356 model, with its welcome boost in power, a new lease on life as a competition car.

The No. 25 Porsche 550A/1500RS Coupe of Richard von Frankenberg/ Wolfgang von Trips awaits scrutineering before the start of the 1956 event. Note, just aft of the door, the distinctive sharklike gills located within a small inspection flap that allowed technicians to access parts of the engine. *Corporate Archives Porsche AG*

Ferry Porsche gives the factory cars a last inspection before the start of the 1956 race. Leaning over the car on the right-hand side is Porsche mechanic Egon Alber, while on the left (with head just visible) is Hubert Mimler. *Corporate Archives Porsche AG*

Leading here is the No. 28 550 RS Spyder (chassis 0032) of Claude Storez/Helmut Polensky, which retired on lap 46 with ignition failure. Immediately behind is the No. 25 550A-RS Coupe (chassis 0104), driven by Wolfgang Graf Berghe von Trips/Richard von Frankenberg to a commendable fifth overall and first in class. *Corporate Archives Porsche AG*

The No. 26 356 Carrera GT 1500 of Max Nathan/Helm Glöckler lies against the fencing after the accident on lap 61. The No. 21 Ferrari 500 Testa Rossa of Pierre Mayrat/Fernand Tavano (visible in the distance) spun and collided with Glöckler, after which the Porsche went up in flames. Glöckler was pulled out of the burning car with a broken leg. *Corporate Archives Porsche AG*

The No. 24 550A-RS Spyder of Maglioli/Herrmann would drop out with engine trouble on lap 136. *Corporate Archives Porsche AG*

Richard von Frankenberg/ Wolfgang von Trips raced the No. 25 Porsche 550A-RS Coupe to fifth overall place in the 1956 Le Mans, securing a first place in the Sports 1500 class. *Corporate Archives Porsche AG*

1956 Race Results

Pos.	Car/Model	No.	Driver(s)	Entered	Class	Cl. Pos.	Laps	Reason
5	550A/1500RS Coupe (0104)	25	Richard von Frankenberg (DE)/Wolfgang von Trips (DE)	Porsche	Sports 1500	1	282	
13	356 A (56007)	34	Roland Bourel (FR)/Michel Slotine (FR)	Rene Bourel	Sports 1500	3	212	
DNF	550A/1500RS Coupe (0103)	24	Umberto Maglioli (IT)/Hans Herrmann (DE)	Porsche	Sports 1500		136	Engine/piston
DNF	356 Carrera	26	Max Nathan (DE)/Helmut Glöckler (DE)	Porsche	Sports 1500		61	Accident/fire
DNF	550 RS Spyder (0041)	27	Mathieu Hezemans (NL)/Carel Godin de Beaufort (NL)	Porsche	Sports 1500		48	Suspension
DNF	550 RS Spyder (0032)	28	Claude Storez (FR)/Helmut Polensky (DE)	Gustave Olivier	Sports 1500		46	Ignition

1957

June 22–23

Some might argue that Jaguar's finest hour at Le Mans occurred in 1957, when they occupied five of the first six places. The race also turned out to be one of Porsche's most dismal performances to date, with just one finish from six entrants. Mike Hawthorn set the fastest lap in a Ferrari 335S, exceeding the 124 mile-per-hour (200 kilometer-per-hour) mark for the first time at Le Mans, pegging the bar at 125.869 miles per hour (203.015 kilometers per hour) but bowing out on lap 56 with engine trouble.

The Porsche contingent in 1957 was a real mixed bag, consisting of their latest 550A model as well as a modified 718 and a trusty 356 A. The new 550A/1500RS Spyder had been further refined and featured modified bodywork, all of which enabled the car to achieve a higher top speed of 150 miles per hour (240 kilometers per hour). The 718 RSK featured twin rear fins, which helped with stability down the long Mulsanne Straight.

With a lighter chassis and improved air penetration and gearing, the output of the 1500 RS was increased to 148 horsepower. In order to be competitive in the Hillclimb Championship for cars up to 2.0-liter, however, Porsche experimented with the Type 547/3 engine, producing first the 1,600cc and then the 1,700cc engines while retaining the 66.0-millimeter stroke. The experiments proved extremely successful, contributing to Porsche's ascendancy on the World Championship stage and in the hotly contested Targa Florio.

Claude Storez/Ed Crawford, who had driven a solid race in their No. 34 Porsche 550A/1500RS (chassis 0120), were classified as "not running at finish" (NRF), having run out of fuel after 275 laps. *Corporate Archives Porsche AG*

718 RSK INTERNATIONAL RACING SPECIFICATIONS

Engine size	1,498cc	1,587cc	1,678cc
Power output (@ 8,000rpm)	148 bhp	150 bhp	170 bhp
Bore & stroke (mm)	85.0 x 66.0	87.5 x 66.0	90.0 x 66.0
Maximum speed	up to 155 miles per hour/250 kilometers per hour (depending on gearing and circuit requirements)		

The 550 RS Spyder of Ed Hugus/Carel Godin de Beaufort is scrutineered prior to the 1957 race. *Corporate Archives Porsche AG*

Italian driver Umberto Maglioli, usually seen behind the wheel of a Maserati or Ferrari (he won the last Carrera Panamericana in 1954 driving a Ferrari 375), is shown here at speed in the new finned Porsche 718 RSK. He enjoyed a decade of driving with the Stuttgart manufacturer, winning the Targa Florio with Vic Elford in a Porsche 907 in 1968. The No. 32 Porsche 718 RSK (chassis 718001) of Umberto Maglioli/Edgar Barth was involved in an accident on lap 129. *Corporate Archives Porsche AG*

Carel Godin de Beaufort (seated left) and Ed Hugus (seated right) had good reason to celebrate after finishing eighth overall in the 1957 race. The No. 35 Porsche 550A/1500RS was the only Porsche finisher that year, which also saw them take first place in the Sports 1500 class. *Corporate Archives Porsche AG*

1957 Race Results

Pos.	Car/Model	No.	Driver(s)	Entered	Class	Cl. Pos.	Laps	Reason
8	550A/1500RS (0132)	35	Ed Hugus (US)/Carel Godin de Beaufort (NL)	Ed Hugus	Sports 1500	1	286	
NRF	550A/1500RS (0120)	34	Claude Storez (FR)/Ed Crawford (US)	Porsche	Sports 1500		275	Out of fuel
DNF	718 RSK (718001)	32	Umberto Maglioli (IT)/Edgar Barth (DE)	Porsche	Sports 1500		129	Accident
DNF	550A/1500RS (0131)	33	Hans Herrmann (DE)/Richard von Frankenberg (DE)	Porsche	Sports 1500		87	Ignition
DNF	550A (550-082)	60	Claude Dubois (BE)/Georges Hacquin (BE)	Jacques Swaters	Sports 1500		70	DQ – illegal refuel
DNF	356 A (83203)	36	Michel Slotine (FR)/Roland Bourel (FR)	Michel Slotine	Sports 1500		26	Engine/piston

1958

June 21–22

Now just a decade old, the Porsche company had shown those in the top echelons of the sport that they were a significant race car manufacturer, and they fully intended to challenge the big players. Sporting a larger 1,587cc engine, the 718 RSK sports racer, an evolution of the 550A, was a potent machine and now had to run in the Sports 2000 class.

Porsche was clearly producing potentially race-winning cars: the third-place pair of Jean Behra and Hans Herrmann was beaten to the line by nothing less than a Ferrari 250 Testarossa and an Aston Martin DB3S in the 1958 Le Mans—and not by very many laps. This result of 3–4–5 must have gone down very well in Stuttgart, especially because the three top Porsches managed to fend off another pair of Testarossas in sixth and seventh places, nine and ten laps down respectively.

Porsche's third-place finish put them on the podium at Le Mans for the first time in the company's short history, but importantly it showed the Stuttgart engineers that the four-cam Type 547 Fuhrmann engine had a lot to offer by way of further development and increases in displacement.

With significant amounts of standing water on the circuit, driving was sometimes hazardous. The No. 31 718 RSK, driven by Porsche stalwarts Edgar Barth and Belgian journalist-cum-racer Paul Frère, calls in to the pits en route to a convincing fourth-place finish and a first in the Sports 1500 class. This was the only Porsche to feature the twin vertical tail fins in 1958. *Corporate Archives Porsche AG*

Race director Huschke von Hanstein (with camera) briefs Porsche driver Jean Behra on the pit wall prior to the 1958 race in the No. 29 718 RSK (chassis 005). Now featuring a larger 1,587cc engine, this car raced in the Sports 2000 class. *Corporate Archives Porsche AG*

The No. 34 Porsche 550 RS (1,498cc), driven by the French pairing of Jean Kerguen/ Jacques Dewez, finished tenth overall and third in the Sports 1500 class. *Corporate Archives Porsche AG*

The No. 32 Porsche 550 RS of Carel Godin de Beaufort/ Herbert Linge negotiates the Esses on its way to fifth place overall, making it a 3–4–5 finish for the Stuttgart manufacturer. *Corporate Archives Porsche AG*

1958 Race Results

Pos.	Car/Model	No.	Driver(s)	Entered	Class	Cl. Pos.	Laps	Reason
3	718 RSK (005)	29	Jean Behra (FR)/Hans Herrmann (DE)	Porsche	Sports 2000	1	291	
4	718 RSK (003)	31	Edgar Barth (DE)/Paul Frére (BE)	Porsche	Sports 1500	1	290	
5	550A RS (0145)	32	Carel Godin de Beaufort (NL)/Herbert Linge (DE)	Carel Godin de Beaufort	Sports 1500	2	288	
10	550A RS (0142)	34	Jean Kerguen (FR)/Jacques Dewez 'Franc' (FR)	Jean-Paul Colas	Sports 1500	3	254	
DNF	718 RSK (004)	30	Richard von Frankenberg (DE)/Claude Storez (FR)	Porsche	Sports 2000		55	Accident

1959

June 20–21

If Porsche thought, after the results of the 1958 Le Mans race, that they would simply need to develop the 718 further in order to repeat their previous year's results, they were in for a rude awakening at the 1959 event.

Of the six Porsche's listed on the race program, not one finished. Three of the cars were private entrants, while the remaining three were factory cars. Half of Porsche's total contingent that year retired because of clutch- and gearbox-related maladies.

This was the first year in which the test session for the teams was held over the full race circuit in the April preceding the race, where the No. 55 Porsche 550 RS of Kerguen posted the ninth-fastest time. After such an encouraging test, expectations must have been running high in the Stuttgart race department.

The No. 32 Porsche 718 RSK of Hans Herrmann/Umberto Maglioli awaits its turn at the scrutineering compound. Standing by are, *from left*: Werner Enz (with back turned), unknown, Eberhard Storz (mechanic), Willi Enz (factory gearbox expert), Ludwig Schmidt (mechanic), unknown, and Wilhelm Hild (with hat). Werner and Willi were colleagues and not related. *Corporate Archives Porsche AG*

Waiting for the start on the grid shortly before the start of the 1959 race are the No. 31 Porsche 718 RSK of Jo Bonnier/Wolfgang von Trips and the No. 32 718 RSK of Hans Herrmann/Umberto Maglioli. *Corporate Archives Porsche AG*

Lined up in their grid positions shortly before the start of the 1959 race: the No. 34 Porsche 718 RSK (chassis 006), driven by the German pairing of Edgar Barth/Wolfgang Seidel, with the No. 35 550 A Spyder of Jean Kerguen/Robert Lacaze just behind. *Corporate Archives Porsche AG*

In the Porsche pit garage during the 1959 race. *From left*: Huschke and Ursula von Hanstein, Carel Godin de Beaufort, Dorothea Porsche, and Ferry Porsche. *Corporate Archives Porsche AG*

Joakim Bonnier negotiates a curve in the No. 31 718 RSK. The Bonnier/von Trips Porsche (Sports 2000 class) retired after 182 laps with clutch trouble. *Corporate Archives Porsche AG*

1959 Race Results

Pos.	Car/Model	No.	Driver(s)	Entered	Class	Cl. Pos.	Laps	Reason
NRF	718 RSK (024)	37	Ed Hugus (US)/Ernie Erikson (US)	Ed Hugus	Sports 1500		240	Engine
NRF	550 A-RS (0142)	35	Jean Kerguen (FR)/Robert Lacaze (FR)	Jean Kerguen	Sports 1500		229	Clutch
DNF	718 RSK (027)	36	Carel Godin de Beaufort (NL)/Christian Heins (BR)	Carel Godin de Beaufort	Sports 1500		186	Engine
DNF	718 RSK (008)	31	Joakim Bonnier (SE)/Wolfgang von Trips (DE)	Porsche	Sports 2000		182	Clutch
DNF	718 RSK (006)	34	Edgar Barth (DE)/Wolfgang Seidel (DE)	Porsche	Sports 1500		168	Gearbox
DNF	718 RSK (007)	32	Hans Herrmann (DE)/Umberto Maglioli (IT)	Porsche	Sports 2000		78	Ignition/fuel

CHAPTER 2

1960s

Poleman Jo Siffert sprints to his car for a good start in 1968, but it was Rolf Stommelen in the No. 33 car who led the starters. Gerhard Mitter filled third spot in the No. 32 Porsche with Joe Buzzetta in the No. 34 908 making it a Porsche 1–2–3–4. *Corporate Archives Porsche AG*

Laying the Foundation

Now racing in its tenth year at Le Mans, Porsche had progressed from its single entry in 1951 to a total of six cars in 1960. In those ten action-packed years, Porsche's presence at Le Mans had increased from a handful of race-prepared road cars to a more meaningful squad of purebred racers.

In 1951, the sole 1,100cc Porsche 356 SL completed 210 laps at Le Mans, finishing twentieth overall and first in the 751–1,100cc class. Ten years later, the highest-finishing Porsche 356 B Carrera GTL Abarth of Linge/Walter crossed the line tenth overall and first in the Sports 1600 class after completing 269 laps. In that first decade, Porsche had also secured its first podium finish at Le Mans, claiming third place in 1958, but only after a disastrous year in 1959 in which not one Porsche car crossed the finish line. With this setback, the company was determined to make amends.

History will show that the 1960s was the decade of the greatest motorsports development and innovation at Porsche: the sheer number and variety of race cars produced by the company astounded many. Both the 356 Carrera Abarth and the 718 looked instantly old-fashioned when the 904 was introduced in 1964, but it is of course inaccurate and untrue to refer to these two racers in this manner, especially when one can even see some familiar 904 design cues in the 718 GTR of 1963. In truth, however, the 904 did offer a far more flexible platform on which future models could be based. With this model, Porsche was finally able to shrug off the converted road-going race car image associated with earlier sports cars from Stuttgart.

This pattern of development continued as the 904 gave way to the 906, 910, 907, and 908, all of which were dedicated, purpose-built race cars. This extraordinary run of technologically advanced race cars quickly rose to prominence, but the best was yet to come: the decade ended with the appearance of one of the most revered sports racers of all time, the Porsche 917.

One could almost be forgiven for thinking that the innovative technology present in the Porsche race cars of 1969 was developed by a completely different company when compared with the cars' design in 1960. Engines had grown from the 160-horsepower, four-cylinder 1,600cc Fuhrmann-derived unit in the 718 RS 60 of 1960 to the mighty twelve-cylinder 4.5-liter monster pushing out 560 horsepower in the space of ten short years.

This unprecedented rollercoaster of development was all due to one man: Dr. Ferdinand Piëch. A nephew of Ferry Porsche, Piëch, besides being keen to make a name for himself, was also fiercely ambitious and determined to guide Porsche to the top step of the winner's rostrum, with the Le Mans crown being his ultimate goal. He achieved this in the following decade, but the road to Le Mans victory for Porsche was characterized by the continuous improvement of new race car models. While future decades would continue to see Porsche's success on the tracks of the world grow with each passing year, this was achieved through the development of a smaller number of race car types.

The pace of development and innovation within the race car department at Stuttgart would never again reach the same levels of intensity and diversity seen in the 1960s. It was, though, unquestionably the most dynamic time in the sport and, as a continuous period, it ran from the early 1960s to the mid-1970s.

1960

June 25–26

A new decade, a fresh start. Following the company's disappointing showing at the 1959 race, Porsche approached the 1960s with a purpose and determination to occupy the leaderboards and podiums of the major European motorsports championships.

Up to this point, Porsche had benefited from Sports Car Club of America (SCCA) rules. In America, these classified a race car by its engine displacement, which ensured that their lightweight, Fuhrmann-engined sports cars had an advantage over the field. In Europe, though, Porsche were coming under increasing pressure from the likes of Lotus and Alfa Romeo. Although still dominant in their class, Porsche had reached its competition limit with their 356 coupe-based Carrera racers.

In order to counter this encroachment by its European competition, Porsche was encouraged to explore the idea of a lightweight racer featuring a streamlined, aluminum-bodied coupe based on the 356 B floor pan. With the unmistakable influence of Italian design, and sharing the same front-end design as the 718 RS 60, the 356 B 1600 GS Carrera GTL Abarth Coupe (to give it its full name) represented the pinnacle of 356 performance at that time.

The Carrera Abarth proceeded to dispose of the competition in its class all over Europe in the early 1960s, taking victories at the Nürburgring, Le Mans, and in the Targa Florio. It was the same in America, where the sports racer showed its speed and agility with wins at Sebring and Daytona.

Also on the sporting menu for 1960 was the larger-engined 718 RS 60, now with 1,600cc displacement, replacing the previous year's 1,500cc RSK. Pushing out 160 horsepower, the RS 60 was slightly heavier and featured a higher windscreen, but still managed the same 161 mile-per-hour (260 kilometer-per-hour) top speed as the RSK.

The No. 35 Porsche 356 B 1600 GS Carrera GTL Abarth Coupe of Herbert Linge and Swiss driver Heini Walter is put through scrutineering. *Corporate Archives Porsche AG*

Porsche factory cars, the No. 35 Carrera GTL Abarth Coupe of Herbert Linge and Heini Walter (*rear*) and the No. 34 718 RS 60 of Maurice Trintignant and Hans Herrmann (*front*) undergo scrutineering prior to the 1960 race. *Corporate Archives Porsche AG*

Race mechanics Eberhard Storz (*left*) and Werner Enz (*right*) carry out some substantial repairs to the engine of a Porsche 718 RS 60 Spyder in the pit lane while interested onlookers watch. *Corporate Archives Porsche AG*

Edgar Barth (*left*) and Wolfgang Seidel (*right*) alongside their No. 39 Porsche 718 RS 60. Barth and Seidel finished eleventh overall and second in the Sports 1600 class. *Corporate Archives Porsche AG*

Herbert Linge sweeps through a curve in the No. 35 Porsche 356 Carrera GTL Abarth Coupe ahead of the Ferrari 250GT SWB of Graham Whitehead/Henry Taylor. The Carrera Abarth would finish tenth overall. *Corporate Archives Porsche AG*

The No. 35 Porsche 356 Carrera GTL Abarth of Linge/Walter crosses the line at the end of the race (note the finish time on the clock) in tenth place overall and first in the Sports 1600 class after completing 269 laps. *Corporate Archives Porsche AG*

1960 Race Results

Pos.	Car/Model	No.	Driver(s)	Entered	Class	Cl. Pos.	Laps	Reason
10	356 B 1600 GS Carrera GTL Abarth (1001)	35	Herbert Linge (DE)/Heini Walter (CH)	Porsche	Sports 1600	1	269	
11	718 RS60 (042)	39	Edgar Barth (DE)/Wolfgang Seidel (DE)	Porsche	Sports 1600	2	264	
DNF	718 RS60 (044)	33	Joakim Bonnier (SE)/Graham Hill (GB)	Porsche	Sports 2000		191	Engine
DNF	718 RSK (055)	38	Carel Godin de Beaufort (NL)/Dick Stoop (GB)	Carel Godin de Beaufort	Sports 2000		180	Engine
DNF	718 RS60	36	Jean Kerguen (FR)/Robert Lacaze (FR)	Jean Kerguen	Sports 1600		92	Engine/camshaft
DNF	718 RS60 (043)	34	Maurice Trintignant (FR)/Hans Herrmann (DE)	Porsche	Sports 2000		57	Engine/piston

1961

June 10–11

The upgraded 718 RS 61 of 1961 replaced the previous year's RS 60 model. Still using the same 1,600cc engine, the RS 61 now featured completely new rear bodywork with a raised engine cover to improve streamlining. The new car was also significantly longer at 158 inches (4,020 millimeters), the result of a 4-inch (100-millimeter) extended wheelbase (90.5 inches/2,300 millimeters). Although Porsche had been using mid-rear-engined sports racers for some time, Ferrari too had seen the advantage as they rolled out their 246SP at the 1961 Le Mans with great results.

One of the most significant introductions for Porsche in 1961 was the 718 W-RS Spyder, a sports racer that would race in events in Europe, California, the Bahamas, and Puerto Rico. The "W" in the car's moniker stood for World Championship, reflecting Porsche's plan to use this racer in the 2.0-liter sports car class of that series. As a result of its varied life as both a track racer and hill climb champion, the 718 W-RS Spyder that competed between 1961 and 1964 was affectionately known within the factory as the "*Grossmutter*" ("Grandmother").

While the 718 W-RS Spyder started out with a four-cam Fuhrmann engine in 1961, the following year it was fitted with a 240 horsepower 2.0-liter eight-cylinder boxer engine. It was this multiple usage of different engine types that made this car one of the most significant Porsche racers of the early 1960s.

The remarkable No. 36 Porsche 356 B 1600 GS Carrera GTL Abarth of factory driver Herbert Linge and Dutchman Ben Pon finished tenth overall and first in the GT 1600 class, while the No. 21 Austin Healey 3000 of Richard Stoop/Jean Beckaert retired because of engine failure after 254 laps. *Corporate Archives Porsche AG*

Powered by a 1,600cc four-cylinder engine, Porsche's No. 32 718 RS 61, driven by stalwarts Hans Herrmann and Edgar Barth, came home in seventh place overall and second in the Sports 2000 class. *Corporate Archives Porsche AG*

Porsche parade! After the finish of the 1961 race, the cars filed past the crowds toward *parc fermé*, located behind the grandstand, for post-race inspection. First in this line of cars is the fifth-place No. 33 718 RS 61 Spyder of Bob Holbert/Masten Gregory, then the tenth-place No. 36 356 B 1600 GS Carrera GTL Abarth of Linge/Pon, followed in turn by the No. 32 718 RS 61 Coupe of Herrmann/Barth, which finished seventh overall. *Corporate Archives Porsche AG*

Crossing the line together, but 25 laps apart, are the No. 33 718 RS 61 of Holbert/Gregory in fifth place overall (*far side*) and the No. 36 Carrera Abarth of Linge/Pon in tenth place. The flag-waving official thought that the finish was worth lifting his hat for. *Corporate Archives Porsche AG*

1961 Race Results

Pos.	Car/Model	No.	Driver(s)	Entered	Class	Cl. Pos.	Laps	Reason
5	718 RS61 (047)	33	Masten Gregory (US)/Bob Holbert (US)	Porsche	Sports 2000	1	309	
7	718 RS61 (045)	32	Edgar Barth (DE)/Hans Herrmann (DE)	Porsche	Sports 2000	2	306	
10	356 B 1600 GS Carrera GTL Abarth	36	Herbert Linge (DE)/Ben Pon (NL)	Porsche	Grand Touring 1600	1	284	
DNF	718 RS61 (046)	30	Joakim Bonnier (SE)/Dan Gurney (US)	Porsche	Sports 2000		262	Engine/oil pipe
DNF	356 B 1600 GS Carrera GTL Abarth	37	Robert Buchet (FR)/Pierre Monneret (FR)	Auguste Veuillet	Grand Touring 1600		261	Engine/oil pipe

1962

June 23–24

For 1962, the Fédération Internationale du Sport Automobile (FIA) shifted its focus toward production-based GT cars, so the World Sportscar Championship, which had seen many "gentleman drivers" in its field since its inception as a series in 1953, was replaced by the International Championship for GT Manufacturers from 1962. Because of changes that year in the rules, which didn't suit Porsche, the factory decided not to enter their eight-cylinder 718s.

This was also the year in which Porsche dipped its toe in the water with its 804-F1 Monoposto Formula 1 race car, so considerable resources, both financial and in terms of manpower, were diverted toward that effort.

This move left the Stuttgart firm with little option but to persist with their trusty Carrera Abarths for the 1962 race. Three similar cars were listed in the program, two of these being entered by the factory, while the third was entered by French Porsche dealer, Auguste Veuillet.

Prerace preparations go ahead for the only two successful Porsches in the 1962 race. In the foreground is the No. 34 356 B GS Carrera GTL Abarth of factory drivers Hans Herrmann and Edgar Barth, who finished seventh. Just ahead of that car is the No. 35 Carrera Abarth of Robert Buchet/Heinz Schiller, which finished twelfth. *Corporate Archives Porsche AG*

1962 Race Results

Pos.	Car/Model	No.	Driver(s)	Entered	Class	Cl. Pos.	Laps	Reason
7	356 B 1600 GS Carrera GTL Abarth	34	Edgar Barth (DE)/Hans Herrmann (DE)	Porsche	Grand Touring 1600	1	287	
12	356 B 1600 GS Carrera GTL Abarth	35	Robert Buchet (FR)/Heinz Schiller (CH)	Auguste Veuillet	Grand Touring 1600	2	272	
DNF	356 B 1600 GS Carrera GTL Abarth	30	Robert Buchet (FR)/Carel Godin de Beaufort (NL)	Porsche	Grand Touring 1600		35	Ignition

More prerace pit action sees the Nos. 34 and 35 Carrera Abarths being prepared during the test sessions ahead of the 1962 event. *Corporate Archives Porsche AG*

Another photo of the prerace preparations in 1962. While mechanics run this way and that, a gendarme strides purposefully by the two 356 B GS Carrera GTL Abarths, keeping a watchful eye on proceedings. *Corporate Archives Porsche AG*

1963

June 15–16

The 7-series cars appeared for the last time at Le Mans in 1963. The 3s, 5s, and 7s had done the company proud, but the next season ushered in a new generation of racers. With only four Porsches on the entry list, they would have their work cut out for them if they were to make their presence felt. As it happened, only one would finish.

Under similar race conditions, the average speed of the winners in 1963 increased by 3 miles per hour (5 kilometers per hour) over the previous year. With just this small increase, it was clear that the world of motorsports was on the move.

With high expectations ahead of their departure from the factory, cars No. 29 and No. 30 are loaded and ready for the journey to Le Mans. Neither *Dreikantschaber* finished the 1963 race, both dropping out around one-third distance.
Corporate Archives Porsche AG

The No. 28 Porsche 718 W-RS Spyder, driven by factory drivers Edgar Barth and Herbert Linge, was the highest-finishing Porsche—eighth overall and third in the Prototype 3000 class. Here the driver vaults into the cockpit at the start. *Corporate Archives Porsche AG*

The No. 28 Porsche 718 W-RS Spyder of Barth/Linge is chased by the No. 23 Ferrari 250 P of John Surtees/Willy Mairesse, but it was the Porsche that prevailed, with the Ferrari retiring after 252 laps because of a fire. *Corporate Archives Porsche AG*

The Barth/Linge 718 W-RS Spyder calls in to the pits during the 1963 race. *Corporate Archives Porsche AG*

Nicknamed *Grossmutter* ("Grandmother"), the 718 W-RS Spyder (chassis 718-047) was raced in many different motorsports events and was powered by several different engines, from four to eight cylinders. In the 1963 race, Barth/ Linge brought the *Grossmutter* home in eighth place overall and third in the Prototype GT 3000 class. *Corporate Archives Porsche AG*

1963 Race Results

Pos.	Car/Model	No.	Driver(s)	Entered	Class	Cl. Pos.	Laps	Reason
8	718/8 WRS (047)	28	Edgar Barth (DE)/Herbert Linge (DE)	Porsche	Prototype GT 3000	3	300	
DNF	356B 2000GS GT (122-991)	30	Heinz Schiller (CH)/Ben Pon (NL)	Porsche	Grand Touring 2000		115	Engine
DNF	718 GTR (046)	27	Joakim Bonnier (SE)/Tony Maggs (ZA)	Porsche	Prototype GT 3000		109	Accident
DNF	356B 2000GS GT (122-992)	29	Gerhard Koch (DE)/Carel Godin de Beaufort (NL)	Porsche	Grand Touring 2000		94	Engine

1964

June 20–21

Aimed at the FIA 2.0-liter Grand Touring category, 1964 saw the introduction of the Porsche 904 Carrera GTS, the first of the so-called "plastic" Porsches. An extremely sleek and strong race car, the 904 was intended to be fitted with the new 2.0-liter, six-cylinder boxer engine from the 911. As development of the engine in early 1963 was not sufficiently advanced to endure the demands of the track, however, the 904 was modified to accept a variety of engines. These included the four-cam, four-cylinder Type 587/3 Fuhrmann engine (1,966cc), the new 1,991cc Type 901 six-cylinder engine used in the 911, and a 2.0-liter flat eight-cylinder unit (Type 771).

The construction method used by Porsche in the 550 and 718, namely a traditional space frame with an aluminum body, would prove too costly and time-consuming for the 904, which was to be made in greater numbers than any of the company's previous race cars. The FIA stipulated that one hundred examples of the 904 were required in order to meet homologation requirements. Since Porsche was unlikely to sell that quantity of full-blown racers, this meant that a road-going version would also be needed.

F. A. "Butzi" Porsche was responsible for the styling of the 904, which resulted in a low drag coefficient of just 0.33 thanks to the car's low, streamlined shape. The car's chassis was fabricated from pressed steel sections, while the glass-reinforced plastic (GRP) body, a first for the Stuttgart manufacturer, was bonded and riveted to the chassis, creating an immensely strong but lightweight shell.

Importantly for Porsche, this construction method permitted making inexpensive repairs to the 904, as the body molds could be easily modified if needed. It also meant that the engineers and designers could further develop the concept as the rules of competition dictated.

It had been ten years since Porsche introduced its first dedicated racer, the 1953 550-1500 S, whose 78-horsepower 1,488cc engine offered a top speed of around 124 miles per hour (200 kilometers per hour); the 904/8 was now producing 240 horsepower and was capable of a top speed of around 162 miles per hour (262 kilometers per hour). In 1964, seven 904s were entered at Le Mans, made up of five 2.0-liter GTS cars and two eight-cylinder 904/8 cars. It would be the proven 2.0-liter models that went the distance, as the bigger-engined cars had not had the same running time and were thus still unproven.

Before the start, Heinz Schiller poses with his camera on the front fender of Porsche 904 that he would share with Gerhard Koch in the 1964 race.
Corporate Archives Porsche AG

PORSCHE 904—THE FIRST OF THE PLASTIC PORSCHES

Butzi Porsche, grandson of the company's founder, was given the not insignificant task of creating a successor to the much-loved 356 sports car. In 1963, the Porsche 911 was publicly launched at the Internationale Automobil-Ausstellung (IAA) in Frankfurt. Some responded with reservation, while others greeted the newcomer with unbounded praise and admiration. The 911 has gone down as one of the most successful sports cars of all time.

Just a year later, Butzi Porsche introduced the world to his latest race car, the 904 Carrera GTS. Right from the start, the 904 was accepted by many as one of the most stylish and functional sports racers to date, while the noted American motor magazine, *Road & Track*, labeled it, perhaps

realistically, as a bit of a compromise, since the 904 was expected to win on the track as well as be welcomed by its road-going customers.

Designed first and foremost as a race car, though, the 904 would bridge the gap between Porsche's Spyder era and the sleek, big-league players that followed. It was clear from the start that the 904 would be different. In compliance with the FIA rules requiring one hundred examples, Porsche turned to GRP, glass reinforced plastic, for its bodywork. Being both easier and quicker to fabricate, GRP importantly offered a platform from which Porsche could develop the family of lightweight racers that flowed from the Stuttgart race department in the years that followed.

The engineers in Stuttgart weren't familiar with GRP, so Porsche contracted aircraft manufacturer Heinkel to produce the fiberglass body of the 904, which consisted of fifty separate panels.

While Heinkel produced the bodies at a rate of two per day, Porsche could only fabricate one steel ladder frame chassis in the same time. The finished bonded bodyshell and chassis frame created a more rigid structure than the space frame used in the 5- and 7-series racers.

The 904 was so versatile that it was fitted with four-, six- and eight-cylinder engines and was successfully campaigned in many race series around the world.

The last of the 904 finishers was the No. 32 of Jacques Dewez/Jean Kerguen, who crossed the line in twelfth place. This superb color shot highlights the sleek lines and proportions of the 904. *Corporate Archives Porsche AG*

One of the eight-cylinder 904s, this one driven by Porsche stalwarts Herbert Linge and Edgar Barth, waits in the pits before the start. The No. 29 Porsche 904/8 would retire with clutch problems, as its eight-cylinder sibling would later. *Corporate Archives Porsche AG*

The No. 30 Porsche 904/8 of Colin Davis/Gerhard Mitter lasted only until lap 244 before retiring with clutch trouble. *Corporate Archives Porsche AG*

Back in 1964, it was still permissible for drivers to push their vehicles to their pit garage, although the practice would be outlawed in the future for safety reasons. Here the driver of the No. 32 Porsche 904 puffs his way toward his pit garage as an interested band of journalists and photographers record the happenings. Whether this situation was due to a flat tire, electrical, mechanical, or fuel reasons is unclear, but the Porsche driven by the French pairing of Jacques Dewez/Jean Kerguen would continue to finish twelfth overall. *Corporate Archives Porsche AG*

Finishing in eleventh place, the No. 35 904 of Herbert Müller/ Claude Sage speeds past the pits. Müller went on to drive many Porsches, finishing second at Le Mans in 1971 and again in 1974. *Corporate Archives Porsche AG*

1964 Race Results

Pos.	Car/Model	No.	Driver(s)	Entered	Class	Cl. Pos.	Laps	Reason
7	904 GTS (021)	34	Robert Buchet (FR)/Guy Ligier (FR)	Auguste Veuillet	Grand Touring 2000	1	322	
8	904 GTS (055)	33	Ben Pon (NL)/Henk van Zalinge (NL)	Racing Team Holland	Grand Touring 2000	2	318	
10	904 GTS (006)	31	Gerhard Koch (DE)/Heinz Schiller (CH)	Porsche	Grand Touring 2000	3	314	
11	904 GTS (075)	35	Herbert Müller (CH)/Claude Sage (CH)	Scuderia Filipinetti	Grand Touring 2000	4	308	
12	904 GTS (041)	32	Jacques Dewez (FR)/Jean Kerguen (FR)	Jacques Dewez	Prototype GT 3000	1	307	
DNF	904/8 (008)	30	Colin Davis (GB)/Gerhard Mitter (DE)	Porsche	Prototype GT 3000		244	Clutch
DNF	904/8 (009)	29	Edgar Barth (DE)/Herbert Linge (DE)	Porsche	Prototype GT 3000		139	Clutch

1965

June 19–20

For all intents and purposes, 1965 was the high watermark for anti-Ferrari feelings in America, and Italian sentiment for the Americans was pretty much the same. Ford's foiled attempts to buy the Italian company a couple of years before had not been forgotten, and Ford's dogged determination to beat Ferrari at all costs had escalated to something of an all-out war between the two marques. European manufacturers regarded Le Mans as the showcase for Continental and British engineering and racing technology, but it was a party that the Americans were keen to crash.

While the temperature between American and Italian camps was heating up, Porsche were quietly getting on with the development of their 904 model, which had shown great promise. Fitted with the six-cylinder boxer engine, the 904 demonstrated once again the racer's versatility, as the top Porsche finisher featured a six-pot engine followed immediately by another 904 powered by a four-pot, Fuhrmann-derived engine.

Ferrari entered a total of ten cars in both the Prototype and GT classes, while Ford entered no fewer than eleven cars spread across the same classes. The well-known journalist,

Denis Jenkinson, writing in *Motor Sport* in July 1965, noted that Ford was even offering cars to teams whose entry into Le Mans had been accepted by the ACO but for whatever reason found themselves without a car as the day approached.

Despite a tornado causing one of the sessions to be canceled on the first evening of practice, the weather for the race itself was clear and ideal for racing. This did not help the American and Italian stables, however; both steadily lost cars as the race progressed, all of which allowed the Porsches to make their way up the field. Although the Porsches were not without their own problems, a fourth- and fifth-place finish was an extremely good conclusion for the Stuttgart manufacturer, considering the strength of the opposition.

The start of the Le Mans race is always packed with excitement and action. In the foreground are two 904s: *at left*, the No. 32 904/6 of Herbert Linge/Peter Nöcker and, *at right*, the No. 33 904/8 of Gerhard Mitter/Colin Davis. *Corporate Archives Porsche AG*

The duties of a Le Mans driver in the 1960s included digging one's own car out of the sand should your enthusiasm get the better of you, as the crew of the No. 43 Alfa Romeo TZ 2 found out on the first lap—their car stayed where it was! The Porsche No. 32 of Linge/Nöcker (finished fourth, the highest-finishing Porsche) flashes past, followed by the No. 31 Rover-BRM of Graham Hill/Jackie Stewart (tenth), while the No. 35 904/6 of Günther Klass/Dieter Glemser ("did not finish," DNF) can be seen in the background. *Corporate Archives Porsche AG*

The No. 33 Porsche 904/8 of Mitter/ Davis puts in a good turn of speed. Competing in the Prototype GT 2000 class, the No. 33 Porsche retired after just twenty laps because of clutch problems. *Corporate Archives Porsche AG*

The four-cylinder No. 36 904
of Gerhard Koch/Anton "Toni"
Fischhaber finished fifth overall and
first in the Grand Touring 2000 class.
Corporate Archives Porsche AG

1965 Race Results

Pos.	Car/Model	No.	Driver(s)	Entered	Class	Cl. Pos.	Laps	Reason
4	904/6 (906-001)	32	Herbert Linge (DE)/Peter Nöcker (DE)	Porsche	Prototype GT 2000	1	336	
5	904 GTS (091)	36	Gerhard Koch (DE)/Anton 'Toni' Fischhaber (DE)	Porsche	Grand Touring 2000	1	325	
DNF	904 GTS (021)	37	Robert Buchet (FR)/Ben Pon (NL)	Auguste Veuillet	Grand Touring 2000		224	Engine/oil leak
DNF	904/6 (906-012)	35	Günther Klass (DE)/Dieter Glemser (DE)	Porsche	Prototype GT 2000		202	Engine/camshaft
DNF	904 GTS (041)	38	Jacques Dewez (FR)/Jean Kerguen (FR)	Jacques Dewez	Grand Touring 2000		130	Out of fuel
DNF	904/8 (008)	33	Colin Davis (GB)/Gerhard Mitter (DE)	Porsche	Prototype GT 2000		20	Clutch
DNF	904 GTS (100)	62	Rolf Stommelen (DE)/Christian Poirot (FR)	Christian Poirot	Grand Touring 2000		13	Gearbox

1966

June 18–19

Reporting for *Motor Sport*, Denis Jenkinson wrote, "[T]he atmosphere at Le Mans was much stronger than Ford versus Ferrari, it was America versus Europe." His comments were motivated by the armada of Ford entrants consisting of eight 7.0-liter Mk II Ford coupes supported by a flotilla of five 4.7-liter GT40s. In the other corner, Ferrari fielded three works 330/P3s and no fewer than eleven factory-supported Ferraris of differing description. Together, these two manufacturers accounted for twenty-seven cars, almost half of the field of fifty-five starters, which makes Jenkinson's comments quite relevant.

In yet another corner was Porsche. Their battle was perhaps not for top honors, as they could not realistically hope to dislodge the likes of Ford and Ferrari, but they were there to pick up the positions as vacated by the big names during the twenty-four-hour battle. With the launch of the new 906, introduced immediately in both shorttail (KH, for Kleinheck) and longtail (LH, for Langheck) form, the potential top speed of the Porsche down the Mulsanne Straight was significantly increased over its predecessor.

Of Porsche's seven starters, six were of the new 906 variant, with five being entered by the factory and one by French Porsche importer Auguste Veuillet, while a single privateer 911 made up the Stuttgart total. In near-standard trim, this No. 35 Porsche 911 finished strongly in fourteenth place.

In the race itself, Ford appeared to dominate proceedings early on as the Ferrari cars fell by the wayside one after the other, with none of the works cars finishing the race. The highest-placed Ferrari was the factory-supported 275 GTB, entered by Ronnie Hoare, which finished in eighth place behind the three top-placed Fords and five Porsches—a comprehensive trouncing of the Italian marque if ever there was one.

Interestingly, the highest-finishing Porsche from the previous year, the fourth-place 904/6 of Linge/Nöcker, completed 336 laps having started from twenty-second place on the grid with a qualifying time of 4:03.1. Fitted with a similar engine, the highest-placed 906 LH in 1966, driven by Siffert/Davis, also finished in fourth place, having started from twenty-second on the grid with a qualifying time of 3:51.0, completing 339 laps. One of the shorttail 906s in the 1966 race was the works-entered car of Klass/Stommelen, which posted a qualifying time of 3:55.8; in reality, this was only slightly slower than its long-tail sibling down the Mulsanne Straight, accounting for the difference in the car's qualifying times.

Jo Siffert and Colin Davis drove one of the new Porsche 906 LH cars at the 1966 event (chassis 906-153). *Corporate Archives Porsche AG*

PORSCHE 906—A NEW GENERATION OF DEDICATED RACE CARS

With each new Porsche racer, it seemed that the engineers created another first. The 904 represented the company's first use of fiberglass and was a clear move away from the Spyder body toward an enclosed body style. For the company, the 906 was once again a clear shift away from any form of hybrid road/race format, as the newcomer was a race-only vehicle and clearly showed the direction Porsche's future race car styling would take.

Where the 904 had introduced Porsche to the creative properties of GRP, this model's body was formed in the tried-and-tested method of hand-laying fiberglass cloth strips directly in the mold. This method produced a strong shell, though it suffered from inconsistent skin thicknesses throughout.

The lessons learned in the development of the 904 gave the Porsche engineers invaluable experience in the creation of their next racer, the 906, or Carrera 6. In a departure from the 904,

where the combined chassis and body were stressed as a unitary construction, the 906 employed a stressed tubular frame chassis combined with a thinner-gauge fiberglass body, which also reduced weight and remained unstressed.

Wanting to take the 906 to new levels of technology, Ferdinand Piëch, as head of motorsports development, ordered a new rear suspension based on the latest Lotus Formula 1 unit. The rushed nature of the 906's development, however, meant that the racing department still had a large quantity of 904 rear suspensions planned for the "Mk II" version of that car, which Piëch no longer intended to use. This did not please Ferry, who responded by insisting that the 904 suspensions be used in the new 906. Piëch had no option but to toe the line.

Debuting at the Manufacturers' Championship Daytona 24 Hours in February 1966, Herrmann/Linge brought the new 906 home sixth overall (first in the Prototype 2000 class), followed by a fourth place (again first in class) in the 12 Hours of Sebring in March that year.

The Targa Florio, one of the most important events on the World

Manufacturers' Championship calendar at the time, saw 906s finishing in 1–3–5–8–15 positions, a remarkable result in anyone's book. The 24 Hours of Le Mans offered another opportunity for the 906 to prove itself yet again. By finishing in positions 4–5–6–7, one might consider this a success by any measure, but for Piëch it was still not enough.

The 906 offered Porsche the versatility seen in the 904, where multiple engines could be fitted; by now, though, the four-cylinder boxer engine was no longer an option. A modified version of the 1,991cc engine as used in the 911 road car was the engine of choice, but the 906 was also fitted with a longtail, which gave the car a higher top speed at Le Mans.

With victory in the French endurance race still at the top of Piëch's list of priorities, the 906's replacement, the 910, was already on the drawing board by mid-season. This time Piëch was not going to use the old 904 suspension: he wanted to make sure that the rest of the paddock knew what Porsche's intentions were.

The Porsche 906 LH of Siffert/Davis (chassis 906-153) finished first in class and fourth overall, behind a brace of Ford Mk IIs in the 1966 Le Mans. The top Porsche averaged 118.12 miles per hour, which in 1963 would have been sufficient to win the race. *Corporate Archives Porsche AG*

Looking remarkably like a Ferrari 250LM, the No. 24 car is in fact a Serenissima-ATS Spider, which bowed out on lap 24. Here the No. 32 Porsche 906 of Udo Schütz/Peter de Klerk is followed by a direct competitor of Porsche, the No. 36 Dino 206S, with the No. 58 906 LH of Günter Klass/Rolf Stommelen just entering the corner. *Corporate Archives Porsche AG*

Udo Schütz and South African sports car ace Peter de Klerk drove their 906 LH to a sixth-place finish in the 1966 race. *Corporate Archives Porsche AG*

The No. 31 906 LH of Hans Herrmann/Herbert Linge leads the No. 26 Ferrari 275 GTB of Giampiero Biscaldi/Michel de Bourbon-Parme that retired with a broken gearbox at around two-thirds distance. The Porsche, driven by the veteran works pairing, finished fifth overall and second in the Prototype 2000 class. *Corporate Archives Porsche AG*

Throughout the second half of the race, the Porsche 906s reeled off one lap after the other in formation—in order Nos. 30, 31, 32, and 58—until the No. 33 906 of Gregg/Axelsson came into the pits with what *Motor Sport*'s Denis Jenkinson described as a "dead engine." They had completed 321 laps compared with the 339 of the top-placed 906 at full time, therefore being classified as "not running at finish," as opposed to "did not finish." *Corporate Archives Porsche AG*

The short "chopped" tail of the 906 is easily distinguished from its long-tailed sibling. Race director Baron Huschke von Hanstein (*right-hand side*) makes his way toward the Günter Klass/Rolf Stommelen No. 58 car in the pit lane before it was sent on its way once again. They would finish in seventh place overall. *Corporate Archives Porsche AG*

1966 Race Results

Pos.	Car/Model	No.	Driver(s)	Entered	Class	Cl. Pos.	Laps	Reason
4	906 LH (153)	30	Jo Siffert (CH)/Colin Davis (GB)	Porsche	Prototype 2000	1	339	
5	906 LH (143)	31	Hans Herrmann (DE)/Herbert Linge (DE)	Porsche	Prototype 2000	2	338	
6	906 LH (152)	32	Udo Schütz (DE)/Peter de Klerk (ZA)	Porsche	Prototype 2000	3	337	
7	906 Carrera 6 (111)	58	Günter Klass (DE)/Rolf Stommelen (DE)	Porsche	Sports 2000	1	330	
NRF	906 Carrera 6 (112)	33	Peter Gregg (US)/Sten Axelsson (SE)	Porsche	Sports 2000		321	Engine
14	911 S	35	Jacques Dewez (FR)/Jean Kerguen (FR)	Jacques Dewez	Grand Touring 2000	1	284	
DNF	906 Carrera 6 (104)	34	Robert Buchet (FR)/Gerhard Koch (DE)	Auguste Veuillet	Sports 2000		110	Accident

1967

June 10–11

Another new year, another new model from Porsche. Although the 906 would soldier on for some years, the 910 represented the company's latest technology. On paper there was little to choose distinguish the 906 from the 910, as both models featured six-cylinder and eight-cylinder engines, but there was the small matter of the 910 being 220 pounds (100 kilograms) lighter than its predecessor.

While the 910 was perhaps a slightly smoother, more rounded design, it was the chassis that was particularly innovative in that several of the tubes were used to carry oil to the forward-mounted cooler and back to the engine again. The 910 was one of the first Porsche race cars to benefit from wind-tunnel research, which resulted in a lower wing height, although this was countered by a wider track, giving the 910 much the same frontal area and aerodynamic efficiency as the 906. The 910 also benefited from the Formula 1–based rear suspension system, which really turned this race car into a winner. Ferdinand Piëch had finally gotten his way, as this car used the suspension he had intended for the 906.

The 910 did not enjoy a full testing program, however, and was thrust straight into battle in the European Hill Climb Championship series at the end of 1966. Class wins came the 910's way at the first four races of the season: Daytona, Sebring, Monza, and the Spa. But the 910's greatest achievements were to come by way of a 1–2–3 finish at the 1967 Targa Florio and the 1–2–3–4 clean sweep at the Nürburgring 1,000 Kilometers.

The 910 would not enjoy the limelight as a factory racer for long, though, because hot on its heels came the Porsche 907, introduced midway through the 1967 season just in time for Round 7 of the Manufacturer's Championship at Le Mans. For Porsche, the 907 represented the company's most advanced racer to date, featuring a teardrop cabin shape. This allowed the wind to slide off the upper body and cabin structure more efficiently, as the teardrop was tapered rearwards.

A significant departure for Porsche with the 907 was the steering, which was located on the right-hand side. This was not in anticipation of sales of the racer in road-going form in Britain, but rather because most European circuits were run clockwise and a right-hand drive made it easier to negotiate tight corners on these circuits. Instead of leaving the gear change in the central position, the lever was in fact located on the right-hand side of the vehicle, too, with the linkage crossing to the center of the car behind the driver's seat.

Although the Porsche entry looked promising, the 907 was still a bit of an unknown quantity, so a pair of 910s (as used in the Targa Florio) and a pair of 906s were brought in to bolster the squad. All the 910 and 907 prototype entries were running with six-cylinder fuel-injected engines. The prototypes all ran on Dunlop tires, on wheels with Porsche's new center-lock nuts, but when the 917 was introduced two years later, the Dunlops were replaced with Firestone rubber, giving the car much better top speed.

The 1960s were all about color! The green-nosed No. 41 Porsche 907 LH of Jo Siffert/Hans Herrmann lines up before the start of the 1967 Le Mans. Fitted with a 901/21 six-cylinder engine, this car (chassis 907-004) would finish in fifth place overall. The purple-nosed No. 40 Porsche 907 LH of Gerhard Mitter/Jochen Rindt can be seen just behind. *Corporate Archives Porsche AG*

Starting from forty-fifth place on the grid, the No. 42 Porsche 911 S, driven by Robert Buchet/ Herbert Linge, finished fourteenth overall and first in the Grand Touring 2000 class. *Corporate Archives Porsche AG*

This photo was probably taken during an evening practice session. *From front to back:* No. 39 910 (chassis 910-026), driven by Joe Buzzetta/Udo Schütz; No. 38 910 (chassis 910-017), driven by Rolf Stommelen/Jochen Neerpasch; No. 37 906 (chassis 906-154), driven by Vic Elford/Ben Pon; No. 66 906 (chassis 906-156), driven by Christian Poirot/Gerhard Koch. *Corporate Archives Porsche AG*

A pair of glamour girls bring a sparkle to the No. 37 Porsche 906 KH before the race. Vic Elford and Ben Pon would drive this car to an overall seventh place and first in the Sports 2000 class. Just behind is the No. 38 910, which finished sixth. *Corporate Archives Porsche AG*

Driving into the sun was the No. 66 Porsche 906 KH of Gerhard Koch/Christian Poirot. They would finish eighth overall and second in the Sports 2000 class. *Corporate Archives Porsche AG*

The No. 38 Porsche 910/6 Coupe of Rolf Stommelen/Jochen Neerpasch finished the race in sixth position overall. The Porsche 910 would replace the 906; although it ran the same six-cylinder engine, it was both lighter and stiffer than its predecessor. Stommelen and Neerpasch would finish second in the Prototype 2000 class. *Corporate Archives Porsche AG*

1967 Race Results

Pos.	Car/Model	No.	Driver(s)	Entered	Class	Cl. Pos.	Laps	Reason
5	907 LH (004)	41	Jo Siffert (CH)/Hans Herrmann (DE)	Porsche	Prototype 2000	1	358	
6	910 (017)	38	Rolf Stommelen (DE)/Jochen Neerpasch (DE)	Porsche	Prototype 2000	2	351	
7	906 Carrera 6 (154)	37	Vic Elford (GB)/Ben Pon (NL)	Porsche	Sports 2000	1	327	
8	906 Carrera 6 (156)	66	Gerhard Koch (DE)/Christian Poirot (FR)	Christian Poirot	Sports 2000	2	321	
14	911 S (308-176 S)	42	Robert Buchet (FR)/Herbert Linge (DE)	Auguste Veuillet	Grand Touring 2000	1	308	
DNF	911 S (307-823 S)	67	Pierre Boutin (FR)/Patrice Sanson (FR)	Pierre Boutin	Grand Touring 2000		134	DQ – early oil fill
DNF	911 S	60	André Wicky (CH)/Philippe Farjon (FR)	Philippe Farjon	Grand Touring 2000		126	Engine/big end bearing
DNF	907 LH (003)	40	Gerhard Mitter (DE)/Jochen Rindt (AT)	Porsche	Prototype 2000		103	Engine/camshaft
DNF	910 (017)	39	Udo Schütz (DE)/Joe Buzzetta (US)	Porsche	Prototype 2000		84	Engine/oil pressure
DNF	911 S (308-101 S)	43	Jacques Dewez (FR)/Toni Fischhaber (DE)	Jacques Dewez	Grand Touring 2000		2	Clutch

1968

September 28–29

Held later than usual on September 28–29 due to workers' strikes in France around the time of the originally scheduled dates, this rescheduled race improved the chances of the Prototypes versus the Sports cars, as the new prototype cars could benefit from further development during the season. The September date meant a change in the rules, because the longer hours of darkness, compared to June, placed additional strain on the cars' electrical systems as they would run longer with their lights on. This meant that a battery change was permitted during the race.

Being run as the last round on the 1968 World Manufacturers' Championship calendar, Le Mans also saw the race for the title that year go right down to the wire, with Ford and Porsche on equal points at the start of the September race.

This year saw the arrival of yet another new race car from the Stuttgart-Zuffenhausen race department. While the 3.0-liter eight-cylinder Porsche 908 debuted at the 1,000 Kilometers of Monza, it finished in a rather unflattering nineteenth place, while the trusty 907 had been reliably picking up first and second places since the beginning of the season. But at the Nürburgring 1,000

Kilometer, the 908 took the checkered flag ahead of a 907, and it followed up that victory with a few top finishes before grabbing first and second at the Austrian Sports Car Grand Prix in August.

Le Mans 1968 was perhaps not the roaring success for the 908 that Porsche had hoped it would be. The four 3.0-liter prototypes proved troublesome, and the sole 908 survivor was beaten into third place overall by its smaller, older sibling, taking second behind the winning Ford GT40. Despite leading the race in the opening stages, the three other 908s dropped out of contention one after the other with a combination of clutch trouble and alternator belt failures.

Despite being so near at the flag, yet so far, for Piëch no further proof was needed to show that his plans to produce a Le Mans–winning race car were not just on track but getting close to realization. Although deeply disappointed at not having taken the victory, he had clearly demonstrated Porsche's intentions and capabilities to the rest of the motorsports world. The 1968 Le Mans result showed that the prototype Porsche 908 with its (relatively) small 3.0-liter eight-cylinder engine was capable of beating the best in the world. The future looked bright for Porsche.

This superb view of the cars lined up before the start of the 1968 Le Mans shows Porsches occupying the first three places on the grid: No. 31 Porsche 908 LH, driven by Siffert/ Herrmann with a qualifying time of 3:35.4 minutes at a speed of 139.876 miles per hour (225.109 kilometers per hour); No. 33 Porsche 908 LH, driven by Stommelen/Neerpasch; No. 32 Porsche 908 LH, driven by Mitter/Elford. Porsche decided to fit the cars with slicks and not wet tires; as it can be seen in this photograph, it had been raining just prior to the start. This decision paid off, as the Porsches built up a considerable lead early in the race. *Corporate Archives Porsche AG*

The No. 33 Porsche 908 LH of Rolf Stommelen/Jochen Neerpasch streaks past the pit complex in the early evening hours. This Porsche was fitted with a 3.0-liter eight-cylinder engine and, despite Porsche's midrace woes, this car was the highest-finishing 908 as it came back strongly in the latter stages of the race. *Corporate Archives Porsche AG*

Despite having set the fastest qualifying time and having set the early pace, the No. 31 Porsche 908 LH of Jo Siffert/Hans Herrmann was disappointingly halted out on the track with a broken clutch on lap 59. *Corporate Archives Porsche AG*

The No. 35 907 KH of Alex Soler-Roig/Rudi Lins speeds past the pits followed by the No. 67 907 of Robert Buchet and factory test driver Herbert Linge. The latter car was disqualified on lap 102 for having carried out an illegal alternator swap, the same destiny befalling the No. 32 Mitter/Elford Porsche 908 LH a few laps later. *Corporate Archives Porsche AG*

The No. 32 Porsche 908 LH, driven by Gerhard Mitter/Vic Elford, was disqualified (lap 111) for fitting a replacement alternator after the car had thrown several belts. Elford picks up the story: "It was around 8:00 p.m. on Saturday night, and I believe Gerhard was driving and he came into the pits as the alternator had failed. In those days you were not allowed to change the alternator, you could repair it, but you couldn't change it. So in preparation for repairing it, and it was obviously going to be very hot when it came off the car, the mechanics had got a huge tub of cold water. So the car pulled in and they lifted the back up and they took the alternator out, dropped it in the bucket of water and let it cool off for a couple of minutes, then they pulled it out and fiddled with it a bit, and then they put it back on the car, having repaired it. Except, unfortunately for us, there was a real smart *commissaire* there who just before the car was going to leave said, 'One moment,' and he put his hand in the bucket of water and came out with the old broken alternator. So we were disqualified on the spot." *Corporate Archives Porsche AG*

The No. 66 2.2-liter 907 LH Coupe (chassis 907-003), entered by Squadra Tartaruga and driven by Dieter Spoerry/Rico Steinemann, is followed by the privately entered No. 35 907 of Alex Soler-Roig/Rudi Lins, which fell out on lap 145 with engine trouble. The Spoerry/Steinemann 907 ran well to finish in second place overall and first in the Prototype 3000 class. *Corporate Archives Porsche AG*

The privateer Squadra Tartaruga team had good reason to be jubilant: by finishing second overall and first in the Prototype 3000 class, the Spoerry/Steinemann 2.2-liter Porsche 907 LH had beaten many other cars of much larger capacity. Here the car makes it way to post-race scrutineering. Steinemann would later succeed race director and PR supremo Huschke von Hanstein at Porsche, and so his time behind the wheel was a valuable step in this direction. *Corporate Archives Porsche AG*

1968 Race Results

Pos.	Car/Model	No.	Driver(s)	Entered	Class	Cl. Pos.	Laps	Reason
2	907 LH (008)	66	Rico Steinemann (CH)/Dieter Spoerry (CH)	Squadra Tartaruga	Prototype 3000	1	326	
3	908 (013)	33	Rolf Stommelen (DE)/Jochen Neerpasch (DE)	Porsche	Prototype 3000	2	325	
12	911 T	43	Jean-Pierre Gaban (BE)/Roger van der Schrick (BE)	Jean-Pierre Gaban	Grand Touring 2000	1	281	
13	911 T	64	Claude Laurent (FR)/Jean-Claude Ogier (FR)	Claude Laurent	Grand Touring 2000	2	276	
NRF	910 (007)	45	Jean-Pierre Hanrioud (FR)/André Wicky (CH)	Jean-Pierre Hanrioud	Prototype 2000		248	Engine/rockers
DNF	911 T (118 2 0779)	44	Guy Chasseuil (FR)/Claude Ballot-Léna (FR)	Auguste Veuillet	Grand Touring 2000		224	Engine
DNF	906 Carrera 6	42	Christian Poirot (FR)/Pierre Maublanc (FR)	Christian Poirot	Sports 2000		202	DQ – engine running at pit stop
DNF	907 (005)	35	Alex Soler-Roig (ES)/Rudi Lins (AT)	Alex Soler-Roig	Prototype 3000		145	Oil loss/cam follower
DNF	908 (014)	34	Joe Buzzetta (US)/Scooter Patrick (US)	Porsche	Prototype 3000		115	Electrics/alternator
DNF	908 (016)	32	Gerhard Mitter (DE)/Vic Elford (GB)	Porsche	Prototype 3000		111	DQ – illegal alternator repair
DNF	907 2.2 (006)	67	Robert Buchet (FR)/Herbert Linge (DE)	Philippe Farjon	Prototype 3000		102	DQ – illegal alternator repair
DNF	908 (015)	31	Jo Siffert (CH)/Hans Herrmann (DE)	Porsche	Prototype 3000		59	Gearbox/clutch
DNF	911 T	60	Willy Meier (DE)/Jean de Mortemart (FR)	Wicky Racing Team	Grand Touring 2000		30	Accident

1969

June 14–15

If the 917 was a history maker, then the 904, 906, 910, 907, and 908 were all instrumental in the development of this awesome racer, as incrementally they all played their part in bringing Porsche to this point.

But the Porsche 917 almost didn't happen. Piëch's dogged determination to lift the Le Mans trophy undoubtedly drove him to develop the ultimate racing machine. This single-mindedness, however, brought him into conflict with none other than his uncle, Ferry Porsche, who was understandably worried about the potential risk the project posed, to say nothing of the resultant damage that it might cause the company should it not succeed.

Such thoughts, however, did not enter Piëch's mind, and as a young and ambitious engineer he was determined to see his plans through. Although his 908 had not won Le Mans, the sweet smell of success was tantalizingly close. Besides, plans for the next generation of racer were already well advanced.

History will show that the 917 was to become the single most successful sports racer of its time. Although it did not have an easy birth, with many drivers refusing to get behind the wheel, the handling and stability problems were soon sorted out. The Porsche 917 has, in fact, gone down in the record books as one of the all-time greats, and it is thanks to the determination of a visionary engineer that it came about at all.

The 1969 World Manufacturers' Championship had already been decided by the time that year's Le Mans came around, with Porsche having secured outright victories at the first five races of the year. Perhaps other manufacturers would have questioned the need to race at Le Mans, or indeed the remaining events that year, thereby saving costs and the possibility of embarrassing defeats should things go wrong. But for Porsche the prize of Le Mans still eluded them, and this was incentive enough for them to treat this like any other race.

Fortunately for the spectators, the race could not have provided a more exciting finale, as the two main players, Porsche and Ford, fought it out tooth and nail for the whole race, the winner being decided by a distance of just 75 yards. Before the start of the race, the opposition could have been forgiven for having felt demoralized by the speed of the 917s, but as they retired one by one, the reliability of the Ford GT40 eventually assured victory for the Detroit manufacturer.

Porsche was worried that the brakes of their leading 908 would not hold out to the end of the race, so Hans Herrmann was obliged to drive the last lap with caution in order to at least secure second place if he was unable to hold onto the lead. Jacky Ickx, driving an aging Ford, swapped places with the Porsche throughout the last lap, eventually taking the lead for the final time and holding his place to cross the line ahead of the Porsche. To this day, this finishing gap remains the closest finish.

VIC ELFORD DESCRIBES HIS FIRST LAPS AT LE MANS WITH THE 917

"At the start, we both made a good start, Rolf was off first and I was right behind him except that as I had jumped in, on the 917 the door used to open upwards, and normally we would just let it go and it would slam itself shut, which I did as I got in and turned the engine on, except it didn't shut properly. On the first lap, we were all supposed to have a *commissaire* standing beside the car to make sure we all put our seat belts on—what a joke! So although the seat belt *commissaire* was looking, he couldn't really see into the car, and so we all made a show of it and took off and on the way down the Mulsanne Straight on the first lap, I was steering with my knees while I put the belt on, and I am sure I wasn't alone, everybody was doing the same thing. Then I turned my attention to the door because the door hadn't closed properly, but the car was a bit of a monster that year s o the only time I had anything like a free hand was on the [Mulsanne] Straight. But then the air pressure was such that I couldn't get the door open. So on the two straights that mattered, I was steering with one hand and trying to push the door open with my other hand to get it to slam again, but I couldn't get it open so after five laps I had to stop and come in and get the mechanics to close the door for me."

Porsche's 917 LH Coupe T-car is prepared in the pits during the 1969 Le Mans practice session. *Corporate Archives Porsche AG*

The No. 20 Siffert/Redman 908/02 Spyder was wheeled into the pit garage with a broken gearbox after four hours and sixty laps. *Corporate Archives Porsche AG*

By 2:00 a.m. on Sunday morning, the No. 12 917 LH Coupe (chassis 917-008), driven by Vic Elford/Richard Attwood, was four laps clear of the second-place 908 of Mitter/Schütz and well ahead of the rest of the field, therefore able to throttle back slightly to preserve the car. The speed differential between the 917 and the other cars was significant, as Elford explains: "The car was very unstable because we were in the realms of where we had never been before. Nobody had ever been over about 200 miles per hour before in anything, and suddenly this monster was doing 220 miles per hour, but it wandered all over the road while doing it. I am sure pretty well everybody at one point had come across the 917 and was frightened silly by it. And it wasn't a bad thing because we found that when we came down through the Esses, through Tertre Rouge onto the straight, everybody else was queued up on the right and they waited until we had gone by. And that carried on pretty well all the time except at one point in the middle of the night, I came around Tertre Rouge and started accelerating down the straight. And there I was doing 220 miles per hour and there were a couple of 911s on the right side and the guy at the back obviously didn't realize that a 917 was coming. About halfway down the straight decided he would start to overtake the car in front of him. Well, I was doing 220 miles per hour and they were both probably doing about 160, so it would have taken the guy forever to pass a similar car. There was no question of stopping, and so I had to go by with two wheels on the grass and two wheels on what was left of the road. So really that was the only problem, until the bell housing and clutch problem in the morning, which was a shame." *Corporate Archives Porsche AG*

After qualifying fourth on the grid, the No. 22 Porsche 908 LH of Rudi Lins/Willi Kauhsen dropped out in the twenty-second hour with a failed gearbox while running in sixth place. They were classified as NRF, rather than a DNF, as the car had completed more than 70 percent of the winning Ford's total distance. *Corporate Archives Porsche AG*

Having qualified on pole, the No. 14 Porsche 917 of Rolf Stommelen/ Kurt Ahrens was forced to retire with transmission trouble before the halfway mark (148 laps), having driven a strong race. The small front winglets on the left and right side of the car were prone to breakage in the hard world of racing; these were discarded by the end of the season. *Corporate Archives Porsche AG*

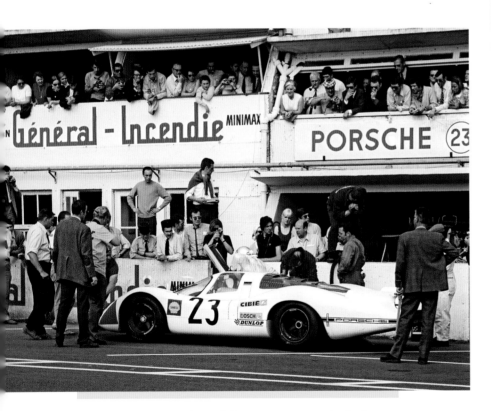

The No. 23 908 LH of Mitter/Schütz receives attention in the pits, but a crash at the end of the Mulsanne Straight with Schütz behind the wheel in the early hours before dawn (lap 199) saw the car burst into flames. It was completely burnt out, but luckily the driver escaped unharmed. *Corporate Archives Porsche AG*

PORSCHE BREAKS INTO THE BIG LEAGUE WITH ITS LEGENDARY FLAT TWELVE-CYLINDER ALL-CONQUERING 917

It had long been Porsche's dream to win the 24-Hours of Le Mans, but to date the Stuttgart manufacturer had had to be content with class honors despite some promising victories in other major events such as Daytona, Sebring, and Nürburgring in 1968, as well as a second place at Le Mans that year. Although these results by both the 907 and 908 showed that Porsche was on the right track, they needed a heavyweight contender in order to make it onto the top step of the podium at the Circuit de la Sarthe.

During the summer of 1968, work began on a successor to the 908 that would take advantage of a loophole in the rules allowing race cars of up to 5.0 liters to compete in the World Manufacturers' Championships Group 4 class. Although the CSI (the FIA's competition wing) was trying to reduce engine sizes, it continued to allow cars to compete with larger engines between 1968–1971 in order to boost numbers, as few manufacturers would have had sufficient time to develop new engines to meet the new 3.0-liter Prototype limit. No one at the CSI thought that a manufacturer would have the required resources to design, develop, and produce a completely new race car to fit through this loophole in time, but they hadn't taken into account the determination and resourcefulness of Ferdinand Piëch.

Using the 908 chassis as his starting point, Piëch designed a more streamlined body, but a whole new engine would be required to propel this new race car to speeds not yet seen at Le Mans. Chassis weight was kept down through the use of aluminum instead of steel, while the body was constructed of fiberglass and epoxy resin, a fabrication method with which Porsche had extensive experience and knowledge.

Piëch faced many technical and logistical hurdles before the project looked like it was going anywhere, but his problems weren't only confined to these matters. Closer to home, while Piëch was trying to convince Ferry Porsche of the 917's viability, the FIA homologation team was not keen to give his new racer the green light.

Against all the odds, though, Piëch had the first car ready for display at the Geneva Motor Show on March 12, 1969, with the first batch of cars ready for the CSI's inspection at Stuttgart on March 20. Homologation required a total production of twenty-five cars. When the CSI delegation arrived, however, they were shown three completed cars with a further eighteen in various stages of completion and parts sufficient to complete the balance. This time the CSI's attitude was different, as Porsche had exploited a loophole in the rules and produced a whole new car rather than adapting an existing race car, according to the spirit of the rules, and so the CSI refused to approve the car for homologation. A later date was set and the CSI returned to Stuttgart on April 21, where they were confronted by twenty-five complete 917s.

In retrospect, that was the *easy* part: the 917 proved to be a real beast to tame on the track, and handling was so bad that many drivers declined an invitation to drive the car in competition. Brian Redman was among the first drivers to be summoned to Stuttgart to test the vehicle, but racing partner Jo Siffert advised Brian not to go, noting the cars' reputation for dire handling. "I was unavoidably detained in England," Redman laughed when he recalled the incident later.

The 917 was first driven in public at the Le Mans test weekend on April 29–30, where Rolf Stommelen set the fastest qualifying time for the June race. On May 11 the 917 was taken to the Spa 1,000 kilometers, where it again set the fastest lap in practice in the hands of Jo Siffert, but the Swiss driver elected to drive the 908 in the race itself. At the 24 Hours of Le Mans in June, the stage was set for what many regarded as the 917's real race debut: Three of the new cars were entered, two factory cars and one privateer entry by John Woolfe.

Once again Piëch came up against officialdom when the FIA ruled that the movable flaps on the 917 were illegal and had to be fixed. Vic Elford recounts the incident:

That year the car was difficult to drive to say the least, and then there was a big hoopla [at Le Mans] because it had actually been homologated with movable rear flaps. The FIA said you can't have movable rear flaps, they are illegal, and Piëch said well it might be but you homologated the car like that, so you homologated an illegal car, that's your problem, tough. And so eventually Stommelen went out and did a lap and they said that they have got to be fixed, so they fixed them on the 917 and Stommelen went out again and did a masterful lap with the car totally out of control everywhere, apparently, and came back in again and Piëch said, "There you see the car is undriveable without it, and you homologated the car." So eventually they came to a compromise and on the 917 we were allowed to have our flaps but they fixed them on the 908.

Sadly, when the race eventually got underway, privateer John Woolfe was killed on the first lap in his 917, but that was more because of his inexperience and the fact that he had allegedly not fastened his seat belt in his haste to pull away at the start. Of the remaining two 917s, the No. 12 car of Vic Elford/Richard Attwood completed 327 laps versus the winning Ford GT40 with 372 laps, and was classified as "not running at finish" (NRF) with a broken clutch. The 917 had shown that, despite its dubious handling characteristics, it would be a serious contender at Le Mans in the future.

The 4,494cc engine was not strictly a flat twelve-cylinder engine, but rather a 180-degree V-12 with two con rods sharing one crankpin. This configuration meant that each pair of pistons did not move in opposite directions with each throw of the crank, but instead moved together in the same direction, creating less air pressure and turbulence in the crankcase. Besides a revised camshaft drive mechanism, the big twelve-cylinder engine otherwise ran with proven Porsche engine technology and produced around 560 horsepower, making it a lot more powerful than any other car on the grid at the time.

Indeed, the Porsche 917 went on to become the standard that many other race car manufacturers sought to emulate, and many of the 917's design and mechanical innovations eventually found their way onto other race cars of the day.

The No. 15 Porsche 917 LH T-car was used in practice at the 1969 Le Mans. *Corporate Archives Porsche AG*

The 917 LH of Vic Elford/Richard Attwood calls into the pits. Elford recalls the lead up to the race, "I kept on with Piëch about having one, and he said, 'No, no, no Vic, if you want to win Le Mans, have a 908 because the 917 is going to break after six hours.' And, indeed, Stommelen's car did break after six hours, but finally he and Bott gave in and said I could have a 917. So I got Richard Attwood to drive with me and we really treated it with kid gloves and it did last, and it went all the way through the night and by the time we retired on Sunday afternoon after 21 hours, what it retired with was nothing at all like they thought originally. It was actually a split bell housing, which allowed the oil through and the clutch was slipping. They tried pouring Coca-Cola on it for a while but that didn't work, and so after 21 hours it was out, by which time we were actually leading by 70 miles." *Corporate Archives Porsche AG*

Until its retirement, the No. 12 Porsche 917 of Vic Elford/Richard Attwood controlled the race and, by 10:00 a.m. on Sunday morning, it held a ten-lap advantage over the No. 6 Ford GT40 of Ickx/Oliver. But Le Mans is about endurance as well as speed, and on lap 327 the Porsche succumbed to what *Motor Sport*'s Jenkinson called "a failing clutch and signs of discontent in its gearbox." *Corporate Archives Porsche AG*

Soon after the No. 12 Porsche 917 of Elford/Attwood had pitted with gearbox trouble, the No. 22 908 LH, driven by Willi Kauhsen, made an unscheduled stop, also suffering from gearbox maladies. The Kauhsen/Lins car would retire on lap 317 just ten laps ahead of the similarly unhealthy 917. *Corporate Archives Porsche AG*

On the final lap, the No. 64 Porsche 908 LH of Hans Herrmann/Gérard Larrousse swapped places with the No. 6 Ford GT40 of Jacky Ickx/Jackie Oliver as many as five times. Despite having lost 35 minutes in the pits due to a faulty wheel bearing, the 908 LH made up four laps on the aging GT40. In the last hour, though, a warning lamp in the cockpit told Herrmann that the brake pads are worn down. The wily German executed the closing laps with care in order not to pit unnecessarily for replacement pads—in fact, a postrace inspection showed that the pads were just fine, it was actually the warning light that was faulty! The two cars were so evenly matched in the closing stages that neither one could hold the lead for an entire lap. The spectators were so caught up in the tension and emotion of the duel that, as the two cars crossed the line, the crowds swarmed onto the track while the rest of the race was still in progress. Even the officials lost control of the situation to the extent that the customary car, driver, and pit crew parade could not take place. Herrmann was so disappointed that he did not reappear after the race, and it was quite some time before even the drivers of the winning Ford could be reunited. The winning margin of 75 yards remains the closest finish in the history of the 24 Hours of Le Mans. *Corporate Archives Porsche AG*

1969 Race Results

Pos.	Car/Model	No.	Driver(s)	Entered	Class	Cl. Pos.	Laps	Reason
2	908 LH (031)	64	Hans Herrmann (DE)/Gérard Larrousse (FR)	Porsche	Prototype 3000	1	372	
NRF	917 LH (008)	12	Vic Elford (GB)/Richard Attwood (GB)	Porsche	Sports 5000		327	Clutch/oil leak
NRF	908 LH (029)	22	Rudi Lins (AT)/Willi Kauhsen (DE)	Porsche	Prototype 3000		317	Gearbox
9	910 (006)	39	Christian Poirot (FR)/Pierre Maublanc (FR)	Christian Poirot	Sports 2000	1	312	
10	911 S	41	Jean-Pierre Gaban (BE)/Yves Deprez (BE)	Jean-Pierre Gaban	Grand Touring 2000	1	306	
11	911 T (118 2 0779)	40	Guy Chasseuil (FR)/Claude Ballot-Léna (FR)	Auguste Veuillet	Grand Touring 2000	2	301	
13	911 T	44	Claude Laurent (FR)/Jacques Marché (FR)	Claude Laurent	Grand Touring 2000	3	287	
14	911 S	67	Philippe Farjon (FR)/Jacques Dechaumel (FR)	Philippe Farjon	Grand Touring 2000	4	286	
DNF	908 LH (030)	23	Gerhard Mitter (DE)/Udo Schütz (DE)	Porsche	Prototype 3000		199	Accident
DNF	911 T	63	René Mazzia (FR)/Pierre Mauroy (FR)	Marcel Martin	Grand Touring 2000		174	Gearbox
DNF	917 LH (007)	14	Rolf Stommelen (DE)/Kurt Ahrens (DE)	Porsche	Sports 5000		148	Clutch/oil leak
DNF	908/02 (028)	20	Jo Siffert (CH)/Brian Redman (GB)	Hart Ski Racing	Prototype 3000		60	Oil leak
DNF	911 T	42	André Wicky (CH)/Edgar Berney (CH)	Wicky Racing Team	Grand Touring 2000		34	Engine/rocker
DNF	910 (007)	60	Jean de Mortemart (FR)/Jean Mesange (FR)	Robert Buchet	Sports 2000		4	Engine/sump damage
DNF	917 K (005)	10	John Woolfe (GB)/Herbert Linge (DE)	John Woolfe Racing	Sports 5000		0	Fatal accident

CHAPTER 3

1970s

With the 1971 race about to get under way, the cars set off on a warm-up lap ahead of the first-ever rolling start at Le Mans. The No. 18 Gulf Porsche 917 LH of Pedro Rodriguez/Jackie Oliver leads the No. 17 Gulf Porsche 917 LH of Jo Siffert/Derek Bell, while the No. 22 Martini Porsche 917 K of Helmut Marko/Gijs van Lennep follows behind. The No. 18 car, driven by Rodriguez/Oliver, dropped out in the twelfth hour with a burst oil pipe while lying in sixth place. *Corporate Archives Porsche AG*

Safety in Numbers

At the start of the previous decade, cars from Modena had dominated Le Mans. The 1960 race kicked off a run of successes, with Ferraris taking six of the top seven places, while the top finishing Porsche came home in tenth place. The average winning speed that year was 109.194 miles per hour (175.730 kilometers per hour) with a total of 313 laps being covered by the winner. The fastest practice lap in 1960 was set by Dan Gurney driving Jaguar's prototype E2A at 123.155 miles per hour (198.199 kilometers per hour), a speed that he later exceeded in the race itself.

Ten years later, the boot was on the other foot, as it was Porsche that now took six of the top ten places, Ferrari claiming an additional three positions and a single Corvette sandwiched in among these heavy hitters. Perhaps of even greater significance was the fact that the average winning speed was now 119.299 miles per hour (191.992 kilometers per hour) with a total of 342 laps being covered by the winner. The fastest lap in qualifying was set by Kurt Ahrens in the No. 25 Porsche 917 LH, at a blistering 150.798 miles per hour (242.685 kilometers per hour), while partner Vic Elford set the fastest race lap at 149.860 miles per hour (241.176 kilometers per hour) in the same car.

This comparison shows in no uncertain terms the progress that had been made in the motorsports field, as race cars now fully embraced the new science of aerodynamics. The increased performance potential highlights what a difference a decade can make.

Porsche's onslaught at Le Mans was most convincing when, of the twelve officially classified finishers in 1971, nine cars came from Stuttgart Zuffenhausen, and a staggering six of those nine Porsches were 911s. The only manufacturer able to offer any form of resistance on the day was Ferrari, who occupied positions 3–4–5.

Although the seventies would not see new race car development at the same furious pace as in the sixties, the decade saw some of Porsche's most significant sports racers, such as the 934, 935 and the 936. The Porsche 935, introduced in 1976, became the most successful sports racer of all time, as it continued to compete around the world well into the 1980s.

Two privateer teams rose to prominence in the seventies: Kremer Racing, from the Ossendorf area of Cologne, and Georg Loos, a property developer in the same town. It is not well known that the Loos outfit was in fact nothing more than an office devoid of any race equipment or cars. John Fitzpatrick, who drove for the Loos team through most of the 1970s explains, "Loos's cars were completely prepared at the factory. The mechanics brought them to the race, the works mechanics looked after them, Loos didn't have anything. All Loos owned was a couple of transporters and he didn't even employ the drivers, they were all Porsche, it was a complete Porsche operation that he paid for out of his own pocket." This made Kremer's achievements all the more admirable, as they were more than equal to the Loos team with far fewer resources.

Following Woolfe's fatal accident in 1969—allegedly due to not fastening his seat belt—the traditional sprint start at Le Mans was banned by the FIA. For the 1970 race, the cars lined up in the same way as before, but the drivers would already be strapped in as the flag dropped at 4:00 p.m. At that moment, the area around Le Mans erupted in a cacophony of sound courtesy of fifty-one highly tuned race engines, and the same manic rush for the first corner ensued in the usual fashion.

1970

June 13–14

If one year had to be nailed to the mast by Porsche as representing the year when the company reached maturity on Europe's racetracks, then it must certainly be the year 1970. Just six years previously, Porsche had rolled out the 904, its latest creation powered mostly by a four-cylinder engine. There can be little doubt that Ferdinand Piëch had a plan in the back of his mind even then, that one day he would develop a world-beater.

Introduced in 1969, the Porsche 917 took the world by storm. As impressive as its arrival was, however, there were several crucial aerodynamic problems that needed sorting out before the new race car could claim the mantle of Porsche's, indeed one of the world's, most revered sports racer ever. It took the expertise of an outside racing team to iron out the 917's wrinkles, but once these modifications had been implemented, the rest of the grid was reduced to scrabbling for the lower positions. The two JWs, John Wyer and John Willment, had run the GT40 program

successfully for Ford for some years under the J.W. Automotive Engineering (JWA) banner, and Ferry Porsche approached them to take over the Porsche Manufacturers' World Championship operation. Together with engineer John Horsman and team manager David Yorke, JWA was a professional race organization familiar with running world-class teams and, more importantly, they had the record to prove it. Porsche was also drawn by the presence of JWA's sponsor partner, Gulf Oil, so JWA and Porsche agreed that the English-based team would run Porsche's entry in the Championship for two seasons.

There was also the small matter of JWA having secured the services of two of the fastest sports car drivers the world had ever seen. Mexican Pedro Rodríguez and Swiss driver Jo Siffert were quite simply a cut above the rest, but there was no such thing as team camaraderie when they got behind the wheel, as they were the fiercest of rivals on the track.

Securely tucked away in their workshop in Teloché, eleven miles from Le Mans, are the Porsche Salzburg 917 KH Coupe (*foreground*) and the Martini-sponsored 917 LH Coupe (*background*). *Corporate Archives Porsche AG*

The day of the battle, Porsche's Martini International 917 LH Coupe (chassis 917-043) awaits warm-up prior to the 1970 race. This psychedelic Martini Porsche was driven by Gérard Larrousse and Willibald Kauhsen. *Corporate Archives Porsche AG*

David Piper and Gijs van Lennep drove the No. 18 Porsche 917 KH Coupe (chassis 917-021), owned by Finnish businessman Antti Aarnio-Wihuri (AAW Racing). Having qualified in eleventh place on the grid, their race would end on lap 112 due to an accident after eleven hours while lying in twentieth place. *Corporate Archives Porsche AG*

Here is the start of the 1970 race, and the year in which Porsche rose to dominance. The pole-sitting No. 25 Porsche 917 LH powers away while the second car on the grid, the No.6 Ferrari 512 S, has already lost ground to the No. 20 Gulf Porsche 917 KH. None of these first three cars was classified as a finisher, but the spoils of the battle would go to the No. 23 Porsche KH (not pictured here), which started from fifteenth place. *Corporate Archives Porsche AG*

Best of the 911 finishers in 1970 were the familiar Porsche stalwarts Erwin Kremer/Nicolas Koob in the No. 47 911 S 2.3-liter. They crossed the line in ninth place but were officially classified in seventh position; good enough to take first place in the Grand Touring 2500 class. *Corporate Archives Porsche AG*

It began to rain during the early evening hours, and the weather got worse as night fell, changing the nature of the race entirely. As the hours passed, cars spun out or retired through mechanical maladies, but the No. 23 Porsche Salzburg 917 kept going. Having lost the title by a whisker the previous year, Hans Herrmann could hardly believe his good fortune as the smaller-engined 4.5-liter 917 didn't miss a beat. *Corporate Archives Porsche AG*

After 225 laps, the No. 25 Salzburg 917 LH ingested an inlet valve, which left Porsche regulars, Vic Elford and Kurt Ahrens, high and dry. *Corporate Archives Porsche AG*

A surprise top finisher at the 1970 race was the Porsche 914/6 GT driven by the French pairing of Guy Chasseuil/ Claude Ballot-Léna. A steady and trouble-free run by the No. 40 car saw them finish in seventh place (officially sixth) and first in the Grand Touring 2000 class. *Corporate Archives Porsche AG*

Porsche's proven 908/02 Spyder, driven by Rudi Lins/Helmut Marko, dropped from second place to third following an errant wheel nut, which delayed the car in the pits long enough to let the No. 3 Martini Porsche 917 pass. The No. 27 908 Spyder was able to hold station to the end, finishing in third place. *Corporate Archives Porsche AG*

Richard Attwood remembers, "The factory rung me in February and they asked what car I would like to take to Le Mans. So I said I wanted the short tail with the small engine [4.5-liter] because the gearbox had broken in the other 4.9-liter-engined cars, so I did not want a big engine." In his interview with the author, Attwood admitted that he had made a mistake, as the larger 4.9-liter engine had been resolved by the time of the race, but he did not want to take that chance back in February 1970. After ten hours they found themselves in the lead; from then on, they had to defend that lead to the end in the heavy rain. According to Attwood, "It was a question really of not making mistakes, but we still had to drive with total concentration in those conditions."
Corporate Archives Porsche AG

1970 Race Results

Pos.	Car/Model	No.	Driver(s)	Entered	Class	Cl. Pos.	Laps	Reason
FL	917 LH (042)	25	Vic Elford (GB)/Kurt Ahrens (DE)	Porsche Salzburg	Time: 3:21.050 minutes		Speed: 241.176km/h; 149.860mph	
1	917 K (023)	23	Hans Herrmann (DE)/Richard Attwood (GB)	Porsche Salzburg	Sports 5000	1	343	
2	917 LH (043)	3	Gérard Larrousse (FR)/Willi Kauhsen (DE)	Martini International Racing	Sports 5000	2	338	
3	908/02 LH (005)	27	Rudi Lins (AT)/Helmut Marko (AT)	Martini International Racing	Prototype 3000	1	335	
7	914/6 GT (043-1020)	40	Guy Chasseuil (FR)/Claude Ballot-Léna (FR)	Auguste Veuillet	Grand Touring 2000	1	285	Officially sixth
NC	908/02 (022)	29	Herbert Linge (DE)/Jonathan Williams (GB)	Solar Productions	Prototype 3000	2	282	NC, eighth, film car
9	911 S	47	Erwin Kremer (DE)/Nicolas Koob (LX)	Ecurie Luxembourg	Grand Touring 2500	1	282	Officially seventh
NC	911 S	62	René Mazzia (FR)/Pierre Mauroy (FR)	René Mazzia	Grand Touring 2500	2	275	Eleventh
NC	911 T	42	Guy Verrier (FR)/Sylvain Garant (CH)	Wicky Racing Team	Grand Touring 2000	2	271	Twelfth
NC	911 S	67	Jean-Claude Parot (FR)/Jacques Dechaumel (FR)	Jacques Dechaumel	Grand Touring 2000	3	271	Thirteenth
NC	911 S	45	Claude Laurent (FR)/Jacques Marché (FR)	Claude Laurent	Grand Touring 2500	4	262	Fourteenth
NC	911 S	64	Jean Sage (FR)/Pierre Greub (CH)	Claude Haldi	Grand Touring 2000	3	254	Fifteenth
NC	911 S	66	Claude Sweitlik (FR)/Jean-Claude Lagniez (FR)	Eric van der Vyver	Grand Touring 2000	4	231	
DNF	917 LH (042)	25	Vic Elford (GB)/Kurt Ahrens (DE)	Porsche Salzburg	Sports 5000		225	Engine over-revved
DNF	907 (005)	61	André Wicky (CH)/Jean-Pierre Hanrioud (FR)	Wicky Racing Team	Prototype 2500		161	Throttle/stuck injection
DNF	917 KH (043)	20	Jo Siffert (CH)/Brian Redman (GB)	JW Automotive	Sports 5000		156	Engine over-revved
DNF	911 S	63	Jacques Rey (CH)/Bernard Chenevière (CH)	Jacques Rey Racing	Grand Touring 2500		132	Accident
DNF	910 (007)	60	Willy Meier (DE)/Daniel Rouveyran (FR)	Guy Verrier	Sports 2000		128	Brakes/scored discs
DNF	911 S	65	Claude Haldi (CH)/Arthur Blank (CH)	Hart Ski Racing	Grand Touring 2500		124	Gearbox/gear lever
DNF	910 (045)	46	Christian Poirot (FR)/Ernst Kraus (DE)	Christian Poirot	Sports 2000		120	Engine
DNF	917 KH (021)	18	David Piper (GB)/Gijs van Lennep (NL)	David Piper/Team AAW	Sports 5000		112	Accident
DNF	911 S	43	Jean-Pierre Gaban (BE)/Willy Braillard (BE)	Jean-Pierre Gaban	Grand Touring 2500		109	Gearbox
DNF	911 S	59	Jean Egreteaud (FR)/Jean Mésange (FR)	Jean Egreteaud	Grand Touring 2500		70	Engine
DNF	917 KH (031)	22	Mike Hailwood (GB)/David Hobbs (GB)	JW Automotive	Sports 5000		49	Accident
DNF	917 KH (016)	21	Pedro Rodriguez (MX)/Leo Kinnunen (FI)	JW Automotive	Sports 5000		22	Engine/cooling

1971

June 12–13

Stuttgart invasion! You weren't likely to see an entry list more heavily weighted with Porsches for many years after 1971, with sports cars and race cars from Zuffenhausen totaling no fewer than thirty-three qualifiers and a further fourteen "did not qualify"s and "did not attend"s. Spectators could almost be forgiven for playing a game of "spot the non-Porsche" on the grid with such a formidable armada of boxer-engined cars from Stuttgart.

The appearance of Porsche dominating the international motor racing stage so overwhelmingly showed that the marque had come an awfully long way in twenty-one years. Of the thirty-three Porsche starters, nineteen were 911s and seven were 917s, with the balance consisting of a 907, a squad of four 908s, and a pair of 914/6s.

If betting was your thing, you would have been quite safe putting money on a Porsche winning the race, but having *seven* Porsche finishers in the top ten that year is nevertheless a remarkable achievement in anyone's book. One crown that had eluded John Wyer and the Gulf Porsche team was the Le Mans event; despite the team's valiant effort, it didn't happen in 1971 either, as the highest JWA car finished in second place by just two laps. All of the 917s in the 1971 race were powered by the bigger 4.9-liter engine, with the exception of the No. 57 Zitro car, which ran with a 4.5-liter unit.

Impressively, the 911 S, driven by the French pairing of Raymond Touroul/André Anselme, finished a lap ahead of the lone 907, while none of the 908s crossed the finish line. As with all competitions, people only remember the winning car, but that night the Stuttgart manufacturer could really celebrate the fulfillment of Piëch's goal. Porsche had finally succeeded in dominating the sports car scene in international motorsports. The loophole in the rules that had allowed the 917 to be born had finally closed in 1971—at least as far as Le Mans was concerned.

However, this year is likely best remembered for the astonishing Le Mans lap and race records set by the winning 917. The No. 22 winning Porsche 917 of Helmut Marko/Gijs van Lennep set an as yet unbroken race record for the circuit (prior to the installation of the two chicanes on the Mulsanne Straight in 1991) of 3,315.216 miles (5,335.313 kilometers) at an average speed, including pit stops, of 138.134 miles per hour (222.305 kilometers per hour). Not wanting to miss an opportunity, Vic Elford was clocked at 241.25 miles per hour (388 kilometers per hour) down the Mulsanne Straight, a record that stood for many years.

Willi Kauhsen and Reinhold Joest drove the "Sau" or "Pink Pig" entered by the Hans-Dieter Dechent Martini team. The 917/20 was Porsche's attempt at combining the high-speed stability of the shorttail 917 K with the improved Langheck bodywork, which gave the 917 LH a straight-line speed advantage on the Mulsanne Straight. This theory proved out, as the redesigned front end also minimized airflow under the car, which in the early 917 days contributed frontal lift and caused instability. The car qualified in seventh place and ran as high as third overall, but later crashed at Arnage under braking with Joest at the wheel, while lying in fifth position. *Corporate Archives Porsche AG*

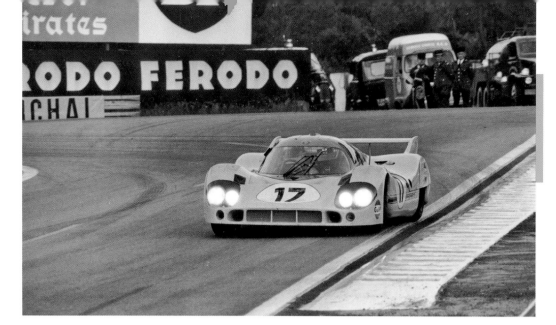

Jo Siffert and Derek Bell's No. 17 Gulf Porsche 917 LH lost time in the pits with a broken suspension, finally retiring on Sunday with terminal engine failure. *Corporate Archives Porsche AG*

By qualifying the No. 21 Martini Porsche 917 LH second on the grid, expectations in the Gérard Larrousse/Vic Elford camp were no doubt high. Lying in third place at the six-hour mark, the sleek Martini 917 engine finally lost its cool, literally, when the engine lost its cooling fan. The car retired with just 74 laps on the board. *Corporate Archives Porsche AG*

Richard Attwood and Herbert Müller qualified their No. 19 Gulf Porsche 917 K in eleventh place on the grid and, despite gearbox troubles, the only short-tailed JWA car kept up its steady progress, finishing in second place overall and second in the Sports 5000 class. In the background can be seen the No. 23 "Sau" of Willi Kauhsen/Reinhold Joest. *Corporate Archives Porsche AG*

Like soldiers standing to attention, the Gulf Porsche 917s lineup for a photo shoot ahead of the 1971 race. *In the foreground*: the No. 19 917 K (chassis 917-026) of Richard Attwood and Herbert Müller qualified back in eleventh on the grid; the No. 18 917 LH, driven by Pedro Rodriguez and Jackie Oliver (Rodriguez set the fastest qualifying time of 3:13.9 at a speed of 155.386 miles per hour (250 kilometers per hour); the No. 17 917 LH, driven by Jo Siffert/Derek Bell qualified in third place for the race. *Corporate Archives Porsche AG*

A LAP RECORD
FOR ETERNITY

Jackie Oliver recalls how they broke the lap record in the Gulf Porsche 917 LH during the test session and the actual race at the 1971 Le Mans: "I remember the aerodynamics during that period were very basic. The long-term aim was to make it more slippery, but there was concern that the rear wing was going to disturb the balance of the car."

Oliver was the only Porsche driver present at the April test session and, as Porsche were still developing the car, they discussed the aerodynamic imbalance of the new Langheck body at speed. Not having any telemetry in those days, Oliver asked the Porsche engineers, "Where do you think the imbalance is going to happen?" to which they replied, "Well, as we start to approach 180–220 miles per hour, that sort of area." Jackie Oliver's reply probably had them worried, but he suggested, "What I will do is, I will weave across the road to see whether the front wheels would still keep their adhesion [at that speed]."

After two laps he returned to the pits and reported that the car had remained stable and was very well balanced. "In fact I took the Mulsanne Kink flat out on the last flying lap," he added. And all the engineers went, "Wow!" Oliver laughed.

They started to go for times following that positive result, as Oliver recalls: "The White House curves are where all the time came from, apart from the car's terminal velocity, we were flat, really flat. And of course I just annihilated the lap record. The car had so much flipping energy."

When the teams returned to Le Mans for the race in June, Pedro Rodriguez set the fastest qualifying time in the No. 18 Gulf 917 LH of 3:13.9 for a lap speed of 155.386 miles per hour (250.069 kilometers per hour). During the race itself, it was Jackie Oliver's turn to set a lap record of 3:18.4 for a lap speed of 151.862 miles per hour (244.397 kilometers per hour). These lap times stand to this day as the fastest at Le Mans. With the introduction of the two chicanes ("kinks") down the Mulsanne Straight, it is unlikely they will ever be bettered.

None of the four Porsche 908s finished the 1971 race. Here the No. 28 Sonauto 908/02 Spyder, driven by French pairing Claude Ballot-Léna/Guy Chasseuil, leads the similar No. 30 car of Louis Cosson/Helmut Leuze. The latter vehicle was disqualified after sixteen hours because of illegal oil replenishment, while the No. 28 car had an accident. *Corporate Archives Porsche AG*

Despite setting the fastest time in qualifying in the No. 18 Gulf Porsche 917 LH, Pedro Rodriguez and Jackie Oliver's race would come to a disappointing end. A big early lead was built up by Rodriguez/Oliver, followed by the usual problems associated with twenty-four-hour racing, and the positions of the leading cars seesawed, with Rodriguez dropping back. The Mexican then fought back to second place, but at 2:00 a.m. on Sunday the oil line came off inside the cockpit, spraying Rodriguez with hot oil. At that stage they were a lap and a half in front, but that incident signaled the end of No. 18's run. *Corporate Archives Porsche AG*

Three in a row—the No. 36 911 S 2.4-liter of Bernard Cheneviére/Björn Waldegaard leads a trio of 911s in the 1971 race. This No. 36 car was the last of the official finishers, being fourteenth across the line, but since it had completed less than 70 percent of the winner's total laps, the 911 was not classified at the finish. *Corporate Archives Porsche AG*

The highest-finishing 911 was the No. 63 2.4-liter car, driven by the French pair of Raymond Touroul/André Anselme. They finished in sixth place overall, taking the laurels in the Grand Touring 2000 class in the process. Here the No. 63 Porsche leads a group of six other Porsches through Indianapolis. *Corporate Archives Porsche AG*

The No. 22 Martini 917 K, driven by Helmut Marko and Gijs van Lennep, was victorious in the 1971 race, making it two in a row for Porsche. Driving steadily throughout, Marko and van Lennep surprised all by setting the fastest-ever average lap speed for the circuit (138.134 miles per hour/222.305 kilometers per hour) as well as the greatest distance covered (3,315.216 miles/5,335.313 kilometers) in a twenty-four-hour race. *Corporate Archives Porsche AG*

1971 Race Results

Pos.	Car/Model	No.	Driver(s)	Entered	Class	Cl. Pos.	Laps	Reason
FL	917 LH (043)	18	Jackie Oliver (GB)	JW Automotive	Time: 3:18.040 minutes		Speed: 244.397km/h; 151.861mph	
1	917 KH (053)	22	Helmut Marko (AT)/Gijs van Lennep (NL)	Martini International Racing	Sports 5000	1	397	
2	917 KH (031)	19	Richard Attwood (GB)/Herbert Müller (CH)	JW Automotive	Sports 5000	2	395	
6	911 S	63	Raymond Touroul (FR)/André Anselme (FR)	ASA Cachia Bundi	Grand Touring 2500	1	306	
7	907 (005)	49	Walter Brun (CH)/Peter Mattli (CH)	André Wicky Racing Team	Prototype 2000	1	306	
8	911 S	38	René Mazzia (FR)/Jürgen Barth (DE)	René Mazzia	Grand Touring 2500	2	303	
9	911 S	42	Jean Mésange (FR)/Gerard Merlin (FR)	Jean Mésange	Grand Touring 2500	3	298	
10	911 S	26	Nicolas Koob (LX)/Erwin Kremer (DE)	Nicolas Koob	Grand Touring 2500	4	292	
11	911 S	39	Guy Verrier (FR)/Gerard Foucault (FR)	A.G.A.C.I.	Grand Touring 2500	5	290	
12	911 S	44	Paul Vestey (GB)/Richard Bond (GB)	Paul Watson Race Organisation	Grand Touring 2500	6	286	
NC	911 S	36	Bernard Chenevière (CH)/Björn Waldegaard (SE)	Ecurie Jean Sage	Grand Touring 2500	7	263	
DNF	917 KH (025)	57	Dominique Martin (CH)/Gérard Pillon (CH)	Zitro Racing Team/ Ortiz Patino	Sports 5000		*	Gearbox
DNF	911 S	35	Pierre Greub (CH)/Sylvain Garant (CH)	Pierre Greub	Grand Touring 2500		*	Engine/ camshaft
DNF	908/02 (009)	29	André Wicky (CH)/Max Cohen-Olivar (MA)	André Wicky Racing Team	Prototype 3000		*	Gearbox
DNF	917 LH (045)	17	Jo Siffert (CH)/Derek Bell (GB)	JW Automotive	Sports 5000		*	Engine/ crankcase split
DNF	911 S	47	Jean-Jacques Cochet (CH)/Jean Selz (CH)	André Wicky Racing Team	Grand Touring 2500		*	Gearbox
DNF	908/02 (016)	30	Louis Cosson (FR)/Helmut Leuze (DE)	Louis Cosson	Prototype 3000		*	DQ – oil replenishment
DNF	914/6 GT	69	Gerd Quist (DE)/Dieter Krumm (DE)	Autohaus Max Moritz	Grand Touring 2000		*	Gearbox
DNF	917 LH (043)	18	Pedro Rodriguez (MX)/Jackie Oliver (GB)	JW Automotive	Sports 5000		*	Oil pipe
DNF	908/02 (026)	28	Claude Ballot-Léna (FR)/Guy Chasseuil (FR)	A. Veuillet – Sonauto	Prototype 3000		*	Accident
DNF	917/20 (001)	23	Willi Kauhsen (DE)/Reinhold Joest (DE)	Martini International Racing	Sports 5000		*	Accident
DNF	911 S	65	Jean-Claude Parot (FR)/Jacques Dechaumel (FR)	Jacky Dechaumel	Grand Touring 2500		*	Engine/oil pressure
DNF	914/6 GT	46	Paul Keller (CH)/Jean Sage (FR)	Porsche Club Romand	Grand Touring 2000		*	Oil pressure
DNF	911 S	40	Jean Egreteaud (FR)/Jean-Marie Jacquemin (FR)	Jean Egreteaud	Grand Touring 2500		*	Gearbox
DNF	911 S	34	Alan Johnson (US)/Elliot Forbes-Robinson (US)	Richie Ginther Racing Inc.	Grand Touring 2500		*	Engine/oil pipe
DNF	911 S	41	Jean-Pierre Gaban (BE)/Willy Braillard (BE)	Jean-Pierre Gaban	Grand Touring 2500		*	Engine
DNF	911 S	37	Pierre Mauroy (FR)/Jean-Claude Lagniez (FR)	Pierre Mauroy	Grand Touring 2500		*	Gearbox
DNF	908/02	60	Hans-Dieter Weigel (DE)/Claude Haldi (CH)	Claude Haldi	Prototype 3000		*	Gearbox
DNF	911 S	33	Jacques Rey (CH)/Jean-Pierre Cassegrain (FR)	Jacques Rey Racing	Grand Touring 2500		*	Gearbox
DNF	917 LH (042)	21	Vic Elford (GB)/Gérard Larrousse (FR)	Martini International Racing	Sports 5000		*	Overheating/ fan drive
DNF	911 S	66	Jean-Claude Guérie (FR)/Claude Mathurin (FR)	Jacques Rey Racing	Grand Touring 2500		*	Fuel system/ timing chain
DNF	911 S	48	Mario Ilotte (IT)/Jean-Pierre Hanrioud (FR)	Jean-Pierre Hanrioud	Grand Touring 2500		*	Engine/piston
DNF	911 S	43	Jean-Pierre Bodin (FR)/Gilbert Courthiade (FR)	François Migault	Grand Touring 2500		*	Engine/over-revved
DNF	910	27	Christian Poirot (FR)/Jean Claude Andruet (FR)	Christian Poirot	Prototype 3000		*	Accident/spin damage

*Completed laps are not available for these nonfinishers.

1972

June 10–11

The 917 era at Le Mans had come and gone. For those who marveled at the car's achievements, it was over too quickly; for others, the opposition in particular, it couldn't be over fast enough. The 917 had come, it had conquered, and as far as the French twenty-four-hour race was concerned, it was now consigned to the history books.

Although not present in 1972 in any official capacity, Porsche was represented by six privately entered 908s, a 907, and a 910, together with a light sprinkling of 911s. The factory's absence could perhaps be put down to a combination of factors, including the fact that the window of opportunity allowing the 917's participation had now closed. For the first time in the postwar period, Ferrari had stayed away from Le Mans, and the absence of its main competitor was another factor that reduced the need for Porsche to prove anything.

In addition, the new 3.0-liter engine capacity limit meant that Porsche's regular 2,997cc eight-cylinder boxer engine would have to suffice, as the company could not justify developing a completely new unit. Of great significance was the great Porsche and Piëch family management shakeup that took place in 1972. With all family members having vacated their company positions, the company's serious motorsports development halted for a time. Moreover, the ACO was doing everything it could to encourage the entry of Grand Touring cars in the twenty-four-hour race, which gave Stuttgart a strong indication of the direction that their future development should take.

Yet another factor in Porsche's temporary withdrawal from racing was the recognition by race organizers of the benefit of accepting a three-man driver combination, as this allowed the drivers to take more frequent rests during the long race.

The leading Porsche in this photograph, the No. 45 911 S, driven by Fernand Sarapoulos/Dominique Bardini/Raymond Touroul, retired just after the halfway mark with engine trouble. The No. 41 911 S of Jürgen Barth/Michael Keyser/Sylvain Garant soldiered on to the end, however, and it was the only 911 still running when the checkered flag fell. *Corporate Archives Porsche AG*

Falling victim to an accident on the 244th lap was the No. 6 Porsche 908/02 Spyder driven by the German pairing of Hans-Dieter Weigel and Helmut Krause. *Corporate Archives Porsche AG*

The No. 24 Porsche 907 was driven by Peter Mattli/Hervé Bayard/Walter Brun, finishing in eighteenth place overall and second in the Sports 2000 class. *Corporate Archives Porsche AG*

The Escuderia Montjuich–entered No. 5 Porsche 908/03 Spyder, driven by Juan Fernandez/Francesco Torredemer/Eugenio Baturone, was classified as NRF following an accident after 278 laps while lying in eighth position. *Corporate Archives Porsche AG*

Driving the No. 41 Porsche 911 S 2.5 were Michael Keyser, Jürgen Barth, and Sylvain Garant. This car made it to the end, the only 911 still running when it crossed the finish line in thirteenth place overall and sixth in the Grand Touring class. *Corporate Archives Porsche AG*

Owned by Jo Siffert, the No. 60 Porsche 908 Coupe LH was driven by Reinhold Joest, Michel Weber, and Mario Casoni. It finished third overall and was the highest-finishing Porsche. *Corporate Archives Porsche AG*

1972 Race Results

Pos.	Car/Model	No.	Driver(s)	Entered	Class	Cl. Pos.	Laps	Reason
3	908/01 LH (026)	60	Reinhold Joest (DE)/Mario Casoni (IT)/ Michel Weber (DE)	Reinhold Joest	Sports 3000	3	325	
13	911 S	41	Jürgen Barth (DE)/Michael Keyser (US)/ Sylvain Garant (CH)	Louis Meznarie	Grand Touring	6	285	
NRF	908/03 (013)	5	Juan Fernandez (ES)/Francesco Torredemer (ES)/ Eugenio Baturone (ES)	Escuderia Montjuich	Sports 3000		278	Accident
18	907 (005)	24	Peter Mattli (CH)/Hervé Bayard (FR)/ Walter Brun (CH)	Wicky Racing Team	Sports 2000	2	252	
NRF	908/02	6	Hans-Dieter Weigel (DE)/Helmut Krause (DE)	Hans-Dieter Weigel	Grand Touring 2000		244	Accident
DNF	911 S	42	Claude Haldi (CH)/Paul Keller (CH)/ Gerard Darton Merlin (FR)	Claude Haldi	Grand Touring		208	Engine/cylinder head
NC	908/02 (013)	67	Christian Poirot (FR)/Philippe Farjon (FR)	Christian Poirot	Sports 3000		206	Officially NC
DNF	910	65	Louis Cosson (FR)/Jean-Louis Ravenel (FR)	Louis Cosson	Sports 3000		188	Wheel bearing
DNF	911 S	45	Fernand Sarapoulos (GR)/Dominique Bardini (FR)/ Raymond Touroul (FR)	Raymond Touroul	Sports 3000		183	Engine
DNF	908/02	76	Jean-Claude Lagniez (FR)/Raymond Touroul (FR)	Jean Egreteaud	Sports 3000		83	Out of fuel
DNF	911 S	44	Jean Sage (FR)/Georg Loos (DE)/Franz Pesch (DE)	Georg Loos	Grand Touring		64	Engine
DNF	911 S	80	Erwin Kremer (DE)/John Fitzpatrick (GB)	Kremer Racing Team	Grand Touring		39	Engine/crankshaft
DNF	911 S	79	Hermes Delbar (BE)/Roger van der Schrick (BE)	Jean-Pierre Gaban	Grand Touring		36	Gearbox
DNF	908/02	58	Otto Stuppacher (AT)/Walter Roser (AT)	Otto Stuppacher Bosch Racing Team	Sports 3000		11	Accident
DNF	911 S	40	Pierre Mauroy (FR)/Marcel Mignot (FR)	René Mazzia	Grand Touring		2	Engine/crankshaft

1973

June 9–10

The rise of the 911! For most manufacturers, the year 1973 fell between two stools, but for Porsche the arrival of their new 936 race car in 1976 was a few years away, so it was up to privateer teams to get their hands on a Carrera RSR if they wanted a racer from Stuttgart. The potent 2,993cc engine produced a whopping 330 horsepower and could propel the RSR to a top speed of more than 174 miles per hour (280 kilometers per hour).

Back at the factory, Porsche was working on extracting ever more power out of the tireless boxer six-cylinder engine,

but the benefits of that work weren't to be put to the test in international competition until the following year. Meanwhile, a young engineer by the name of Norbert Singer was given the enviable task of looking after the two factory racers in 1973, and over the years he would show his employer just how talented he was.

On the production car front, Porsche had just launched its iconic 911 Carrera RS 2.7, and so it fell to such a sports car to lead the racers around the track on their warm-up lap.

The cars set off on their warm-up lap at the start of the 1973 race. This photo shows the No. 46 Martini Carrera RSR of Gijs van Lennep/Herbert Müller, followed by the similar No. 47 car driven by Reinhold Joest/Claude Haldi; the No. 3 Porsche 908/03 of Bernard Chenevière/ Juan Fernandez/Francesco Torredemer can be seen in the background. *Corporate Archives Porsche AG*

First developed in 1968, the Porsche 908 was amazingly still competitive in 1973. The 908/03 was built at the same time as the first 917 in early 1969 and stands as a testament to the car's excellent, yet simple design. The No. 3 car, driven by Juan Fernández/Bernard Chenevière/Francesco Torredemer, finished a superb fifth overall. *Corporate Archives Porsche AG*

It's all action as the No. 4 Porsche 908/02 Spyder of Ecuadorian duo Guillermo Ortega/Fausto Merello arrives in the pits. The fuel man on the left delivers gasoline, drivers change over, and oil is carefully replenished while the wheelman on the right of the picture attends vigorously to the wheel nut. This car finished seventh overall and sixth in the Sports 3000 class. *Corporate Archives Porsche AG*

The No. 42 Porsche 911 Carrera RSR of French duo Pierre Mauroy/Marcel Mignot finished seventeenth overall and fifth in the Grand Touring 3000 class. *Corporate Archives Porsche AG*

Georg Loos (later of Gelo Racing fame) and Jürgen Barth shared the No. 63 911
Carrera RSR 2.8 putting in a good showing by finishing tenth overall and second
in Grand Touring 3000 class. *Corporate Archives Porsche AG*

Looking battle scarred, the 2.8-liter No. 45 Kremer Racing Carrera RSR of well-known
Porsche drivers Clemens Schickentanz/Paul Keller/Erwin Kremer chases down a Ferrari
Daytona and a BMW 3.0 CSL. The Kremer Porsche finished eighth overall and first in
the Grand Touring 3000 class. *Corporate Archives Porsche AG*

Driven by Porsche regulars Herbert Müller/ Gijs van Lennep, the No. 46 Martini Carrera RSR 3.0-liter continued its successful streak in the Group 5 Prototype class. Around sixty production Carrera RS 2.7 cars were taken from the main assembly line and prepared for racing in the old Werk 1 building in Stuttgart.

The engine of the RSR was bored out to yield 2,993cc and, with domed pistons and slide throttles fitted, output was raised to 330 horsepower. This car finished fourth overall at Le Mans in 1973 and fourth in the Sports Prototype 3000 class. *Corporate Archives Porsche AG*

1973 Race Results

Pos.	Car/Model	No.	Driver(s)	Entered	Class	Cl. Pos.	Laps	Reason
4	Carrera RSR	46	Gijs van Lennep (NL)/Herbert Müller (CH)	Porsche Martini Racing Team	Sports 3000	4	329	
5	908/03 (013)	3	Bernard Chenevière (CH)/Juan Fernandez (ES)/ Francesco Torredemer (ES)	Escuderia Monjuich – Tergal	Sports 3000	5	320	
7	908/02 (018)	4	Guillermo Ortega (EC)/Fausto Merello (EC)	Guillermo Ortega Ecuador	Sports 3000	6	317	
8	911 Carrera RSR (73/02)	45	Clemens Schickentanz (DE)/Paul Keller (CH)/ Erwin Kremer (DE)	Kremer Racing Team	Grand Touring 3000	1	317	
10	911 Carrera RSR	63	Georg Loos (DE)/Jürgen Barth (DE)	Gelo Racing Team	Grand Touring 3000	2	312	
14	911 Carrera RSR	48	Peter Gregg (US)/Guy Chasseuil (FR)	Porsche Sonauto BP Racing	Grand Touring 3000	3	299	
16	911 Carrera RSR	41	Jean Selz (CH)/Florian Vetsch (CH)	Heinz Schiller Racing Team	Grand Touring 3000	4	298	
17	911 Carrera RSR	42	Pierre Mauroy (FR)/Marcel Mignot (FR)	René Mazzia	Grand Touring 3000	5	291	
21	908/02 (009)	52	André Wicky (CH)/Max Cohen-Olivar (MA)/ Philippe Carron (CH)	André Wicky Racing Team	Sports 3000	9	271	
DNF	910	22	Raymond Touroul (FR)/Jean-Pierre Rouget (FR)	Raymond Touroul	Sports 2000		142	Out of fuel
DNF	911 Carrera RSR	49	Jean Egreteaud (FR)/Jean-Claude Lagniez (FR)	Jean Egreteaud	Grand Touring 3000		139	Axle/transmission
DNF	911 Carrera RSR	44	Jean-Francois Piot (FR)/Peter Zbinden (CH)	Porsche Club Romand	Grand Touring 3000		110	Gearbox
DNF	911 Carrera RSR	43	Gerd Quist (DE)/Manfred Laub (CH)/Jürgen Zink (DE)	Max Moritz Racing Team	Grand Touring 3000		103	Accident
DNF	911 Carrera RSR	78	Hervé Bayard (FR)/René Ligonnet (FR)	Jean Sage	Grand Touring 3000		95	Head gasket
DNF	911 Carrera RSR	47	Reinhold Joest (DE)/Claude Haldi (CH)	Porsche Martini Racing Team	Grand Touring 3000		65	Out of fuel

1974

June 15–16

Following the successful years with the 917, Porsche went on to further develop the racer, which resulted in the turbocharged 917/10 and 917/30 versions. The former, with its 5.0-liter engine, dominated the European Interserie, while the latter version, with its monstrously powerful 5.4-liter turbocharged engine, produced around 1,100 horsepower in race trim with flash power bursts of up to 1,500 horsepower. This turbocharging experience was not lost on the engineers back at Stuttgart once the 917 had been retired, and new racing applications were sought that could use this rich bank of knowledge.

Enter the 911 Carrera RSR. Although it was a racer in production car "silhouette" form, the racer was embarrassingly quick, and this model would provide a solid platform on which future, higher-performing versions of the car would be based. Produced for the 1974 season in anticipation of the forthcoming Silhouette prototype formula planned for the following year's World Manufacturers' Championship, the 2.1-liter Carrera RSR Turbo was the only turbo-powered 911 to be given the Carrera name.

The Martini-backed Carrera RSR Turbo produced between 450–500 horsepower (depending on boost) from its 2,142cc engine, a capacity arrived at by Singer, as the 1.4 multiplication factor, applied by the ACO to turbocharged cars, would allow this racer to compete in the Prototype Sports 3000 class. Singer also raised the rear roofline and attached a huge rear wing to this substantially aerodynamically revised 911. The result was a very fast Carrera, but still not quite fast enough to compete on an equal footing with the purpose-built racing prototypes. For that, more work was needed before the 911 could claim some major wins. With no fewer than seventeen Carrera RSRs in the field, however, these cars were certain to make their presence felt.

Changes in the rules meant that the Prototype Sports 5000 cars of 1971—such as the Porsche 917, which set qualifying times of 3:18.4 completing 396 laps and covering 3,315.216 miles—would not be seen again for many years. The fastest qualifying time set by the Matra Simca in 1974 in the top Prototype Sports 3000 class was just 3:35.7 by comparison, where the winning car completed 337 laps for a distance of 2,862.395 miles. In this year the 2.1-liter Carrera RSR Turbo posted a qualifying time of 3:52.4.

The 1974 Le Mans test session was held on March 24. Teams could enter the three-hour race as part of preparation for the real thing. Seen here for the test is the No. 38 Carrera RSR 3.0 of Bernard Chenevière/Peter Zbinden; athough they didn't finish this race, they *did* start in the Le Mans proper with car No. 66. The No. 35 Carrera RSR 3.0 was driven by the all-French squad of Raymond Touroul/Denis Rua/ Henri Cachia/Jacques Borras, with No. 70 as their starting number for the twenty-four-hour race. *Corporate Archives Porsche AG*

Four 908s were entered in the 1974 race, none of which would seriously compete for overall honors. The No. 65 908/02 Spyder, driven by Christian Poirot/ Jean Rondeau, was the only one of the four to finish, and that was in nineteenth place. *Corporate Archives Porsche AG*

Calling in to the pits is the No. 22 Carrera RSR Turbo 2.1 of Herbert Müller and Gijs van Lennep. This car ran like clockwork in second place until the eighteenth hour, when the lead Matra Simca was worryingly garaged with a failed gearbox. With this repaired, the Matra reentered the race just ahead of the No. 22 Porsche, which had closed to within a lap of the pitted leader. Soon after, it was the Porsche's turn to have its gearbox attended to, and it too resumed the race, still in second place. *Corporate Archives Porsche AG*

The distinctive No. 70 ASA Cachia-entered Carrera RSR, driven by the French trio of Raymond Touroul/Henri Cachia/Denis Rua, finished fourth in the Grand Touring class and a fine tenth overall. *Corporate Archives Porsche AG*

The battered and bandaged No. 73 Carrera RSR of Michael Keyser/Milt Minter/Paul Blancpain finished twentieth overall and eleventh in the Grand Touring 3000 class. *Corporate Archives Porsche AG*

Bernard Chenevière/Peter Zbinden/Michel Dubois drove their No. 66 911 Carrera RSR to a seventh place overall and third in the Grand Touring 3000 class. This car was the second RSR home and the highest-placed privateer Porsche. *Corporate Archives Porsche AG*

Cocking its front right wheel, the No. 22 Porsche 911 2.1-liter Carrera RSR Turbo of Herbert Müller and Gijs van Lennep powers its way out of the Esses on its way to a second-place finish in the 1974 race. *Corporate Archives Porsche AG*

1974 Race Results

Pos.	Car/Model	No.	Driver(s)	Entered	Class	Cl. Pos.	Laps	Reason
2	911 Carrera RSR	22	Gijs van Lennep (NL)/Herbert Müller (CH)	Porsche Martini Racing Team	Sports 3000	2	332	
7	911 Carrera RSR	66	Bernard Chenevière (CH)/Peter Zbinden (CH)/ Michel Dubois (FR)	Porsche Club Romand	Grand Touring	3	312	
10	911 Carrera RSR	70	Raymond Touroul (FR)/Henri Cachia (FR)/ Denis Rua (FR)	ASA Cachia	Grand Touring	4	288	
12	911 Carrera RSR	69	Lucien Nageotte (FR)/Pierre Laffeach (FR)	Claude Haldi	Grand Touring	6	277	
13	911 Carrera RSR	59	Pierre Mauroy (FR)/Anny-Charlotte Verney (FR)/ Martine Rénier (FR)	Pierre Mauroy	Grand Touring	7	276	
14	911 Carrera RSR	63	Jean-Claude Lagniez (FR)/Jean Egreteaud (FR)/ Gérard Meo (FR)	Jean-Claude Lagniez	Grand Touring	8	274	
19	908/02 (016)	65	Christian Poirot (FR)/Jean Rondeau (FR)	Christian Poirot	Sports 3000	7	251	
20	911 Carrera RSR	73	Michael Keyser (US)/Milt Minter (US)/ Paul Blancpain (CH)	Paul Blancpain Toad Hall	Grand Touring	11	246	
DNF	911 Carrera RSR	72	Jürgen Barth (DE)/Franz Pesch (DE)	Polifac Gelo Racing Team	Grand Touring		232	Engine
DNF	911 Carrera RSR	62	Richard Bond (GB)/Hughes de Fierlandt (BE)	Jacques Swaters Ecurie Francorchamps	Grand Touring		227	Clutch
DNF	911 Carrera RSR	67	William Vollery (CH)/Eric Chapuis (CH)/ Roger Dorchy (FR)	Porsche Club Romand	Grand Touring		225	Engine
DNF	910 (014)	44	Gérard Cuynet (FR)/Yves Evrard (FR)/ Jean-Louis Gama (FR)	Gérard Cuynet	Sports 2000		143	Out of fuel
DNF	911 Carrera RSR	64	Georg Loos (DE)/Clemens Schickentanz (DE)	Polifac Gelo Racing Team	Grand Touring		134	Ignition/ distributor
DNF	908/02 (013)	17	Guillermo Ortega (EC)/Fausto Merello (EC)/ Lothar Ranft (EC)	Ortega Ecuador Marlboro Tea	Sports 3000		122	Accident
DNF	911 Carrera RSR	61	Claude Ballot-Léna (FR)/Vic Elford (GB)/ Bob Wollek (FR)	Robert Buchet	Grand Touring		117	Gearbox/ driveshaft
DNF	911 Carrera RSR	21	Manfred Schurti (FL)/Helmuth Koinigg (AT)	Porsche Martini Racing Team	Sports 3000		87	Engine/fire
DNF	911 Carrera RSR	68	Hans Heyer (DE)/Erwin Kremer (DE)/ Paul Keller (CH)	Samson Kremer Team	Grand Touring		65	Engine
DNF	911 Carrera RSR	46	Guillermo Rojas (MX)/Hector Rebaque Sr. (MX)/ Freddie van Beuren Jr. (MX)	Rebaque-Rojas Racing Team	Sports 3000		60	Distributor
DNF	911 Carrera RSR	58	Claude Haldi (CH)/José-Maria Fernandez (ES)/ Jean-Marc Seguin (FR)	José-Maria Fernandez Escuderia Montjuich	Grand Touring		43	Engine/valves
DNF	908/02 (009)	19	Jacques Boucard (FR)/Louis Cosson (FR)	Wicky Racing Team	Sports 3000		41	Gearbox
DNF	911 Carrera RSR	60	Hubert Striebig (FR)/Hughes Kirschoffer (DE)/ Jean-Louis Chateau (FR)	Louis Meznarie	Grand Touring		23	Accident
DNF	908/03 (013)	31	Francesco Torredemer (ES)/Juan Fernandez (ES)/ Bernard Tramont (FR)	Francesco Torredemer Ecurie Tibidabo	Sports 3000		12	Gearbox

1975

June 14–15

The 1975 Le Mans will hardly go down in history as the ACO's greatest race. The absence of the big prototype players such as Matra, Alpine, Ferrari, and Alfa Romeo, and the ACO's introduction of an overriding fuel economy factor, left the event without many of its big draw cards.

No doubt with one eye on the oil crisis of a few years earlier, the new fuel consumption requirements forced race cars to be as much as 25 percent more fuel efficient than before, even more in some cases. And drivers were adopting a more economical attitude toward racing, which seems rather at odds with the fundamental principle of why teams and drivers go racing in the first place. The result was that the quickest race lap was around 11 seconds slower than the previous year's fastest lap.

Porsche did not enter a factory team that year, and even the Stuttgart engineers were absent from the circuit as they had their hands full with the development and launch of the company's new 911 Turbo model. Despite their nonattendance, Porsche had its eyes on the future, with the appearance of the Group 4 and 5 Grand Touring cars the following year.

It is little wonder then that the big teams stayed away from the event, as the ACO seemed to be going about their fuel consumption strategy in quite the wrong way. Fuel efficiency is, in any event, of prime concern for any race car manufacturer, with the car's weight being the biggest challenge. Carrying unnecessary fuel around the racetrack is counterproductive, which means that race cars are by their very nature fuel efficient in terms of the power they deliver. The imposition of a fuel improvement factor of 25 percent seems to have been the final straw that broke the camel's back: with the big names absent, crowd attendance at this race was significantly lower.

This situation played into the hands of the GT contenders, with the result that twenty-eight of the fifty-five entrants had a Porsche badge on the nose. Of those twenty-eight Porsches, twenty-five were 911s of varying description, which ranged from the S model through to the Carrera RSR. The remaining two Porsches were a pair of non-turbo 908/02s and a single 908/03.

Driven by Reinhold Joest/Mario Casoni/Jürgen Barth, the Joest-entered Porsche 908/03 drove steadily to a fourth-place finish. The aging 908 was no match for the winning Gulf Ford GR8, which had been built specifically for the 1975 rules. *Corporate Archives Porsche AG*

Driving the No. 67 911 Carrera RSR 3.0 was the all-French, all-female trio of Anny-Charlotte Verney, Corinne Tarnaud, and Yvette Fontaine. They would finish a solid eleventh overall and second in the GT Series class. *Corporate Archives Porsche AG*

Kremer Racing and Vaillant Heating would team up regularly to form a formidable combination in the future. In 1975 Erwin Kremer stepped back from his role as a driver, allowing a full-time professional team to take the helm at Le Mans. Here the battle-scarred No. 65 Kremer Carrera RSR (or Carrera RSK to the Kremer mechanics) of American Billy Sprowls and Mexicans Juan-Carlos Bolanos/Andres Contreras speeds toward a solid ninth-place overall after having qualified in twenty-sixth place on the grid. *Corporate Archives Porsche AG*

The No. 69 Porsche 911 Carrera RSR of Jean Blaton/Nick Faure/John Cooper exits the Esses on its way to an overall sixth place finish and second in the Grand Touring class. *Corporate Archives Porsche AG*

John Fitzpatrick, Toine Hezemans, Gijs van Lennep, and Manfred Schurti brought the 58 Georg Loos–entered Porsche 911 Carrera RSR 3.0 home in a fine fifth place overall and first in the GT class. *Corporate Archives Porsche AG*

During the night, the Joest/Casoni/Barth Porsche 908/03 hit a slower-moving car at the Mulsanne Corner, resulting in valuable time lost in the pits to repair the front left wing. The Porsche continued in spite of the challenges to finish in fourth place overall, eleven laps down on the winning Gulf. *Corporate Archives Porsche AG*

1975 Race Results

Pos.	Car/Model	No.	Driver(s)	Entered	Class	Cl. Pos.	Laps	Reason
4	908/03	15	Reinhold Joest (DE)/Mario Casoni (IT)/ Jürgen Barth (DE)	Joest Racing	Sports 3000	4	326	
5	911 Carrera RSR	58	John Fitzpatrick (GB)/Gijs van Lennep (NL)/ Toine Hezemans (NL)	Gelo Racing Team	Grand Touring	1	316	
6	911 Carrera RSR	69	Jean Blaton (BE)/Nick Faure (GB)/John Cooper (GB)	Jean Blaton	Grand Touring	2	312	
7	911 Carrera RSR	53	Jacques Borras (FR)/Pascal Moisson (FR)/ Henri Cachia (FR)	Henri Cachia Asa Cachia Bondy	Grand Touring	3	310	
8	911 Carrera RSR	55	Claude Ballot-Léna (FR)/Jacques Bienvenue (CA)	Ecurie Robert Buchet	Grand Touring	4	305	
9	911 Carrera RSR	65	Billy Sprowls (US)/Juan-Carlos Bolanos (MX)/ Andres Contreras (MX)	Jägermeister Kremer	Grand Touring	5	305	
10	911 Carrera RS	84	Gerhard Maurer (DE)/Christian Beez (DE)/ Eugen Strähl (CH)	Gérard Maurer	GT Series	1	296	
11	911 Carrera RS	67	Anny-Charlotte Verney (FR)/Yvette Fontaine (FR)/ Corinne Tarnaud (FR)	Anny-Charlotte Verney	GT Series	2	295	
DNF	911 Carrera RS	78	Bob Wollek (FR)/Cyril Grandet (FR)	Ecurie Buchet C. Grandet	GT Series		294	DQ – early refueling
15	911 Carrera RSR	20	Bernard Béguin (FR)/Peter Zbinden (CH)/ Claude Haldi (CH)	Porsche Club Romand	Le Mans GTX	1	291	
17	911 Carrera RS	77	Thierry Sabine (FR)/Philippe Dagoreau (FR)/ Jean-Pierre Aeschlimann (CH)	Philippe Dagoreau	GT Series	3	285	
18	911 Carrera RS	80	Raymond Touroul (FR)/Philippe Hesnault (FR)	X Racing	GT Series	4	284	
19	911 Carrera RS	63	Jean-Claude Bering (CH)/Klaus Utz (DE)/ Horst Godel (DE)	Porsche Club Romand	GT Series	5	284	
20	911 S	87	René Boubet (FR)/Philippe Dermagne (FR)	X Racing	GT Series	6	282	
23	911 Carrera RSR	61	Christian Bussi (FR)/Patrick Metral (FR)	Ecurie Armagnac Bogorre	Grand Touring	9	266	
25	911 Carrera RS	71	Joël Laplacette (FR)/Alain Leroux (FR)/ Dominique Pigeon (FR)	Joël Laplacette	Grand Touring	10	258	
NRF	908/02 (016)	3	Christian Poirot (FR)/Gérard Cuynet (FR)/ Guillermo Ortega (EC)/Jean-Claude Lagniez (FR)	Christian Poirot	Sports 3000		249	Driveshaft/transmission
NC	Carrera RSR	50	Hubert Striebig (FR)/Hughes Kirschoffer (DE)/ Pierre Mauroy (FR)	Louis Meznarie	Grand Touring		243	28th o/v, twelfth class
DNF	908/02 (009)	1	Max Cohen-Olivar (MA)/Philippe Carron (CH)/ Joël Brachet (FR)	Wicky Racing Team	Sports 3000		161	Clutch
DNF	911 Carrera RSR	59	Tim Schenken (AU)/Howden Ganley (NZ)	Gelo Racing Team	Grand Touring		106	Gearbox
DNF	911 Carrera RSR	52	William Vollery (CH)/Roger Dorchy (FR)/ Eric Chapuis (CH)	Ecurie du Nord	Grand Touring		93	Engine/valves
DNF	911 Carrera RS	68	Guy Verrier (FR)/Florian Vetsch (CH)/ Jean-Robert Corthay (CH)	Guy Verrier	Grand Touring		91	Engine/head gasket
DNF	911 Carrera RS	96	Lucien Nageotte (FR)/Gérard Picard (FR)	Bonnemaison – Thiaw	Grand Touring		48	Ignition
DNF	911 Carrera RSR	16	Clemens Schickentanz (DE)/Hartwig Bertrams (DE)	Joest Racing	Grand Touring		42	Engine
DNF	911 Carrera RSR	60	Toine Hezemans (NL)/Manfred Schurti (LI)	Gelo Racing Team	Grand Touring		41	Accident/off course
DNF	911 Carrera RSR	57	John Rulon-Miller (US)/Tom Waugh (US)/ Serge Godard (FR)	Gante Racing	Grand Touring		16	Oil system/oil leak
DNF	911 Carrera RS	83	Jean-Yves Gadal (FR)/Andre Gahinet (FR)	Jean-Yves Gadal	Grand Touring		6	Engine/ignition

1976

June 12–13

Having received rather a fright in 1975 with the low public attendance, the Le Mans organizers sought to spice things up a little, proceeding to invite all manner of entrants, including stock cars from America.

The main contenders were still to be drawn from the sports racers and GT cars traditionally seen at Le Mans. No longer referred to as Prototypes by the ACO, the top classification was now called Group 6, which included two-seater sports racing cars, ably supported by the Group 5 Silhouette racers and the Group 4 GT cars.

Porsche's new 936 Spyder model was seen for the first time in 1976. The product of the creative minds of Stuttgart's engineers

Norbert Singer and Helmut Flegl, the 936 essentially replaced the 908, which was still being run by some privateers but in danger of being cast into the "geriatric" class, as it had first seen action back in 1968. In motorsports terms, a lifespan of eight years is almost unheard-of, but the 908's successes had silenced many critics in its time.

A period of international sports car dominance for Porsche began in 1976 with their 935 and 934 sports racers. The more powerful 935 would be regarded by many racing enthusiasts as the most successful race car in its class in the world. During an eight-year period, from 1976 through 1984, the Porsche 935 won over 150 races that included over twenty class victories.

Qualifying second on the grid, the No. 20 Martini Porsche 936 of Jacky Ickx/Gijs van Lennep (the No. 19 Renault-Alpine pole sitter is already out of the picture) starts the warm-up lap alongside the No. 40 Martini Porsche 935, driven by Rolf Stommelen/Manfred Schurti, had qualified third for the start. Just behind is the No. 18 Martini Porsche 936, the factory's original test car, driven by the well-known factory pairing of Reinhold Joest/Jürgen Barth. *Corporate Archives Porsche AG*

The No. 20 Group 6–winning Porsche 936 of Jacky Ickx/Gijs van Lennep having passed under the Dunlop Bridge. Twenty minutes into the race, Jacky Ickx took the 936 into the lead, building up a useful cushion, which allowed the team to carry out repairs later in the race without losing the lead. *Corporate Archives Porsche AG*

PORSCHE 936 SPYDER

For 1976, the ACO decided to split the top class into the Group 5 category, which encompassed the Silhouette cars, and Group 6, also known as the Sports category. Word got out that Renault was taking the Group 6 challenge seriously and developing a new Spyder, which prompted Porsche to take up the challenge, although their racer was kept under wraps until the last moment.

The Stuttgart Group 6 contender was actually assembled out of the parts bins at Weissach, being built around the 908's tubular chassis, though with the wheelbase set at 94.5 inches (2,400 millimeters) it was 4 inches (100 millimeters) longer than the older car. Powered by the tried-and-tested 2,142cc flat six engine turbocharged to produce 540 horsepower, the 936 was capable of a top speed of 217.5 miles per hour (350 kilometers per hour) despite its 1,631 pounds (740 kilograms). The racer was fitted with 917 brakes, gearbox, and driveshafts (remember the 917 was itself based on the 908 chassis), while safety cells located behind the front wheels protected the fuel tank.

Externally, the 936 was characterized by a large, full-width rear wing structure (similar to the 917 LH of 1971), while engine breathing was aided by the fitment of a tall airbox that protruded, statue-like, above the driver's head.

The final body style of the 936/76 featured a high rear bulkhead and bodywork behind the driver's seat. The extended framework supported the lightweight rear bodywork. *Corporate Archives Porsche AG*

Finishing in eleventh place overall was the No. 54 Porsche 934 of French trio Hubert Striebig/Anny-Charlotte Verney/Hughes Kirschoffer. *Corporate Archives Porsche AG*

With shadows lengthening, it was time to light up those BBQs. On the track, meanwhile, this very bright orange Egon Evertz–entered No. 63 Porsche Carrera RSR was driven by the German trio of Heinz Martin/ Hartwig Bertrams/Egon Evertz. Here the Porsche, which finished ninth overall and third in Group 5, is seen doing battle with the No. 1 Inaltéra Ford-Cosworth, which finished eighth, three laps ahead of the ever-reliable RSR. *Corporate Archives Porsche AG*

Porsche stalwart Leo Kinnunen was partnered by Egon Evertz in the No. 16 Porsche 908/03 Spyder, but the car retired on the 124th lap with engine trouble. *Corporate Archives Porsche AG*

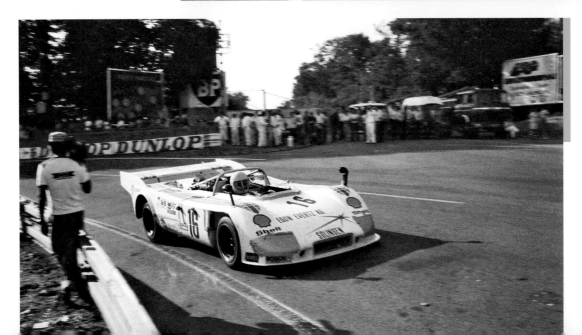

Joest Racing's No. 17 Porsche 908/03 Spyder, driven by Ernst Kraus/Günther Steckkönig, was always going to be outclassed, but did well to finish seventh. It is interesting to compare the longer rear bodywork with the No. 16 car, which has a more abrupt tail with airfoil. *Corporate Archives Porsche AG*

Rolf Stommelen and Manfred Schurti brought their No. 40 Porsche 935 home in fourth place overall. The 935 had to survive a spate of scares, though, including a broken alternator belt, a collapsed rear suspension pickup, and a damaged rear wing that required repair. Most significant was the replacement of the complete turbo unit by the Porsche mechanics in just ten minutes. *Corporate Archives Porsche AG*

Despite the setback with its cracked exhaust and errant turbo, the No. 20 Martini Porsche 936 was victorious, finishing eleven laps ahead of the second-place Mirage. The two drivers, Gijs van Lennep (*left, with champagne*) and Jacky Ickx (*right*) sit in the car after winning the race. *Corporate Archives Porsche AG*

1976 Race Results

Pos.	Car/Model	No.	Driver(s)	Entered	Class	Cl. Pos.	Laps	Reason
1	936 (002)	20	Jacky Ickx (BE)/Gijs van Lennep (NL)	Porsche Martini Intl. Racing	Sports 3000	1	350	
4	935 (002)	40	Rolf Stommelen (DE)/Manfred Schurti (LI)	Porsche Martini Intl. Racing	Group 5	1	332	
6	911 Carrera RSR	52	Raymond Touroul (FR)/Alain Cudini (FR)/René Boubet (FR)	Gérard Méo	Group 5	2	315	
7	908/03 (008)	17	Ernst Kraus (DE)/Günther Steckkönig (DE)	Joest Racing	Sports 3000	5	314	
9	911 Carrera RSR	63	Heinz Martin (DE)/Hartwig Bertrams (DE)/Egon Evertz (DE)	Egon Evertz KG	Group 5	3	303	
11	934	54	Hubert Striebig (FR)/Anny-Charlotte Verney (FR)/Hughes Kirschoffer (FR)	Louis Meznarie	Group 5	5	299	
12	911 Carrera RSR	71	Andre Gahinet (FR)/Marcel Ouviére (FR)/Jean-Yves Gadal (FR)	Andre Gahinet	Grand Touring	1	293	
13	911 Carrera RSR	53	Thierry Sabine (FR)/Philippe Dagoreau (FR)/Jean-Claude Andruet (FR)/Henri Cachia (FR)	A.S.A. Cachia	Group 5	6	289	
14	911 Carrera RS	77	Tom Waugh (US)/John Rulon-Miller (US)/Jean-Pierre Laffeach (FR)	Tom Waugh	IMSA GT	1	284	
16	934	57	Tim Schenken (AU)/Toine Hezemans (NL)	Gelo Racing Team	Grand Touring	2	278	
17	911 Carrera RSR	67	Joël Laplacette (FR)/Alain Leroux (FR)/Georges Bourdillat (FR)	Joël Laplacette	Grand Touring	3	274	
18	911 Carrera RSR	50	Thierry Perrier (FR)/Guy de Saint-Pierre (FR)/Martine Rénier (FR)	Thierry Perrier	Group 5	7	274	
NRF	935	47	Juan-Carlos Bolanos (MX)/Hans Heyer (DE)/Eduardo Lopez Negrete (MX)/Billy Sprowls (US)	Porsche Kremer Racing	Group 5		272	Fire
19	934	65	Marie-Claude Beaumont (FR)/Didier Pironi (FR)/Bob Wollek (FR)	Porsche Kremer Racing	Grand Touring	4	271	
DNF	934	58	Bernard Cheneviére (CH)/Peter Zbinden (CH)/Nicolas Bührer (CH)	Club Romand Claude Haldi	Grand Touring		270	Engine/valves
23	911 Carrera RSR	55	Christian Poirot (FR)/René Boubet (FR)/Jean-Claude Lagniez (FR)	Almeras Fréres	Group 5	8	246	
DNF	934	69	Claude Haldi (CH)/Florian Vetsch (CH)	Heinz Schiller Racing Team	Grand Touring		219	Engine/valves
DNF	936 (001)	18	Reinhold Joest (DE)/Jürgen Barth (DE)	Martini Racing Joest	Sports 3000		218	Engine
NC	934	61	Jean-Claude Andruet (FR)/Henri Cachia (FR)/Jacques Borras (FR)	A.S.A. Cachia	Grand Touring		204	Twenty-sixth
NC	934	70	Jean Blaton (BE)/Nick Faure (GB)/John Goss (AU)	Jean Blaton	Grand Touring		169	Twenty-seventh
DNF	911 Carrera RSR	78	Diego Febles (PR)/Alec Poole (IE)/Hiram Cruz (US)	McMahon/Febles	IMSA GT		144	Gearbox
DNF	908/03	16	Leo Kinnunen (FI)/Egon Evertz (DE)	Egon Evertz KG	Sports 3000		124	Engine
DNF	911 Carrera RS	72	Jean-Pierre Aeschlimann (CH)/Roger Dorchy (FR)/William Vollery (CH)	William Vollery	Le Mans GTX		82	Electrics/battery
DNF	911 Carrera RSR	62	Christian Bussi (FR)/Philippe Gurdjian (FR)/Christian Gouttepifre (FR)	Philippe Dagoreau	Grand Touring		79	Engine
DNF	911 Carrera RSR	49	Clemens Schickentanz (DE)/Howden Ganley (NZ)	Gelo Racing Team	Group 5		74	Drive shaft/transmission
DNF	934	48	Jean-Louis Chateau (FR)/Dominique Fornage (FR)/Jean-Claude Guérie (FR)	Jean-Louis Chateau	Group 5		9	Gearbox

1977
June 11–12

Being a law unto itself, the ACO could basically do whatever it wanted and, in a rude gesture to the CSI, they proceeded to populate the grid with a pleasingly wide range of cars by allowing a mixed entry of both production-based sports cars and two-seater sports racers, or prototypes, as they used to be known.

Porsche came along to the party with three Martini-sponsored cars made up of a pair of 936s and a single 935/77. One of the 936s was to be driven by Jacky Ickx/Henri Pescarolo and the other by Jürgen Barth/Hurley Haywood, although this arrangement would change midrace.

The Porsche factory effort was supported by a pair of potent 935s entered by the well-known Porsche driver George Loos's Gelo team. Another two silhouette cars were entered by the Cologne-based Kremer organization, these being a 935/K2 (Kremer's own modified 935) and a 934, the latter of which was performing extremely well.

Now featuring twin turbos and a longer tail section than their 1976 models, the Porsche 936s entered the fray almost unnoticed when compared with the well-publicized Renault onslaught in 1977. Here the No. 4 car heads the No. 7 Alpine-Renault at the end of the main straight, followed by the No. 39 Gelo Porsche 935 (retired on lap 269). In the background can be seen the No. 8 Alpine-Renault with the second No. 38 Gelo 935 (retired on lap 15), and the No. 3 Porsche 936 behind that.
Corporate Archives Porsche AG

The No. 61 Porsche 911 Carrera RS of French trio Christian Gouttepifre/Philippe Malbran/Alain Leroux would finish in tenth place overall in the 1977 race. Ironically, the No. 50 BMW 320i, seen just behind the Porsche here, would finish in ninth place, while the No. 48 Carrera behind that would retire on lap 90 with gearbox trouble. *Corporate Archives Porsche AG*

Henri Pescarolo overrevved the engine of the No. 3 Martini Porsche 936 going into Arnage, causing that car to exit the race on lap 45. As a result of its departure, Jacky Ickx joined the Barth/Haywood team in the No. 4 Martini Porsche 936/77, where the Belgian ace was put to good use setting the fastest lap of 3:36.8 in that car. *Corporate Archives Porsche AG*

The Kremer-entered No. 58 Porsche 934, driven by Bob Wollek/J. P. Wielemans/Philippe Gurdjian, came home in seventh place overall and first in the Grand Touring class in the 1977 race. *Corporate Archives Porsche AG*

PORSCHE 935—THE MOST SUCCESSFUL GT RACER EVER PRODUCED

Introduced back in 1975, Porsche's 934 and 935 were attempts by the Stuttgart company to take advantage of the ACO's new Silhouette rules intended for that season, but the rules were actually only implemented in 1976. The 934 was created to race in Group 4, and these cars were intended for Porsche's customers. The Group 5 935, on the other hand, was a hairy-chested brute reserved for the factory's drivers.

The rules governing Group 5 cars allowed the manufacturers a fair degree of flexibility as long as the race car closely resembled the silhouette of the production car (911 Turbo) and any additional aerodynamic aids did not extend beyond the basic shape of the car when viewed from the front. Norbert Singer was clearly in his element with these rules as, in the 935, he produced one of the most successful sports racers in the history of the sport.

Big spoilers were the order of the day, but under the engine cover lurked a turbocharged 3.0-liter engine that in 1976 developed in the order of 650 horsepower. Braking was courtesy of 917 calipers, while the cooling fan was placed in a horizontal position as opposed to the vertical unit in the production car.

Kremer was undoubtedly the most adventurous of the privateer teams to use the early 935s, as their K1 (1976) and K2 (1977) models used their own in-house-developed turbo intercooler. In 1977, the K2 was fitted with secret higher lift cams, but the No. 42 car was a nonfinisher in the race that year. The engineers at Porsche would never admit to it, but several modifications developed by Kremer for their K cars would make their way to the factory 935s, which made the Cologne boys even prouder.

The 935 went on to dominate the World Manufacturers' Championship from 1976 through 1981, until the introduction of Group C specifications for 1982. Despite this move, the 935 continued in competition on both sides of the Atlantic, ultimately amassing more than 150 race wins and twenty class victories.

Some drivers loved the 935, while others clearly did not like the car. Jochen Mass comments, "It was not the car which made the heart beat particularly. It had good performance, but it was a sort of wildly overpowered 911. You knew it was OK to drive but there was nothing fine about it, it was a muscle car from a power perspective and a muscle car in the way you had to drive it."

Porsche driver John Fitzpatrick drove 935s well into the eighties:

"Well, the 935 was a fantastic car. I mean it had terrific grip with enormous rear wheels and tires and, depending on the race, you would run anything from say 700–850 horsepower. When I got into a corner, I would start to accelerate through it and I used to turn the boost right up so it used to shoot off the corners, and then I would turn it right back so that when the engine ran up to 8,000–9,000 revs on the straight it wasn't on massive boost, so it didn't damage the engine. But I used to fiddle with the boost through and out of the corners and, of course, the guys in America didn't know about all that. It was just a great car."

Pictured here outside the Weissach Motor Sport department is the No. 41 Porsche 935/77 (chassis 005) driven by Rolf Stommelen/Manfred Schurti in the 1977 race. This car suffered from a loose rocker shaft, which caused persistent oil loss after just eight laps, eventually retiring with a blown head gasket three hours later. *Corporate Archives Porsche AG*

This was the 935's second year of competition. After a promising fourth-place finish in 1976, it was the turn of Frenchman Henri Cachia's 935 to shine in 1977 as the team of Claude Ballot-Léna/Peter Gregg/Jacques Borras brought the No. 40 car home in an impressive third place overall and first in the Group 5 class. *Corporate Archives Porsche AG*

Taking the checkered flag in the No. 4 Martini Porsche 936/77 at the end of the 1977 race was a very relieved Jürgen Barth. Barth revealed to the author that the rev counter had stopped working around two hours after the start, and the racing experience of both Ickx (who joined this car after his own retired) and Barth enabled them to change gear according to the sound of the engine. Haywood's driving style, however, was different and he found that he could not drive the car in the same way. An overrevved engine in the No. 4 car resulted in a burnt piston because of low oil pressure; in the final hour of the race, engineer Peter Falk called the car in to the pits. The team had built up such a lead, they calculated that a 30-minute pit stop to rest the engine would still allow them to rejoin the race in the lead. Ickx had already driven his allotted time/laps and, with the car running on just five cylinders, it fell to Barth to nurse the car to the end. The ACO rules stipulated that the winning car must cross the line under its own steam, with the final lap taking no longer than four times the qualifying time set by the car. So it was that Jürgen Barth left the pits for the final time (in fact after a longer-than-anticipated 42-minute stop) with a large clock strapped to his steering wheel showing him the minutes/seconds within which he must complete the final two laps—the out lap and his final lap. With Barth's experience, he was able to keep the revs down to a level that would not further damage the engine, completing the two laps in around six minutes each. In this way, Barth retained the lead and won the race, the second consecutive win for the 936 and Ickx's third straight win at Le Mans. *Corporate Archives Porsche AG*

1977 Race Results

Pos.	Car/Model	No.	Driver(s)	Entered	Class	Cl. Pos.	Laps	Reason
FL	936/77 (001)	4	Jacky Ickx (BE)	Porsche Martini Intl. Racing	Time: 3:36.800 minutes		Speed: 226.494km/h; 140.737mph	
1	936/77 (001)	4	Jürgen Barth (DE)/Hurley Haywood (US)/ Jacky Ickx (BE)	Porsche Martini Intl. Racing	Group 6	1	343	
3	935	40	Claude Ballot-Léna (FR)/Peter Gregg (US)/ Jacques Borras (FR)	JMS Racing Team	Group 5	1	316	
7	934	58	Bob Wollek (FR)/J.P. Wielemans (BE)/ Philippe Gurdjian (FR)	Porsche Kremer Racing	Grand Touring	1	299	
10	911 Carrera RS	61	Christian Gouttepifre (FR)/Philippe Malbran (FR)/ Alain Leroux (FR)	Christian Gouttepifre	Grand Touring	2	282	
12	911 Carrera RSR	70	Simon de Latour (GB)/Jean-Pierre Delaunay (FR)/ Jacques Guérin (FR)	ASA Cachia	IMSA GT	3	276	
14	911 Carrera RS	79	Jean-Louis Ravenel (FR)/Jacques Ravenel (FR)/ Jean-Marie Détrin (FR)	Ravenel Freres	IMSA GT	4	276	
NRF	935	39	Toine Hezemans (NL)/Tim Schenken (AU)/Hans Heyer (DE)	Gelo Racing Team	Group 5		269	Fuel injection
18	911 Carrera RSR	47	Anny-Charlotte Verney (FR)/René Metge (FR)/ Dany Snobeck (FR)/Hubert Striebig (FR)	Anny-Charlotte Verney	Group 5	2	255	
19	934	56	Jean-Louis Bousquet (FR)/Cyril Grandet (FR)/ Philippe Dagoreau (FR)	JMS Racing Team	Grand Touring	3	254	
20	911 Carrera RSR	77	Dennis Aase (US)/Robert Kirby (US)/John Hotchkis Sr. (US)	Kirby/Hitchcock Wynn's International	IMSA GT	6	247	
DNF	911 Carrera RS	96	André Savary (CH)/Jean-Robert Corthay (CH)/ Antoine Salamin (CH)	GVEA – Habethur	Le Mans GTX		211	Engine/head gasket
DNF	911 Carrera RSR	78	John Rulon-Miller (US)/John Cooper (GB)/ Pete Lovett (GB)	Charles Ivey Racing	IMSA GT		198	Engine/ignition
DNF	911 Carrera RS	80	Bernard Béguin (FR)/René Boubet (FR)/ Jean-Claude Briavoine (FR)	Bernard Béguin	IMSA GT		191	Engine/head gasket
DNF	934	59	François Servanin (FR)/Laurent Ferrier (FR)/ Franz Hummel (FR)	Schiller Racing Team	Grand Touring		160	Gearbox
DNF	934	60	Claude Haldi (CH)/Florian Vetsch (CH)/ Angelo Pallavicini (CH)	Schiller Racing Team	Grand Touring		123	Engine
DNF	934	57	Willy Braillard (BE)/Guillermo Ortega (EC)/ Nicolas Koob (LX)	Nicolas Koob	Grand Touring		116	Engine/head gasket
DNF	934	55	Juan Fernandez (ES)/Eugenio Baturone (ES)/ Raphaël Tarradas (ES)	Juan Fernandez Escuderia Monjuich	Grand Touring		115	Engine
DNF	911 Carrera RS	63	Joël Laplacette (FR)/Yves Courage (FR)/ Andre Gahinet (FR)	Joël Laplacette	Grand Touring		100	Engine
DNF	911 Carrera RS	48	Thierry Perrier (FR)/Jean Belliard (FR)	Thierry Perrier	Group 5		90	Gearbox
DNF	934/5	49	Guy Chasseuil (FR)/Hubert Striebig (FR)/ Hughes Kirschoffer (FR)	Hubert Striebig	Group 5		65	Engine/head
DNF	935/77 (005)	41	Rolf Stommelen (DE)/Manfred Schurti (LI)	Porsche Martini Intl. Racing	Group 5		52	Engine
DNF	911 Carrera RS	62	Georges Bourdillat (FR)/Bruno Sotty (FR)/ Alain-Michel Bernhard (FR)	Georges Bourdillat	Grand Touring		52	Engine
DNF	936/77 (002)	3	Jacky Ickx (BE)/Henri Pescarolo (FR)	Porsche Martini Intl. Racing	Group 6		45	Engine
DNF	935	38	Tim Schenken (AU)/Toine Hezemans (NL)/ Hans Heyer (DE)	Gelo Racing Team	Group 5		15	Engine
DNF	935 K2	42	John Fitzpatrick (GB)/Guy Edwards (GB)/ Nick Faure (GB)	Porsche Kremer Racing	Group 5		15	Engine

1978

June 10–11

If Porsche could ever have been charged with playing musical chairs with its drivers at a race, the 1978 Le Mans was that event. Entering a squad of four factory cars, Porsche's three 936s and lone 935/78 offered a mix of innovation and old technology.

The two top 936s, the No. 5 car driven by Jacky Ickx/Henri Pescarolo and the No. 6 car driven by Bob Wollek/Jürgen Barth, featured the relatively small but extremely powerful 2.1-liter engine with the latest twelve-valve, twin overhead camshaft, water-cooled cylinder heads, and a turbocharger-per-cylinder bank. In this form the 936/78 engines developed around 580 horsepower, while the No. 7 936/77 driven by Hurley Haywood/Peter Gregg/Reinhold Joest was fitted with the older single turbo, a slightly less powerful engine from the previous year.

Every so often Porsche produces a real gem of a racer, and the Martini-sponsored 935/78 "Moby Dick" was just such a vehicle. Equipped with a twin-turbo 3.2-liter engine, promising a top speed of around 228 miles per hour (366 kilometers per hour) from its 845 horsepower, this racer was loved by almost all who raced her. Jochen Mass, who didn't drive it at Le Mans, recalls, "That car was nice, I loved that 'Moby Dick,' it was a great car to drive. It was the only type I really fancied of these 935s."

In total, there were ten Porsche 935s in the field. Apart from the single works Martini car (No. 43), there were no fewer than nine privateer teams, consisting of a trio of cars entered by the Kremer team (Nos. 44, 45, and 46), two cars by Dick Barbour (Nos. 90 and 91), and one each by the Georg Loos team (No. 47), Cachia (No. 41), Heinz Schiller (No. 48), and the Whittington brothers (No. 94).

Jacky Ickx, "Mister Le Mans," set the fastest qualifying time of 3:27.6 (146.974 miles per hour/236.5 kilometers per hour) in the No. 5 Martini Porsche 936/78, which annoyed the French driver Jean-Pierre Jabouille so much that, despite being in second place on the grid, crossed the line at the end of the first lap of the race more than 11 seconds ahead of the leading Porsche. This compared with the qualifying lap record of 3:13.9 (155.386 miles per hour/250 kilometers per hour) set by Pedro Rodriguez in 1971 driving the 917 LH. The track, which measured 8.369 miles (13.47 kilometers) then, had been extended slightly to 8.476 miles (13.64 kilometers) in 1978, and engine capacities, which had nudged 5.0-liters in 1971, were now set at 3.0 liters, highlighting the advances made in turbocharging, construction, and aerodynamics in the intervening seven years.

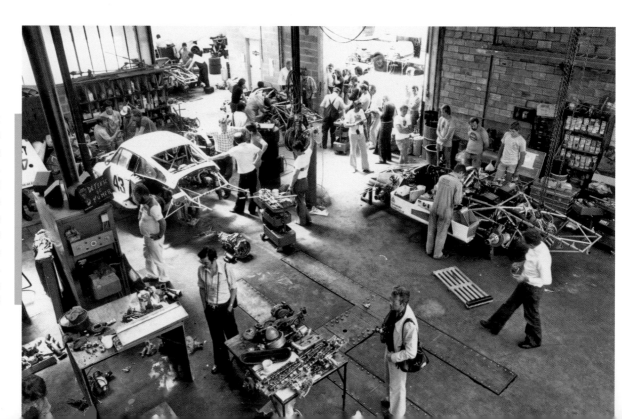

Porsche's quartet of factory cars is prepared in the workshops at Teloché. The No. 43 Martini Porsche 935/78 can be seen on the left of the photo, while the three 936s occupy positions along the far wall. *Corporate Archives Porsche AG*

With all the preparations now behind them, it's time to race as the field is led on the warm-up lap by a Porsche 928 safety car. Jacky Ickx (No. 5) had snatched pole position from the Renaults, while the second-place No. 1 Alpine-Renault A443 can just be made out behind the safety car. On the second row of the grid is the third-place No. 43 Martini Porsche 935/78; alongside is the No. 6 936 of Wollek/Barth, and just behind them is the No. 7 Porsche 936/77 of Haywood/Gregg. *Corporate Archives Porsche AG*

Despite being a certain class winner prior to the race, the No. 43 Martini Porsche "Moby Dick" works car, driven by Rolf Stommelen/Manfred Schurti, suffered a broken piston seal that resulted in excessive oil consumption; it eventually finished eighth overall and third in Group 5. The 935 series saw the introduction of the wheel inserts, which helped with brake cooling around the wheels, a feature only adopted by Formula 1 in recent years. *Corporate Archives Porsche AG*

Almost considered old technology when compared with the potent 935s in the same race, the somewhat international team of Larry Perkins/Gordon Spice/Jim Rullon-Miller brought their No. 97 Carrera RSR 3.0 home in fourteenth place overall and second in the IMSA GTX class. *Corporate Archives Porsche AG*

After a change of turbocharger some five hours into the race, the No. 7 Martini Porsche 936/77, driven by Hurley Haywood/Peter Gregg/Reinhold Joest, finished third overall, proving that the previous year's technology still worked. It's interesting to contrast the tail section of this 1977 car with that of the later 1978 car, which was also fitted with large side air intakes. *Corporate Archives Porsche AG*

The Dick Barbour–entered No. 90 Porsche 935/77A finished fifth. Out of the team of Brian Redman/Dick Barbour/John Paul Sr., Redman, in his first finish at Le Mans, took the lion's share at the wheel. This was the highest-finishing 935 in 1978, which saw the car claiming top spot in the IMSA GTX class. *Corporate Archives Porsche AG*

Driven by the all-American trio of Jim Busby, Rick Knoop, and Chris Cord, the No. 44 Porsche 935/77A finished in a hard-fought sixth place overall and first in the Group 5 class. *Corporate Archives Porsche AG*

Jacky Ickx and Henri Pescarolo were listed as the drivers in the No. 5 Martini Porsche 936/78, but after five hours the car pitted with its fifth gear missing, which required a forty-five minute operation. In the seventh hour it was decided to transfer Ickx to the No. 6 sister car and put Jochen Mass (who was down as reserve driver for both the No. 6 and No. 7 cars) into the No. 5 car. It is no secret that Mass did not like Le Mans because of the huge speed differential between the front and back markers; as a member of the Grand Prix Drivers' Association (GPDA), he had grave concerns about the circuit's safety policies. At one point in the race, he was running on just five cylinders and pushing the car to catch a Renault ahead of him. Another car had just blown its engine right in the Porsche Curves (this section of the circuit added in 1972), which deposited oil on the track. This caused the No. 5 Porsche to skid and hit the Armco barrier on lap 255, resulting in a DNF. *Corporate Archives Porsche AG*

After an eventful 1978 race, the No. 6 Martini Porsche, piloted by Jürgen Barth/ Bob Wollek/Jacky Ickx, finished second. Ickx had started the race in car No. 5, which broke its fifth gear early on, and he was then switched to the No. 6 car, which, ironically also broke its fifth gear early on Sunday morning after the Belgian had climbed as high as second place by midnight on Saturday. Although the gap held by Renault over the No. 6 Porsche had been around eight laps at the time of the gearbox breakage, this had been reduced to five laps when the flag fell at 4:00 p.m. on Sunday. *Corporate Archives Porsche AG*

1978 Race Results

Pos.	Car/Model	No.	Driver(s)	Entered	Class	Cl. Pos.	Laps	Reason
2	936/78 (001)	6	Bob Wollek (FR)/Jürgen Barth (DE)/Jacky Ickx (BE)/Reinhold Joest (DE)	Porsche Martini Intl. Racing	Sports 2000	2	365	
3	936/77 (002)	7	Hurley Haywood (US)/Peter Gregg (US)/Reinhold Joest (DE)	Porsche Martini Intl. Racing	Sports 2000	3	363	
5	935/77A	90	Brian Redman (GB)/Dick Barbour (US)/John Paul (US)	Dick Barbour Racing	IMSA GTX	1	338	
6	935/77A	44	Jim Busby (US)/Chris Cord (US)/Rick Knoop (US)	Porsche Kremer Racing	Group 5	1	337	
7	935	41	Alfredo Guarana (BR)/Paulo Gomes (BR)/Mario Amaral (BR)	ASA Cachia	Group 5	2	330	
8	935/78 (007)	43	Manfred Schurti (FL)/Rolf Stommelen (DE)	Porsche	Group 5	3	327	
12	Carrera RSR	66	Anny-Charlotte Verney (FR)/Xavier Lapeyre (FR)/François Servanin (FR)/Hubert Stiebig (FR)	Anny-Charlotte Verney	Grand Touring	1	280	
14	Carrera RSR	97	Larry Perkins (AU)/Gordon Spice (GB)/John Rulon-Miller (US)	Charles Ivey Racing	IMSA GTX	2	279	
17	934	62	Christian Bussi (FR)/Jean-Claude Briavoine (FR)/Andre Gahinet (FR)	Andre Gahinet	Grand Touring (+3000)	1	260	
DNF	936/78 (003)	5	Jacky Ickx (BE)/Henri Pescarolo (FR)/Jochen Mass (DE)	Porsche Martini Intl. Racing	Sports 2000		255	Accident
NC	Carrera RSR	64	Georges Bourdillat (FR)/Alain-Michel Bernard (FR)/Jean-Luc Favresse (FR)	Georges Bourdillat	Grand Touring	2	242	
NC	935/77	45	Louis Krages (DE)/Dieter Schornstein (DE)/Philippe Gurdjian (FR)	Porsche Kremer Racing	Group 5		183	Distance
DNF	934	68	Edgar Dören (DE)/Gerhard Holup (DE)/Hervé Poulain (FR)/Roman Feitler (LX)	Hervé Poulain	Grand Touring 3000		167	Gearbox
DNF	935	91	Bob Garretson (US)/Steve Earle (US)/Bob Akin (US)	Dick Barbour Racing	IMSA GTX		159	Accident
DNF	935/76	48	Herbert Müller (CH)/Claude Haldi (CH)/Nik Mac Granger (CH)	Heinz Schiller Racing Team	Group 5		140	Gearbox casing
DNF	930	65	Antoine Salamin (CH)/Gérard Vial (CH)/Yves Courage (FR)/Joël Laplacette (FR)	Joël Laplacette	Grand Touring (3000)		116	Brakes/accident
DNF	934	61	Guy Chasseuil (FR)/Jean-Claude Lefévre (FR)	Auto Daniel Urcun	Grand Touring		61	Engine/piston
DNF	935/77A	94	Don Whittington (US)/Bill Whittington (US)/Franz Konrad (AT)	Whittington Brothers Racing	Group 5		41	Accident
DNF	934	69	Willy Braillard (BE)/Philippe Dagoreau (FR)/Jean-Louis Ravenel (FR)/Jacque Ravenel (FR)	Jean-Louis Ravenel	Grand Touring 3000		35	Injection pump
DNF	935/77A	46	Martin Raymond (GB)/J.P. Wielemans (BE)/Mike Franey (GB)	Porsche Kremer Racing/Fison	Group 5		34	Engine
DNF	935/77A	47	John Fitzpatrick (GB)/Toine Hezemans (NL)	Weisberg Gelo Team	Group 5		19	Engine/piston

1979

June 9–10

Four o'clock on Sunday afternoon of June 10, 1979, was probably one of the 935's finest hours, but there can be no doubt that, for the Cologne-based Kremer brothers, it was the realization of a lifelong dream. The small Kremer outfit had first raced at Le Mans back in 1970, and in this, their tenth year of competition in the greatest endurance race of all time, they were to be crowned kings before the great and the good in the motorsports world.

Kremer Racing had learned the art of achieving much with very little, and it was through the dedication of their committed workforce that they were able to compete on a shoestring budget compared with the resources of the big players. From the time of the company's founding in 1962, there had only ever been one qualified engineer at the Kremer workshop, as the team was made up of mechanics who worked with passion and commitment.

As was becoming the norm at Le Mans, the field in 1979 consisted mostly of Porsches, which this year comprised nineteen of the fifty-five starters. Heading up the Stuttgart contingent were a pair of factory 936s sponsored this time by Essex Petroleum. The 936s were of the longtail variety and were fitted with the familiar 2.1-liter twin-turbocharged engine that had powered the marque to victory in 1976 and 1977, albeit now with more robust fifth gears than those that had let them down in previous years.

The 936s were ably supported by a squadron of powerful, very quick 935s, with the main contenders in the Group 5 class being the Cologne-based Gelo and Kremer teams, while the Dick Barbour 935 organization fielded no fewer than four 935s. In total there were fourteen 935s on the starting grid. At the end of the race, the top three places on the podium were filled by Porsche 935s with a 934 in fourth spot.

The traditional starting time of 4:00 p.m. on Saturday was changed to 2:00 p.m. to allow the French public sufficient time to cast their votes for the EEC's new European Assembly.

All four of the Dick Barbour Racing Porsche 935s line up in the pits ahead of the 1979 race, each with the Stars and Stripes draped over the rear wing. *From left to right*: No. 73 935/77 (934 1/2)—John Hotchkiss, Bob Kirby, and Bob Harmon; No. 72 935/77—Bob Garretson, Skeeter McKitterick and Ed Abate; No. 71 935/78—Bob Akin, Roy Woods, and Rob McFarlin; No. 70 935/79—Dick Barbour; the team owner, Rolf Stommelen; and actor Paul Newman. *Corporate Archives Porsche AG*

Being rolled out before the start of the 1979 race is the No. 14 Porsche 936/78. Driven by Bob Wollek/Hurley Haywood/Jürgen Barth, the Essex Petroleum Porsche 936/78 retired after 236 laps with a failed engine. *Corporate Archives Porsche AG*

BRIAN REDMAN RECALLS HIS NEAR ACCIDENT IN 1979

I took over the car from Ickx early in the race, and if you were going into the pits, in those days you had to turn in immediately after you had come through the chicane, and when I went through that second part, which is a right turn, the car didn't feel right. I had a split second to decide whether to pit or to carry on, and I thought, 'Well, it's probably me,' because I was a little out of practice, so I carried on. When I turned into the 180 mile-per-hour (290 kilometer-per-hour) Dunlop Curve, the car spun because the left rear tire had gone down, and that's what I had felt.

"By some miracle I didn't hit anything, but as you can imagine, the tire and the body flew off and I had to stop and cut the tire off the rim with a hacksaw that we carried in the toolkit, and then drive it on the verge at 10 or 15 miles per hour for the seven or eight miles back to the pits. And I thought for sure we were out [of the race], but they repaired it and by midnight we were climbing back up the field. The rain was terrible, and I was standing above the pits with my friend Ian Green when Ickx stopped on the straight. It had broken a fuel pump drive belt, so we changed it and got going again and then he stopped again, and I thought, 'That is definitely it,' but half an hour later Ickx was going again, so I looked down into the pits and they waved for me to come down. I thought that this was my last time, and so I went out in the rain, the thunder and lightning, and I was driving like a madman at 200 miles per hour (322 kilometers per hour) in the dark and the rain. But after I had done about 45 minutes I got a pit signal out of sequence, so I pitted and Norbert Singer the team manager said to me, 'Brian, you can get out—we were disqualified an hour ago!'

"The mechanic had taken a sandwich to throw to Jacky Ickx, who was stuck at the Mulsanne Corner, and inside the sandwich was a fuel pump drive belt."

Redman laughs at the reason for their disqualification now.

K3 IS KREMER RACING'S SECRET WEAPON

Since the company's inception in 1962, Kremer Racing had experimented with innovative technology and weight-saving techniques. In their first year of participation in the French classic endurance race, the 1970 Kremer Porsche 911 S featured fiberglass bumpers, hood, and wings; an aluminum engine lid; a radiator-cooled, limited-slip diff and gearbox; and plexiglass windows (except for the front windscreen). They officially finished in seventh place that year.

Experience gained and lessons learned in the tough world of international motorsports served to sharpen Kremer's resolve to triumph on the racetrack wherever they competed. When Porsche produced their 934 Group 4 and 935 Group 5 racers, it was exactly the kind of factory-built racer that Kremer had been waiting for, as most of the expensive test and development work had been done for them.

Built for the 1976 motorsports season, Kremer's first major project with the 935 was their K1. This car was built up from scratch using the 935 as a base, but the engine and intercooler were developed in-house without the use of any factory parts. This step was quite remarkable in itself, as Kremer had only taken its first tentative steps in the motor racing world eight years earlier, while their first outing at Le Mans had been in 1970.

Although Kremer's attempts with the 935 K1 (1976) and K2 (1977) at Le Mans did not produce a finish, their 934 cars were achieving promising results there and elsewhere in Europe. In 1978, however, their persistence at Le Mans began to pay dividends: The Kremer Porsche 935/77A, driven by the American trio of Busby/Cord/Knoop, brought the team's No. 44 car home in sixth place overall and first in Group 5. The future looked bright, but just how bright no one would have dared predict.

For the 1979 season, Kremer unveiled its latest K3 version of the 935 with which it would take on the world's best. Featuring a widened and lengthened body made mostly of Kevlar, Kremer also lowered the chassis and covered the tubular frame with an aerodynamic body that saw many interesting modifications. The car was developed without the aid of a wind tunnel, with the bodywork specifically designed to funnel air through to the rear wing; this significantly increased the racer's downforce. Modified twin KKK turbochargers with a water-cooled intercooler system further boosted power to the 3.2-liter engine, which, with a compression ratio of 7.2:1 and with the boost up at 1.7 bar, provided an output estimated at 800 horsepower at 8,000 rpm. For the race, however, a boost setting of 1.4 bar gave the engine an output of 740 horsepower at 7,800 rpm, enabling the K3 to reach a top speed well in excess of 200 miles per hour (322 kilometers per hour).

The Whittington brothers, Don and Bill, together with Klaus Ludwig, took the checkered flag in the 1979 Le Mans race—the first privateer Porsche team to do so. This victory resulted in a surge of requests for Kremer to build K3s for other teams, and the small Cologne firm found itself flooded with orders from around the world for 935 K3 body kits. Such was the success of the K3 that no less than thirteen of these modified racers were built by Kremer Racing for other teams.

Pictured in the pit lane before the start of the 1979 race, the winning No. 41 Kremer 935 K3 *at left* of brothers Don and Bill Whittington and Klaus Ludwig sits alongside the No. 45 Kremer Racing 935 K3 *at right* driven by Axel Plankenhorn/Philippe Gurdjian/Louis Krages, which finished thirteenth. *Corporate Archives Porsche AG*

Dick Barbour in the Porsche Chicanes during practice— at least it was dry. Rolf Stommelen, Dick Barbour, and Paul Newman finished second overall and first in the IMSA +2.5 Class. *Corporate Archives Porsche AG*

The No. 73 Porsche, seen here exiting the Esses, was driven by John Hotchkiss/Bob Kirby/Bob Harmon. They would finish ninth overall and fourth in the IMSA GTX class. *Corporate Archives Porsche AG*

Comfortably fastest during practice, the two factory 936s couldn't go the distance. During practice the Porsche shed its tires with alarming regularity, and a last-minute change in wheel size caused brake problems in the 936s. Here the No. 12 Essex Porsche 936 of Jacky Ickx/ Brian Redman is in action, but Ickx would be disqualified for receiving assistance out on the circuit. *Corporate Archives Porsche AG*

The No. 71 car was the IMSA-class-winning car from the 1978 Le Mans race, having finished fifth overall the previous year. It was driven in 1979 by Bob Akin/Roy Woods/Rob McFarlin, but it retired after just seventy-eight laps with a blown head gasket. *Corporate Archives Porsche AG*

Kremer's No. 41 car, driven by the Whittington brothers and Klaus Ludwig, calls in to the pits during a rainy spell. There was understandably a lot of media attention directed at the Cologne-based car. *Corporate Archives Porsche AG*

Against all expectations, the No. 41 Numero Reserve Kremer Porsche 935 K3 triumphed in the 1979 race, the first privateer team to achieve this feat in a Porsche. Driven by the relatively unknown pairing of American brothers Don and Bill Whittington, with the somewhat better-known German driver Klaus Ludwig, the Kremer 935 K3 crossed the line first as much by attrition as by reliable performance. With a top speed of around 220 miles per hour (354 kilometers per hour), this car was quicker than any of the Group 6 cars down the Mulsanne Straight, with the exception of Jacky Ickx in the 936. The No. 41 car found itself leading the field after about fifteen hours, but there was great concern in the pits when a snapped fuel injection pump belt saw Don Whittington stranded out on the circuit. By the time Whittington had effected a Heath-Robinson repair and limped back to the pits, their substantial fifteen-lap lead had shrunk to just three laps. A seized wheel nut cost the No. 70 Porsche four laps in the pits, so the finishing gap between the winning No. 41 Porsche and the No. 70 Porsche was seven laps. Another Kremer 935, that of Laurent Ferrier/François Servanin/François Trisconi, came home in third place, having been delayed by a broken driveshaft, making it a 1–2–3 for the Porsche 935s. *Corporate Archives Porsche AG*

The No. 70 Dick Barbour Porsche 935/79, driven by team owner Rolf Stommelen and the actor Paul Newman, accelerates past the pits through the incessant rain. This car would finish second overall and first in the IMSA GTX class. *Corporate Archives Porsche AG*

1979 Race Results

Pos.	Car/Model	No.	Driver(s)	Entered	Class	Cl. Pos	Laps	Reason
FL	936/78 (003)	12	Jacky Ickx (BE)	Essex Porsche	Time: 3:36.100 minutes		Speed: 227.003km/h; 141.053mph	
1	935 K3	41	Klaus Ludwig (DE)/Don Whittington (US)/Bill Whittington (US)	Porsche Kremer Racing	Group 5	1	307	
2	935/77A	70	Rolf Stommelen (DE)/Paul Newman (US)/Dick Barbour (US)	Dick Barbour Racing	IMSA GTX	1	300	
3	935/77	40	Laurent Ferrier (FR)/François Servanin (FR)/François Trisconi (CH)	Porsche Kremer Racing	Group 5	2	293	
4	934	82	Herbert Müller (CH)/Angelo Pallavicini (CH)/Marco Vanoli (CH)	Angelo Pallavicini Lubrifilm Racing Team	Grand Touring 3000	1	292	
7	935/77A	42	Edgar Dören (DE)/Dieter Schornstein (DE)/Götz von Tschirnhaus (DE)	Dieter Schornstein Sekurit Racing	Group 5	3	284	
8	935	72	Edwin Abate (US)/Bob Garretson (US)/Skeeter McKitterick (US)	Dick Barbour Racing	IMSA GTX	3	279	
9	935	73	Robert Kirby (US)/Bob Harmon (US)/John Hotchkis (US)	Dick Barbour Racing Stanton Barbour	IMSA GTX	4	276	
11	935	43	Claude Haldi (CH)/Rodrigo Teran (PA)/Herbert Loewe (CH)	Claude Haldi	Group 5	4	271	
13	935 K3	45	Axel Plankenhorn (DE)/Philippe Gurdjian (FR)/Louis Krages (DE)	Porsche Kremer Racing	Group 5	5	269	
15	935	39	Jacques Guérin (FR)/Jacques Goujon (FR)/Frédéric Alliot (FR)	ASA Cachia	Group 5	6	265	
16	934	86	Georges Bourdillat (FR)/Pascal Ennequin (FR)/Alain-Michel Bernard (FR)	Alain-Michel Bernard Kores Racing	Grand Touring 3000	2	259	
19	934	84	Anny-Charlotte Verney (FR)/Patrick Bardinon (FR)/René Metge (FR)	Anny-Charlotte Verney	Grand Touring 3000	3	243	
NRF	936/78 (001)	14	Bob Wollek (FR)/Hurley Haywood (US)	Essex Porsche	Sports 2000		236	Engine
DNF	935/77A	36	Manfred Schurti (FL)/Hans Heyer (DE)	Gelo Racing Team	Group 5		201	Engine
DNF	936/78 (003)	12	Jacky Ickx (BE)/Brian Redman (GB)	Essex Porsche	Sports 2000		200	DQ – outside assistance
DNF	935/77A	37	John Fitzpatrick (GB)/Jean-Louis Lafosse (FR)/Harald Grohs (DE)	Gelo Racing Team	Group 5		196	Engine
DNF	934	87	Christian Bussi (F)/Bernard Salam (F)	Christian Bussi	Grand Touring 3000		182	Accident damage
DNF	935/79	68	Ted Field (US)/Milt Minter (US)/John Morton (US)	Ted Field Interscope Racing	IMSA GTX		154	Engine
DNF	935/77A	71	Bob Akin (US)/Roy Woods (US)/Rob McFarlin (US)	Dick Barbour Racing	IMSA GTX		78	Head gasket
DNF	935	74	Jean-Pierre Jarier (FR)/Randolph Townsend (US)/Raymond Touroul (FR)	Jean-Pierre Jarier	IMSA GTX		65	Engine

CHAPTER 4

1980s

Lined up for the photo shoot following
scrutineering for the 1982 race are the
three works Porsche Group C cars.
Corporate Archives Porsche AG

Domination, Porsche Style

At least on the European and American stage, the 1980s began with the knowledge that Group 6 was to be replaced with the FIA's latest Group C rules in 1982. This resulted in a varied collection of contenders at Le Mans in the early part of that decade, as some manufacturers understandably delayed the development of their new cars while others went ahead with theirs. Whether one viewed this situation with pessimism or interest, such a varied grid did provide the race-goer with some entertaining trackside action.

While some manufacturers may have withheld their new cars, in Europe, at least, this situation did play into the hands of the privateer teams such as Loos and Kremer. With Kremer's victory at Le Mans in 1979 came the inevitable demand for performance components from the Cologne company, which served to push Erwin Kremer and his team to produce even more advanced technical innovations for their own as well as their customer's cars.

The expectation was that Kremer would produce a bigger, better version of its formidable K3, which was logically called the K4. Only two 935 K4s were built, one being the right-hand-drive Jägermeister car in that sponsor's familiar orange livery, and the other a similar left-hand-drive vehicle. The K4 featured bigger turbos, an intercooler and oil pump, but the K4's rear body differed substantially from the K3's in that the entire back end was fabricated over the existing rear window so that the team could open the complete rear section of the car as one large piece. This gave the pit crew an advantage during pit stops by allowing much-improved access to the engine, gearbox, wheels, and other vital parts.

In the 1970s, professional drivers still had to be somewhat creative if they were to secure sufficient drives in a year to make a decent living, as John Fitzpatrick recalls: "I can remember when we used to do a season with Kremer or Georg Loos or Ford. In the early to midseventies, driving in the works team or a winning car, we used to earn about DM100,000 a year. In 1980, when I won the Porsche Cup, I won a lot of races that year, I probably made about a maximum of $200,000."

As race car speeds continued to increase, even in the lower ranks, the level of sponsorship, investment in research and development, driver/team professionalism, and subsequently salaries, all rose substantially in the 1980s. Fitzpatrick again: "When I stopped [in 1984], I remember Klaus Ludwig carried on and drove for Mercedes, he was the first touring car driver to have a DM1-million contract."

1980

June 14–15

The 1980 Le Mans event would be the last for Porsche's chief executive, Professor Fuhrmann. Father of the famous four-cam Carrera engine, Fuhrmann had allegedly overstepped the mark when he decided to phase out the 911 by 1984 and replace it with a range of water-cooled, front-engined cars that would meet the more stringent noise and emissions regulations threatening the industry. He dictated that the 936 was also to go, and that the new decade would see a squad of 924 Carrera GTs taking to the Sarthe Circuit.

Once the shock of this announcement had died down at Weissach, it was revealed that, for the 1980 Le Mans race, each of the three 924s to be entered would be driven by representative drivers from the nations of Germany, Britain, and America. The three cars to run in the LM GTP class would be manned by Manfred Schurti/Jürgen Barth in the German car; Andy Rouse/Tony Dron in the British car; and Derek Bell/Al Holbert in the American car, with Bell standing in for the injured Peter Gregg at the last moment.

Despite Fuhrmann's insistence that there would be no more 936 development, a rather modern-looking 908/80 lined up on the grid in Martini colors. Built by Joest and driven by him,

Jacky Ickx, and the late inclusion of Michel Leclère, the 908/80 was fabricated at Joest's Karlsruhe workshop and built around a 908/4 chassis with many "spare" 936 parts.

Although the 924s surprised the most, the move by Fuhrmann had rattled some cages in high places, most significantly that of Ferry Porsche, and by the end of the year Fuhrmann had been given his marching orders.

On the racing front, the ACO was up to some new tricks this year: the grid positions would not be determined by the cars according to their fastest lap times, instead being placed according to the average of the fastest lap times of all the drivers in each car. Thus, when the ACO came to eliminate those cars that had not qualified in each class, there was great consternation and confusion in the paddock, but the ACO conceded by allowing fifty-five cars to start, rather than the fifty that had been previously stipulated.

The start of the 1980 race was a wet affair. Here the pace vehicle, a Porsche 928 S, leads the No. 70 Dick Barbour Racing Porsche 935 K3/80 and the No. 15 Rondeau M379 off the line. *Corporate Archives Porsche AG*

The No. 93 Porsche 911 SC, driven by the French pairing of Thierry Perrier and Roger Carmillet, ran a steady race to finish sixteenth overall, winning the GT class. *Corporate Archives Porsche AG*

The No. 3 Porsche 924 Carrera GT "Le Mans," driven by Derek Bell/Al Holbert, finished thirteenth overall, just behind the Rouse/Dron car. *Corporate Archives Porsche AG*

The No. 4 Porsche 924 Carrera GT "Le Mans," driven by Jürgen Barth/Manfred Schurti, corners hard during its fine run to finish sixth overall. *Corporate Archives Porsche AG*

924 MEMORIES

Tony Dron, who tested the 924 GT Prototype ahead of the 1980 Le Mans race, said, "The 924 Carrera GT Prototype of 1980 was a quite remarkable car. We did a 36-hour test before Le Mans at Ricard with several drivers, and I remember in our car we had Derek [Bell] and Andy [Rouse] and myself and the obvious idea was to drive it for more than 24 hours absolutely flat out."

Norbert Singer was running the test for the works team at Circuit Paul Ricard. The engineers were most concerned about the cylinder head temperatures and the survival of the valves. Dron again: "We had a digital readout of cylinder head temperatures up on top of the dashboard, and up until you got halfway along that long straight at Ricard it just climbed slowly, but between halfway and two thirds of the way along the straight, it went mad and started whizzing in front

of you. So that was a bit of a worry, and sure enough we did have valves burning out after about 18 hours, but that was repaired and so we carried on."

Although the team had done tests at the factory simulating Le Mans laps, they still needed to put in some real-time testing. Dron continued: "I asked whether it would be necessary just to ease off a bit two thirds along the Mulsanne Straight just to look after the valves, and they said 'No, this car will run for 24 hours now.' Well, two of them didn't, and ours (No. 2) was one, which was extremely disappointing."

The cars finished in sixth, twelfth, and thirteenth places, with the latter two struggling home on three and two cylinders respectively. Dron recalled:

"For the last six hours of the race, Andy and I had to run with reduced power. It was still reaching the same speed down the Mulsanne Straight, but it just took much longer to get there, so

we were losing 15 seconds to 20 seconds a lap. But what I do remember that car for is that the wonderful integrity of its chassis, an extremely stiff chassis and the handling of the car, were extraordinarily good. One of the best-handling cars I have ever driven, I really liked the feel of it. We had a great sort of mixture of weather that year, I remember going down the straight and seeing three lots of rain and three lots of sun in front of me on the straight. The car was just fabulous from that point of view and, you know, with 350 horsepower I think it was doing 180–185 miles per hour (290–298 kilometers per hour) on the straight."

The No. 2 Porsche 924 Carrera GT Turbo, driven by Andy Rouse/ Tony Dron, finished twelfth despite being one cylinder short at the flag. *Corporate Archives Porsche AG*

The American father-and-son team of John Paul Sr. and John Paul Jr., together with Briton Guy Edwards, brought their No. 73 Porsche 935 K3 home in ninth place. Despite a severe off-course excursion under the Dunlop Bridge due to a torrential downpour on Sunday, John Paul Sr. was able to extricate himself sufficiently well to continue. *Corporate Archives Porsche AG*

A heavy thunderstorm drenched the circuit just before the start, but John Fitzpatrick, having qualified second on the grid, got the drop on Henri Pescarolo in the No. 15 Rondeau M379 and was ahead of the resultant spray. Driving the No. 70 Dick Barbour Racing–entered 935 K3/80, the extremely experienced trio of John Fitzpatrick/Brian Redman/Dick Barbour managed to finish fifth overall and first in the IMSA GTX class. Fitzpatrick said, "The 935 engine always had problems at Le Mans with burnt pistons. It happened to me in 1980 and 1982, although we did manage to finish both times by disconnecting the cylinder." *Corporate Archives Porsche AG*

Jacky Ickx set both the fastest qualifying time and the fastest race lap in the No. 9 Porsche 908/80. After driving steadily in the first few hours, the car took the lead at the four-and-a-half-hour mark but lost it when Ickx stopped a short while later with a broken fuel injection pump drive belt. However, the car was back in the lead at the halfway mark (4:00 a.m. Sunday). Then, after a delay of almost an hour thanks to the old 936 problem of a broken fifth gear, the Porsche once again regained its composure in the hands of Ickx, staging what looked like a dramatic comeback—if it hadn't been for a gamble to fit rain tires in the dying stages of the race, things may have looked quite different. The Belgian brought the Porsche to the finish line for a fine second place behind the winning Rondeau-Ford. *Corporate Archives Porsche AG*

1980 Race Results

Pos.	Car/Model	No.	Driver(s)	Entered	Class	Cl. Pos	Laps	Reason
FL	908/80 (004)	9	Jacky Ickx (BE)	Martini Racing	Time: 3:40.600 minutes		Speed: 222.373km/h; 138.176mph	
2	908/80 (004)	9	Jacky Ickx (BE)/Reinhold Joest (DE)	Martini Racing	Sports +2000	2	337	
5	935 K3/80	70	John Fitzpatrick (GB)/Brian Redman (GB)/ Dick Barbour (US)	Dick Barbour Racing	IMSA GTX	1	318	
6	924 Carrera GT Turbo	4	Manfred Schurti (FL)/Jürgen Barth (DE)	Porsche	Le Mans GTP	2	317	
8	935/77A	49	Harald Grohs (DE)/Dieter Schornstein (DE)/ Götz von Tschirnhaus (DE)	Dieter Schornstein Vegla Racing Team	Group 5	1	314	
9	935 K3	73	John Paul Sr. (US)/Guy Edwards (GB)/ John Paul Jr. (US)	JLP Racing	IMSA GTX	2	313	
12	924 Carrera GT Turbo	2	Andy Rouse (GB)/Tony Dron (GB)/ Eberhard Braun (DE)/Derek Bell (GB)	Porsche	Le Mans GTP	3	311	
13	924 Carrera GT Turbo	3	Derek Bell (GB)/Al Holbert (USA)	Porsche	Le Mans GTP	4	306	
16	911 SC	93	Thierry Perrier (FR)/Roger Carmillet (FR)	Thierry Perrier	Grand Touring	1	281	
20	935	89	Dany Snobeck (FR)/Hervé Poulain (FR)/ Pierre Destic (FR)	Hervé Poulain	IMSA GTX	6	272	
DNF	934	94	Jacques Alméras (FR)/Jean-Marie Alméras (FR)/Marianne Hoepfner (FR)	Équipe Alméras Fréres	Grand Touring		255	Accident
24	934	90	Georges Bourdillat (FR)/Alain-Michel Bernhard (FR)/Roland Ennequin (FR)	Georges Bourdillat	Grand Touring +2000	2	249	
DNF	935 K3	69	Bob Akin (US)/Ralph Kent-Cooke (US)/ Paul Miller (US)	Mendez/Woods/Akin Racing Associates Inc.	IMSA GTX		237	Gearbox/ driveshaft
DNF	935 K3-80	43	Xavier Lapeyre(FR)/Jean-Louis Trintignant (FR)/Anny-Charlotte Verney (FR)	Malardeau Kremer Racing	Group 5		217	Gearbox/ differential
DNF	935	45	Bob Wollek (FR)/Helmut Kelleners (DE)	Gelo Racing Team	Group 5		191	Engine/piston
DNF	935 K3-80	42	Tetsu Ikuzawa (JP)/Rolf Stommelen (DE)/ Axel Plankenhorn (DE)	Kremer Racing Team	Group 5		167	Engine/head gasket
DNF	934	80	Mandy Gonzalez/(PR) Diego Febles (PR)/ Francisco Romero (YV)	Diego Febles Racing	Grand Touring		164	Accident
DNF	935 K3	44	John Cooper (GB)/Dudley Wood (GB)/ Pete Lovett (GB)	Charles Ivey Racing	Group 5		158	Engine/head gasket
DNF	935 K3	85	Hurley Haywood (US)/Don Whittington (US)/ Dale Whittington (US)	Whittington Brothers Racing	IMSA GTX		151	Differential
DNF	934	91	Christian Bussi (FR)/Bernard Salam (FR)/ Cyril Grandet (FR)	ASA Cachia	Grand Touring		137	Engine
DNF	935 K3	71	Bobby Rahal (US)/Bob Garretson (US)/ Allan Moffat (AU)	Dick Barbour Racing	IMSA GTX		134	Engine/piston
DNF	935 K3-80	41	Ted Field (US)/Danny Ongais (US)/ Jean-Louis Lafosse (FR)	Kremer Racing Team	Group 5		89	Engine/piston
DNF	935/77A	46	Claude Haldi (CH)/Bernard Béguin (FR)/ Volkert Merl (DE)	Claude Haldi Mecarillos Racing	Group 5		37	Engine/ camshaft
DNF	935 K3	68	Skeeter McKitterick/(US)/ Charles Mendez (US)/Leon Walger (AR)	Mendez/Woods/Akin Racing Associates Inc.	IMSA GTX		9	Accident/spin
DNF	935 K3	72	Robert Kirby (US)/Bob Harmon (US)/ Michael Sherwin (US)/Siegfried Brunn (DE)	Dick Barbour Racing/ Wynns Racing	IMSA GTX		7	Collision/ wheel

1981

June 13–14

The use of a pace car was introduced for the first time at Le Mans this year, to be deployed in the event of a potentially dangerous race situation. The aim was to slow the field to a manageable speed, allowing the track crew to clear away debris following a crash or remove a damaged or stopped car from the track.

After the family management upheaval in Stuttgart at the end of 1980 and following the departure of Ernst Fuhrmann, Porsche once again reinstated its motorsports program with the aim of dominating the top step of the podium. This renewed competitive spirit replaced the detuned race program that had been proposed by Fuhrmann, the outgoing chief executive.

Porsche engineer Helmuth Bott was tasked with the responsibility of coming up with a Le Mans winner, and so was born the 936/81. This new racer differed from its predecessors, the 936 Spyder and 936/80, in that it was fitted with a larger 2,650cc engine rescued from the abandoned Indy 500 project. The bigger engine developed 100 horsepower more than the 2,142cc unit that had powered the earlier car. Although this only raised the top speed from 217 miles per hour (350 kilometers per hour) to 224 miles per hour (360 kilometers per hour), the extra capacity handily pushed the maximum power to 640 horsepower. At 195 inches (4,950 millimeters), the 936/81 was longer than its predecessor by 10 inches (254 millimeters), which included a wheelbase that was longer by 0.4 inches (10 millimeters). This, coupled with the much-revised rear spoiler arrangement, aided high-speed stability. Although the car was 10 inches (254 millimeters) higher, it was only 22 pounds (10 kilograms) heavier than the 1977 version. Sponsorship of the new 936/81 was now courtesy of Jules, a newly launched Christian Dior fragrance for men.

Porsche also entered a pair of special cars derived from the 924, the first being the No. 36 Porsche 924 Carrera GTR (1,983cc) driven by Manfred Schurti and Andy Rouse. The second was the No. 1 Porsche 924 GTP Le Mans powered by a 2.5-liter engine, driven by Jürgen Barth and Walter Röhrl. Despite being given a real thrashing by factory drivers Barth and Röhrl, the No. 1 car came home in seventh place overall. Immediately after the race,

Porsche announced the introduction of the new 944 production model, which was coincidentally also powered by the 2.5-liter engine as used by Barth/Röhrl in the twenty-four-hour race that had just been completed.

Not to be left out of the picture, Kremer Racing produced a bit of a shock when the team arrived at Le Mans with a Porsche 917. Having long held the view that the 917 was a superb racing design, the Kremers had been buying up and storing whatever 917 parts they could find. Eventually they had almost enough parts to build two 917s, but this certainly gave them what they needed to build one good car with sufficient spares to keep it running and make repairs. Kremer left the building of the 4.5-liter engine to Porsche itself, as there was no one else around who had more experience with the big twelve-cylinder powerplant.

Activity in Porsche's Teloché workshops prior to the 1981 race was understandably at fever pitch. Here the No. 1 924 GTP Le Mans receives some prerace attention. *Corporate Archives Porsche AG*

The No. 40 Joest Racing 935 J (77-003) of Mauricio de Narváez/Kenper Miller/Günther Steckkönig rounds the bend into the Esses during the 1981 race. Entered in the IMSA GTX class, the car was forced to retire after 152 laps following a fire. *Corporate Archives Porsche AG*

The Kremer K81 was a throwback to the great 917 era, the first and only car of its type not to be constructed at the factory. The engine for the 917 K81 was assembled by the factory, whose engineers clearly had more experience with the flat twelve engine than anyone else. Two versions of this potent powerplant were tried in the Kremer car—the 4.5- and the 4.9-liter—but it was the 4.5 liter engine that was fitted to the K81. Sponsored by the Malardeau real estate company, the No. 10 Kremer 917 K81 featured a specially designed body with a comparatively low rear spoiler. In order to enhance rearward vision, a centrally mounted roof mirror was installed. An engine mount failure at about quarter distance (lap 82) dashed the team's hopes, but in truth the car did not deliver on its expected performance. Behind the 917 is the No. 12 Porsche 936/81 of Jochen Mass/Vern Schuppan/Hurley Haywood. *Corporate Archives Porsche AG*

The all-French team of Thierry Perrier/ Valentin Bertapelle/Bernard Salam drove the Thierry Perrier–entered No. 70 Porsche 934 to first place in the Grand Touring class and seventeenth overall. *Corporate Archives Porsche AG*

In contrast to the No. 11 winning sister car, the factory's No. 12 Porsche 936/81 (2,649cc), driven by Jochen Mass/Vern Schuppan/Hurley Haywood, suffered numerous problems throughout the race and eventually finished second in Group 6 and twelfth overall. *Corporate Archives Porsche AG*

Manfred Schurti and Andy Rouse drove the No. 36 924 Carrera GTR to eleventh place, winning the IMSA GTO class in the process. *Corporate Archives Porsche AG*

Considerable time was lost by the Joest-prepared No. 60 Porsche 935 of the German team of Dieter Schornstein/Harald Grohs/Götz von Tschirnhaus. The trouble was traced to a damaged exhaust, which in turn affected the turbo. The car finished tenth overall, however, and third in Group 5. *Corporate Archives Porsche AG*

The turbocharged 2,476cc Porsche 924 GTP Le Mans (chassis 006) pushed out a whopping 410 horsepower. Two highly experienced factory drivers, Jürgen Barth and Walter Röhrl, drove the No. 1 Porsche to an overall seventh place finish and first in the LM GTP class. *Corporate Archives Porsche AG*

Kremer Racing did brisk business in selling the K3 to several customers around the world, following their Le Mans victory with that model two years earlier. Anny-Charlotte Verney/Bob Garretson/Ralph Kent-Cooke also drove one in the 1981 race, taking the No. 42 Cooke-Woods Racing 935 K3 to a sixth overall finish, which earned them a first in the IMSA GTX class. *Corporate Archives Porsche AG*

Another of Kremer's K3 creations was entered by Claude Bourgoignie, who drove it together with two Britons, John Cooper and Dudley Wood. The No. 55 Porsche 935 K3 would finish first in the Group 5 class and fourth place overall. *Corporate Archives Porsche AG*

An almost trouble-free race by the No. 11 Jules Porsche 936/81 (2,649cc) saw the lead factory car thirteen laps ahead of the field by 10:00 a.m. on Sunday, at which time the team was ordered to ease back slightly. Driven by the talented duo of Jacky Ickx/Derek Bell, the No. 11 car took the checkered flag at 3:00 p.m. for a well-deserved victory. *Corporate Archives Porsche AG*

1981 Race Results

Pos.	Car/Model	No.	Driver(s)	Entered	Class	Cl. Pos	Laps	Reason
FL	936/81 (001)	12	Hurley Haywood (US)	Porsche	Time: 3:34.100 minutes		Speed: 229.231km/h; 142.437mph	
1	936/81 (003)	11	Jacky Ickx (BE)/Derek Bell (GB)	Porsche	Group 6	1	355	
4	935 K3	55	Claude Bourgoignie (BE)/John Cooper (GB)/ Dudley Wood (GB)	Claude Bourgoignie	Group 5	1	331	
6	935 K3	42	Anny-Charlotte Verney (FR)/Bob Garretson (US)/ Ralph Kent-Cooke (US)	Cooke-Woods Racing	IMSA GTX	1	328	
7	944 LM GTR	1	Jürgen Barth (DE)/Walter Röhrl (DE)	Porsche	Le Mans GTP	1	324	
10	935 J	60	Dieter Schornstein (DE)/Harald Grohs (DE)/ Götz von Tschirnhaus (DE)	Dieter Schornstein Vegla Racing Team	Group 5	3	321	
NRF	935 K3	43	Bob Akin (US)/Paul Miller (US)/Craig Siebert (US)	Bob Akin Motor Racing	IMSA GTX		320	Electrics/short-circuit
11	924 LM GTR	36	Manfred Schurti (LI)/Andy Rouse (GB)	Porsche	IMSA GTO	1	316	
12	936/81 (001)	12	Jochen Mass (DE)/Vern Schuppan (AU)/ Hurley Haywood (US)	Porsche	Group 6	2	313	
17	934	70	Thierry Perrier (FR)/Valentin Bertapelle (FR)/ Bernard Salam (FR)	Thierry Perrier	Grand Touring	1	275	
DNF	935/77-A	57	Claude Haldi (CH)/Mark Thatcher (GB)/ Hervé Poulain (FR)	Claude Haldi	Group 5		260	Accident
DNF	935 J	40	Mauricio de Narváez (CO)/Kenper Miller (US)/ Günther Steckkönig (DE)	Joest Racing	IMSA GTX		152	Fire
DNF	917K/81	10	Bob Wollek (FR)/Xavier Lapeyre (FR)/ Guy Chasseuil (FR)	Kremer Racing	Sports +2000		82	Engine mount/frame
DNF	908/80 J	14	Reinhold Joest (DE)/Dale Whittington (US)/ Klaus Niedzwiedz (DE)	Joest Racing	Sports +2000		60	Accident damage
DNF	935 K3	59	Ted Field (US)/Bill Whittington (US)/Don Whittington (US)	Kremer Racing	Group 5		57	Engine/head
DNF	935 L1	69	Jan Lundgardh (SE)/Axel Plankenhorn (DE)/ Mike Wilds (GB)	Jan Lundgardh Tuff-Kote Dinol Racing	Group 5		49	Engine
DNF	935 K3	61	Edgar Dören (DE)/Jürgen Lässig (DE)/ Gerhard Holup (DE)	Edgar Dören Weralit RacingTeam	Group 5		48	Driver ill/out of fuel
DNF	935 K3	41	Preston Henn (US)/Michael Chandler (US)/ Marcel Mignot (FR)	Preston Henn Racing	IMSA GTX		45	Engine/crankshaft pulley
DNF	924 Carrera GTR	73	Jean-Marie Alméras (FR)/Jacques Alméras (FR)	Alméras Freres Eminence Racing Team	Grand Touring		30	Gearbox/engine

1982

June 19–20

With the dawning of the 1982 season, the introduction of the Group C era ushered in a new breed of closed race cars that conformed to a 1,764-pound (800-kilogram) minimum weight requirement among a host of other dimensional and fuel consumption regulations. In many ways, Group C, which ran for eleven years (the final class-legal Group C car took to the Le Mans grid in 1994), pioneered technical and aerodynamic developments that saw speeds rise and lap times fall significantly. During the Group C era, manufacturers undeniably developed sports racers to levels of performance that had not been seen since the heady days of the Porsche 917. With the 956, though, Porsche had once again created a winner that would place the company at the forefront of the motorsports world for several years.

Spectators attend races like the 24 Hours of Le Mans hoping to see fast racing and fierce competition, and to some extent that's what they got. But the regulations on fuel economy did not allow for extended all-out contests between rivals, as drivers and teams always had to keep a close eye on fuel consumption. That being said, this era of racing did provide some of the most exciting and memorable races at Le Mans, between many different teams, the likes of which we are unlikely to see again.

Porsche did not make their new 956 Group C racer available to privateer teams in 1982, and so it was left up to those privateer teams to field cars that made use of the previous year's technology, spiced up with a dash of their own inspiration. In true Kremer style, the Cologne team introduced their own brand of aerodynamic innovations, clothing their racers in sleek, unique bodies, while other teams watched and learned. In this way, Kremer emerged in the 1980s as a forerunner in the privateer stakes as they began to develop a range of Group C sports racers that included the CK5 (1982), CK6 (1988), and the K8 Spyder (1995).

Based on the 908/936, this Kremer evolution was called the CK5—"C" for Group C and "K" for Kremer. This remarkably innovative Group C car was driven by the American trio of Ted Field/Danny Ongais/Bill Whittington, who were all well known to Kremer and Porsche. Sadly, the No. 5 Kremer Racing car with Ted Field at the wheel didn't even complete the first two hours of the race, as a head gasket blew while occupying twelfth place. *Corporate Archives Porsche AG*

BF Goodrich wanted to prove that its road tires could stand the rigors of twenty-four hours of racing. As such, two 924 Carrera GTRs were entered by Jim Busby in grey-and-blue livery, the No. 86 car being driven by Pat Bedard/Paul Miller/Manfred Schurti. The No. 86 car was recorded at 186 miles per hour on the Mulsanne Straight in qualifying, but at 2:00 a.m. on Sunday morning it stopped with a broken clutch. Following a lengthy repair, it went back out again but lost a wheel at Indianapolis and retired after completing 128 laps. *Corporate Archives Porsche AG*

Piloted by the hugely experienced Bob Wollek, with the Martin brothers, Jean-Michel and Philippe, the No. 4 Joest-prepared Porsche 936 C was running extremely well and at the six-hour mark was lying in fifth place behind the works Porsches and a single Rondeau. Having picked up a further place overnight, the car then began to misfire early on Sunday morning, and the problem got progressively worse during the day until, with just ninety minutes to go, the engine blew up with the car lying in third place. *Corporate Archives Porsche AG*

Having qualified twenty-first on the grid, the No. 60 Charles Ivey Racing 935 K3 of John Cooper/Paul Smith/Claude Bourgoignie was putting in good times, but on Sunday morning it came into the pits requiring a turbo replacement. Following an operation lasting longer than an hour, the Porsche went back out again sounding healthy, and eventually finished eighth overall and, for the second year in succession, Cooper and Bourgoignie took top honors in Group 5, this year a sizable eleven laps ahead of the second-placed Lancia in the same group. *Corporate Archives Porsche AG*

It's not often that two drivers strike up a long-term partnership that transcends the highly charged, ego-filled life of a competitive international racing driver. But that is exactly what the Jacky Ickx/Derek Bell partnership became, scoring three Le Mans victories as a team. With only one competitive race at Silverstone in which to shake down the new 956, the team, drivers, and sponsors brought it all together at Le Mans in what some described as a rather lackluster race, but that was perhaps only because Porsche stormed to a 1–2–3 podium finish. The drivers revealed after the race that it was, in fact, an extremely difficult race for them, since the rules only allowed twenty-five fuel stops to take on 22 gallons (100 liters) per stop,

and as the 956 was easily the thirstiest of the Group C cars; some clever driving was needed to ensure they would make it to the flag. The strategy adopted was for Ickx to do what he did best, and that was to drive flat out and build up a lead, which Bell then had to maintain in a more defensive manner. Both drivers said that their style of driving had to change in order to conserve fuel, which meant that they couldn't use the engine to its full potential, but instead they would take corners faster and generally drive on the limit in all areas, thereby reducing the need for aggressive acceleration. The plan worked, giving Ickx his sixth Le Mans victory and Bell his third in the French classic. *Corporate Archives Porsche AG*

PORSCHE 956

It is unlike Porsche to send a newly developed car to a major race without it being thoroughly proven. The new 956 Group C race car, however, made its debut at the 6 Hours of Silverstone on May 16, 1982, just a month before the Le Mans event; importantly, though, it had been raced in England by the two drivers designated to drive it at Le Mans—Derek Bell and Jacky Ickx.

Also worth remembering is the fact that, apart from the all-new suspension, there was very little on the 956 that hadn't been previously run in a test environment. The 956 *did* differ markedly from previous models in its body, which was an aluminum monocoque construction, the conventional space frame chassis having been outlawed for reasons of safety. This deviation was significant for Porsche, as it allowed the introduction of ground effects, which had previously not been a design factor.

The monocoque construction was required to meet certain crash test criteria as laid down by the FIA, and this opened the door for the 956 to incorporate ground effect capability in its design, while help on chassis material came from Dornier, the aircraft manufacturer. Aerodynamic experiments were conducted at Stuttgart University, where it was found that ground effect in a full-width sports car was quite different from that experienced in a Formula 1 open-wheel design. Norbert Singer discovered that the sports car would draw its ground effect from along the side, between the front and back wheels, not from the front, as in a Formula 1 car. The final body design certainly resembled a cleaned-up 917 LH, but that is where the similarities ended, as at 104.4 inches (2,650 millimeters), the wheelbase of the 956 was 13.8 inches (350 millimeters) longer than the 917 LH and, at 1,808 pounds (820 kilograms), the newer racer was slightly heavier too. The comparison

with the 917 is only of interest because of the similar closed-body design. Although the 936 prototype from 1981 featured a space frame chassis and an open body design, this race car was closer in terms of technology to the 956.

Power in the new 956 was courtesy of the same basic engine that had brought success to the 936 in 1981, although this flat six unit was now fitted with twin turbochargers. In 956 guise, the engine capacity was increased to 2,649cc, which delivered up to 620 horsepower, depending on boost pressure. The 956's biggest card was, in fact, the car's reliability, which was so ably demonstrated at the 1982 Le Mans race, where the Rothmans-sponsored cars Nos. 1, 2, and 3 (chassis #002, #003, and #004 respectively) finished in exactly that order, 1–2–3.

The No. 3 Rothmans Porsche 956, driven by Hurley Haywood/ Al Holbert/Jürgen Barth, finished third. Al Holbert experienced firsthand a problem that beset some of the Group C cars when at speed: opening doors. By merely bumping it at the end of the Mulsanne Straight, his car's door simply flew off and into the trees, a result of the extreme forces placed on the body and the differential in pressure between the interior and exterior of the car. It took around twenty minutes to fit a replacement door. The No. 3 car finished third at sixteen laps behind its second-place sister car. *Corporate Archives Porsche AG*

Asked who his favorite driving partner was, John Fitzpatrick replied, "My favorite partner was David Hobbs, because David was 100 percent reliable, he was really quick, and one of the nicest guys you could ever wish to meet, and a very funny guy." The No. 79 Porsche 935 was delivered directly to the track by Reinhold Joest without having put the car to a real test. Starting from twenty-seventh on the grid, the car was up in the top ten after five hours, and by half distance it was up to sixth place. Despite suffering a blown head gasket around sun-up on Sunday morning, the mechanics isolated the errant cylinder and, as "Fitz" commented, they raced on with speed almost undiminished. Their fourth-place finish must, therefore, be viewed in context as the British pairing crossed the line just behind the three works Porsche 956s, despite being one cylinder short! The 935 LM built by Reinhold Joest was modeled on the original factory "Moby Dick" car, as Fitzpatrick told the author. It was built for Le Mans with a 2.6-liter turbo engine because of the fuel restrictions at that time. The team's backer, currency trader J. David (Jerry Dominelli in real life) sponsored the Fitzpatrick Porsche, but he went bust in San Diego in 1981, allegedly taking with him about $250 million of his investors' money. *Corporate Archives Porsche AG*

1982 Race Results

Pos.	Car/Model	No.	Driver(s)	Entered	Class	Cl. Pos	Laps	Reason
1	956 (002)	1	Jacky Ickx (BE)/Derek Bell (GB)	Rothmans Porsche	Group C	1	359	
2	956 (003)	2	Jochen Mass (DE)/Vern Schuppan (AU)	Rothmans Porsche	Group C	2	356	
3	956 (004)	3	Hurley Haywood (US)/Al Holbert (US)/ Jürgen Barth (DE)	Rothmans Porsche	Group C	3	340	
4	935-78/81(Joest JR/2)	79	John Fitzpatrick (GB)/David Hobbs (GB)	John Fitzpatrick Racing	IMSA GTX	1	329	
5	935 K3	78	Dany Snobeck (FR)/François Servanin (FR)/ René Metge (FR)	Ralph Kent Cooke BP – Cooke Racing	IMSA GTX	2	325	
8	935 K3	60	John Cooper (GB)/Paul Smith (GB)/ Claude Bourgoignie (BE)	Charles Ivey Racing	Group 5	1	316	
NRF	936C (JR 005)	4	Bob Wollek (FR)/Jean-Michel Martin (BE)/ Philippe Martin (BE)	Joest Racing	Group C		314	Engine/piston
11	935 K3	77	Anny-Charlotte Verney (FR)/ Bob Garretson (US)/Ray Ratcliff (US)	Bob Garretson Developments	IMSA GTX	5	299	
13	934	90	Richard Cleare (GB)/Tony Dron (GB)/ Richard Jones (GB)	Richard Cleare Racing	Grand Touring	1	291	
16	924 Carrera GTR	87	Jim Busby (US)/Doc Bundy (US)	Jim Busby B.F. Goodrich Co.	IMSA GTO	1	272	
DNF	935 K3	75	Claude Haldi (CH)/Rodrigo Teran (PA)/ Philippe Hesnault (FR)	Claude Haldi	Group 5		141	Gearbox/differential
DNF	924 Carrera GTR	86	Pat Bedard (US)/Paul Miller (US)/ Manfred Schurti (LI)	Jim Busby B.F. Goodrich Co.	IMSA GTO		128	Gearbox
DNF	924 Carrera GTR	84	Andy Rouse (GB)/Richard Lloyd (GB)	Richard Lloyd Canon Cameras – GTi	IMSA GTO		77	Gearbox/transmisson
DNF	935 K3-80	64	Edgar Dören (DE)/Billy Sprowls (US)/ Antonio Contreras (MX)	Edgar Dören	Group 5		39	Engine/out of fuel
DNF	Kremer-Porsche CK5-82	5	Ted Field (US)/Danny Ongais (US)/ Bill Whittington (US)	Interscope Kremer Racing	Group C		25	Engine
DNF	935 L1	76	Bob Akin (US)/Dave Cowart (US)/ Kenper Miller (US)	Bob Akin Motor Racing	IMSA GTX		15	Out of fuel

1983

June 18–19

Domination doesn't come in any more convincing a form than for one manufacturer to take nine out of the top ten positions in a single race with the same model of race car. As from the beginning of the 1983 season, the Porsche 956 was made available to its loyal privateer teams as well. As a result, at the 1983 Le Mans race, 956s filled positions one to eight as well as ten, completing the most convincing set of race results ever recorded in a major international race.

The 956 had become the car of choice if a race team hoped to raise the silverware in any of the major races. At the 1983 Le Mans race, there were no fewer than eleven 956s distributed as follows: three Rothmans-sponsored factory cars (Nos. 1, 2, and 3); just one from Kremer (No. 21); John Fitzpatrick Racing (Nos. 11 and 16); Reinhold Joest (Nos. 8 and 12); Hans Obermaier Racing (No. 18); Richard Lloyd (No. 14); and Preston Henn (No. 47). To this Group C tally could be added the Kremer-entered CK5/83 and the Richard Cleare CK5/82, as well as the Joest 936C, none of which, however, finished the race.

With such an overwhelmingly strong contingent of race cars from Stuttgart, one could perhaps understand the smaller than usual number of French spectators in attendance. On the flip side, this race attracted the largest proportion of British and German race-goers seen in many years. Perhaps the French had a hunch that their national cars and drivers were just not going to measure up to the Stuttgart invasion, and they would have been right, as the highest-finishing WM-Peugeot P83 came home in sixteenth place. Against such a formidable onslaught, there could be little surprise.

However depressing the race prospects might have appeared to the loyal French supporters, the 1983 race was a star-studded affair if ever there was one. Apart from the multiple Le Mans–winning drivers and stars like Ickx, Bell, the Andretti family, Klaus Ludwig, Hurley Haywood, Jochen Mass, Bob Wollek and John Fitzpatrick, a host of Formula 1 drivers also participated, including Michele Alboreto, Derek Warwick, Teo Fabi, Desiré Wilson, and Tiff Needell. Nowhere else on the international motorsports stage could one hope to find such a wealth of driver and team experience in the fifty-plus lineup of powerful machinery on the grid, as you would at Le Mans in this year. And, despite the predictable Porsche victory, nothing is ever assured at Le Mans, as the 1983 event would reveal a sting in the tail for the anxious competitors.

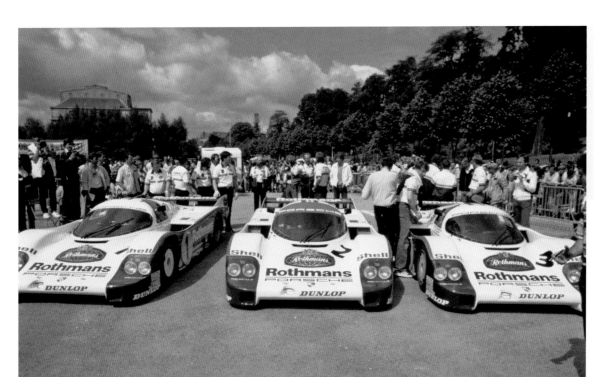

Lined up at scrutineering are the three factory Porsche 956s, *from left*: No.1, driven by Jacky Ickx/Derek Bell; No.2, driven by Jochen Mass/Stefan Bellof; No.3 driven, by Vern Schuppan/Al Holbert/Hurley Haywood. *Corporate Archives Porsche AG*

Despite its innovative and slippery shape, the No. 22 Grand Prix International magazine–sponsored Kremer CK5/83 disappointed, bowing out after just seventy-six laps. Having finished in a promising sixth place at Silverstone the month before, greater things were expected from this racer at Le Mans. When the Derek Warwick/Patrick Gaillard/Frank Jelinski car crawled into the pits at dusk with a broken oil pipe, though, it ended any plans for further participation in the race. *Corporate Archives Porsche AG*

John Fitzpatrick Racing entered two identical 956s in the 1983 race, but the No. 11 car he drove with David Hobbs and Dieter Quester was forced to retire after 135 laps with a sheered fuel metering unit drive. *Corporate Archives Porsche AG*

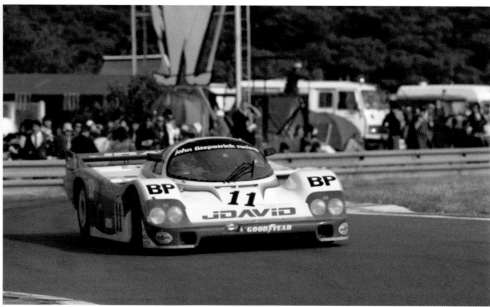

Entered by Claude Haldi, the No. 94 Porsche 930 Turbo 3.3, driven by Claude Haldi/Günther Steckkönig/Bernd Schiller, heads this group of similar 911s. The Group B Porsche failed to finish because of engine failure (piston), exiting on lap 217. *Corporate Archives Porsche AG*

Breaking the monotony of the 956 brigade was the No. 97 Raymond Boutinaud–entered Porsche 928 S, driven by the French team of Raymond Boutinaud/Patrick Gonin/Alain le Page. Although the near-standard 4.7-liter Group B 928 S had 235 laps under its belt at the finish, the car was unclassified because it had failed to complete more than 70 percent of the winner's total laps. *Corporate Archives Porsche AG*

A collision between the No. 14 car driven by Dutchman Jan Lammers and the No. 1 Rothmans car with Ickx behind the wheel; this could potentially have seen both cars out of the race on the second lap. As a group of cars approached the Mulsanne Corner, however, some fancy footwork by Lammers resulted in just a minor bump with little damage. The No. 14 Canon Porsche 956, driven by Jonathan Palmer/Jan Lammers/Richard Lloyd, went on to finish eighth overall. *Corporate Archives Porsche AG*

Following a start from twelfth place on the grid, the No. 18 Boss-sponsored 956, driven by Axel Plankenhorn/Jürgen Lässig/Desiré Wilson and entered by Hans Obermaier Racing, was content in the early stages to put in a consistent performance rather than shoot for the front. This strategy paid off as they moved up to seventh just after midnight before a series of frustrating problems delayed, though did not stop, the team. Eventually the problem was solved by setting a richer mixture, and this enabled the team to get back into the regular swing again and to record a seventh finish overall. *Corporate Archives Porsche AG*

Klaus Ludwig, the fastest of the privateers, qualified the No. 8 Marlboro Porsche 956 in fifth place on the grid, but was still seven seconds behind Ickx's qualifying time. Entered by Joest Racing, No. 8 was identical to its sister car, the No. 12 New Man car, but both 956s differed slightly from the Rothmans factory cars because the Joest cars ran with mechanical fuel injection while the factory cars had electrical injection. The Marlboro 956 was fitted with a new rear section due to damage sustained during a spin by Ludwig on Sunday morning; unable to fit a low-downforce replacement wing, a high wing setup was installed instead. The highly talented team of Bob Wollek/Klaus Ludwig/Stefan Johansson eventually brought the No. 8 car home sixth overall. *Corporate Archives Porsche AG*

Driven by the British squad of John Fitzpatrick/Guy Edwards/Rupert Keegan, the No. 16 Fitzpatrick-entered Porsche 956 finished fifth overall and fifth in the Group C class. *Corporate Archives Porsche AG*

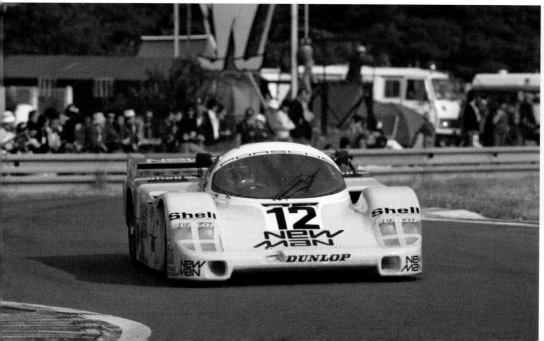

Having qualified in ninth place on the grid, the distinctively colored No. 12 New Man Porsche 956 entered by Joest Racing was piloted by Volkert Merl/Clemens Schickentanz/Mauricio de Narváez. Mechanically, the yellow-and-black Porsche enjoyed the most trouble-free twenty-four hours of all the 956s. One worry was its windscreen: after repeatedly threatening to pop out, it was eventually secured in place by additional brackets. Its excellent fourth-place overall finish was well received by its sponsors, New Man. *Corporate Archives Porsche AG*

The No. 21 Kenwood-sponsored Kremer Racing Porsche 956, driven by the father-and-son team of Mario and Michael Andretti with Frenchman Philippe Alliot, finished third, six laps down on the winning car. *Corporate Archives Porsche AG*

With the Ickx/Bell car having lost two laps in the pits after the second lap shunt with Lammers, the No. 1 works Porsche sliced its way back up through the field, and at the halfway mark they were in second place behind the No. 3 lead car—which is the way things stayed until the checkered flag fell after twenty-four hours. *Corporate Archives Porsche AG*

By midnight, the No. 3 Rothmans 956 of Vern Schuppan/Al Holbert/Hurley Haywood was leading the field by a lap, having started from seventh place on the grid. With just an hour to go and with Holbert behind the wheel, the lead looked secure until a door flew off down the Mulsanne Straight, necessitating a replacement. During the few laps that Holbert stayed out while the new door was being prepared, the airflow over the body to the left side radiator at the rear was affected and the engine began to overheat. With a new door fitted, the battle resumed, but as Holbert approached the pit straight for the last time, a telltale puff of smoke was emitted from the exhaust, indicating that the cylinder head had been terminally damaged. With the Bell car just two minutes behind, there was no time for a last-minute pit stop, so Holbert had to nurse the ailing 956 around the 13-kilometer track once more. As Holbert crossed the line for his first Le Mans victory, Bell was just one minute behind, proving that nothing is assured in this classic French endurance race until the checkered flag has fallen. *Corporate Archives Porsche AG*

NO FORMATION FINISH IN 1983

Dreams of repeating the factory 1–2–3 finish from the previous year were dashed when the No. 2 Rothmans 956 of Jochen Mass/Stefan Bellof was retired three hours from the end with a blown head gasket, having completed 281 laps.

Jochen Mass elaborates, "We had a little water leak in one of the head gaskets, so they said 'no problem, we'll put in some radiator sealant,' but that dissolved all the gaskets, and it got worse until eventually on Sunday afternoon we couldn't start anymore. The water ran out of the exhaust pipes as we poured it in at the top. It was really a shame because we would really have won it easily."

1983 Race Results

Pos.	Car/Model	No.	Driver(s)	Entered	Class	Cl. Pos	Laps	Reason
FL	956	1	Jacky Ickx (BE)	Rothmans Porsche	Time: 3:29.070 minutes		Speed: 233.922km/h; 145.352mph	
1	956 (003)	3	Vern Schuppan (AU)/Al Holbert (US)/Hurley Haywood (US)	Rothmans Porsche	Group C	1	371	
2	956-83 (005)	1	Jacky Ickx (BE)/Derek Bell (GB)	Rothmans Porsche	Group C	2	371	
3	956 (101)	21	Mario Andretti (US)/Michael Andretti (US)/Philippe Alliot (FR)	Porsche Kremer Racing	Group C	3	365	
4	956 (105)	12	Volkert Merl (DE)/Clemens Schickentanz (DE)/ Mauricio de Narváez (CO)	Joest Racing	Group C	4	362	
5	956 (102)	16	John Fitzpatrick (GB)/Guy Edwards (GB)/Rupert Keegan (GB)	John Fitzpatrick Racing	Group C	5	359	
6	956 (104)	8	Bob Wollek (FR)/Klaus Ludwig (DE)/Stefan Johansson (SE)	Joest Racing	Group C	6	355	
7	956 (109)	18	Axel Plankenhorn (DE)/Jürgen Lässig (DE)/Desiré Wilson (ZA)	Hans Obermaier Racing	Group C	7	348	
8	956 (106)	14	Jonathan Palmer (GB)/Jan Lammers (NL)/Richard Lloyd (GB)	Richard Lloyd Racing	Group C	8	340	
10	956 (103)	47	Preston Henn (US)/Claude Ballot-Léna (FR)/ Jean-Louis Schlesser (FR)	Preston Henn/John Fitzpatrick Racing	Group C	10	328	
11	930	93	John Cooper (GB)/Paul Smith (GB)/David Ovey (GB)	Charles Ivey Racing	Group B	1	304	
13	930	92	Heinz Kuhn-Weiss (DE)/Georg Memminger (DE)/ Fritz Müller (DE)	Georg Memminger	Group B	2	300	
NRF	956-83 (008)	2	Jochen Mass (DE)/Stefan Bellof (DE)	Rothmans Porsche	Group C		281	Engine
15	930	95	Jean-Marie Alméras (FR)/Jacques Alméras (FR)/ Jacques Guillot (FR)	Équipe Alméras Fréres	Group B	3	280	
20	930	96	Michel Lateste (FR)/Raymond Touroul (FR)/ Michel Bienvault (FR)	Michel Lateste	Group B	4	265	
NC	928S	97	Raymond Boutinaud (FR)/Patrick Gonin (FR)/Alain le Page (FR)	Raymond Boutinaud	Group B	5	235	
DNF	930	94	Claude Haldi (CH)/Günther Steckkönig (DE)/ Bernd Schiller (DE)	Claude Haldi	Group B		217	Engine/ piston
DNF	956 (110)	11	John Fitzpatrick (GB)/David Hobbs (GB)/Dieter Quester (AT)	John Fitzpatrick Racing	Group C		135	Fuel pump
DNF	Kremer-Porsche CK5/83 (003)	22	Derek Warwick (GB)/Patrick Gaillard (FR)/Frank Jelinski (DE)	Porsche Kremer Racing	Group C		76	Exhaust/ head gasket
DNF	936 C	15	Jean-Michel Martin (BE)/Philippe Martin (BE)/Marc Duez (BE)	Joest Racing	Group C		9	Engine
DNF	Kremer-Porsche CK5/82 (001)	42	Richard Cleare (GB)/Tony Dron (GB)/Richard Jones (GB)	Richard Cleare Racing	Group C		8	Turbocharger
DNF	930	91	Jean-Marie Lemerle (FR)/Alexandre Yvon (FR)/ Michael Krankenberg (DE)	Edgar Dören	Group B		7	Gearbox

1984

June 16–17

A new year and a new version of the 956 became available. Now fitted with the Motronic 1.2 engine-management system for better fuel consumption, the 956B (as it was called) also featured lighter bodywork and a revised front suspension. Nevertheless, the German manufacturer refrained from entering a works team at the 1984 Le Mans in protest of the ACO's constant changing of the rules. This, of course, opened the door for those privateer teams who had entered 956s to have a crack at the title without having to compete against the might of a full factory team. Despite the absence of a works team, the 956 filled eight out of the top ten positions, once again proving that the 956 was a phenomenally successful racer.

There were no fewer than fourteen privateer 956s in the field, plus a pair of 962s. For Porsche at Le Mans, the 956 would prove to be one of the company's most successful race cars to date, with four consecutive wins: the first, with Ickx/Bell, was in 1982, followed by Haywood/Schuppan/Holbert in 1983 and then the win by Pescarolo/Ludwig/Johansson in 1984. Finally, in 1985 Ludwig/Barilla/Krages took the crown.

Returning to the classic French race was the Jaguar team with a pair of Group 44 XJR-5s run by Bob Tullius Racing of America. They kept up a steady performance until the second car retired after running about three quarters of the distance. But it was the 956s that ruled the roost with the following entrants, which included two 962s: Reinhold Joest (Nos. 7 and 8), Kremer Racing (Nos. 11 and 17), Preston Henn (Nos. 26 and 61), John Fitzpatrick Racing (Nos. 33 and 55), Brun Motorsport (Nos. 9 and 20), Schornstein Racing Team (No. 12), Richard Lloyd GTi Engineering (Nos. 14 and 16), Hans Obermaier Racing (No. 47), Charles Ivey Racing (No. 21), and Team Australia (No. 34).

The No. 16 Richard Lloyd GTi Engineering–entered Porsche 956/83, driven by Richard Lloyd/Nick Mason/René Metge, was disqualified after 139 laps for accepting outside assistance. Nick Mason explains what happened: "We had a fuel supply problem and it couldn't be fixed, so the sensible thing was to retire and get the mechanics to repair it, and then get it back to the pits rather than leave it out all race. It happened during the late evening on the Mulsanne." As part of their agreement with sponsor Canon, however, the No. 16 car was fitted with a video camera with the aim of recording the whole race. The monocoque of the Lloyd car was quite advanced when compared with the standard 956, in that it used aluminum honeycomb in place of aluminum sheet, thereby increasing the car's rigidity. Designer Peter Stevens improved the aerodynamics by increasing downforce, and a twin-element rear spoiler setup replaced the single spoiler arrangement. These changes gave the car its moniker: the 956 GTi. *Corporate Archives Porsche AG*

Team Australia's fire-engine-red No. 34 Porsche 956, driven by Larry Perkins/Peter Brock, retired following an accident shortly after midnight (145 laps). *Corporate Archives Porsche AG*

The talented team of Stefan Johansson/Jean-Louis Schlesser/ Mauricio de Narváez never enjoyed the same good fortune that their stablemate would. The No. 8 Joest Racing New Man Porsche 956 retired at 4:30 a.m. on Sunday after 170 laps because of irreparable engine damage. *Corporate Archives Porsche AG*

So popular and dominant were the Group C racers that most other participants hardly got a mention. The Raymond Boutinaud–entered Porsche 928 S, piloted by the all-French team of Raymond Boutinaud/Philippe Renault/Gilles Guinand, gave a good account of itself despite being a relatively heavy car. The No. 107 Porsche finished twenty-second overall and third in Group B behind a BMW M1 and a Porsche 930. *Corporate Archives Porsche AG*

The No. 11 Kremer Racing Porsche 956B briefly took the lead on Saturday afternoon. As the night wore on, a raging battle between this car and the lead Lancia ensued. The Kenwood-sponsored Kremer Porsche, driven by ex-World Formula 1 Champion Alan Jones with fellow Australian Vern Schuppan and Jean-Pierre Jarier, another ex-Formula 1 driver, finished sixth overall. *Corporate Archives Porsche AG*

David Hobbs, a great friend of John Fitzpatrick, partnered with Philippe Streiff and the multi-talented South African ex-rally champion Sarel van der Merwe in the No. 33 Porsche 956B. Fitzpatrick always rated Hobbs highly as a driver. While still breaking in a set of brake pads, the No. 33 car slipped from its sixth place on the starting grid to eighteenth in the opening laps, but fought its way back to sixth again with some spirited driving from the Briton. Sarel van der Merwe was later embroiled in an intense battle with the Lancias and at one stage held second place. The Skoal Bandit–sponsored No. 33 Porsche would finish on the podium in third place. *Corporate Archives Porsche AG*

The Hawaiian Tropic–sponsored No. 26 Porsche 956 was entered under the name of Preston Henn Swap Shop. The colorful Texan, Preston Henn, was no stranger to Le Mans, having entered cars in the race for many years. Better known for his escapades in race cars bearing his own name, Frenchman Jean Rondeau teamed up with the car's owner and John Paul Jr. to record a fine second place result. *Corporate Archives Porsche AG*

It is ironic that the qualifying time of the winning 956 for 1984 was exactly the same as the qualifying time achieved by Jacky Ickx in 1982 in the 956's first year at Le Mans—3:28.4—despite several performance enhancements introduced to the 956 since its debut. Following what could only be described as a slow start, the No. 7 Joest Racing Porsche 956B, driven by Henri Pescarolo/Klaus Ludwig, progressed steadily through the field, climbing to fourth place by midnight, at which point only three laps separated the top seven cars. It was a combination of good tactics, steady driving, and a seemingly trouble-free run that saw the New Man Porsche take the flag at 3:00 p.m. on Sunday. Although Stefan Johansson has his name on the side, he did not in fact drive the car in 1984. *Corporate Archives Porsche AG*

1984 Race Results

Pos.	Car/Model	No.	Driver(s)	Entered	Class	Cl. Pos	Laps	Reason
1	956B (117)	7	Henri Pescarolo (FR)/Klaus Ludwig (DE)	Joest Racing	Group C	1	360	
2	956 (103)	26	Jean Rondeau (FR)/John Paul Jr. (US)/Preston Henn (US)	Preston Henn	Group C	2	358	
3	956B (114)	33	David Hobbs (GB)/Philippe Streiff (FR)/ Sarel van der Merwe (ZA)	John Fitzpatrick Racing	Group C	3	351	
4	956B (116)	9	Walter Brun (CH)/Leopold von Bayern (DE)/Bob Akin (US)	Brun Motorsport	Group C	4	340	
5	956 (105)	12	Volkert Merl (DE)/Dieter Schornstein (DE)/ Louis Krages (DE)	Schornstein Racing Team	Group C	5	340	
6	956B (115)	11	Alan Jones (AU)/Vern Schuppan (AU)/Jean-Pierre Jarier (FR)	Porsche Kremer Racing	Group C	6	337	
7	956 (111)	20	Massimo Sigala (IT)/Oscar Larrauri (AR)/Joël Gouhier (FR)	Brun Motorsport	Group C	7	335	
9	956 (101)	17	Tiff Needell (GB)/David Sutherland (GB)/Rusty French (AU)	Porsche Kremer Racing	Group C	9	321	
16	930	106	Claude Haldi (CH)/Altfrid Heger (DE)/Jean Krucker (CH)	Claude Haldi	Group B	2	285	
17	911 SC	122	Thierry Perrier (FR)/Raymond Touroul (FR)/ Valentin Bertapelle (FR)	Raymond Touroul	IMSA GTO	1	283	
NRF	956 (110)	21	Chris Craft (GB)/Alain de Cadenet (GB)/Allan Grice (AU)	Charles Ivey Racing	Group C		272	Engine
18	930	123	Jean-Marie Alméras (FR)/Jacques Alméras (FR)/ Tom Winters (US)	Équipe Alméras Fréres	IMSA GTO	2	269	
22	928S	107	Raymond Boutinaud (FR)/Philippe Renault (FR)/ Gilles Guinand (FR)	Raymond Boutinaud	Group B	3	256	
DNF	962 (104)	61	Preston Henn (US)/Edgar Dören (DE)/Michel Ferté (FR)	Preston Henn	Group C		247	Ignition
DNF	956 (106)	14	Jonathan Palmer (GB)/Jan Lammers (NL)	Richard Lloyd GTi Engineering	Group C		239	Cooling system/ alternator
DNF	956 (104)	8	Stefan Johansson (SE)/Jean-Louis Schlesser (FR)/ Mauricio de Narváez (CO)	Joest Racing	Group C		170	Engine/overheating
DNF	956 (109)	47	Jürgen Lässig (DE)/George Fouché (ZA)/John Graham (CA)	Hans Obermaier Racing	Group C		147	Accident
DNF	930	121	Paul Smith (GB)/Margie Smith-Haas (US)/David Ovey (GB)	Charles Ivey Racing	IMSA GTO		146	Engine/oil loss
DNF	956 (102)	34	Larry Perkins (AU)/Peter Brock (AU)	Team Australia	Group C		145	Accident
DNF	956/83 (007)	16	Richard Lloyd (GB)/Nick Mason (GB)/René Metge (FR)	Richard Lloyd GTi Engineering	Group C		139	DQ – outside assistance
DNF	962 (105)	55	Rupert Keegan (GB)/Guy Edwards (GB)/ Roberto Moreno (BR)/David Hobbs (GB)	John Fitzpatrick Racing	Group C		72	Accident
DNF	930	114	Michel Lateste (FR)/Michel Bienvault (FR)/ Andre Gahinet (FR)	Michel Lateste	Group B		70	Engine/piston

1985

June 15–16

As the midpoint of the decade was reached, sentiments about the format of the economy-driven Le Mans had reached their nadir. The media noted how cars took turns driving in each other's slipstreams on the long back straight to conserve fuel, and some commentators even described the event as boring.

No matter which way the bettor chose to view things, however, all competitors were faced with the same situation on the track, and the winner of the 1985 race would surely be the team most able to make the best use of the regulations. The only really pure racing came in the qualifying sessions, when Hans Stuck and Jacky Ickx went all-out to grab pole position, but it was Stuck who put in the fastest time of 3:14.8, making him the first driver to lap the new circuit layout at over 250 kilometers per hour, recording a speed of 156.48 miles per hour (251.815 kilometers per hour).

Once again it was almost a certainty that Porsche would be victorious, and it was simply a matter of which team would rise to the occasion. The Stuttgart armada comprised seven 956s and five 962s, with the factory fielding three of the newer 962 racers. To everyone's surprise, the factory cars ended up outclassed from the start, as the works 962s proved very thirsty; within four hours, all three of the Rothmans cars had been lapped, with the privateer teams in the 956s and other 962s managing their speed and fuel allocation far better.

Despite the rather disappointing performance of the works cars, which finished in third and tenth places (with one "did not finish," DNF), a combination of Porsche 956/962s still managed to fill eight of the ten top places that year. By all accounts, an excellent result for Porsche, but perhaps more important for the Stuttgart manufacturer was their tally of Le Mans wins (ten), which now exceeded that of Ferrari's.

A mass of Porsches as far as the eye could see, as the No. 1 works Porsche 962, driven by Jacky Ickx/Jochen Mass, moves into view at the start, followed behind by the eventual winners in the No. 7 New Man Joest Racing Porsche 956, driven by Klaus Ludwig/Paolo Barilla/Louis Krages (or "John Winter," as Krages was known).
Corporate Archives Porsche AG

Driven by Jean-Pierre Jarier/
Mike Thackwell/Franz Konrad,
the Kenwood-sponsored
Kremer Racing No. 11 Porsche
962 C finished ninth overall.
Jarier was drafted in for
Manfred Winkelhock, who
had Formula 1 duties in
the Canadian Grand Prix.
Corporate Archives Porsche AG

PORSCHE 962 C

Porsche introduced the 962 C at the
opening round of the 1985 World Endurance
Championship (WEC) at Mugello in Italy.
Besides the modifications described below,
the factory's main aim was to reduce fuel
consumption in the car in keeping with
the lower fuel allocation that the FIA
planned to introduce in 1984. To Porsche's
great frustration, this standard wasn't
adopted that year, and it seemed that the
development cost incurred to ensure their
cars' compliance would be wasted—or at
any rate would prove premature.

Although visually similar to the 956,
the 962 was once again a significant step
forward for Porsche. To satisfy safety
concerns, Norbert Singer and his engineers
lengthened the 962 by 1.2 inches (30
millimeters) to 189 inches (4,800 millimeters),
but more significantly the wheelbase
was extended forward by 5.7 inches (145
millimeters) to 110 inches (2,795 millimeters).
This modification was primarily to locate the
pedal box behind the axle line to protect the
driver's feet in the event of an accident. The
basic height, width, and weight of the race
car remained unchanged, although track
width was slightly reduced. Apart from the
revised chassis dimensions, the tire size of
the 962 was increased to 19 inches so that it
had a larger footprint on the road.

Originally fitted with a single turbo
2.8-liter engine, the 962 would, in fact, run
with several different engines in its time. For
1985 alone, the engine capacities used in
the 962 included 2,649cc, 2,826cc, 2,869cc,
2,986cc, and 3,164cc, and power output
subsequently varied between 620bhp and
750bhp, depending on the capacity and
compression ratio being used. The engine
was now fully water-cooled and the gearbox
received many upgrades and modifications.
The umbrella series under which these cars
raced in 1986 would be renamed World
Sports Prototype Championship (WSPC),
but by any other name the outcome was
much the same: the 962 C just got better
with age.

All engines used in the 956 and 962
series were based on the basic Type 935,
and even today the Porsche engineers admit
that, with small changes to the engine's
capacity when the bore or stroke differed
slightly, they did not generate a new engine
type number because of the complexities
of registering a new unit. This resulted in
a confusing family of engines where, for
instance, the Type 935/79 engine used in the
962 is listed as being 2,826cc, 2,986cc, and
3,164cc in the same year, 1986.

Photographed at the Weissach test track shortly
before the 1985 race, this No. 1 Porsche 962 C
Kurzheck was to be driven by Jacky Ickx and
Jochen Mass. *Corporate Archives Porsche AG*

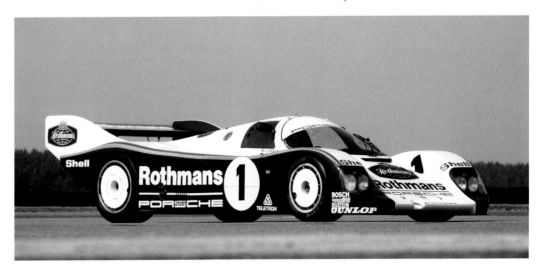

South Africans Sarel van der Merwe and George Fouché, with Swiss driver Mario Hytten, drove the No. 10 Kremer Racing 956 to a fine fifth place. Sponsorship for the Kremer 956 came courtesy of Pretoria Brick, a family firm owned by Fouché's father in Pretoria, South Africa. George Fouché recalls, "In 1985 the car was on the pace, and for the first couple of hours we were right up there with Jonathan Palmer in second place, and we would slipstream him in order to save fuel, as there was a fuel restriction in place at the time. Then we had a clutch pipe burst, which put us back to thirty-seventh place, but we drove without further incident to fifth place at the close of the race." *Corporate Archives Porsche AG*

The No. 33 John Fitzpatrick Racing Porsche 956B, driven by David Hobbs/ Jo Gartner/Guy Edwards, finished fourth behind the No. 2 Rothmans works car of Bell/Stuck. Purchasing a Porsche 956 as a privateer was by no means a cheap venture, as John Fitzpatrick recalls. "In those days the dollar was worth quite a lot, and I remember the 956s were $250,000." *Corporate Archives Porsche AG*

Motor Sport reported that fuel conservation was so high on the teams' list of priorities that some drivers cooperated with each other by taking turns "breaking the air" down Mulsanne Straight. Two such drivers were Jonathan Palmer in the No. 14 Canon Porsche and Klaus Ludwig in the No. 7 New Man car. Their tactics clearly paid off, as the No. 14 car still had 6.6 gallons (30 liters) of fuel left over after the race. The Canon Porsche, however, did not have an altogether smooth passage, as a high water temperature reading was eventually traced to a faulty sender unit, while the car's brakes also needed to be rebedded after seven hours. This was then followed by a slow puncture, but progress remained rapid and the No. 14 Porsche 956, piloted by Jonathan Palmer/James Weaver/Richard Lloyd, crossed the finish line in second place, three laps down from the winning car. *Corporate Archives Porsche AG*

The winning No. 7 New Man Joest Racing Porsche 956B was driven by Klaus Ludwig/Paolo Barilla/Louis Krages. Ludwig drove this same car to victory the previous year, the racer being simply rebuilt for the 1985 race. It was reported in the motoring press of the day that this Porsche led for all but twenty-six of the total of 373 laps. By comparison with the 1983 Rothman works cars, the Joest Porsche covered the equivalent of three more laps in the 1985 race, and still had 22 gallons (100 liters) of fuel left over at the end of the day. This might be put down to weather, safety car periods, negotiating traffic, and a host of other variables, but it does indicate an improvement in the car's fuel consumption. *Corporate Archives Porsche AG*

1985 Race Results

Pos.	Car/Model	No.	Driver(s)	Entered	Class	Cl. Pos	Laps	Reason
FL	962C	1	Jochen Mass (DE)	Porsche	Time: 3:25.100 minutes		Speed: 239.178km/h; 148.618mph	
1	956B (117)	7	Klaus Ludwig (DE)/Paolo Barilla (IT)/Louis Krages (DE)	Joest Racing	Group C1	1	374	
2	956GTi	14	Jonathan Palmer (GB)/James Weaver (GB)/Richard Lloyd (GB)	Richard Lloyd Racing	Group C1	2	371	
3	962C (003)	2	Derek Bell (GB)/Hans-Joachim Stuck (DE)	Rothmans Porsche	Group C1	3	367	
4	956B (114)	33	David Hobbs (GB)/Jo Gartner (AT)/Guy Edwards (GB)	Fitzpatrick Porsche Team	Group C1	4	366	
5	956 (115)	10	Sarel van der Merwe (ZA)/George Fouché (ZA)/Mario Hytten (CH)	Kremer Porsche Racing	Group C1	5	361	
8	956 (109)	26	Jürgen Lässig (DE)/Hervé Regout (BE)/Jésus Pareja-Mayo (ES)	Obermaier Racing Team	Group C1	8	357	
9	962C (110)	11	Jean-Pierre Jarier (FR)/Mike Thackwell (NZ)/Franz Konrad (AT)	Kremer Porsche Racing Group C1 Kenwood	Group C1	9	356	
10	962C (002)	1	Jacky Ickx (BE)/Jochen Mass (DE)	Rothmans Porsche	Group C1	10	348	
NRF	956 (111)	18	Oscar Larrauri (AR)/Massimo Sigala (IT)/Gabriele Tarquini (IT)	Brun Motorsport	Group C1		323	Engine
NRF	962C (107)	19	Walter Brun (CH)/Didier Theys (BE)/Joël Gouhier (FR)	Brun Motorsport	Group C1		304	Accident
DNF	962C (004)	3	Al Holbert (US)/John Watson (GB)/Vern Schuppan (AU)	Rothmans Porsche	Group C1		299	Engine
DNF	956 (104)	8	Mauricio de Narváez (CO)/Kenper Miller (US)/Paul Belmondo (FR)	Joest Racing	Group C1		277	Accident
DNF	911 SC	156	Raymond Touroul (FR)/Thierry Perrier (FR)/Philippe Dermagne (FR)	Raymond Touroul	Group B		107	Head gasket

1986

May 31–June 1

Porsche has always used motorsports as a proving ground for new technology, and as such the racetracks and podiums of the world are where the company's reputation has been built, where lessons have been learned and victories earned the hard way.

It was perhaps a foregone conclusion then that with the advent of the company's flagship production model of the day, the road-going 959, would eventually be put to the test in the motorsports arena. A four-wheel-drive system is, of course, better suited to rallying where every ounce of grip is needed on a loose or uneven surface, but once the 959 had proved itself in the Paris–Dakar rally (1984, first; 1986, first, second, and sixth) and the Pharaohs Rally (1985, first), it was time to put the technology to work on the racetrack as, although the expensive and sophisticated 4x4 system could not be economically adapted for a road car, neither could it be left to gather dust on a workshop shelf.

However sophisticated and advanced the 959 was, the car's potential performance was hampered by its somewhat boxy design and the rather weighty four-wheel-drive system. Works driver René Metge, who had scored several rally victories in the car, was charged with the responsibility for qualifying a special 959 (chassis 10016) for the 1986 Le Mans. Specifically prepared for the event, Metge had no trouble in prequalifying the car for the race at the spring test day.

The field was otherwise liberally sprinkled with 956s and 962s, including the well-prepared factory Rothmans 962s, as well as a lone 936 C entered by Joest Racing. Almost the entire grid was made up of Group C1 and C2 cars, with the odd IMSA GTP entry and the single Porsche 961, which was entered in the invitational IMSA GTX class.

Qualifying was run at a blistering pace, which saw Mass record the fastest time of 3:15.99 (154.409 miles per hour/248.486 kilometers per hour), but this was still down from Stuck's time of 3:14.8 (156.483 miles per hour/251.824 kilometers per hour) the year before. Second on the grid was the No. 1 Rothmans works car of Stuck/Bell/Holbert, while Klaus Ludwig in the No. 7 Taka Q Joest Racing 956B car was in third place.

Ludwig recorded the fastest race lap of 3:23.3 (148.857 miles per hour/239.551 kilometers per hour) and was also the quickest through the Hunaudières speed trap at 232 miles per hour (373 kilometers per hour).

A major development of the 962 C six-cylinder engine was that this power unit now featured a water-cooled block as well as water-cooled heads, a solution that did away with the traditional horizontal fan that did not always provide even cylinder cooling. The Porsche 962 C was so successful that, between 1986 and 1994, no fewer than 148 of these all-conquering sports racers were produced.

Another big step for Porsche was the introduction of the Porsche Doppel-Kupplung (PDK) twin-clutch transmission system. Although the No. 3 Rothmans works car driven by Vern Schuppan/Drake Olson was fitted with such a system, it retired while in fifth place after two-and-a-half hours on lap 41, when the PDK gearbox input shaft failed. Schuppan was subsequently transferred to the Mass/Wollek No. 2 Rothmans works car, but that was later involved in an accident. Porsche eventually perfected this innovative gearbox, reaping the benefits in the years that followed.

The No. 1 T Porsche 962 C training car of Al Holbert makes its way through a crowded paddock area. *Corporate Archives Porsche AG*

JOCHEN MASS RECALLS THE JO GARTNER ACCIDENT

"I had another accident with the 962 [in 1986]. A car blew up in front of me and it spun and blocked the road, and he was still moving toward the guardrail, then he started to come back onto the road, so I went to go behind him and I skidded on his oil and hit the Armco [barrier]. My wing fell off and I had a puncture front left and left rear, and then I hit him on the nose, so I had three punctures and couldn't go anywhere.

"Meanwhile, there was another dreadful accident somewhere else on the circuit involving Jo Gartner, an Austrian, who was killed in a Kremer Porsche. But I didn't know about that, so I saw the safety car going round and round and so eventually I walked back [to the pits] because my accident was at the Porsche Corner. When I got back to the pits they looked at me and they said, 'Where did you come from?' because officially it had been announced that Gartner and I had tangled up and we were both in flames and goodness knows what, and of course I had no idea this had happened.

"So that was it for me and I drove home, and it was such a beautiful morning. Gartner was a nice guy, I knew him, and I felt very sorry for him and I was really sad. So I drove through the forest on this crispy morning on my way home, and I pulled into some little lane. I got out of the car and you could smell the summer morning with a very light drizzle . . . but sometimes this feeling of being alive hits you, and it was amazing. It was a very grateful feeling, and I was suddenly terribly aware of life, and just how short it can be. It was remarkable."

The No. 2 Rothmans works Porsche 962 C (chassis 004), driven by Jochen Mass/Bob Wollek/Vern Schuppan, had an accident on lap 180 and retired. *Corporate Archives Porsche AG*

The No. 7 Taka-Q Joest Racing Porsche 956B of Klaus Ludwig/Paolo Barilla/Louis Krages only managed 196 laps before being parked with engine failure. Just before half distance, the race was brought up behind the pace car following the accident in which Jo Gartner was killed. The entire field circulated behind the pace car for three hours while the barriers were rebuilt, which affected some race cars' cooling systems and engines. The No. 7 Joest Porsche was one of the cars forced to retire. *Corporate Archives Porsche AG*

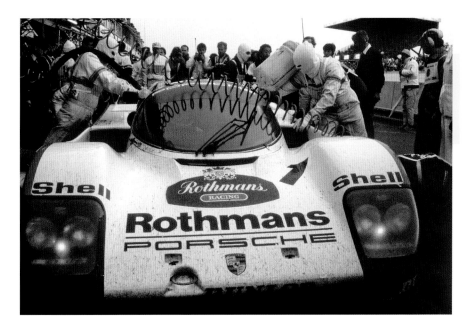

The No. 1 Rothmans works Porsche 962 C (chassis 003), driven by Hans-Joachim Stuck/ Derek Bell/Al Holbert, stops in the pits for refueling. *Corporate Archives Porsche AG*

The No. 180 Porsche 961 factory entry attracted a lot of interest in the 1986 race. Driven by the French pairing of René Metge/Claude Ballot-Léna, the one-off Porsche 961 (chassis 10016) finished a remarkable seventh overall and first in the IMSA GTX class (it was the only car in this class!), despite a broken throttle linkage and a high-speed blowout, which required a new driveshaft to be fitted. The 961 was the first four-wheel-drive car ever to race at Le Mans, completing 321 laps against the 368 laps of the winning factory 962. The Type 961 was powered by a twin-turbocharged 2,847cc engine and, with a maximum output of 680 horsepower, it was close to the Group C spec engine. The 961 could reach a top speed of 205 miles per hour (330 kilometers per hour) down the Mulsanne Straight, but weighing in at 2,535 pounds (1,150 kilograms) she was no lightweight, being more than 662 pounds (300 kilograms) heavier than a Group C car, which makes its seventh-place finish all the more remarkable. *Corporate Archives Porsche AG*

For the spectators camped alongside the track in tents, sleeping must have been a bit of a challenge with the likes of the Group C cars flashing by continuously. After a shunt at the Tertre Rouge by the No. 9 Obermaier Racing Porsche 956, in which the front of the car was damaged by Jürgen Lässig, the German driver, his teammates Fulvio Ballabio and Dudley Wood recovered well to record a fifth overall placing. *Corporate Archives Porsche AG*

The No. 33 John Fitzpatrick Racing Danone Porsche 956B finished fourth overall. Listed as drivers were Emilio de Villota/George Fouché/Fermin Velez/Juan Fernandez, but Fernandez only drove a few laps in practice before deciding not to continue. Karl Jennings, Fitzpatrick's team manager, recalls, "Emilio was a real gentleman and Fermin Velez was a nice guy too but very small . . . his seat was so far forward that he could hardly see into the side mirrors. They were both steady, constant drivers that year in the WEC." *Corporate Archives Porsche AG*

Appropriately called the "Spirit of America" because of its distinctive livery, the No. 8 Joest Racing Porsche 956 was driven by John Morton/George Follmer/Kenper Miller/Paolo Barilla to a promising third place overall. *Corporate Archives Porsche AG*

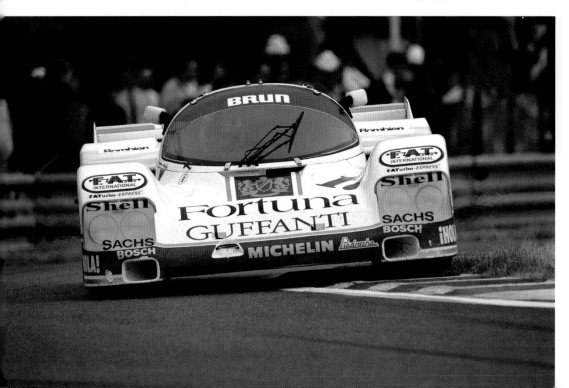

The No. 17 Brun Motorsport Porsche 962 C (chassis 115) finished second overall, after a spirited fight with the TWR Silk Cut Jaguar of Warwick/Cheever/Schlesser. The Porsche, however, driven by Oscar Larrauri/Joël Gouhier/Jésus Pareja-Mayo, kept up its pace to finish eight laps down on the winning Rothmans car. *Corporate Archives Porsche AG*

It was perhaps appropriate that the No. 1 Rothmans Porsche 962 C (chassis 003) should finish in first place, but it wasn't all easy going for the well-seasoned team of Hans-Joachim Stuck/Derek Bell/Al Holbert. Bell had an almighty fight with the Joest Racing 956B of Klaus Ludwig/Paolo Barilla/Louis Krages, as the two Porsches bumped door handles with each other down the Mulsanne Straight, and the lead swapped back and forth between these two. It was only during the prolonged pace car period (almost three hours) that the Ludwig car was retired to the pits after it ran too cold and suffered engine failure. This gave the leading Porsche a nine-lap margin and enabled them to rein back slightly on power and conserve fuel. The list of record achievements that flowed from this victory were many, as Bell and Holbert were the first Porsche drivers to win both the Daytona and Le Mans in the same year. The Le Mans victory also gave Porsche its eleventh title in the famous French race, stretching its lead over Ferrari, which had nine wins. Importantly for Derek Bell, it made him England's most victorious driver at Le Mans, with four wins to his name. *Corporate Archives Porsche AG*

1986 Race Results

Pos.	Car/Model	No.	Driver(s)	Entered	Class	Cl. Pos	Laps	Reason
FL	956B (117)	7	Klaus Ludwig (DE)	Joest Racing	Time: 3:23.300 minutes		Speed: 239.551km/h; 148.850mph	
1	962C (003)	1	Hans-Joachim Stuck (DE)/Derek Bell (GB)/Al Holbert (US)	Rothmans Porsche	Group C1	1	368	
2	962C (115)	17	Oscar Larrauri (AR)/Joël Gouhier (FR)/Jésus Pareja-Mayo (ES)	Brun Motorsport	Group C1	2	360	
3	956 (104)	8	John Morton (US)/George Follmer (US)/Kenper Miller (US)	Joest Racing	Group C1	3	355	
4	956B (114)	33	Emilio de Villota (ES)/George Fouché (ZA)/Fermin Velez (ES)	John Fitzpatrick Danone Porsche Espana	Group C1	4	349	
5	956 (109)	9	Jürgen Lässig (DE)/Fulvio Ballabio (IT)/Dudley Wood (GB)	Obermaier Racing	Group C1	5	345	
6	936CJ	63	Siegfried Brunn (DE)/Ernst Schuster (DE)/Rudi Seher (DE)	Ernst Schuster	Group C1	6	344	
7	961	180	René Metge (FR)/Claude Ballot-Léna (FR)	Porsche	IMSA GTX	1	321	
9	956B	14	Mauro Baldi (IT)/Price Cobb (US)/Rob Dyson (US)	Richard Lloyd Liqui Moly	Group C1	7	318	
10	962C (112)	55	Philippe Alliot (FR)/Michel Trollé (FR)/Paco Romero (ES)	John Fitzpatrick Racing	Group C1	8	312	
DNF	956B (117)	7	Klaus Ludwig (DE)/Paolo Barilla (IT)/Louis Krages (DE)	Joest Racing	Group C1		196	Engine
DNF	962C (004)	2	Jochen Mass (DE)/Bob Wollek (FR)/Vern Schuppan (AU)	Rothmans Porsche	Group C1		180	Accident
DNF	962C (118)	10	Sarel van der Merwe (ZA)/Jo Gartner (AT)/Kunimitsu Takahashi (JP)	Porsche Kremer Racing	Group C1		169	Accident fatal
DNF	956 (105)	12	Pierre Yver (FR)/Hubert Striebig (FR)/Max Cohen-Olivar (MA)	Porsche Kremer Racing	Group C1		160	Withdrawn after No. 10 fatal accident
DNF	962C (106)	19	Thierry Boutsen (BE)/Alain Ferté (FR)/Didier Theys (BE)	Brun Motorsport	Group C1		89	Accident
DNF	962C (117)	18	Massimo Sigala (IT)/Frank Jelinski (DE)/Walter Brun (CH)	Brun Motorsport	Group C1		75	Engine/valves
DNF	962C (002)	3	Vern Schuppan (AU)/Drake Olson (US)	Rothmans Porsche	Group C1		41	PDK transmission

1987

June 13–14

During the second half of the 1980s, Jaguar put in a determined effort to return to the top of the sport, and in 1986 and 1987 the Tom Walkinshaw–prepared XJRs certainly made their presence felt, although success eluded the British team. This development, however, served to give Porsche a bit of a wake-up call, as the Jaguars had proved to be faster than expected.

The Porsche attack fizzled out steadily and rather alarmingly with the pole-sitting No. 18 Rothmans Porsche 962 C retiring within the first hour, while the two Joest 962 Cs, driven by Sarel van der Merwe/Chip Robinson/David Hobbs (No. 7) and Frank Jelinski/Hurley Haywood/Stanley Dickens/David Hobbs (No. 8), dropped out after four laps and seven laps respectively.

In a race that saw intermittent rain, the lone works Rothmans Porsche, driven by Hans-Joachim Stuck/Derek Bell/Al Holbert (No. 17), kept going, and in the words of *Motor Sport* correspondent Michael Cotton, "This race must have been one of Porsche's most satisfying victories, a triumph in the face of adversity."

Changes to the circuit included the installation of a chicane on the rise up to and just before the Dunlop Bridge. This alteration was an attempt to slow the cars down from the high speeds attained down the main pit straight before they reached the Esses.

The Brun Motorsport No. 2 Porsche 962 C of Oscar Larrauri/Jésus Pareja-Mayo/Uwe Schäffer was involved in a frightening accident on lap 40, when the car, driven by Schäffer at the time, spun and landed outside of the barriers at the Porsche Curves. Here the Porsche is followed by the No. 62 Kouros Racing Sauber Mercedes-Benz C9 of Johnny Dumfries/Chip Ganassi/Mike Thackwell that retired after thirty-seven laps with severe damage to the car's undercarriage because of a flat tire. *Corporate Archives Porsche AG*

KEES NIEROP ON THE PORSCHE 961

"I was first introduced to the 961 at Daytona in the fall of 1986 after the car had already run the 1986 Le Mans race. I had been very close to several people at Porsche and I finally got my chance to join the factory team, I was so proud to be chosen.

"I remember that we had some issues with the car [at Daytona], it was hot . . . *very* hot, mostly due to the fact that there was a radiator mounted in the front, and it washed the car with hot air. The driver's fresh air duct also got filled with hot air.

"It felt big and powerful, it was hard work to drive but I enjoyed it. At Le Mans I was scheduled to drive a 962 but due to the earlier crash by Price Cobb I was invited to drive the 961 again. It was much easier to drive this time around as it had bigger tires and wider fenders, a better AWD system and an improved aero package. My memory flashes back to going down the Mulsanne Straight at full speed and having Hans Stuck just

creep by me. This [961] was a big car with the same horsepower as the 962, it was just aerodynamics that kept it from going faster."

The crash came on Sunday at around 10:00 a.m.

"I came into Indy corner at full speed and I went from sixth to fourth at 180 miles per hour . . . or so I thought, but it had actually slipped into second and started to lock the rear tires. Of course, the engine could not rev up fast enough to keep traction at 180 miles per hour in second gear . . . I caught the tach and realized what had happened and depressed the clutch again in time to not overrev the engine, but the damage was already done. The rear of the car came out and hit the guardrail and then swung the car around and the front impacted the barrier also."

Following the impact, the engine was still running. Despite much of the broken fiberglass bodywork hanging loose, Nierop was able to continue driving. Unbeknown to him, though, a piece of the rear bodywork was touching the hot turbo and it started a fire that wasn't

visible in his mirrors. Nierop's aim was to get back to the pits, but while making his way along the track he heard Peter Falk's voice over his radio, "Stop the car and get out!" Falk and the crew could see on the TV monitors that the car was burning, so Nierop pulled over and got out. As it turned out, by the time he received the frantic order, he was midway between two marshal posts; by the time the fire marshals reached his car it was completely engulfed in flames.

Nierop continues:

"They had to run a long way to get to me and so all I could do was stand on the side line and watch this million-dollar car burn up. The car was structurally OK, the actual impact against the barrier didn't do that much damage. I still watch the TV clip of my final moments in the 961 while it was on fire. It was so sad, if only I had been told that it was on fire, I would have stopped at a fire station.

"As the car was only entered in three races over its life, I was lucky enough to be chosen twice to drive it."

Dutchman Kees Nierop (now living in Canada) spun out on lap 199 following a gear selection problem, and a car fire ensued while lying in tenth place and third in class, thus terminating any chance of another fine finish for the No. 203 works Porsche 961 (chassis 10016). This incident brought the 961's career to an unceremonious, premature end. *Corporate Archives Porsche AG*

Now resplendent in Rothmans livery, the No. 203 Porsche 961, driven by René Metge/Claude Haldi/Kees Nierop, returned to Le Mans in 1987. A seventh-place finish in the 1986 Le Mans was followed by an overall twenty-fourth place in the 3 Hours of Daytona same year because of tire problems encountered on the steep banking. The 1987 Le Mans race didn't give the car a favorable sendoff into retirement. *Corporate Archives Porsche AG*

Hans Obermaier had good reason to celebrate, as two of his Primagaz-sponsored Porsches finished in the second and third places. Pictured here, the No. 72 Porsche 962 C of Pierre Yver/Bernard de Dryver/Jürgen Lässig drove a steady race, stayed out of trouble, and finished second, albeit twenty laps down on the winning works Porsche. *Corporate Archives Porsche AG*

Several safety car periods, combined with consistent and determined progress, resulted in yet another remarkable finish for three remarkably talented drivers, making it a second consecutive win for this trio. Starting from second on the grid, the No. 17 Rothmans Porsche 962 C LH, driven by Hans-Joachim Stuck/ Derek Bell/Al Holbert, completed 355 laps, marking a fifth Le Mans victory for Bell. *Corporate Archives Porsche AG*

1987 Race Results

Pos.	Car/Model	No.	Driver(s)	Entered	Class	Cl. Pos	Laps	Reason
1	962C (006)	17	Hans-Joachim Stuck (DE)/Derek Bell (GB)/Al Holbert (US)	Rothmans Porsche	Group C1	1	355	
2	962C (130)	72	Pierre Yver (FR)/Bernard de Dryver (BE)/Jürgen Lässig (DE)	Obermaier Racing Primagaz Competition	Group C1	2	335	
4	962C Thompson (118)	11	George Fouché (ZA)/Wayne Taylor (ZA)/Franz Konrad (AT)	Porsche Kremer Racing	Group C1	4	327	
DNF	961	203	René Metge (FR)/Claude Haldi (CH)/Kees Nierop (CA)	Rothmans Porsche	IMSA GTX		199	Accident/fire
DNF	962C Thompson (001BM)	3	Bill Adam (CA)/Scott Goodyear (CA)/Richard Spenard (CA)	Brun Motorsport	Group C1		120	Engine
DNF	962C (106B)	15	Jonathan Palmer (GB)/James Weaver (GB)/Price Cobb (US)	Équipe Liqui Moly	Group C1		112	Fire
DNF	962C (117)	1	Michel Trollé (FR)/Paul Belmondo (FR)/Pierre de Thoisy (FR)	Brun Motorsport	Group C1		88	Accident damage
DNF	962C (115)	2	Oscar Larrauri (AR)/Jésus Pareja-Mayo (ES)/Uwe Schäfer (DE)	Brun Motorsport	Group C1		40	Accident
DNF	962C (008)	18	Bob Wollek (FR)/Jochen Mass (DE)/Vern Schuppan (AU)	Rothmans Porsche	Group C1		16	Engine
DNF	962C Thompson (116)	8	Frank Jelinski (DE)/Hurley Haywood (US)/Stanley Dickens (SE)	Joest Racing	Group C1		7	Engine
DNF	962C Thompson (110)	10	Volker Weidler (DE)/Kris Nissen (DK)/Kunimitsu Takahashi (JP)	Porsche Kremer Racing	Group C1		6	Engine
DNF	962C (129)	7	Sarel van der Merwe (ZA)/Chip Robinson (US)/David Hobbs (GB)	Joest Racing	Group C1		4	Engine

1988

June 11–12

It was almost inevitable that Porsche's winning streak would not, or could not, continue forever. Their record of twelve wins since 1970, including an unbroken run of victories since 1981, was unprecedented, and would take an almighty effort by any team to surpass. In 1988 it was Jaguar that rose to the challenge, but the Coventry manufacturer's winning margin was a mere two-and-a-half minutes.

Even if Porsche did not occupy the top step of the podium that year, it completely dominated the scoreboard, filling nine of the top eleven places, and Jaguar was the only team able to spoil the party by taking first and fourth spots. The Porsche 962 C was the only game in town if you had any plans of competing for the leading positions, but it was the No. 17 Shell-sponsored 962 C of Stuck/Bell/Ludwig that Jaguar's Tom Walkinshaw saw as his major threat.

Looking at the car's specifications, the 1,942-pound (881 kilogram) Jaguar was powered by a mighty 7.0-liter V-12 fuel-injected engine developing 750 horsepower and capable of 245 miles per hour (394 kilometers per hour). By comparison, the 962 C, which weighed in at just 1,808 pounds (820 kilogram), was fitted with Porsche's bullet-proof and well-tested twin-turbocharged 2,994cc six-cylinder boxer engine, which developed around 780 horsepower and was capable of 220 miles per hour (354 kilometers per hour). These are the statistics made available to the media, but in reality the performance potential and power output figures were a closely guarded secret, as gearing could in any event be changed at the circuit to suit conditions.

Reports do suggest that the Jaguar had the edge on straight-line speed, but on the race day, this is also only of academic interest: The driver behind the wheel made the difference in lap times. The Jaguar XJR-9LM and the Porsche 962 C were in fact very closely matched and the lead was swapped countless times throughout the race, much to the delight of the spectators.

Standing next to the No. 17 Porsche 962 C LH: *on the left, front to back,* Derek Bell, Klaus Ludwig, Michael Andretti, and John Andretti with, *on the right, front to back,* Mario Andretti, Bob Wollek, Hans-Joachim Stuck, and Sarel van der Merwe. *Corporate Archives Porsche AG*

Through the first half of Saturday night, the No. 18 works car of Bob Wollek/Sarel van der Merwe/Vern Schuppan kept the pressure on the lead Jaguar, exchanging the lead many times. In the wee hours of the morning and approximately around the halfway mark (192 laps), the No. 18 car was retired from the race with engine problems. *Corporate Archives Porsche AG*

The No. 10 Kenwood-sponsored Kremer Racing 962 C (CK6/88), driven by Kunimitsu Takahashi/Hideki Okada/Bruno Giacomelli, finished ninth. The "CK6" suffix refers to the longer Kremer chassis and special Langheck tail of this car. *Corporate Archives Porsche AG*

Just as with the tobacco wars between the likes of Marlboro, Silk Cut, and Rothmans, the big audio companies used motor racing to promote their wares. Blaupunkt sponsored the Joest Racing cars this year, while Kremer had enjoyed the support of Kenwood. The No. 7 Joest Racing 962 C Thompson, seen here, was driven to a fine fifth place by David Hobbs/Didier Theys/Franz Konrad. *Corporate Archives Porsche AG*

"F.A.T. International, a transport company based in Paris, was a faithful sponsor of ours during these days," explained a Joest Racing spokesman. Stanley Dickens/Louis Krages/Frank Jelinski brought their No. 8 F.A.T.-sponsored Joest Racing Porsche 962 C home third to secure a place on the podium. *Corporate Archives Porsche AG*

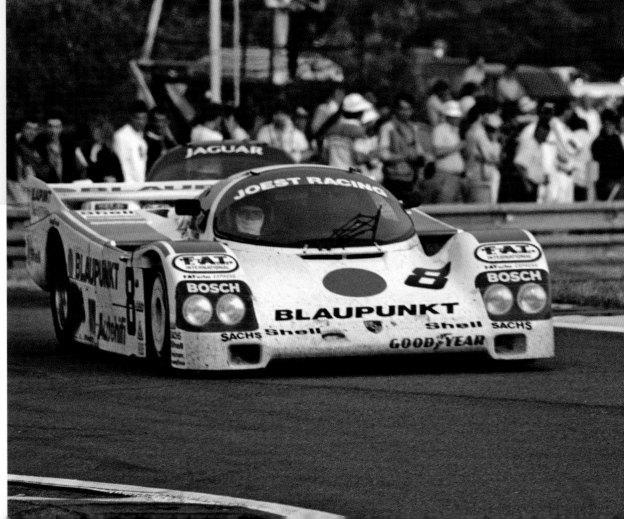

The No. 17 Shell-sponsored works 962 C, driven by Stuck/Ludwig/Bell, was beaten to the flag by the 7.0-liter V12 Jaguar XJR-9LM of Lammers/Dumfries/Wallace by a mere 2:36.85 minutes. This margin would have been reduced somewhat had the Porsche been allowed to finish the race in the normal manner on the circuit, but, with the crowds swamping the area around the finish line, the Porsche was flagged into the pit lane to cross the finish line there, at a much slower speed. In the end it didn't make any difference to the result of the race, but the crowds went home after twenty-four hours having witnessed a duel between Jaguar and Porsche that had held their attention for the full duration of the contest. *Corporate Archives Porsche AG*

1988 Race Results

Pos.	Car/Model	No.	Driver(s)	Entered	Class	Cl. Pos	Laps	Reason
FL	962C (010)	17	Hans-Joachim Stuck (DE)	Porsche	Time: 3:22.500 minutes		Speed: 240.622km/h; 149.516mph	
2	962C (010)	17	Hans-Joachim Stuck (DE)/Klaus Ludwig (DE)/Derek Bell (GB)	Porsche	Group C1	2	394	
3	962C (004)	8	Stanley Dickens (SE)/Louis Krages (DE)/Frank Jelinski (DE)	Joest Racing	Group C1	3	385	
5	962C (116)	7	David Hobbs (GB)/Didier Theys (BE)/Franz Konrad (AT)	Joest Racing	Group C1	5	380	
6	962C (008)	19	Mario Andretti (US)/Michael Andretti (US)/John Andretti (US)	Porsche	Group C1	6	375	
7	962C (115)	5	Jésus Pareja-Mayo (ES)/Massimo Sigala (IT)/Uwe Schäfer (DE)	Brun Motorsport	Group C1	7	372	
8	962C Thompson (118)	11	Kris Nissen (DK)/Harald Grohs (DE)/George Fouché (ZA)	Porsche Kremer Racing	Group C1	8	371	
9	962C (CK6/88)	10	Kunimitsu Takahashi (JP)/Hideki Okada (JP)/Bruno Giacomelli (IT)	Porsche Kremer Racing	Group C1	9	370	
10	962C (123)	33	Brian Redman (GB)/Eje Elgh (SE)/Jean-Pierre Jarier (FR)	Takefuji Schuppan Racing	Group C1	10	359	
11	962C (130)	72	Jürgen Lässig (DE)/Pierre Yver (FR)/Dudley Wood (GB)	Obermaier Racing Primagaz Competition	Group C1	11	356	
DNF	962C (007)	18	Bob Wollek (FR)/Sarel van der Merwe (ZA)/Vern Schuppan (AU)	Porsche	Group C1		192	Engine
DNF	962C (117)	4	Walter Lechner (AT)/Franz Hunkeler (CH)/Manuel Reuter (DE)	Brun Motorsport	Group C1		91	Accident

1989

June 10–11

In this year, the highest-finishing Porsche crossed the line in the relatively lowly position (for Porsche at least) of third place, with only three Porsches finishing in the top ten. The media attributed this rather sorry state of affairs to a lack of development by the factory and to the rise in recent years of two significant old rivals—Jaguar and Mercedes-Benz.

A war of words between the FIA and the ACO did not help calm the manufacturers' nerves either. As the flag fell for the start of the 1989 Le Mans race, the conflict around whether it should be brought back into the World Championship remained unresolved. In the lead-up to the June race, the FIA, having taken control of the World Sports Prototype Championship

(WSPC), decreed that all teams would have to participate in all ten rounds of the series or face stiff financial penalties for any nonappearance. The ACO felt that this did not suit their agenda and withdrew the Le Mans race from the WSPC calendar a matter of weeks before the event.

On the track, however, the next four years would see many 962 Cs entered in the classic French race by Porsche's customer teams. Although the Stuttgart manufacturer did have a favorite—namely Joest Racing—in 1989 no fewer than seventeen 962 Cs were listed in the race program, but only five would cross the finish line, the others falling victim to fires, accidents, and a range of engine failures and related problems.

The No. 15 Richard Lloyd Racing Porsche 962 C leads a group of cars past the pits in the early stages of the race. This car was driven by Steven Andskär, David Hobbs, and Damon Hill, but it retired after 228 laps with engine failure. *Corporate Archives Porsche AG*

Fearing a repeat of the car fires that so many other 962s had suffered, Vern Schuppan parked the No. 55 blue Omron-sponsored Team Schuppan 962 C in the pits, taking it out with just enough time to cross the line in thirteenth place. The car was driven by its owner, Vern Schuppan, with Swede Eje Elgh and Le Mans debutant Gary Brabham. *Corporate Archives Porsche AG*

The No. 14 Richard Lloyd Racing 962 C was full of promise, but suffered as a result of an accident in Wednesday's practice with Tiff Needell. Despite being repaired in time, and featuring super-slick, covered-in rear wheels, the star-studded trio of Derek Bell, James Weaver, and Tiff Needell were classified as NRF at the checkered flag. *Corporate Archives Porsche AG*

Although its sister car, the No. 7 Joest Porsche, retired with a blown engine quite early in the race, the No. 8 Blaupunkt 962 C, driven by the French trio of Henri Pescarolo/Claude Ballot-Léna/Jean-Louis Ricci, soldiered on and finished sixth. *Corporate Archives Porsche AG*

Having inherited the lead around the six-hour mark, a warning light in Joest Racing's No. 9 car, driven by Bob Wollek/Hans-Joachim Stuck, around midnight signaled a rising water temperature. The fault persisted and required regular attention, which dropped the car back into second place. Later, oil seeping into the clutch housing caused further delays and the team was forced to change tactics to see the race through, a defensive move that served them well, with the Joest car securing a third-place finish. *Corporate Archives Porsche AG*

1989 Race Results

Pos.	Car/Model	No.	Driver(s)	Entered	Class	Cl. Pos	Laps	Reason
3	962C (145)	9	Bob Wollek (FR)/Hans-Joachim Stuck (DE)	Joest Racing	Group C1	3	383	
6	962C (004)	8	Henri Pescarolo (FR)/Claude Ballot-Léna (FR)/ Jean-Louis Ricci (FR)	Joest Racing	Group C1	6	372	
10	962C (128)	16	Uwe Schäfer (DE)/Harald Huysman (NO)/ Dominique Lacaud (FR)	Brun Motorsport	Group C1	8	352	
NRF	962C	14	Derek Bell (GB)/James Weaver (GB)/ Tiff Needell (GB)	Richard Lloyd Racing	Group C1		339	Fire
13	962C (008)	55	Vern Schuppan (AU)/Eje Elgh (SE)/ Gary Brabham (AU)	Team Schuppan	Group C1	10	322	
15	962C (138)	20	Tim Lee-Davey (GB)/Tom Dodd-Noble (GB)/ Katsunori Iketani (JP)	Team Lee-Davey	Group C1	11	309	
NRF	962C (CK6-03)	10	Kunimitsu Takahashi (JP)/Giovanni Lavaggi (IT)/ Bruno Giacomelli (IT)	Kremer Racing	Group C1		303	Fire
DNF	962C (150)	17	Oscar Larrauri (AR)/Walter Brun (CH)/ Jésus Pareja-Mayo (E)	Brun Motorsport	Group C1		242	Engine
DNF	962C	15	David Hobbs (GB)/Steven Andskär (SE)/ Damon Hill (GB)	Richard Lloyd Racing	Group C1		228	Engine
DNF	962C Thompson (110)	34	Jacques Alméras (FR)/Jean-Marie Alméras (FR)/ Alain Ianetta (FR)	Équipe Alméras Fréres	Group C1		188	Accident
DNF	962C (007)	7	Frank Jelinski (DE)/Pierre-Henri Raphanel (FR)/ Louis Krages (DE)	Joest Racing	Group C1		124	Engine/water leak
DNF	962C (117)	27	Franz Konrad (AT)/Rudi Seher (DE)/ Andres Vilarino (ES)	Brun Motorsport	Group C1		81	Brakes/turbo
DNF	962C Thompson	5	Harald Grohs (DE)/Akihiko Nakaya (JP)/ Sarel van der Merwe (ZA)	Brun Motorsport	Group C1		78	Electrics/ gearbox
DNF	962C (143)	33	Will Hoy (GB)/Jean Alesi (FR)/Dominic Dobson (US)	Team Schuppan	Group C1		69	Fire
DNF	962C (130)	72	Jürgen Lässig (DE)/Pierre Yver (FR)/ Paul Belmondo (FR)	Obermaier Racing/ Primagaz	Group C1		61	Accident
DNF	962C Thompson	6	Walter Lechner (AT)/Roland Ratzenberger (AT)/ Maurizio Sala (BR)	Brun Motorsport	Group C1		50	Tyres/ puncture damage
DNF	962C (CK6-04)	11	George Fouché (ZA)/Hideki Okada (JP)/ Masanori Sekiya (JP)	Kremer Racing	Group C1		42	Accident

CHAPTER 5

1990s

In 1995 veteran Hans-Joachim Stuck complained bitterly about the handling of the Motul-sponsored No. 4 Kremer Racing K8: run in very wet conditions, the car lacked downforce and therefore grip. Nevertheless, the highly experienced team of Thierry Boutsen/Hans-Joachim Stuck/Christophe Bouchut were able to finish sixth overall in the 2,994cc Kremer Spyder WSC02, earning them second place in the WSC class. *Corporate Archives Porsche AG*

Privateers Rule

Looking at the entry list for the four-year period from 1990 to 1993, we can see that the Porsche 962 continued to dominate the grid, but the results were disappointing by Porsche standards even if these were customer cars. Until the arrival of the 911 GT1 during the second half of the decade, the only bright spots were the win in 1994 with the Dauer 962 LM, followed by the WSC95 victories by Joest Racing in 1996 and 1997. These three wins in the nineties were all achieved by privateer teams, but the 1998 victory by McNish/Ortelli/Aiello in the factory GT1 capped a return to the fray begun by the Porsche factory team two years earlier.

The playing field in the upper echelons of international sports car racing was most certainly changing, as the big Japanese manufacturers, in the form of Mazda, Nissan and Toyota, were making their presence felt. This development was in addition to the factory effort by Mercedes-Benz, who had won the previous year's race, and of course Jaguar, who were threatening to dominate the scene at Porsche's expense. Anticipation among the teams and the spectators alike ran high, since the winner could just as easily have come from any of these five main players (excluding Mercedes-Benz, as they had decided not to continue competing at Le Mans). At the end of the day, this was exactly what the fans had come to see: an action-packed race.

Of significance were the changes to the circuit, which altered the character of the long Hunaudières straight with the inclusion in 1991 of two chicanes, initially named the Nissan Chicane and the Carte S Chicane. The first chicane was located 1¼ miles (2 kilometers) down the famous back straight and was kinked to the right, while the second was a further 1¼ miles down the track, but this time it kinked to the left. These two chicanes were intended to slow the cars down, which they did, but their effectiveness was brought into question because of the additional stresses and strains placed on the cars' suspension, brakes, tires, and other mechanical components, as well as on the drivers themselves.

The ACO had also taken heed of the teams' complaints over the years that the pit and paddock area was simply inadequate and, as cars were being transported in larger carriers than ever before, space behind the existing pits was at a premium. With the expansion of the sport, thanks to growing financial support from eager sponsors, sports car racing was becoming a much bigger operation in all aspects of the game, and more equipment was required to be carried from race to race. Although the construction of the new pit and media center, with sponsors' suites and spectator stands above, was still a year away, at least the teams could see that things were moving in the right direction.

1990

June 16–17

On the Saturday afternoon when the race got underway, the starting grid for the 1990 race looked very different. On pole was Nissan, with Porsche in second and sixth places, and Nissan again in third, fourth, and fifth places. The Jaguars were placed back in seventh, eighth, and ninth, with Toyota taking the tenth spot. Of course, the starting grid seldom reflects the order of the winning cars, but it did signal that things were not going to be the same in the international sports car arena for much longer. Despite Porsche officially staying away from the French race, there were no fewer than eighteen 962s in the entry list. Most prominent were the familiar teams of Brun Motorsport (Nos. 15 and 16), Kremer Brothers (Nos. 10 and 11), Joest Racing (Nos. 6, 7, and 9), Hans Obermaier (Nos. 26 and 27), Vern Schuppan (Nos. 33 and 55), and Richard Lloyd Racing (Nos. 43 and 44), to which could be added Japanese entrant Tomei Engineering (No. 45), Trust Engineering (No. 63), Team Davey (Nos. 19 and 20), and Momo Gebhardt Racing (No. 230).

In 1990 the Kremer brothers came up with another development of the 962, which merited the "K" designation. The strikingly colored Le Mans car, the 962 CK6, had a short tail, a single center-post spoiler, and covered wheel arches that gave the Porsche a distinct appearance. The Kremer Racing 962 CK6 raced at Le Mans from 1990 to 1993, although toward the end of this period it appeared without the covered wheels. This innovation, however, shows how creative the privateer teams could become in the absence of any development on the 962s by the factory.

By comparison with a decade earlier, the fastest car on the track did not come from Germany, but from the Land of the Rising Sun—how things had changed! At the 1980 race, Jacky Ickx set a fastest qualifying lap of 3:41.5 (137.615 miles per hour/221.464 kilometers per hour) in the No. 9 Porsche 908/80, a time that he bettered in the race itself with a lap of 3:40.6 (138.176 miles per hour/222.367 kilometers per hour). Ten years later, it was the No. 24 Nissan R90CK of Mark Blundell who set the fastest qualifying time of 3:27.02 (146.954 miles per hour/236.493 kilometers per hour), with the fastest Porsche, the No. 16 962 C of Walti Brun, which posted a lap of 3:33.06 in second place on the starting grid. For the record, the track was officially 88.6 feet (27 meters) shorter in 1990 than it had been ten years earlier.

During practice, the Japanese pairing of Kunimitsu Takahashi and Hideki Okada, together with South African Sarel van der Merwe, tested the No. 10 Kremer car, which had been fitted with the new 3.2-liter engine, but they instead chose to run with the proven 3.0-liter unit, which promptly blew up on Wednesday. The fire-engine-red No. 10 962 CK6 finished twenty-fourth overall and twenty-first in the Group C1 class. *PCGB*

Kremer Racing's No. 11 Thompson-chassied 962 CK6 was driven by Patrick Gonin/Philippe Alliot/Bernard de Dryver to sixteenth place. This strikingly colorful car was painted by Lübeck-born pop artist Peter Klasen. *Corporate Archives Porsche AG*

Nobody was going to miss the unusual pink No. 44 Italiya Sports–sponsored Richard Lloyd Racing 962 C (chassis 161), driven by John Watson/Bruno Giacomelli/Allen Berg who, incidentally, looked resplendent in their matching pink racing overalls. Despite the unique color scheme, the car finished eleventh, having started from twenty-first on the grid. *PCGB*

Almost immediately after the start, the No. 9 Mizuno-sponsored Joest Racing 962 C (the Joest Porsches were all fitted with longtail bodywork) of Bob Wollek/Stanley Dickens/Louis Krages ("John Winter") pulled into the pits to have more downforce added to the rear spoiler. Bob Wollek was the only member of this threesome not to have lifted the coveted Le Mans trophy (Krages in 1985, Dickens in 1989), an accolade that he was destined never to achieve. In 1990 this car finished eighth. *Corporate Archives Porsche AG*

Despite being fitted with a larger 3.2-liter works engine, the No. 7 Blaupunkt Joest Racing 962 C, driven by Porsche stalwarts Hans-Joachim Stuck/Derek Bell/Frank Jelinski, could only manage a fourth-place finish. With the Joest car requiring a new turbo wastegate on Sunday around midday, the No. 45 Tomei Engineering Alpha Racing Team car took the opportunity to slip by and into third place. *Corporate Archives Porsche AG*

The No. 16 Repsol-sponsored Brun Porsche sister car, driven by the owner himself, Walter Brun, together with Oscar Larrauri and Jésus Pareja-Mayo, breathed its last just four laps from the end after a spirited fight throughout the preceding twenty-three-and-three-quarter hours—but that's Le Mans for you: tough and unrelenting. *PCGB*

The No. 45 Tomei Engineering Alpha Racing Team of Tiff Needell/David Sears/ Anthony Reid finished third. The all-British team had driven faultlessly throughout the twenty-four hours and deserved their place on the podium after a solid performance. *Corporate Archives Porsche AG*

1990 Race Results

Pos.	Car/Model	No.	Driver(s)	Entered	Class	Cl. Pos	Laps	Reason
NRF	962C (160)	16	Oscar Larrauri (AR)/Jésus Pareja-Mayo (ES)/Walter Brun (CH)	Brun Motorsport	Group C1		355	Engine
3	962C (154)	45	Tiff Needell (GB)/David Sears (GB)Anthony Reid (GB)	Tomei Engineering Alpha Racing Team	Group C1	3	352	
4	962C (015)	7	Hans-Joachim Stuck (DE)/Derek Bell (GB)/Frank Jelinski (DE)	Joest Racing	Group C1	4	350	
8	962C (145)	9	Louis Krages (DE)/Stanley Dickens (SE)/Bob Wollek (FR)	Joest Racing	Group C1	8	346	
9	962C (902)	27	Jürgen Lässig (DE)/Pierre Yver (FR)/Otto Altenbach (DE)	Obermaier Racing	Group C1	9	341	
10	962C Thompson	15	Harald Huysman (NO)/Massimo Sigala (IT)/Bernard Santal (CH)	Brun Motorsport	Group C1	10	335	
11	962C (161)	44	John Watson (GB)/Bruno Giacomelli (IT)/Allen Berg (CA)	Richard Lloyd Racing	Group C1	11	335	
12	962C (146)	33	Hurley Haywood (US)/Wayne Taylor (ZA)/Rickard Rydell (SE)	Team Schuppan	Group C1	12	332	
13	962C (159)	63	George Fouché (ZA)/Steven Andskär (SE)/Shunji Kasuya (JP)	Trust Racing Team	Group C1	13	330	
14	962C (144)	6	Jean-Louis Ricci (FR)/Henri Pescarolo (FR)/Jacques Laffite (FR)	Joest Racing	Group C1	14	328	
15	962C (TS01C)	55	Eje Elgh (SE)/Thomas Danielsson (SE)/Thomas Mezera (AU)	Team Schuppan	Group C1	15	326	
16	962CK6 Thompson	11	Patrick Gonin (FR)/Philippe Alliot (FR)/Bernard de Dryver (BE)	Kremer Racing	Group C1	16	319	
19	962C (138/02)	20	Tim Lee-Davey (GB)/Giovanni Lavaggi (IT)/Max Cohen-Olivar (MA)	Team Davey	Group C1	19	306	
24	962CK6 Thompson	10	Kunimitsu Takahashi (JP)/Sarel van der Merwe (ZA)/Hideki Okada (JP)	Kremer Racing	Group C1	21	279	
26	962C (138/001)	19	Max Cohen-Olivar (MA)/Katsunori Iketani (JP)/Patrick Trucco (FR)	Team Davey	Group C1	22	260	
DNF	962C GTi	43	Manuel Reuter (DE)/James Weaver (GB)/J. J. Lehto (SF)	Richard Lloyd Racing	Group C1		188	Pit fire
DNF	962C Thompson	26	Jürgen Oppermann (DE)/Harald Grohs (DE)/Marc Duez (BE)	Obermaier Racing	Group C1		145	Gearbox
DNF	962C Thompson	230	Gianpiero Moretti (IT)/Nick Adams (GB)/Günter Gebhardt (DE)	Momo Gebhardt Racing	IMSA GTP		141	Gearbox

1991

June 22–23

This was the first year in which the teams, press, and spectators could marvel at the brand-new, state-of-the-art pit complex. Comprising a widened pit lane with larger pit garages at track level, the building ran the full length of the pit lane and rose several stories high, with a futuristic race control tower looming at the pit lane entrance.

On the track, however, one could be forgiven for asking if the shine was beginning to wear off the 962, a vehicle that had entered competitive life in 1985. Six years at the top of the motorsports pyramid for a single model is almost unheard-of in international racing, and yet the 962 was not finished. No fewer than thirteen 962s were on the 1991 entry list for Le Mans, but what was different was that more teams were listed with fewer cars per team. The highest-placed Porsche 962 C on the starting grid was the No. 11 Kremer Racing Porsche 962 CK6 driven by Manuel Reuter/Harri Toivonen/J. J. Lehto, which was placed well back in fifteenth place.

The Le Mans returned to the World Championship fold again in 1991, but one rule that slipped through the cracks almost unnoticed by the established European teams was that the Group C cars were to weigh a minimum of 2,205 pounds (1,000 kilograms), while an exemption allowed the quad-rotor Mazda at a weight of only 1,830 pounds (830 kilograms). This weight rule for 1991 was to prove the undoing of the familiar Group C cars such as Porsche, Jaguar, and Mercedes-Benz.

It was evident in 1991, however, that once again the playing field was being tilted in favor of manufacturers and teams from the Far East, who were renewing their efforts to make their presence felt in European production car markets. Mazda was a name that stood out prominently in 1991: at the end of the twenty-four-hour race that year, they could claim the first rotary-engined victory at Le Mans.

The No. 57 Porsche 962 C was an early retirement due to an overheating engine. Entered by Konrad Motorsport, the car completed 197 laps in the hands of Bernd Schneider/Henri Pescarolo/Louis Krages. *Corporate Archives Porsche AG*

The No. 52 Team Salamin Primagaz (Team Schuppan) 962 C, piloted by Eje Elgh/Roland Ratzenberger/Will Hoy, completed 202 laps before retiring with a blown head gasket. The Austrian Roland Ratzenberger was later killed during practice for the 1994 San Marino Grand Prix at Imola in only his third Formula 1 race, the same race that claimed the life of Ayrton Senna that fateful weekend. *Corporate Archives Porsche AG*

The No. 53 Porsche 962 C was driven by James Weaver/Hurley Haywood/Wayne Taylor. Entered under the Vern Schuppan team banner, they would finish thirteenth overall. *Corporate Archives Porsche AG*

A broken suspension during the late-night hours cost Manuel Reuter/Harri Toivonen/J. J. Lehto several laps, but the No. 11 Kenwood-sponsored Kremer Racing 962 CK6 crossed the finish line in ninth place. *Corporate Archives Porsche AG*

THAT ALL-IMPORTANT HORSEPOWER

One of the most experienced race mechanics at Kremer Racing, Walter Heuser, began his apprenticeship with Kremer back in 1972. Heuser worked at the Cologne-based workshop through the company's heyday; he remembers their jubilation when Kremer won the 1979 Le Mans with the K3. Following his apprenticeship, he moved on to engine assembly and specialized in this area for over thirty years. Today, Heuser talks proudly of Kremer's achievements and the fun they had as a team.

Back in 1991, Heuser and a colleague set about building the perfect 3.2-liter flat six engine for one of Kremer's 962 race cars, with the aim of seeing what kind of power they could get out of it. A challenge was laid down whereby these two highly skilled colleagues would try to produce the first 1,000 horsepower six-cylinder Porsche engine. The engine in normal race trim was usually good for around 700–750 horsepower, but when fitted to the dyno and with the boost turned up to 1.3 bar, the Heuser engine developed a massive 850 horsepower, all from a twin turbo 3.2-liter powerhouse.

When asked by the author during a visit back in 2008, Heuser eagerly produced the engine build records to show the power curve and related technical data achieved during the test session, a truly remarkable achievement, even if it fell short of their rather ambitious 1,000 horsepower target.

Walter Heuser stands proudly alongside the 3.2-liter Porsche 962 engine that he and a colleague tuned to produce a mighty 850 horsepower. *Glen Smale*

The Kremer 3.2-liter 962 engine that Heuser and a colleague worked on hoping to generate the first 1,000 horsepower flat six output. *Glen Smale*

Driver change for the No. 58 Konrad Motorsport (Joest Porsche) 962 C as Derek Bell stands ready at the front of the car. Not even the combined experience of Hans-Joachim Stuck/Derek Bell/Frank Jelinski could manage better than seventh place at the flag, but that experience had helped them get that far, as their mount suffered a persistent water leak during the late-night hours. *Corporate Archives Porsche AG*

1991 Race Results

Pos.	Car/Model	No.	Driver(s)	Entered	Class	Cl. Pos	Laps	Reason
7	962C (012)	58	Hans-Joachim Stuck (DE)/Derek Bell (GB)/Frank Jelinski (DE)	Konrad Motorsport (Joest Porsche)	Gr C1/Cat 2	7	348	
9	962CK6	11	Manuel Reuter (DE)/Harri Toivonen (FI)/J. J. Lehto (FI)	Kremer Racing	Gr C1/Cat 2	9	344	
10	962C (177)	17	Oscar Larrauri (AR)/Jésus Pareja-Mayo (ES)/Walter Brun (CH)	Repsol Brun Motorsport	Gr C1/Cat 2	10	339	
13	962C (146)	53	Hurley Haywood (US)/James Weaver (GB)/Wayne Taylor (ZA)	Vern Schuppan Team Salamin Primagaz	Gr C1/Cat 2	12	317	
NRF	962C (159)	49	George Fouché (ZA)/Steven Andskär (SE)	Trust Engineering Courage Compétition	Gr C1/Cat 2		316	Gearbox
DNF	962C (901)	51	Otto Altenbach (DE)/Jürgen Lässig (DE)/Pierre Yver (FR)	Team Salamin Primagaz/Hans Obermaier	Gr C1/Cat 2		232	Suspension
DNF	962C (02C)	52	Eje Elgh (SE)/Roland Ratzenberger (AT)/Will Hoy (GB)	Team Schuppan Team Salamin Primagaz	Gr C1/Cat 2		202	Engine/head gasket
DNF	962C (014)	57	Louis Krages (DE)/Bernd Schneider (DE)/Henri Pescarolo (FR)	Konrad Motorsport (Joest Porsche)	Gr C1/Cat 2		197	Overheating
DNF	962C (160)	16	Harald Huysman (NO)/Robbie Stirling (CA)/Bernard Santal (CH)	Repsol Brun Motorsport	Gr C1/Cat 2		138	Head gasket
DNF	962C (157)	14	Antoine Salamin (CH)/Max Cohen-Olivar (MA)/Marcel Tarrés (FR)	Team Salamin Primagaz	Gr C1/Cat 2		101	Overheating
DNF	962C (Thompson)	21	Franz Konrad (AT)/Anthony Reid (GB)/Pierre-Alain Lombardi (CH)	Konrad Motorsport	Gr C1/Cat 2		98	Engine
DNF	962C (EAF-001)	50	Jacques Alméras (FR)/Jean-Marie Alméras (FR)/Pierre de Thoisy (FR)	Courage Compétition Almera Freres	Gr C1/Cat 2		86	Accident
DNF	962CK6 (Thompson)	46	Tomas Lopez (MX)/Gregor Foitek (CH)/Tiff Needell (GB)	Kremer Racing	Gr C1/Cat 2		18	Accident

1992

June 20–21

Porsche entered a two-year period of stagnation, akin to a yachtsman sailing into the doldrums. To the outsider it looked like the company's motorsports program had come to a standstill and that they were doing nothing to regain their place at the top of the sport. Only the privateers were entering Le Mans in this period, and even their numbers were vastly reduced. In fact, only five 962s were listed on the scrutineer's schedule for the 1992 prerace check, plus three other Group C Porsche-engined Cougar cars entered by Courage Compétition.

In reality, the lower number of Stuttgart-Zuffenhausen race cars had more to do with the Group C rules, which limited engine size to 3.5 liters, as required by FIA to run in the Sportscar World Championships. This resulted in just twenty-four cars entering this class at Le Mans, and so the grid was boosted by a gaggle of smaller-engined cars that ran in a local French championship series. As a consequence, the 1992 race-goers witnessed the smallest field of cars seen at any Le Mans race for decades. This year would see the end of the Group C era from a purist's point of view, as the rules were to change in 1993 because of the ACO's withdrawal from the Sportscar World Championships.

There were moves afoot in Stuttgart to give the 911 an injection of power, however, preparing this stalwart to contest Le Mans once again. It was this development work that kept Porsche's focus away from producing a 962 upgrade or replacement. The revived 911 *did* appear at the following year's race and later competitions, where it once again made its presence felt in no uncertain terms.

Suspension damage as a result of an accident put the No. 68 Team Alméras Chotard 962 C of Jean-Marie/Jacques Alméras/Max Cohen-Olivar out of the running after just eighty-five laps. *Corporate Archives Porsche AG*

The No. 53 ADA Engineering 962 C GTi, driven by the father-and-son team of Derek and Justin Bell, together with the amiable Tiff Needell, finished in a disappointing twelfth place because of faulty brakes. The car covered just 284 laps, compared with 352 laps by the winning Peugeot, making this Porsche the last classified finisher in 1992. *Corporate Archives Porsche AG*

Kremer Racing's No. 52 962 CK6 (Thompson) featured the trademark Kremer shorttail with a center-post rear spoiler. Driven by Robin Donovan/Charles Rickett/ Almo Coppelli, the Hawaiian Tropic–sponsored Porsche finished eleventh. *John Brooks*

During prerace practice, the No. 51 Kremer Racing 962 CK6 is seen experimenting with various setups, in this case without its rear wheel covers. This shot was taken in the late afternoon, with Manuel Reuter behind the wheel before actually going out on to the track, as the car is very clean (!) and the left door is slightly ajar. Kremer also had a No. 51 T-car at Le Mans in identical livery, but that car featured a distinctive roof-mounted air scoop and had a white "Kremer Kenwood" windscreen decal. Driven by Manuel Reuter/John Nielsen/Giovanni Lavaggi, the car pictured here was the highest-placed Porsche in the 1992 race, finishing seventh. *Corporate Archives Porsche AG*

1992 Race Results

Pos.	Car/Model	No.	Driver(s)	Entered	Class	Cl. Pos	Laps	Reason
7	962CK6	51	Manuel Reuter (DE)/John Nielsen (DK)/Giovanni Lavaggi (IT)	Kremer Racing	Gr C1	2	334	
10	962C (Thompson)	67	Otto Altenbach (DE)/Jürgen Lässig (DE)/Pierre Yver (FR)	Obermaier Racing	Gr C1	3	297	
11	962CK6 (Thompson)	52	Robin Donovan (GB)/Charles Rickett (GB)/Almo Coppelli (IT)	Kremer Racing	Gr C1	4	297	
12	962C GTi	53	Derek Bell (GB)/Justin Bell (GB)/Tiff Needell (GB)	ADA Engineering	Gr C1	5	284	
DNF	962C (Thompson)	68	Jean-Marie Alméras (FR)/Jacques Alméras (FR)/Max Cohen-Olivar (MA)	Team Alméras Chotard	Gr C1		85	Accident

1993

June 19–20

The 911 returned to Le Mans in 1993, posting some meaningful numbers after an absence of more than ten years. Of the eighteen Porsches that started, eleven were 911s, with eight of those being classified as finishers. The late seventies and early eighties saw the rise of the 930, 934, and 935 variants, but throughout the middle and late eighties the Group C cars ruled, with the 956s and 962s taking center stage. But the writing was on the wall for the 962 by 1993: in the words of the *Motor Sport* correspondent that year, "The aging Porsches were soundly beaten."

No doubt Porsche engineers had been watching closely the direction the ACO was heading with its regulations, as the French race organizers sought to restrict the speeds of the Group C cars and to introduce a production sports car based on the Grand Touring class. This development opened the doors for Porsche to expand its work on their Grand Touring 911 program, which resulted in the appearance of the 911 Turbo S Le Mans GT at the 1993 race. Clearly this new car was not vying for top honors, but by putting such stalwarts as Walter Röhrl, Hans-Joachim Stuck, and Hurley Haywood behind the wheel, Porsche obviously wanted the most accurate feedback possible under full race conditions to further aid its development program.

This year also saw the reintroduction of the spring test day, which teams had supported to a wildly varying degree. This year was different, however, in that the teams regarded the prerace contest as important to their race preparation, and the good attendance was encouraging.

Never short of a new idea, Kremer Racing arrived at the May test session with a new model that wasn't intended for Le Mans, but which participated in the European Interserie. By this time Group C had fallen away. Replacing the CK6, the new K7 was allowed out for a brief run by way of an exemption from the ACO. The K7 was not simply a 962 with the roof chopped off; rather it featured a completely new chassis created by Kremer, with a substantially strengthened rollover bar, different mirrors to ensure improved airflow to the rear, and revised air ducts. The K7 was without ground effects, as this had been outlawed in both Europe and America, and the car was fitted with Kremer's now-familiar covered rear wheels. Only three examples of the hugely successful 3.2-liter K7 were made, but this car led to the development of the K8, which was to race at Le Mans in 1994.

Once the dust had settled at the end of the 1993 race, the Tom Walkinshaw Jaguar XJ220C, which had finished fifteenth overall and first in the Grand Touring class, was retrospectively disqualified for not having a catalytic converter fitted, as per the IMSA rules under which the car had been entered. This lifted the No. 47 Porsche Carrera RSR of Joël Gouhier/Jürgen Barth/Dominique Dupuy into a class-winning position by default.

Walter Röhrl/Hans-Joachim Stuck/Hurley Haywood drove the No. 46 factory-entered 911 Turbo S LM, pictured here in the pits before the start.
PCGB

The No. 49 Team Paduwa Carrera 2 Cup (3.6-liter), driven by Bruno Ilien/ Alain Gadal/Bernard Robin, finished twenty-sixth overall and tenth in the Grand Touring class. *PCGB*

Konrad Motorsport's 911 Carrera 2 Cup finished fifth in the new Grand Touring class in the hands of Franz Konrad/Jun Harada/Antonio Hermann, and in nineteenth overall. *Corporate Archives Porsche AG*

In sixteenth spot overall and second place in the Grand Touring class was the No. 78 Carrera RSR of Jésus Pareja-Mayo/Jack Leconte/Pierre de Thoisy. Jack Leconte was the founder of Larbre Compétition, which still runs a number of different sports cars today, including Porsche, in various racing series. *Corporate Archives Porsche AG*

Monaco Media International, the Monaco-based media agency established by ex-Formula 1 driver Jean-Pierre Jarier, sponsored the No. 47 Larbre Compétition Carrera RSR (3.8-liter) to be driven by Joël Gouhier/Jürgen Barth/Dominique Dupuy. Entered into the Grand Touring class, the white-and-blue Porsche RSR finished first in class and fifteenth overall. *PCGB*

The No. 23 Team Guy Chotard 962 C, driven by French trio Denis Morin/Didier Caradec/Alain Sturm, completed 309 laps; they finished fourteenth overall and ninth in the Group C1/Cat 2 class. *Corporate Archives Porsche AG*

Just slipping into the top ten finishers was Joest Racing's highest-placed car, driven by Le Mans veterans Bob Wollek/Henri Pescarolo/Ronny Meixner, claiming ninth spot overall and fourth in class. *Corporate Archives Porsche AG*

The surprise of the 1993 race was the No. 21 Obermaier Racing 962 C, which claimed seventh place behind the works Peugeots and Toyotas that occupied the first six places. Otto Altenbach/Jürgen Oppermann/Loris Kessel completed 355 laps against the winning 376 laps of the Peugeot, but the car's reliability was enough to secure the team third place in the Group C1/Cat 2 class. The Obermaier car was fitted with carbon brakes, which were thought to have contributed to its impressive result. *Corporate Archives Porsche AG*

1993 Race Results

Pos.	Car/Model	No.	Driver(s)	Entered	Class	Cl. Pos	Laps	Reason
7	962C (155)	21	Otto Altenbach (DE)/Jürgen Oppermann (DE)/Loris Kessel (CH)	Obermaier Racing	Gr C1/Cat 2	3	356	
9	962C (014)	18	Bob Wollek (FR)/Henri Pescarolo (FR)/Ronny Meixner (DE)	Joest Racing	Gr C1/Cat 2	4	352	
12	962CK6	10	Jürgen Lässig (DE)/Giovanni Lavaggi (IT)/Wayne Taylor (ZA)	Kremer Racing	Gr C1/Cat 2	7	329	
13	962CK6	11	Andy Evans (US)/Tomas Saldaña (ES)/François Migault (FR)	Kremer Racing	Gr C1/Cat 2	8	317	
14	962C (Thompson)	23	Denis Morin (FR)/Didier Caradec (FR)/Alain Sturm (FR)	Team Guy Chotard	Gr C1/Cat 2	9	309	
15	Carrera RSR	47	Joël Gouhier (FR)/Jürgen Barth (DE)/Dominique Dupuy (FR)	Monaco Media International	Grand Touring	1	305	
16	Carrera RSR	78	Jésus Pareja-Mayo (ES)/Jack Leconte (FR)/Pierre de Thoisy (FR)	Jack Leconte	Grand Touring	2	302	
17	Carrera RSR	65	Ulli Richter (DE)/Dirk Ebeling (DE)/Karl-Heinz Wlazik (DE)	Dirk Ebeling Heico Dienstleistungen	Grand Touring	3	300	
18	Carrera RSR	77	Claude Haldi (CH)/Olivier Haberthur (CH)/Charles Margueron (FR)	Scuderia Chicco d'Oro Guido Haberthur	Grand Touring	4	300	
19	Carrera 2 Cup	62	Franz Konrad (AT)/Jun Harada (JP)/Antonio Hermann (BR)	Konrad Motorsport	Grand Touring	5	294	
NRF	962C (013)	17	Manuel Reuter (DE)/Frank Jelinski (DE)/Louis Krages (DE)	Joest Racing	Gr C1/Cat 2		282	Engine
21	Carrera RS	66	Gustl Spreng (DE)/Sandro Angelastri (CH)/Fritz Müller (DE)	Mühlbauer Motorsport Gustl Spreng	Grand Touring	6	277	
22	Carrera 2 Cup	40	Philippe Olczyk (BE)/Josef Prechtl (DE)/Gérard Dillmann (FR)	Obermaier Racing	Grand Touring	7	275	
26	Carrera 2 Cup	49	Bruno Ilien (FR)/Alain Gadal (FR)/Bernard Robin (FR)	Team Paduwa	Grand Touring	10	267	
DNF	962CK6	15	Almo Coppelli (IT)/Robin Donovan (GB)/Steve Fossett (US)	Kremer Racing	Gr C1/Cat 2		204	Fuel pump
DNF	911 Turbo S LM	46	Walter Röhrl (DE)/Hans-Joachim Stuck (DE)/Hurley Haywood (US)	Porsche	Grand Touring		79	Accident
DNF	Carrera 2 Cup	76	Enzo Calderari (CH)/Luigino Pagotto (IT)/Lilian Bryner (CH)	Cartronic Motorsport Enzo Calderari	Grand Touring		64	Accident
DNF	Carrera 2 Cup	48	Harald Grohs (DE)/Jean-Paul Libert (BE)/Didier Theys (BE)	Team Paduwa	Grand Touring		8	Overheating/engine

1994

June 18–19

There was life in the old dog yet, as the 962 was given another chance to show its credentials. Some considerable effort was made by the ACO to narrow the gap between the two main classes, and this meddling with the rules resulted in the revised homologation requirement, where only one road-going example of a car needed to exist in order to qualify for the Grand Touring class.

Jochen Dauer had produced a road-going 962, which was on display at the 1993 Frankfurt Motor Show. A sharp-eyed Norbert Singer spotted it at the show and approached Dauer with a view to entering this car in the GT class at Le Mans in 1994. Alain Bertaut, the ACO's race director, was responsible for the wording of the 1994 rules. While many felt that the Dauer 962 LM did not belong in the GT class, it was correct to the letter of the law. Dauer's name was on the car, Joest

entered it in the race, and Porsche supplied the crew and managed the team at the track. The result was that Porsche won the race giving the manufacturer its thirteenth victory at Le Mans, which very nearly became a 1-2 finish, as the No. 2 factory car was surpassed at the post by less than a second by the No. 1 Toyota.

In 1994, Porsche privateers Kremer Racing risked a one-year "affair" with the Japanese manufacturer Honda by fielding a trio of NSX cars. In true Kremer style, the three GT2 cars were meticulously prepared and finished in fourteenth, sixteenth, and eighteenth places, although the latter two cars were not classified, having failed to complete sufficient laps. Despite this relative success, Kremer felt that it had cheated its lifelong partner, Porsche, and returned to the Stuttgart manufacturer the following season.

The all-British team of Ray Bellm/Harry Nuttall/Charles Rickett retired their No. 66 Carrera RSR in the second hour after just thirty-four laps. A failed engine in the Bristow Racing Porsche 911 GT2 LM was the cause of the car's withdrawal. *Corporate Archives Porsche AG*

The No. 50 Carrera RSR of French trio Pierre Yver/ Jack Leconte/Jean-Luc Chéreau, entered by Larbre Compétition, had an accident during the early night hours and fell out of contention after sixty-two laps. *Corporate Archives Porsche AG*

Another victim of an accident was the No. 58 Seikel Motorsport 968 Turbo RS Coupe (chassis 820065). Piloted by John Nielson/Thomas Bscher/Lindsay Owen-Jones, the front-engined LM GT2 entry exited the competition after eighty-four laps. *Corporate Archives Porsche AG*

Norbert Singer had calculated well: the prototype Toyotas were pitting every forty minutes for fuel, while the Dauer cars were running an hour between stops. At that rate, their times were comparable with the top prototype contenders. This was confirmed as the two 962 Dauer LM GTs were leading the field at the two-hour mark. Here the No. 36 car driven by Mauro Baldi, Yannick Dalmas, and Hurley Haywood leads the No. 35 car through the Ford Chicane. *Corporate Archives Porsche AG*

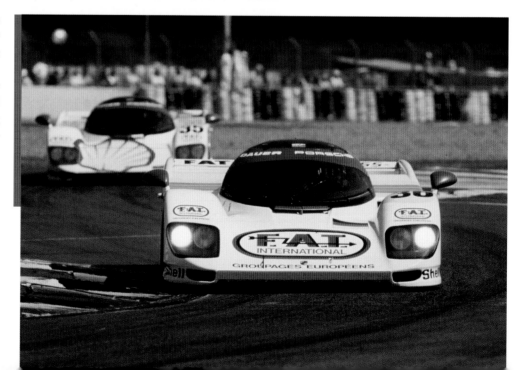

Entered by Austrian-born race car tuner Franz Konrad of Konrad Motorsport, the No. 59 Carrera RSR finished tenth overall and second in the LM GT2 class in the hands of Cor Euser/Patrick Huisman/Matjaz Tomlje. Huisman later became a highly successful in Porsche's Supercup series, winning the European Championship four years in a row, 1997–2000. *Corporate Archives Porsche AG*

The No. 54 Porsche 911 Carrera RSR 3.8 was prepared by Stadler Motorsport and entered under the Swiss-based Ecurie-Biennoise team banner. Drivers Lilian Bryner, Enzo Calderari, and Renato Mastropietro finished ninth overall and second in the GT2 class. *Corporate Archives Porsche AG*

The No. 52 Larbre Compétition 911 Carrera RSR 3.8 put in an impressive performance in the hands of Jesús Pareja-Mayo, Dominique Dupuy and Carlos Palau. They drove a consistent race and kept up the pressure in the GT2 class to finish eighth overall, adding class honors to their weekend haul. *Corporate Archives Porsche AG*

Nuremberg-based race car constructor, Jochen Dauer, built a street legal 962 GT, which was spotted by Norbert Singer. The ACO rules for the 1994 Le Mans required that just a single street legal car be built in order to qualify for the Grand Touring class that year. Porsche took over the construction of the race cars and proceeded to build two cars for Le Mans. Jochen Dauer remained as the constructor; since Porsche didn't have a racing license that year, the two race cars were entered by Joest Racing (hence the sponsorship by Joest Racing partner F.A.T.). The mechanics and logistics were all supplied by Porsche at the track. The No. 36 Porsche, seen here late on the Saturday night, was driven by Mauro Baldi/Yannick Dalmas/Hurley Haywood to claim first place in a hard-fought race over 345 laps, where the top three cars were separated by just one lap. *Corporate Archives Porsche AG*

1994 Race Results

Pos.	Car/Model	No.	Driver(s)	Entered	Class	Cl. Pos	Laps	Reason
FL	Dauer 962 LM Porsche (GT003/176)	35	Thierry Boutsen (BE)	Porsche	Time: 3:52.540 minutes		Speed: 210.544km/h; 130.826mph	
1	Dauer 962 LM Porsche (GT003/176)	36	Yannick Dalmas (FR)/Hurley Haywood (US)/Mauro Baldi (IT)	Porsche	LM GT1	1	345	
3	Dauer 962 LM Porsche (GT002/173)	35	Hans-Joachim Stuck (DE)/Danny Sullivan (US)/Thierry Boutsen (BE)	Porsche	LM GT1	2	344	
6	Kremer K8	5	Derek Bell (GB)/Robin Donovan (GB)/Jürgen Lässig (D)	Gulf Oil Racing	LMP1/C90	3	316	
8	911 Carrera RSR	52	Jésus Pareja-Mayo (ES)/Dominique Dupuy (FR)/Carlos Palau (ES)	Larbre Compétition	LM GT2	1	308	
9	911 Carrera RSR	54	Enzo Calderari (CH)/Lilian Bryner (CH)/Renato Mastropietro (IT)	Ecurie Biennoise	LM GT2	2	299	
10	911 Carrera RSR	59	Cor Euser (NL)/Patrick Huisman (NL)/Matjaz Tomlje (SK)	Konrad Motorsport	LM GT2	3	295	
NC	Porsche 962 GTi	6	Jun Harada (JP)/Tomiko Yoshikawa (JP)/Masahiko Kondo (JP)	A.D.A. Engineering/Team Nip	LMP1/C90		189	
DNF	911 S LM Turbo	33	Franz Konrad (AT)/Antonio Hermann (BR)/Bernd Netzeband (DE)	Konrad Motorsport/Patrick Néve Racing	LM GT2		100	Engine
DNF	911 Carrera RSR	49	Jacques Laffite (FR)/Jacques Alméras (FR)/Jean-Marie Alméras (FR)	Fylmo Mobil Alméras	LM GT2		94	Accident
DNF	968 RS Turbo	58	Thomas Bscher (DE)/Lindsay Owen-Jones (GB)/John Nielsen (DK)	Seikel Motorsport	LM GT2		84	Accident
DNF	911 Carrera RSR	50	Pierre Yver (FR)/Jack Leconte (FR)/Jean-Luc Chéreau (FR)	Larbre Compétition	LM GT2		62	Accident
DNF	911 Carrera RSR	45	Ulli Richter (DE)/Karl-Heinz Wlazik (DE)/Dirk Ebeling (DE)	Heico Service GmbH	LM GT2		57	Engine
DNF	911 Turbo	56	Olivier Haberthur (CH)/Patrice Goueslard (FR)/Patrick Vuillaume (FR)	Elf Haberthur Racing	LM GT2		42	Turbocharger
DNF	911 Carrera RSR	66	Ray Bellm (GB)/Harry Nuttall (GB)	Erik Henriksen	LM GT2		34	Engine

1995

June 17–18

Porsche's reentry into the endurance racing world with a works team was still another year away, so it was left to the privateers to fly the Stuttgart flag. Leading the privateer charge in 1995 was the Kremer Racing team with their K8, bristling with confidence and fresh from their victory with their new car in the 24 Hours of Daytona in February that year.

The K8, the direct descendent of the K7, was powered by a 2,994cc Porsche flat six, twin-OHC engine with four valves per cylinder and fitted with twin KKK K27 turbos. Bosch Motronic electronic ignition and a 9.5:1 compression ratio ensured maximum power of 560 horsepower. According to Kremer, however, the K8's engine (Type 935/76) was a bit of a hybrid in that it used the basic 962 unit with an intake system and airbox similar in structure to the forthcoming GT1.

The K8 was based on the Porsche 962 but with its roof removed, which resulted in an open-cockpit Spyder that was lighter than the closed-body style. The K8 body retained its two-seater layout as found in the CK6, however. Designed by Erwin Kremer, it was created to qualify for use in several international racing series, including the IMSA GT Championship, the International Sports Racing Series (ISRS) and Europe's own Interserie. The K8 had a full carbon-fiber monocoque chassis built by John Thompson's Northamptonshire-based TC Prototypes, the same company responsible for building many 962 chassis for other Porsche customers.

Also in the field for 1995 was a squadron of 911s entered by a wide range of teams from well-known names, as well as some newcomers. *Motor Sport* reported that the ACO had restricted the Porsche contingent to no more than a quarter of the entry list. If a company was looking for any more of a compliment regarding the dominance of its machinery, it couldn't be more convincing.

The race was run for sixteen of its twenty-four hours under a persistent drizzle, which meant that the drivers had to contend with constant spray and slippery going. The dry periods toward the end of the race did not make the going any easier, however, as the rain showers were relentless, making tire choices for the teams difficult.

Here the No. 3 Kremer K8 Spyder is lifted up for inspection during the scrutineering session. This event always presents other teams and photographers with an opportunity to get close to the opposition's cars for a peek at what they're doing—which explains the army of Honda mechanics on the prowl in these photographs. This car was driven by Jürgen Lässig/Franz Konrad/Antonio Hermann, but it retired with electrical problems after 163 laps. *Corporate Archives Porsche AG*

Another early Porsche retirement was the No. 55 Larbre Compétition 911 GT2 Evo, driven by the French team of Pierre Yver/Jean-Luc Chéreau/Jack Leconte. The silver GT1 contender was involved in an accident on lap 40, thereby ending its race. *Corporate Archives Porsche AG*

Based on the 993 chassis, Porsche developed the GT2 Turbo for 1995. This 3.6-liter race car developed 480 horsepower and was eligible for the GT2 class. The Repsol-sponsored No. 91 car, driven by Tomas Saldaña/Miguel Ángel de Castro/ Alfonso de Orleans, was the third of Kremer's entries in 1995, but it was involved in a race-ending accident early on, with Saldaña at the wheel. *Corporate Archives Porsche AG*

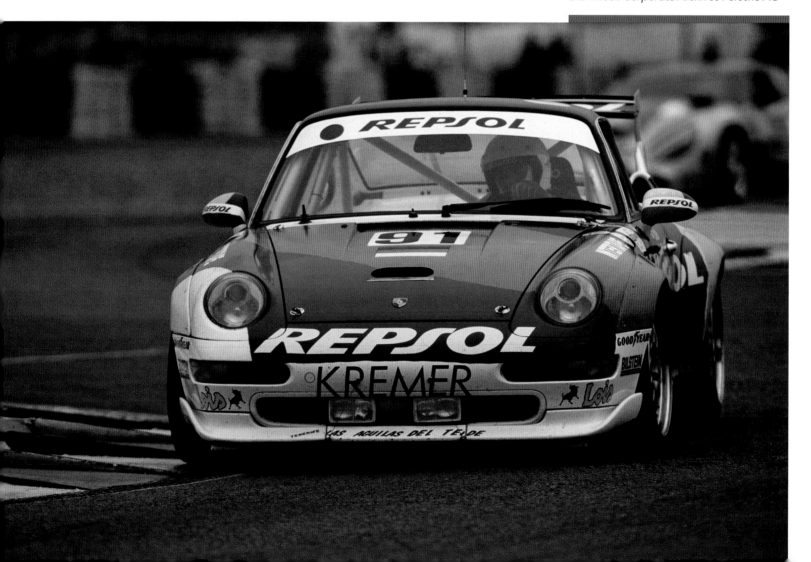

Karlsruhe-based Freisinger Motorsport entered this interesting 911 in the 1995 race. Based on the standard 993, this vehicle featured a bi-turbo 3.8-liter engine, whereas the factory GT2 version was fitted with a 3.6-liter unit. The GT2 body is easily distinguished from the 993 body in its bolt-on wheel flares. It's possible that Freisinger chose to use the 993 seen here because of its narrower frontal area, which made it more aerodynamic. The No. 54 car did acquit itself well in competition with the big guns in the GT1 class, and Wolfgang Kaufmann/Yukihiro Hane/Michel Ligonnet finished nineteenth overall and tenth in the GT1 class. *Corporate Archives Porsche AG*

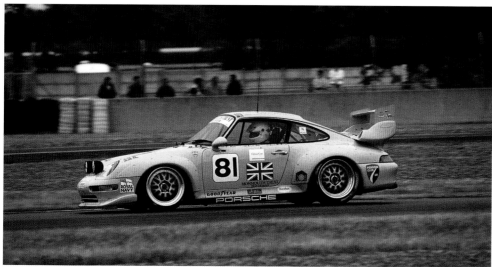

The all-British team of Nick Adams/ Richard Jones/Gérard MacQuillan brought the No. 81 Richard Jones Racing 3.6-liter turbo 911 GT2 home in seventeenth place, despite a three-quarter-hour turbo replacement. This earned the team a sixth place in the GT2 class. *Corporate Archives Porsche AG*

1995 Race Results

Pos.	Car/Model	No.	Driver(s)	Entered	Class	Cl. Pos	Laps	Reason
6	Kremer K8 (Thompson)	4	Thierry Boutsen (BE)/Hans-Joachim Stuck (DE)/Christophe Bouchut (FR)	Kremer Racing	WSC	2	290	
15	911 GT2	77	Guy Kuster (FR)/Karel Dolejší (CZ)/Peter Seikel (DE)	Seikel Motorsport	GT2	4	264	
16	911 GT2	78	Eric van de Vyver (BE)/Didier Ortion (FR)/Jean-François Véroux (FR)	Jean-Francois Veroux	GT2	5	263	
17	911 GT2	81	Nick Adams (GB)/Richard Jones (GB)/Gérard MacQuillan (GB)	Richard Jones	GT2	6	251	
19	993 BiTurbo	54	Wolfgang Kaufmann (DE)/Yukihiro Hane (JP)/Michel Ligonnet (FR)	Freisinger Motorsport	GT1	10	230	
DNF	Kremer K8 (Thompson)	3	Jürgen Lässig (DE)/Franz Konrad (AT)/Antonio Hermann (BR)	Kremer Racing	WSC		163	DQ – electrics
DNF	911 GT2 Evo	37	Dominique Dupuy (FR)/Emmanuel Collard (FR)/Stéphane Ortelli (FR)	Larbre Compétition	GT1		82	Accident
DNF	911 GT2	79	Enzo Calderari (CH)/Lilian Bryner (CH)/Andreas Fuchs (DE)	Stadler Motorsport	GT2		81	Accident
DNF	911 GT2	91	Tomas Saldaña (ES)/Miguel Ángel de Castro (ES)/Alfonso de Orleans (ES)	Heico Motorsport	GT2		63	Accident
DNF	911 GT2 Evo	36	Jean-Pierre Jarier (FR)/Jésus Pareja-Mayo (ES)/Erik Comas (FR)	Larbre Compétition	GT1		58	Accident
DNF	911 GT2 Evo	55	Pierre Yver (FR)/Jean-Luc Chéreau (FR)/Jack Leconte (FR)	Larbre Compétition	GT1		40	Accident
DNF	911 GT2	82	Charles Margueron (CH)/Pierre de Thoisy (FR)/Philippe Siffert (CH)	Elf Haberthur Racing	GT2		13	Accident

1996

June 15–16

In a departure from tradition, the ACO decided to start the open sports cars on the left of the grid, with the GT cars lined up on the right in an effort to give both race car types an equal opportunity within their respective classes at the start. This move might have caused chaos at the start, as the quicker prototypes mixed with the Grand Tourers straightaway off the start line, but in reality, it made little difference to the grid: many of the LM GT1 cars, such as Porsche and McLaren, were just as quick as the open sports cars anyway.

A pair of TWR Porsche WSC95s were entered by Joest Racing, but it was surely the farsightedness of Reinhold Joest alone that recognized the potential for an ex-Jaguar chassis powered by a Porsche 2,994cc flat six engine to win the Le Mans crown. In the late-night talks that followed a Christmas party in 1995, Joest had asked Porsche R&D boss Horst Marchant if he could use these two chassis, so the recycled Jaguar chassis

were duly prepared at Weissach and tested in the wind tunnels at the test center. The outcome was a win for the No. 7 Joest Porsche, not a bad result for a frame that was just gathering dust in the workshop.

This year marked the return of Porsche with a factory team, headed by the new 911 GT1. Although this newcomer did not win Le Mans in its debut year, the two works cars did fill second and third places.

For some years the factory had concentrated its development work around the 993 model, but the GT1 project (see sidebar) was prompted by Porsche's need to respond to the success of the McLaren F1. The McLaren challenge was just too much of an opportunity for Norbert Singer to ignore, so he set about building a sports racer around a 600 horsepower mid-engined concept that would once again carry the Stuttgart manufacturer's flag high.

Kremer's No. 2 Porsche K8, driven by Steve Fossett/George Fouché/ Stanley Dickens, awaits the start of the 1996 race. *PCGB*

The perfect twins! Works Porsche GT1 Nos. 25 and 26 line up on the starting grid before the 1996 race. With many years of racing experience behind them, Hans-Joachim Stuck/Thierry Boutsen/Bob Wollek piloted the No. 25 car, while Karl Wendlinger/Yannick Dalmas/Scott Goodyear were behind the wheel of the No. 26 car. *PCGB*

At the start, Porsche GT1 No. 26 (chassis 003) and No. 25 (chassis 002) begin their assault on the 1996 race, and the No. 8 Joest Racing WSC95 can be seen just behind. *Corporate Archives Porsche AG*

Team owner Reinhold Joest discusses race progress with 24-year-old Alexander Wurz in the No. 7 Joest Racing TWR Porsche WSC95 during a pit stop. Wurz was already well known to Joest Racing through his participation in the team's FIA International Touring Car Championship Opel Calibra entry. *Joest Racing*

Kremer Racing endured a weekend that they would sooner forget, losing both of their cars early in the race. Their No. 1 F.A.T.-sponsored Kremer K8, driven by the extremely experienced team of Christophe Bouchut/Jürgen Lässig/Harri Toivonen, went out after just 110 laps with engine problems. *Corporate Archives Porsche AG*

The No. 77 Seikel Porsche GT2 is put through its paces during the test session on Sunday, April 28, 1996. During the test, owner Peter Seikel drove the car with Manfred Jurasz and Takaji Suzuki, but for the race itself Seikel vacated his seat to make way for Frenchman Guy Kuster. Sharp eyes will confirm the name of Peter Seikel on the roof of the car, which is without any Le Mans stickers at this point. In the race, the car finished fifth in the LM GT2 class and eighteenth overall. *Corporate Archives Porsche AG*

At around 10:00 a.m. on Sunday, Stéphane Ortelli brought the No. 83 New Hardware Racing/Parr Motorsport 911 GT2 into the pits looking decidedly unhealthy. Up to this point, the car had been running in third place in the GT2 class, and Ortelli had been pushing hard to narrow the gap with the No. 71 sister car in front when he blew the left turbo. Team manager Paul Robe said, "We mended it in about twenty minutes and he went out again." No. 83 was also driven by Andy Pilgrim/Andrew Bagnall, and would eventually finish seventeenth overall, slipping to fourth in the LM GT2 class because of the turbo repair. *Corporate Archives Porsche AG*

It's time to look alert as the No. 8 TWR Porsche WSC95 LMP1 car comes in for refueling during the night. Driven by Didier Theys/Michele Alboreto/Pierluigi Martini, this car wouldn't finish the race because of electrical problems, which caused it to retire in the nineteenth hour. *Joest Racing*

The No. 79 Roock Racing Porsche 911 GT2 put in an extremely good performance. Piloted by Guy Martinolle/Ralf Kelleners/Bruno Eichmann, the red 911 finished twelfth overall and first in the LM GT2 class, completing 317 laps. Kelleners would win the German Carrera Cup series in 1996. *PCGB*

Despite all three drivers adding their own chapter to the list of damages that the No. 26 factory Porsche GT1 sustained in the 1996 race, the ending was a happy one. The vastly experienced team of Karl Wendlinger/ Yannick Dalmas/Scott Goodyear brought the 911 GT1 home in third place overall and second in the LM GT1 class. Yannick Dalmas took a trip through the gravel and caught a stone in his brake caliper, which required a replacement, while Wendlinger spun the car at the Dunlop Chicane, clipping the wall and requiring a new nose and underbody. It was left to Goodyear to exact his own damage on the car, which drew the last underbody panel from the factory stock. Apart from this self-inflicted damage, the car ran a mechanically faultless race. *Corporate Archives Porsche AG*

By regulation, the open-topped sports car carried twenty liters less fuel than the Porsche 911 GT1s, which in itself counted against them over the course of twenty-four hours. But with a slight speed advantage over the coupe-bodied Porsches— and fitted with the slightly smaller 3.0-liter engine—it was this car, in the hands of Alexander Wurz/ Manuel Reuter/Davy Jones, that prevailed, completing 354 laps and winning the race by a single lap from the second-place works No. 25 Porsche GT1. *Corporate Archives Porsche AG*

PORSCHE GT1

A mere nine months lay between the decision to produce a near-standard yet competitive LM GT1 class racer and the time set for the car's first race. A direct descendent of the 935/78 Moby Dick, the 911 GT1 was more than a class winner: it almost beat the winning LMP1 car in 1996.

Powered by a 600 horsepower 3,164cc twin-turbocharged flat six engine, the GT1 was made to be recognizable as a member of the 911 family through the use of the 911's steel monocoque. This worked wonders for the company's marketing, as the front section and profile resembled that of the GT2, and therefore took after their other 911 road-going cars as well. In keeping with the rules for homologation, Porsche had to make a road-going car first, and

in March 1996 the first body panels were delivered. This was followed later the same month by the car's first test at Estoril in the hands of Bob Wollek and Yannick Dalmas.

In a break with tradition, the 911 GT1 was the first of the 911 family to be water cooled. For cost reasons, it had to carry several steel body components over from the 911, incorporating a reinforced roll cage in the center section.

What made it resemble its smaller sibling ended there, though, as the engine unit was not in the rear position, but instead located centrally, with the engine just ahead of the rear axle and the gearbox just behind, significantly improving overall weight distribution. This, and the fact that no cooling fan was required, also allowed for a more tapered rear body. A roof-mounted air scoop fed air to the intercoolers, which were located behind the gearbox.

Merely turning the gearbox around to sit behind the engine would have resulted in six reverse gears and one forward gear, so the gearbox had to be completely remade, and it was strengthened in the process. Much of the internal controls were derived from the 911 to save costs.

The result was a devastating racer, weighing just 2,315 pounds (1,050 kilograms) and capable of a top speed of 199 miles per hour (320 kilometers per hour). Although the 911 GT1 was some 30 inches (750 millimeters) longer than its road-going 911 siblings, it was still recognizable as a 911 derivative.

The No. 25 works Porsche 911 GT1 of Thierry Boutsen/ Bob Wollek/Hans-Joachim Stuck speeds into the dusk during the 1996 race. *Corporate Archives Porsche AG*

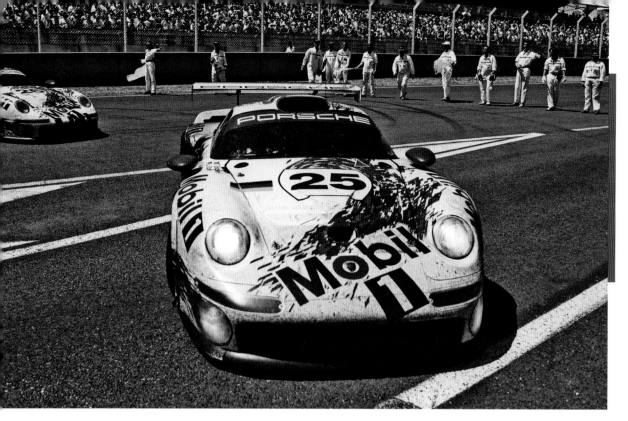

Both factory GT1 cars were fitted with the larger 3,200cc engine. With the marshals forming an arc, the No. 25 car (second place) and its sibling the No. 26 car (third place) turn into the *parc fermé* following their lap of honor after twenty-four hours of battle and an eventful 2,991 miles covered. Because of several delays encountered by the No. 26 car, the two were separated by twelve laps. *PCGB*

1996 Race Results

Pos.	Car/Model	No.	Driver(s)	Entered	Class	Cl. Pos	Laps	Reason
1	TWR Porsche WSC 95	7	Davy Jones (US)/Alexander Wurz (AT)/Manuel Reuter (DE)	Joest Racing	LM P1	1	354	
2	911 GT1 (002)	25	Hans-Joachim Stuck (DE)/Thierry Boutsen (BE)/Bob Wollek (FR)	Porsche AG	LM GT1	1	353	
3	911 GT1 (003)	26	Karl Wendlinger (AT)/Yannick Dalmas (FR)/Scott Goodyear (CA)	Porsche AG	LM GT1	2	341	
NRF	TWR Porsche WSC 95	8	Didier Theys (BE)/Michele Alboreto (IT)/Pierluigi Martini (IT)	Joest Racing	LM P1		317	Electrics
12	911 GT2	79	Guy Martinolle (FR)/Ralf Kelleners (DE)/Bruno Eichmann (CH)	Roock Racing Team	LM GT2	1	317	
14	911 GT2	71	Bill Farmer (NZ)/Greg Murphy (NZ)/Robert Nearn (GB)	New Hardware Racing/Parr Motorsport	LM GT2	2	313	
17	911 GT2	83	Stéphane Ortelli (FR)/Andy Pilgrim (US)/Andrew Bagnall (NZ)	New Hardware Racing/Parr Motorsport	LM GT2	4	299	
18	911 GT2	77	Guy Kuster (FR)/Manfred Jurasz (AT)/Takaji Suzuki (JP)	Seikel Motorsport	LM GT2	5	297	
20	911 GT2	82	Patrice Goueslard (FR)/André Ahrlé (DE)/Patrick Bourdais (FR)	Larbre Compétition	LM GT2	6	284	
22	911 GT2 Evo	27	Jean-Luc Chéreau (FR)/Pierre Yver (FR)/Jack Leconte (FR)	Société Chéreau Sports	LM GT1	13	279	
DNF	Kremer K8 (Thompson)	1	Christophe Bouchut (FR)/Jürgen Lässig (DE)/Harri Toivonen (FI)	Kremer Racing	LM P1		110	Engine
DNF	911 GT2 Evo	37	Franz Konrad (AT)/Antonio Hermann (BR)/Wido Rössler (DE)	Konrad Motorsport	LM GT1		107	Accident
DNF	911 GT2 Evo	55	Jean-Pierre Jarier (FR)/Jésus Pareja-Mayo (ES)/Dominic Chappell (GB)	Roock Racing Team	LM GT1		93	Engine
DNF	Kremer K8 (Thompson)	2	Steve Fossett (US)/George Fouché (ZA)/Stanley Dickens (SE)	Kremer Racing	LM P1		58	Accident
DNF	911 GT2	73	Michel Neugarten (BE)/Toni Seiler (CH)/Bruno Ilien (FR)	Elf Haberthur Racing	LM GT2		46	Gearbox
DNF	911 GT2	70	Steve O'Rourke (GB)/Guy Holmes (GB)/Soames Langton (GB)	Steve O'Rourke	LM GT2		32	Engine

June 14–15

It was a case of the old beating the new, as Joest Racing's TWR Porsche WSC95 stepped up to the plate for the sixty-fifth Le Mans with a driver combination that included both experience and youthful flair. Although the two factory GT1s were the fastest and looked to be the most reliable on the day, team boss Norbert Singer was handed a double headache that robbed Porsche of victory.

For Joest Racing, it was a case of "if it ain't broke, don't fix it," as the 1996 car was wheeled out to do battle once more against the might of the much-improved factory GT1s. After the race, even the engineers at Joest Racing admitted that their car did not have the legs to match the works GT1s and that the factory cars should have won—but for a split oil pipe, they would have.

In an effort to bring some equality to the grid between the Prototypes and the GT cars—and while trying to retain similar performance levels from the two classes—the ACO reduced the fuel tank capacity of the faster, open prototypes to just 17½ gallons (80 liters). This meant that, while the Prototypes were quicker, they would have to make more frequent stops to refuel, thereby leveling the playing field with the GT-class cars that were only marginally slower. In theory this worked, but the pace of development progress in the GT world meant that the Porsches and McLarens were surprisingly fast, and the privateer teams were quick to snap up the Porsche GT1s that were available to select customers.

The fans were in for a real treat, as no fewer than eight Porsche GT1s took to the grid for the 1997 race. In the end, only two were classified as finishers. Race-goers were still treated to a spectacular display of close racing as the two factory GT1 Evos showed the rest of the field a clean pair of heels during their time on the track. The Joest car was just one lap behind the second remaining factory car when it went up in smoke.

The Porsche team delivers its No. 25 works 911 GT1 Evo to the scrutineering station for the 1997 race. The latest model now featured the 996's front lights in an effort to cement its heritage with the road-going car. In addition, the new GT1 boasted improved aerodynamics, a new front axle with a wider track and optimized suspension, and revised engine management, making it an all-round better race car. *Corporate Archives Porsche AG*

The No. 25 works GT1 Evo is put through its paces in practice by the hugely experienced team, comprising Frenchman Bob Wollek, longstanding factory driver Hans-Joachim Stuck, and the talented Belgian ex-Formula 1 driver Thierry Boutsen. *Corporate Archives Porsche AG*

Joest Racing's team manager Ralf Jüttner (*left*), in the dark top and leaning on the car) discusses the start with Michele Alboreto ahead of the 1997 race. The No. 7 TWR Porsche WSC95 was driven by Michele Alboreto/Stefan Johansson/Tom Kristensen. *Joest Racing*

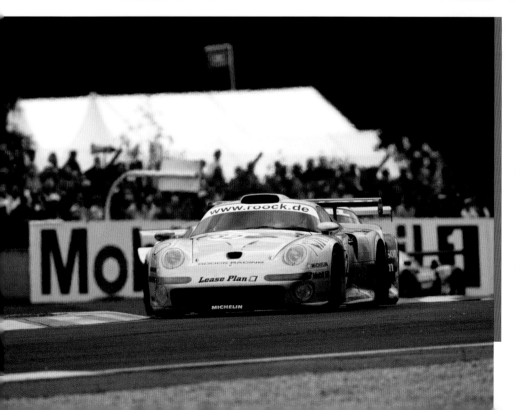

With a Porsche contract in hand at the beginning of 1997, McNish was loaned out to Fabian Roock to gain some "Porsche" experience. The Le Mans program was already fixed, so there was no space for him in the works team. Driving the No. 32 Roock Racing Porsche GT1, Allan McNish, Stéphane Ortelli, and Karl Wendlinger formed a formidable team, but the race was to end disastrously for them after just eight laps, as McNish put the GT1 into the wall in the Porsche Curves. McNish recalls what happened: "Coming into the left-hander, it sort of stepped and walked, and then just walked into the wall, because it is quick and also there was no run-off area. There was just a little bit of grass and then wall. But you know, once you are in any off-form shape through there, that's it. They looked at the data and they thought it could be damper failure, but there was quite heavy damage and it was difficult for them to trace it back, but there was something odd in the right rear." *Corporate Archives Porsche AG*

Despite the best efforts of the Hawaiian Tropic girls, the 2,995cc Kremer K8 Spyder (Thompson) was out after only 103 laps with a blown engine. *Corporate Archives Porsche AG*

A failed damper delayed the No. 30 Kremer GT1 for about half an hour, but it was an overheating engine after 207 laps that finally ended the race for Christophe Bouchut/ Bertrand Gachot/Andy Evans. Kremer Racing was serious about their racing, employing top international drivers to pilot their Cologne car, which was the leading privateer GT1 at the time of their untimely retirement. *Corporate Archives Porsche AG*

Ralf Kelleners had an oil line split about two hours from the end (327 laps) while at full speed down the Mulsanne Straight, bringing their race to an abrupt end. Kelleners shared the No. 26 factory Porsche 911 GT1 with the extremely experienced French duo, Emmanuel Collard and Yannick Dalmas. *Corporate Archives Porsche AG*

Roock Racing's No. 74 Porsche GT2, driven by Bruno Eichmann/Andy Pilgrim/André Ahrlé, finished tenth overall, and second in the GT2 class despite a catalogue of mechanical woes that included two blown turbochargers. *Corporate Archives Porsche AG*

Reliability was the key to the GT2 class win for the No. 78 Elf Haberthur Racing Porsche GT2. Finishing inside the top ten in a GT2 car is no easy task, particularly when that car loses a wheel near the entrance to the pits. After much heaving and shoving, the driver Jean-Claude Lagniez got the car over the line that marked the entrance to the pit lane, at which point the team was able to assist in getting the car to their pit garage. With a new wheel fitted, the Michel Neugarten/Jean-Claude Lagniez/Guy Martinolle–driven car ran faultlessly to the end, claiming ninth place. *Corporate Archives Porsche AG*

Michele Alboreto/Stefan Johansson/Tom Kristensen drove a trouble-free race to bring the No. 7 Joest Racing TWR Porsche WSC95 home in first place after having covered 361 laps. Alboreto had set the fastest qualifying lap putting the car on pole, while the young and talented Tom Kristensen claimed the fastest race lap. *Corporate Archives Porsche AG*

The first Porsche GT1 across the finish line in 1997 was the private entry of Schübel Engineering. The No. 33 car, driven by Armin Hahne/Pedro Lamy/Patrice Goueslard, required a brake pad change after four hours, and an hour later Hahne spun the car and had to bring it back into the pits again for front disc replacement and another pad change. After a further stop of fifty-one minutes for engine cooling problems just after midday Sunday, the car continued to the end of the race without any more issues. Despite the stops, the total time spent in the pits was less than two hours; the car finished fifth and took third place in the GT1 class. *Corporate Archives Porsche AG*

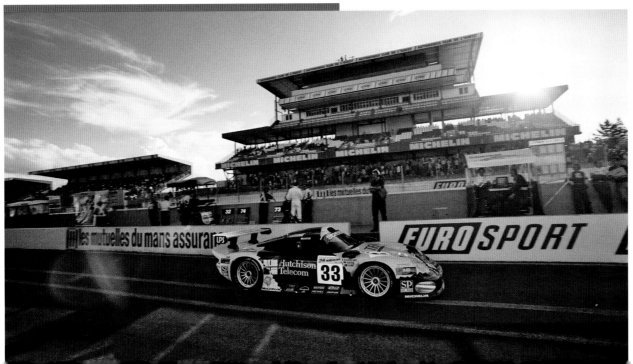

THE EVERGREEN TWR PORSCHE WSC95 (001)

The Joest Porsche WSC95 was one of only three cars in the history of Le Mans to win the race back to back. Incredibly, one other of the three was also a Joest car, namely the Porsche 956/117 that won in both 1984 and 1985.

The story of the WSC95 begins back in 1990–1991, when TWR's then-engineering director Ross Brawn designed a chassis for the XJR-14 Silk Cut Jaguar with which Tom Walkinshaw's Oxfordshire-based Jaguar sports car team won the 1991 FIA World Sportscar Championship. Davy Jones drove the TWR in the 1992 IMSA GTP Championship as a Jaguar, winning at Michelin Raceway Road Atlanta and Mid-Ohio Sports Car Course, after which the two cars languished in a workshop in Indiana until Porsche showed an interest in them.

Needing a car to contest the classic endurance events in 1995 (Daytona, Sebring, and Le Mans), Porsche approached TWR to see if the chassis could be converted to house a flat six turbo. Two distinguishing features that set the XJR-14 apart, however, were the center gear-change position and the torsion bar front suspension, while the deep venturi in the floor had to be blanked off, as the regulations demanded flat bottoms. The coupe roof was removed in the car's conversion to a Spyder design, and intercooler ducts were incorporated, after which the two cars were made ready for trials at Daytona in December 1994.

From the start, IMSA didn't like them, and their way of showing disapproval was to slow the cars down still further by reducing the size of the inlet air restrictors; this reduced power by as much as 80 horsepower and increased weight by 100 pounds (45 kilograms). These measures rendered the WSC cars totally uncompetitive, and Porsche's entries for Daytona and Sebring were canceled immediately.

In 1995, Reinhold Joest approached Porsche's management with the proposal that he run the two cars at Le Mans in 1996. The plan was approved and, after several tests and numerous modifications incorporating completely new bodywork that improved the cars significantly, in early 1996 the two Joest Racing TWRs passed the mandatory qualifying procedure. The two cars performed beyond all expectations, with Pierluigi Martini qualifying the No. 8 car in pole position and the No. 7, driven by Alexander Wurz, Davy Jones, and Manuel Reuter, winning the race outright.

With the Porsche factory fully focused on the 911 GT1 program, this left Joest Racing free to campaign the two TWR WSC95s again in 1997. Sponsored this time by Hagenuk Telecom GmbH and their regular sponsor, the transport company F.A.T., Joest Racing ran the same car (chassis 001), but this time with some changes and improvements, mainly to aerodynamics, suspension, and the area around the engine.

The young Danish driver, Tom Kristensen, joined as the third driver partnering Michele Alboreto and Stefan Johansson. After a close battle with the factory GT1s, the No. 7 TWR WSC95 took the flag by a clear lap. This memorable achievement must set Joest Racing apart as the most successful private team in the history of Le Mans, with no fewer than four outright victories to its credit, and all with Porsches bearing the number 7!

Michele Alboreto behind the wheel of the No. 7 TWR Porsche WSC95.
Joest Racing

The vast experience of Michele Alboreto and Stefan Johansson combined with the youthful talent of rising star Tom Kristensen was enough to ensure victory for the No. 7 Joest Racing TWR Porsche WSC95. Here, Michele Alboreto raises both hands as he crosses the finish line at the end of the race. Tom Kristensen went on to enjoy the most wins at Le Mans, a staggering nine victories by the time of his retirement in 2014, surpassing the record previously held for so many years by Jacky Ickx. *Joest Racing*

1997 Race Results

Pos.	Car/Model	No.	Driver(s)	Entered	Class	Cl. Pos	Laps	Reason
FL	TWR-Porsche WSC 95	7	Tom Kristensen (DK)	Joest Racing	Time: 3:45.068 minutes		Speed: 217.614km/h; 135.219mph	
1	TWR-Porsche WSC 95	7	Michele Alboreto (IT)/Stefan Johansson (SE)/Tom Kristensen (DK)	Joest Racing	LMP	1	361	
5	911 GT1 (102)	33	Armin Hahne (DE)/Pedro Lamy (PT)/Patrice Goueslard (FR)	Schübel Engineering	GT1	3	331	
DNF	911 GT1 (005)	26	Emmanuel Collard (FR)/Yannick Dalmas (FR)/Ralf Kelleners (DE)	Porsche AG	GT1		327	Fire
8	911 GT1 (106)	27	Pierluigi Martini (IT)/Christian Percatori (IT)/Antonio Hermann (BR)	BMS Scuderia Italia	GT1	4	317	
9	911 GT2	78	Michel Neugarten (BE)/Jean-Claude Lagniez (FR)/Guy Martinolle (FR)	Elf Haberthur Racing	GT2	1	307	
10	911 GT2	74	Bruno Eichmann (CH)/Andy Pilgrim (US)/André Ahrlé (DE)	Roock Racing	GT2	2	306	
11	911 GT2	73	Manuel Mello-Breyner (PT)/Pedro Mello-Breyner (PT)/Tomas Mello-Breyner (PT)	Roock Racing	GT2	3	295	
13	911 GT2	80	Claudia Hürtgen (DE)/Hugh Price (GB)/John Robinson (GB)	GT Racing Team AG	GT2	4	287	
DNF	911 GT1 (004)	25	Bob Wollek (FR)/Hans-Joachim Stuck (DE)/Thierry Boutsen (BE)	Porsche AG	GT1		238	Gearbox
DNF	911 GT1 (101)	29	Alain Ferté (FR)/Olivier Thévenin (FR)/Jürgen von Gartzen (DE)	JB Racing	GT1		236	Engine
DNF	911 GT1 (104)	30	Christophe Bouchut (FR)/Bertrand Gachot (BE)/Andy Evans (US)	Kremer Racing	GT1		207	Overheating
DNF	911 GT2	75	Patrick Bourdais (FR)/André Lara Resende (BR)/Peter Kitchak (US)	Larbre Compétition	GT2		205	Gearbox
DNF	911 GT1 (109)	28	Mauro Baldi (IT)/Robert Nearn (GB)/Franz Konrad (AT)	Franz Konrad Motorsport	GT1		138	Accident
DNF	911 GT2	79	Michel Ligonnet (FR)/Toni Seiler (CH)/Larry Schumacher (US)	Franz Konrad Motorsport	GT2		126	Engine
DNF	Kremer K8 (Thompson)	5	Tomas Saldaña (ES)/Carl Rosenblad (SE)/Jürgen Lässig (DE)	Kremer Racing	LMP		103	Engine
DNF	911 GT2	84	Enzo Calderari (CH)/Lilian Bryner (CH)/Angelo Zadra (IT)	Stadler Motorsport	GT2		98	Oil leak
DNF	911 GT2	77	Jean-Pierre Jarier (FR)/Jean-Luc Chéreau (FR)/Jack Leconte (FR)	Chéreau Sports	GT2		77	Gearbox
DNF	911 GT1 (108)	32	Allan McNish (GB)/Stéphane Ortelli (FR)/Karl Wendlinger (AT)	Roock Racing	GT1		8	Accident

1998

June 6–7

Now significantly lower and far more streamlined, the Porsche 911 GT1-98 was a much-revised model of the original GT1. It had become apparent, from the results of the two preceding years, that the GT1 was not delivering the performance needed to win Le Mans, which had long been Porsche's measure of success. The engineers realized that the GT1 would have to be constructed as a full GT prototype with no production links, in reality making it a thoroughbred race car.

No longer could the GT1 be built around the steel monocoque of the 911, as Michael Hölscher, general project manager for the Carrera GT, told the author in 2005: "I can say that the 1998 GT1 was a full carbon-fiber car." Replacing the steel monocoque with one fabricated from carbon-fiber not only reduced the GT1's weight by around 220½ pounds (100 kilograms), but it also increased the car's rigidity.

Despite the fact that Porsche still homologated the GT1-98 by producing a road-legal model, the road-going version was instead engineered from the race spec model, which drove the project. The GT1-98 was a racing prototype first and foremost, but it retained its 3.2-liter twin-turbo engine and the 911 looks, a stipulation from Stuttgart's management. But the famous flat six unit had reached its maximum operating capacity and, as the GT class was in any event on its way out thanks to the behavior—or, rather misbehavior—of another Stuttgart manufacturer in this class, Porsche was thinking ahead and already planning its next power unit.

For the 1998 event, however, Porsche team boss Norbert Singer opted to run with a reliable combination of proven technology, mating the bulletproof 3.2-liter engine with a synchromesh box, while many in the pit lane chose the new sequential boxes for their ease of operation and replacement time in case of repairs. The old-style gearbox was both slower in gear change operation and in replacement time, should a repair be necessary, but it was a known entity, so Singer stuck with it.

A break from tradition, in fact a fifty-year tradition, saw the installation of Porsche's new water-cooled engine that powered the 911. Porsche had long known that a four-valve head was required to produce more power, but this had not been possible with the air-cooled engine. Developed toward the end of 1997, the new water-cooled engine was to power the revolutionary 996 version of Porsche's evergreen 911 from 1998 onwards, in the process taking the company's motorsports program to a new level.

The pressure was well and truly on for a Porsche victory, as 1998 marked the fiftieth anniversary since the manufacture of the company's first 356 sports car back in Gmünd, Austria. Company boss Dr. Wendelin Wiedeking made it quite clear that nothing less than a victory would be acceptable, so Porsche hedged its bets by backing the two Joest Racing TWR WSC open cars to bolster its chances, renaming them LMP1-98. These cars were entered under the Porsche factory name but were managed by Joest Racing.

The GT2 class was populated by no fewer than a dozen 911s, so with all bases supposedly covered, the stage was set for an onslaught by the Stuttgart-Zuffenhausen team.

Entered by Porsche AG but managed by Joest Racing, the No. 7 Porsche LMP1-98, driven by Michele Alboreto/Stefan Johansson/Yannick Dalmas, qualified ninth on the grid. Here Alboreto speeds down the pit straight, but despite reaching the top six by the seventh hour, the No. 7 car failed to finish, retiring on lap 107 with electrical problems. *Corporate Archives Porsche AG*

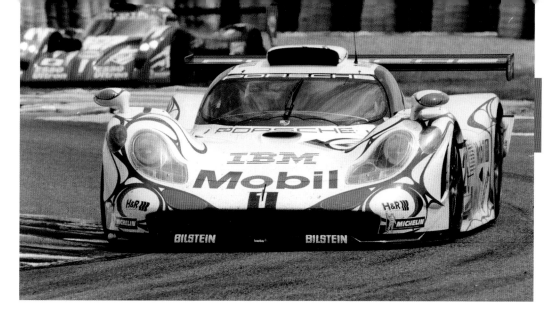

Allan McNish/Stéphane Ortelli/
Laurent Aiello took the works
Porsche 911 GT1 to victory in the
1998 race. *Corporate Archives
Porsche AG*

The No. 25 factory GT1-98 reports
for scrutineering. This car was
piloted by German drivers Jörg
Müller and Uwe Alzen, with
Frenchman Bob Wollek. Someone
surveying race-goers on the day
would probably have found that
most agreed Wollek, more than
any other driver, deserved to win
the classic French race after so
many attempts—and near misses.
Corporate Archives Porsche AG

The calm before the storm. The No. 65 Roock Racing Porsche GT2, driven by André Ahrlé/Dave Warnock/Robert Schirle, awaits the start of the twenty-four-hour contest. *Corporate Archives Porsche AG*

ALLAN MCNISH RECALLS HIS 1998 VICTORY

Allan McNish only had two years of racing a Porsche at Le Mans, and although he is a household name in sports car racing today behind the wheel of an Audi, his brief time with Porsche left a lasting impression.

McNish admitted in an interview with the author, "I liked it [the GT1-98] more than the '96 version and the '97 version, it was more of a racing car, I could throw it around, it had better downforce, less shudder, it was just more aggressive, and for me it was a good step forward. At Le Mans, with the variety of conditions that you get there, it was in its natural environment.

"Certainly as a company, the names Le Mans and Porsche went hand in hand. Their motorsports department was set up very much around endurance racing. When we would arrive at Le Mans it was like arriving at just another part of the house. Although it was in France, for them it might as well have just been at the other side of Weissach. They were very much at home, and all the guys just seemed to sit down in the same place just as they had done the previous fifteen years, and they knew exactly what was going to happen."

In 1997 McNish was signed by Porsche, who farmed him out to the Fabian Roock racing team to gain some experience. Arriving at Le Mans that year, McNish approached Singer, complaining that the Roock car had excessive oversteer in the corners. Singer quickly narrowed the problem down to the differential setting, as McNish explains.

"It was obvious to him that that was not the way to run at Le Mans, and it suddenly became a completely different car. But if you've got a new engineer and a new team trying to learn these things, then they basically start from behind. And that was something that I found with Porsche. That depth of experience, that knowledge of what was required, made it a lot easier for us drivers because we didn't have to think about it. We just drove, because they were the ones who were 95 percent in control of the car before we even got to the track, and the last 5 percent was tuning."

Roock had some good technical people in the team, as McNish added later, but the 1997 race did not end happily for the Scotsman when he hit the wall in the Porsche Curves. McNish picks up the story: "Obviously it was a bit of a shock, and it was a lesson in terms of getting the car back to the pits, that's for sure. They looked at the data; they thought it could be damper failure, but there was quite heavy damage to the car, so it was difficult for them to piece it back together."

The following year was a completely different situation for McNish.

"There was a massive difference in terms of experience, in terms of capability, in terms of everything—technology, the lot. You couldn't compare the two. One had the capability to have good results in some races some of the time, but the Porsche factory team had the capability to have good results all of the time. We had all the appropriate physios, we had the dietitians, and we had the areas to rest. And that was not an optional extra, that was a standard. It wasn't something where they thought, "Oh, let's try this," they already knew about it as they had been doing it for a long time. And that's where factory teams and private teams start to separate.

"But, for me, Stéphane Ortelli was very good because he taught me a lot, he taught me about where to go and where not to go at Le Mans. He was very good, and so I would say that Stéphane was quite important to that success in '98."

On the podium, the formalities were interrupted with some fun and games, as McNish recalls, "Standing on the podium in '98 at Le Mans, we had been given these wee Instamatic cameras, and Stéphane and Laurent and I were taking these pictures of each other. It was like three beach bums that had just struck gold, if you like, and that was one of the funniest, most surreal experiences."

But the importance of the occasion was not lost on the drivers, as this victory coincided with the fiftieth anniversary of the Porsche car company's birth, and McNish admitted that there had been a tremendous amount of prerace pressure because of that.

"The board was there, everybody expected a victory, and anyway it would have been a pretty bad celebration if we had finished third, wouldn't it? Herbert Ampferer, who was the boss who put his trust, against a lot of people's opinions, in three young guys who had nothing in terms of a record for Le Mans, and by going against the board to say these are the ones we want to put in the car, his neck was probably on the line. But he felt that was the right way to go. There was also pressure

because we had been beaten in all the races up until then by Mercedes. And so there was that expectation, too, that we had built a new car but we hadn't succeeded yet, but we did succeed in the big one."

The actual anniversary was on the Monday, the day after Le Mans, and McNish noted with a smile, "We basically celebrated on the Sunday night into the Monday morning."

Sadly, Ferry Porsche, the driving force behind the Porsche company for so many years, had passed away on March 27, 1998, at the age of eighty-eight, just seventy-four days before the company's anniversary. As the postrace celebrations went into full swing, many stopped to reflect on their own memories of that great man and what he meant to the company.

The winning factory Porsche calls in for a quick splash-'n'-dash before resuming its bid for victory. Allan McNish is at the wheel. *Corporate Archives Porsche AG*

In the opening stages, the ex-Formula 1 driver Jean-Pierre Jarier led the GT2 field in the No. 60 Chéreau Sports (Larbre) Porsche GT2. The Porsche, driven by Jean-Pierre Jarier/Carl Rosenblad/Robin Donovan, was sidelined on lap 164 with transmission trouble. *Corporate Archives Porsche AG*

Lasting a bit longer than its sister car, the No. 8 Porsche LMP1-98, piloted by Pierre-Henri Raphanel/James Weaver/David Murry, lay in fifth place at midnight. After sixteen hours and while on lap 218, the rear wing was damaged in a spin at the first of the Mulsanne chicanes (known as the Toyota Chicane in 1998) in the rain with Murry at the wheel. Repairs were carried out in the pits, but several bodywork mounting points had been damaged and the car retired soon after returning to the action. *Corporate Archives Porsche AG*

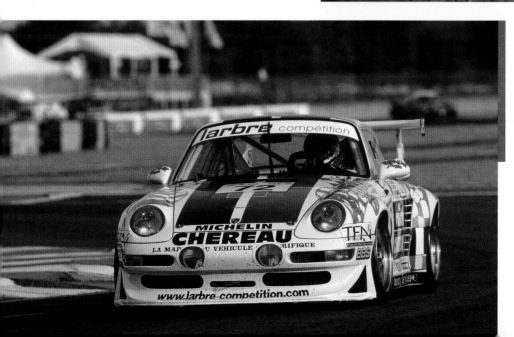

The No. 72 Larbre Compétition Porsche GT2 of French trio Patrice Goueslard/Jean-Luc Chéreau/Pierre Yver was unclassified at the end of the race, having not completed the required number of laps (only 240). The team was nevertheless classified ninth in the GT2 class. *John Brooks*

The No. 64 Roock Racing 911 GT2 of Claudia Hürtgen/ Michel Ligonnet/Robert Nearn required a new gearbox at 11:00 a.m. on Sunday, losing them two hours and dropping them down to seventeenth overall and third in the GT2 class. *John Brooks*

Positioned in fifth place on the grid and just behind its No. 25 sister car, the No. 26 factory GT1-98 delivered victory against some really strong opposition in 1998. The victory meant everything to the team and management at Porsche on the eve of the company's fiftieth anniversary. The No. 26 factory car, driven by Laurent Aiello/Allan McNish/Stéphane Ortelli, did not have a trouble-free run, however, as McNish brought the car into the pits around dawn with an overheating engine; the split water pipe was found to be the cause, and it took more than half an hour to repair, allowing the Toyota to take the lead at 7:00 a.m. The No. 26 car returned to do battle, and with just an hour and a half to go (2:00 p.m. finish) the Toyota suffered terminal gearbox failure, allowing the Porsche to retake the lead, which it held to the flag. At the finish, the No. 26

and No. 25 factory Porsches lined up to take the flag in formation, separated by a single lap, in what was one of the company's most memorable victories. McNish had this to say about the GT1-98: "You know at the end of the day, it was built by people who had been brought up with, and breathed, racing, who didn't sit in little offices never seeing the sunlight, and I think that is a big point. Weissach is quite a tight little community, but they put 'Made in Flacht' on the back of the car, because it's not really made in Weissach." To explain the distinction: Weissach and Flacht are two small towns that back on to each other, but the Weissach plant straddles both towns. Although the plant is all under one roof, the race car development section lies in Flacht. Local pride runs high in the area, so the GT1-98 is regarded as their "baby." *Corporate Archives Porsche AG*

Powered once again by the Porsche 2,995cc flat six engine, the No. 16 Kremer K8, driven by Almo Coppelli/Riccardo "Rocky" Agusta/Xavier-Alan Pompidou, finished twelfth overall and second in the LMP1 class. Uwe Sauer, general manager at Kremer Racing, explained: "Problems with the gearbox were traced to an internal filter that was blocked, causing the oil pump in the gearbox to fail. This slowed the car due to the temperature in the gearbox being far too high, but the car crossed the finish line under its own steam, albeit slowly." *Corporate Archives Porsche AG*

1998 Race Results

Pos.	Car/Model	No.	Driver(s)	Entered	Class	Cl. Pos	Laps	Reason
1	911 GT1 (003)	26	Allan McNish (GB)/Laurent Aiello (FR)/Stephane Ortelli (FR)	Porsche AG	GT1	1	352	
2	911 GT1 (002)	25	Jörg Müller (DE)/Uwe Alzen (DE)/Bob Wollek (FR)	Porsche AG	GT1	2	351	
12	Kremer K8/2 (Thompson)	16	Riccardo 'Rocky' Agusta (IT)/Almo Coppelli (IT)/Xavier Pompidou (FR)	Kremer Racing	LM P1	2	315	
17	911 GT2	64	Claudia Hürtgen (DE)/Michel Ligonnet (FR)/Robert Nearn (GB)	Roock Racing	GT2	3	286	
DNF	911 GT2	71	Manuel Monteiro (PT)/Michel Monteiro (PT)/Michel Maisonneuve (FR)	Estoril Racing Communications	GT2		277	Engine failure
18	993 GT2 Evo	69	Michel Nourry (FR)/Thierry Perrier (FR)/Jean-Louis Ricci (FR)	Michel Nourry	GT2	4	277	
20	911 GT2	68	Eric Graham (FR)/Hervé Poulain (FR)/Jean-Luc Maury-Laribiére (FR)	Elf Haberthur Racing	GT2	6	269	
22	911 GT2	65	André Ahrlé (DE)/Dave Warnock (GB)/Robert Schirle (GB)	Roock Racing	GT2	8	248	
23	911 GT2	72	Patrice Goueslard (FR)/Jean-Luc Chéreau (FR)/Pierre Yver (FR)	Larbre Compétition	GT2	9	241	
DNF	LMP1-98	8	James Weaver (GB)/Pierre-Henri Raphanel (FR)/David Murry (US)	Porsche AG	LM P1		218	Bodywork/chassis
DNF	911 GT2	67	Michel Neugarten (BE)/David Smadja (FR)/Jean-Claude Lagniez (FR)	Elf Haberthur Racing	GT2		198	Accident
DNF	911 GT2	60	Jean-Pierre Jarier (FR)/Carl Rosenblad (SE)/Robin Donovan (GB)	Chéreau Sports (Larbre)	GT2		164	Accident
DNF	911 GT2	62	John Morton (US)/Harald Grohs (DE)/John Graham (CA)	CJ Motorsports	GT2		164	Accident
DNF	LMP1-98	7	Michele Alboreto (IT)/Stefan Johansson (SE)/Yannick Dalmas (FR)	Porsche AG	LM P1		107	Electrics
DNF	911 GT2	61	Bernhard Müller (DE)/Michael Trunk (DE)/Ernst Palmberger (DE)	Krauss Race Sports Intl.	GT2		71	Engine failure
DNF	911 GT2	70	Franz Konrad (AT)/Larry Schumacher (US)/Nick Ham (US)	Konrad Motorsport	GT2		24	Spin/accident
DNF	911 GT2	73	Toni Seiler (CH)/Peter Kitchak (US)/Angelo Zadra (IT)	Konrad Motorsport	GT2		2	Engine failure

1999

June 12–13

Over a period of almost three decades of competing at Le Mans, Porsche had racked up sixteen wins, putting them well ahead of any other manufacturer. With a record approaching a win rate of 60 percent at the end of the 1998 season, Porsche announced that it would not compete with a factory team at Le Mans in 1999.

What followed for Porsche was a period of preparing and supplying cars to customer teams who would compete privately. Despite the absence of an official factory team, development work at Weissach proceeded apace. For the 1999 Le Mans, two of Porsche's new racing 911 GT3 Rs appeared, one under the name of well-known Manthey Racing, located near the legendary Nürburgring, while the other was entered by Dave Maraj's Florida-based Champion Racing stable.

Porsche 911s were entered in two different classes this year. The Type 993 GT2 Evo, powered by a 600-horsepower twin-turbo version of Porsche's 3.6-liter air-cooled flat six engine (two-valve head), was entered in the LM GTS class. Its sibling,

the Type 996 GT3 R, was fitted with a water-cooled, fuel-injected 3.6-liter flat six engine (four-valve head) developing 415 horsepower and was entered in the LM GT class.

Behind the scenes, and in fact under a cloud of great secrecy, Porsche had begun developing an altogether new prototype racer. Known as the LMP 2000, this racer was planned to run at Le Mans powered by a new 5.5-liter V-10 engine, but ultimately this project was canceled by the board and the engine eventually found its way into the Carrera GT road car.

On the afternoon of June 12, a group of eleven Porsche 911s lined up on the grid for the start of the race, only five of which would be classified as finishers twenty-four hours later.

The No. 66 Estoril Racing Communications Porsche 911 GT2 (LM GTS class), driven by Manuel Monteiro/ Michel Monteiro/Michel Maisonneuve, failed to finish, completing just 123 laps. Maisonneuve collided with the Toyota GT1 of Thierry Boutsen, landing the Belgian in hospital. *Corporate Archives Porsche AG*

The French trio of Thierry Perrier/Jean-Louis Ricci/Michel Nourry brought the No. 84 Perspective Racing 993 Carrera RSR home in twenty-first place overall and third in the GT class. *John Brooks*

Despite spending ninety minutes in the pits having its gearbox changed, the No. 62 Roock Racing 993 GT2 Evo of Claudia Hürtgen/André Ahrlé/Vincent Vosse finished twentieth overall and eighth in the GTS class. *Corporate Archives Porsche AG*

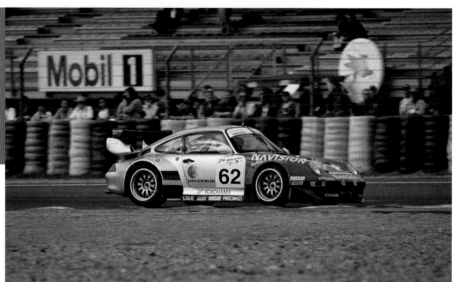

The No. 80 Porsche 996 GT3 R of Dave Maraj's Champion Racing team finished nineteenth in the hands of Dirk Müller/Bob Wollek/Bernd Mayländer. Running in the LM GT class, the GT3 R lost nine laps because of gearbox trouble, completing 293 laps. *Corporate Archives Porsche AG*

Austrian Franz Konrad was partnered by Americans Charles Slater and Peter Kitchak in the No. 64 Konrad Motorsport 911 GT2. The No. 64 GTS class Porsche finished 18th overall and seventh in class. *Corporate Archives Porsche AG*

The No. 81 Manthey Racing Porsche 996 GT3 R, driven by Uwe Alzen/Patrick Huisman/Luca Riccitelli, placed thirteenth overall, making it the top finisher from Stuttgart-Zuffenhausen. The No. 81 car completed 318 trouble-free laps, taking first place in the LM GT class. *Corporate Archives Porsche AG*

1999 Race Results

Pos.	Car/Model	No.	Driver(s)	Entered	Class	Cl. Pos	Laps	Reason
13	996 GT3 R	81	Uwe Alzen (DE)/Patrick Huisman (NL)/Luca Riccitelli (IT)	Manthey Racing	GT	1	318	
18	911 GT2	64	Franz Konrad (AT)/Charles Slater (US)/Peter Kitchak (US)	Konrad Motorsport	GTS	7	294	
19	996 GT3 R	80	Dirk Müller (DE)/Bob Wollek (FR)/Bernd Mayländer (DE)	Champion Racing Dave Maraj	GT	2	293	
20	911 GT2	62	Claudia Hürtgen (DE)/André Ahrlé (DE)/Vincent Vosse (BE)	Roock Racing Intl. Motorsport	GTS	8	291	
21	993 Carrera RSR	84	Thierry Perrier (FR)/Jean-Louis Ricci (FR)/Michel Nourry (FR)	Perspective Racing	GT	3	289	
NC	911 GT2	65	Jean-Luc Chéreau (FR)/Patrice Goueslard (FR)/Pierre Yver (FR)	Chéreau Sports	GTS		240	
DNF	911 GT2	63	Hubert Haupt (DE)/Hugh Price (GB)/John Robinson (GB)	Roock Racing Intl. Motorsport	GTS		232	Engine
DNF	911 GT2	61	Wolfgang Kaufmann (DE)/Michel Ligonnet (FR)/Ernst Palmberger (DE)	Freisinger Motorsport	GTS		157	Engine
DNF	911 GT2	67	Patrick Bourdais (FR)/Pierre de Thoisy (FR)/Jean-Pierre Jarier (FR)	Larbre Compétition	GTS		134	Engine
DNF	911 GT2	66	Manuel Monteiro (PT)/Michel Monteiro (PT)/Michel Maisonneuve (FR)	Estoril Racing Communications	GTS		123	Accident
DNF	911 GT2	60	Ray Lintott (AU)/Manfred Jurasz (AT)/Katsunori Iketani (JP)	Freisinger Motorsport	GTS		24	Accident

CHAPTER 6

200s

In the first six hours of the 2008 race, a fascinating battle was waged between the No. 34 van Merksteijn Porsche and the No. 31 Team Essex Porsche, with the lead swapping constantly and no quarter given by either team. The lead eventually swung the Dutch team's way at around 9:30 p.m. on Saturday when the Danish Porsche pitted for an unscheduled tire change. Although van Merksteijn and Bleekemolen were racing in their third Le Mans, it was the first appearance by ex-Formula 1 driver Jos Verstappen in the French classic. *Corporate Archives Porsche AG*

Regrouping for the New Millennium

As the new millennium approached, the world was faced with fears that resulted from reports that a global computer catastrophe loomed as 1999 rolled into 2000. This impending phenomenon, known as the millennium bug, threatened to render computer systems useless because of the practice of abbreviating a four-digit year as just two digits. No one knew how computers would handle the transition from "99" to "00."

No such concerns were evident in the Audi camp at the end of the first Le Mans of the new millennium, as three Team Joest-prepared Audi R8s rolled across the finish line in a 1–2–3 formation. Such a display of dominance had not been seen since Peugeot's similar demonstration in 1993 with their 905 Evos.

Although Porsche had not sent a factory team to Le Mans since their victory of 1998, there were still fourteen 911s that had been entered privately. These consisted of both GT2 and GT3 R versions. The first decade of the new millennium, in fact, would not see a Porsche factory car take to the grid at Le Mans, despite rumors of a brand-new racer in the wings.

The LMP 2000 project was initially planned for Le Mans, though in the end it was not built. Much of the development work, including the new V-10 engine, was instead channeled into the Carrera GT road car. In 2005 Porsche announced that it would contest the American Le Mans Series (ALMS) with its first purpose-built racer since the GT1 of 1998. In an effort to evoke its 1950s and 1960s, the RS Spyder, as it was named, no doubt utilized some ideas and components from the LMP 2000 development project and was aimed at the LMP2 class.

The RS Spyder was powered by a 3,397cc V-8 engine developing 503 horsepower, weighing in at just 1,709 pounds/775 kilograms (which accorded with ACO regulations for the LMP2 class). It was set to be a winner right out of the box. Although this racer was built by Porsche, the project was in fact inspired by Roger Penske, primarily for use in the ALMS series; nevertheless, Porsche had configured it for entry in the European LMS series, or at Le Mans itself.

The RS Spyder *did* do battle in the 2008 and 2009 Le Mans race, two cars in total being entered by two privateer teams.

Although Porsche made it known to the media and the wider racing public that the RS Spyder had inherited its DNA from the RS race cars of old, the factory still held off entering the fray with its own factory team. It seemed that the company had forgotten how it had grown into the sports car manufacturer that it now was, turning away from the very heritage it had built on a committed factory racing presence.

It's one thing to manufacture race cars for privateers to compete in around the world—and in the process make a lot of money selling such cars—but Porsche had built its reputation on the many victories achieved in its official capacity as a factory team. According to the common wisdom, racing on Sunday brings sales on Monday, and this result is best achieved by a factory entering and running its own teams. When a privateer team driving your car wins that race, the team gets the publicity, not the manufacturer. In the first decade of the new millennium, Audi took advantage of this fact with its victorious run at Le Mans: although the Ingolstadt motorsports program was run by the Joest team, it was Audi's name that enjoyed the limelight when victory was achieved, thanks no doubt to Audi touting its win wherever it could.

On the other side of the coin, Porsche only had privateer teams running their cars in the LMP2 and GT2 classes, and it was exactly from these lower classes that Porsche fought to lift itself in the 1960s and 1970s, a goal accomplished through the mighty efforts of the 917. The result back then was a huge boost in global awareness of the brand—and a handsome increase in international sales. Perhaps the new millennium would prove a good time for Porsche to acknowledge its racing roots, as motorsports has always been the backbone of the company's innovation and development.

2000

June 17–18

All twelve contestants in the GT class of the 2000 Le Mans fielded a Porsche 911 GT3 R (each one a different race team). In the GTS class it was slightly different, though, as the 911 GT2 came up against the fearsome V-10 Chrysler Viper GTS-R and the works Corvette C5R. The top six positions in the GTS class that year were taken by these American muscle cars.

The starting time was set for the customary 4:00 p.m., and the race was run in hot and dry conditions throughout the twenty-four hours. Of the twelve 911 GT3 R GT class entrants, seven were classified as finishers, while the top Porsche finisher in the GTS class came a disappointing seventh in class.

The first Porsche to drop out of the running was the No. 71 911 GT3 R driven by the American trio of Shane Lewis/Cort Wagner/Bob Mazzuoccola. This happened after just twenty-two laps because of an accident. *John Brooks*

The No. 81 Haberthur Racing 911 GT3 R of Michel Ligonnet/ Gabrio Rosa/Fabio Babini was forced to retire after 310 laps following a late duel that resulted in a coming together with the No. 73 Porsche driven by Hideo Fukuyama; the latter car finished sixteenth overall. *John Brooks*

Tomas Saldaña/Jesús Diez de Villaroel/Giovanni Lavaggi were also the victims of an accident in the No. 72 911 GT3 R. The Racing Engineering Porsche went out after seventy-eight laps. *Corporate Archives Porsche AG*

The No. 59 Freisinger Motorsport 911 GT2, driven by Wolfgang Kaufmann/Yukihiro Hane/ Katsunori Iketani, retired after 313 laps with suspension failure. *Corporate Archives Porsche AG*

Located within shouting distance of the Nürburgring circuit in Germany, the Manthey Racing Team had enjoyed a long association with Porsche. The No. 75 911 GT3 R, driven by the American trio of Gunnar Jeannette/Michael Lauer/ Mike Brockman, finished twenty-seventh overall. *Corporate Archives Porsche AG*

Belgians Philippe Verellen/Kurt Dujardyn/Rudi Penders brought their No. 80 Club-Renstal Excelsior–entered 911 GT3 R in to twenty-fourth place overall and fifth in the GT class. *Corporate Archives Porsche AG*

The No. 83 Dick Barbour Porsche 911 GT3 R took GT class honors and finished thirteenth overall, having led the class the whole race, which allowed Wollek to claim a class victory—or so he thought. Once again, though, the luckless Wollek walked away empty handed, as the car was later disqualified for having an oversized fuel tank. The disappointment for drivers Dirk Müller/Bob Wollek/Lucas Lühr must have been crushing. After three decades of sports car racing, and with four 24 Hours of Daytona victories to his name, 2000 would be Wollek's last race at Le Mans; the likeable and talented French driver was killed in a cycling accident in early 2001. *John Brooks*

Frenchmen Thierry Perrier and the father-and-son team of Jean-Louis and Romano Ricci brought their No. 79 Perspective Racing 911 GT3 R home in twenty-third place overall and fourth in the GT class. *Corporate Archives Porsche AG*

The No. 76 Seikel Motorsport 911 GT3 R of Michel Neugarten/ Tony Burgess/Max Cohen-Olivar finished eighteenth overall and third in the GT class. *John Brooks*

As a result of the postrace disqualification of the No. 83 Dick Barbour car, the No. 73 Team Taisan Advan 911 GT3 R, driven by Hideo Fukuyama/Bruno Lambert/Atsushi Yogo, was elevated to sixteenth overall and was retrospectively awarded GT class honors. *Corporate Archives Porsche AG*

The drama of nighttime racing at Le Mans is captured in this photograph of the No. 60 Konrad Motorsport 911 GT2, driven by Jürgen von Gartzen/Charles Slater/Tom Kendall. This GTS car was initially beaten to the line by the Barbour Porsche, but that car's subsequent disqualification resulted in the Konrad car becoming the first Porsche home in fourteenth place overall, and seventh in the GTS class. *Corporate Archives Porsche AG*

The No. 82 Skea Racing International 911 GT3 R, driven by David Murry/Sascha Maassen/Johnny Mowlem, was vaulted into third place in class and seventeenth place overall thanks to a clash between the No. 81 and No. 73 911s, the former retiring while the latter car finished sixteenth overall. *John Brooks*

2000 Race Results

Pos.	Car/Model	No.	Driver(s)	Entered	Class	Cl. Pos	Laps	Reason
DNF	Porsche 911 GT3-R	83	Dirk Müller (DE)/Bob Wollek (FR)/Lucas Lühr (DE)	Dick Barbour	GT		319	DQ – oversize fuel
14	Porsche 911 GT2	60	Jürgen von Gartzen (DE)/Charles Slater (US)/Tom Kendall (US)	Konrad Motorsport	GTS	7	317	
DNF	Porsche 911 GT2	59	Wolfgang Kaufmann (DE)/Yukihiro Hane (JP)/Katsunori Iketani (JP)	Freisinger Motorsport	GTS		313	Suspension
16	Porsche 911 GT3-R	73	Hideo Fukuyama (JP)/Bruno Lambert (BE)/Atsushi Yogo (JP)	Team Taisan Advan	GT	1	310	
DNF	Porsche 911 GT3-R	81	Michel Ligonnet (FR)/Gabrio Rosa (IT)/Fabio Babini (IT)	Harberthur Racing	GT		310	Accident
17	Porsche 911 GT3-R	82	David Murry (US)/Sascha Maassen (DE)/Johnny Mowlem (GB)	Skea Racing International	GT	2	304	
18	Porsche 911 GT3-R	76	Michel Neugarten (BE)/Tony Burgess (CA)/Max Cohen-Olivar (MA)	Seikel Motorsport	GT	3	302	
23	Porsche 911 GT3-R	79	Thierry Perrier (FR)/Jean-Louis Ricci (FR)/Romano Ricci (FR)	Perspective Racing	GT	4	286	
24	Porsche 911 GT3-R	80	Philip Verellen (BE)/Dujardin (BE)/Rudi Penders (BE)	Club-Renstal Excelsior	GT	5	285	
27	Porsche 911 GT3-R	75	Gunnar Jeannette (US)/Michael Lauer (US)/Mike Brockman (US)	Olaf Manthey	GT	6	261	
DNF	Porsche 911 GT3-R	72	Tomas Saldaña (ES)/Jesús Diez de Villaroel (ES)/Giovanni Lavaggi (IT)	Racing Engineering	GT		78	Engine
DNF	Porsche 911 GT3-R	77	Christophe Bouchut (FR)/Patrice Goueslard (FR)/Jean-Luc Chéreau (FR)	Larbre Compétition	GT		34	Accident
DNF	Porsche 911 GT3-R	78	Jean-Luc Maury-Laribiére (FR)/Angelo Zadra (IT)/Bernard Chauvin (FR)	Jean-Luc Maury-Laribiére	GT		32	Accident
DNF	Porsche 911 GT3-R	71	Shane Lewis (US)/Cort Wagner (US)/Bob Mazzuoccola (US)	Michael Colucci	GT		22	Accident

2001
June 16–17

A squadron of ten 911s competed in the GT class for 2001, with the sole non-Porsche entrant being a lone Callaway C12R. Porsche's ten-strong GT contingent was dominated by eight 911 GT3 RS cars, with just two 911 GT3 Rs. This year Porsche could claim a race-finishing rate of 80 percent.

The 4:00 p.m. start was followed almost immediately by a heavy rainstorm. As the race progressed, more and more cars succumbed to the elements. Perhaps more than any other race in recent years, this year's event was characterized by torrential downpours that necessitated no fewer than four safety car periods. Despite the atrocious weather conditions, the highest-placed Porsche finished in an amazing sixth position overall, with six of the top twelve places (except eighth place) going to the Stuttgart manufacturer.

This year it was Seikel Motorsport's turn to show its colors: the race team started by Peter Seikel back in 1968 could now claim to have equaled the highest-placed GT class finisher at Le Mans. This result would rank alongside the team's other highlight when they took class wins in the 6 Hours of Vallelunga and the 1000 Kilometres of Monza events.

Perhaps lost in all the emotion and atmosphere of the impending twenty-four-hour battle was the fact that the two chicanes down the back straight had new names. The first chicane was now called the PlayStation Chicane, while the second would be known as the Michelin Chicane; today these are simply referred to as the first and second chicanes.

The No. 71 Racing Engineering 911 GT3 R, driven by Robin Donovan/Terry Lingner/Chris MacAllister, retired after just thirty-eight laps because of an accident in the treacherous and slippery conditions. The car was one of only two GT3 Rs in the race, and this was Lingner's first outing at Le Mans, although it was Donovan who had the dubious honor of being at the wheel when the first Porsche was forced to withdraw from the race following his crash during the hours of darkness. *John Brooks*

Driving the other 911 GT3 R was the all-French team of Luc Alphand/Michel Ligonnet/Luis Marques. The Luc Alphand Adventures Team was created in 1998 when Alphand, 1997 World Cup skiing champion, joined with Philippe Poincloux to compete in the Dakar rally that year. The No. 74 car finished seventeenth overall and eighth in class. *John Brooks*

The No. 76 PK Sports GT3 RS ran as high as first in class at one stage, but an accident suffered by Stephen Day and Mike Youles delayed progress slightly, while Dave Warnock had a trip through the gravel. Warnock remembers that it rained for most of the race, and that the general appetite among the drivers to get behind the wheel was quite low. "When it is raining on one side of the track and completely dry on the other, and you get this radio message saying, 'it's absolutely hammering it down in the pits' and you are going down the Mulsanne where it is dry, you think 'what do I do now?' because you are just waiting to hit the Porsche Curves when it is suddenly damp and you are on slicks. It was really scary, to be honest." The PK Sports car finished seventh in the GT class and sixteenth overall, out of just twenty classified finishers. *John Brooks*

Team Seikel fielded two 911 GT3 RSs in the 2001 race. In action here is the No. 82 car, driven by Max Cohen-Olivar/Andrew Bagnall/Tony Burgess, which finished twelfth overall and sixth in class. *John Brooks*

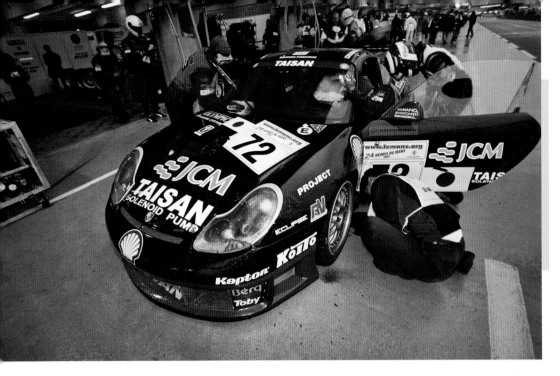

Formed in 1984, Team Taisan won the Japanese Sports Car Championship for three consecutive years, from 1985–1987, also taking the Japan Touring Car Championship in 1989, so this was no startup team. Here is the team's No. 72 GT3 RS, driven by the all-Japanese crew of Kazuyuki Mishizawa/Atsushi Yogo/Hideo Fukuyama, seen in the pits in the early evening during one of the many wet periods. The car finished eleventh overall and fifth in class. *Corporate Archives Porsche AG*

Supported by longtime Porsche sponsor, F.A.T. International, the No. 80 Larbre Compétition Chéreau 911 GT3 RS was driven to tenth place by Jean-Luc Chéreau/Sébastien Dumez/Patrice Goueslard, earning them fourth place in class. *John Brooks*

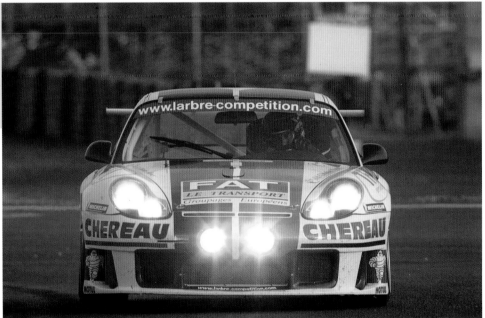

The No. 75 Perspective Racing 911 GT3 RS, driven by Thierry Perrier/Michel Neugarten/Nigel Smith, finished ninth overall. The car was the third 911 across the finish line, also finishing third in the LM GT class. *Corporate Archives Porsche AG*

Crossing the line in a remarkable seventh place, just a lap down on the Seikel Porsche, was the No. 77 Freisinger Motorsport car driven by Gunnar Jeannette/Philippe Haezebrouck/Romain Dumas. At just eighteen years of age in the previous year's race, Gunnar Jeannette was certainly one of the event's youngest competitors to race at Le Mans. His race in 2001 was one to remember, as the young American put in a quality performance. The Freisinger team finished second in the GT class. *Corporate Archives Porsche AG*

Driving the No. 83 Seikel 911 GT3 RS was the Italian trio of Luca Drudi, Gabrio Rosa, and Fabio Babini, who edged out their class rivals, Freisinger Motorsport, by a single lap. A fascinating battle with Freisinger kept the class alive, and by early Sunday morning the car had built up a two-lap lead, but this was reversed when a holed radiator cost the Seikel car four laps in the pits. The Seikel Porsche prevailed, however, finishing in sixth place, thereby equaling the highest overall placing ever for a GT class car at Le Mans (the No. 63 Porsche 911 S of French pairing Raymond Touroul/André Anselme finished sixth in 1971), a result that also netted them first in class. At the same time, the team received the École Supérieure de Commerce des Réseaux de l'Automobile (ESCRA) prize for the best technical assistance by a pit crew during the race. *John Brooks*

2001 Race Results

Pos.	Car/Model	No.	Driver(s)	Entered	Class	Cl. Pos	Laps	Reason
6	911 GT3 RS	83	Lucas Drudi (IT)/Gabrio Rosa (IT)/Fabio Babini (IT)	Seikel Motorsport	LM GT	1	283	
7	911 GT3 RS	77	Gunnar Jeannette (US)/Philippe Haezebrouck (FR)/Romain Dumas (FR)	Freisinger Motorsport	LM GT	2	282	
9	911 GT3 RS	75	Thierry Perrier (FR)/Michel Neugarten (BE)/Nigel Smith (GB)	Perspective Racing	LM GT	3	275	
10	911 GT3 RS	80	Jean-Luc Chéreau (FR)/Sébastien Dumez (FR)/Patrice Goueslard (FR)	Larbre Compétition Chéreau	LM GT	4	274	
11	911 GT3 RS	72	Kazuyuki Mishizawa (JP)/Atsushi Yogo (JP)/Hideo Fukuyama (JP)	Team Taisan Advan	LM GT	5	273	
12	911 GT3 RS	82	Max Cohen-Olivar (MA)/Andrew Bagnall (NZ)/Tony Burgess (CA)	Seikel Motorsport	LM GT	6	272	
16	911 GT3 RS	76	Dave Warnock (GB)/Stephen Day (GB)/Mike Youles (GB)	PK Sport Ltd, Ricardo	LM GT	7	265	
17	911 GT3 R	74	Luc Alphand (FR)/Michel Ligonnet (FR)/Luis Marques (FR)	Luc Alphand Adventures	LM GT	8	265	
NC	911 GT3 RS	79	Georges Forgeois (US)/Sylvain Noel (FR)/Jean-Luc Maury-Laribière (FR)	Del Bello Noel	LM GT		193	NC
DNF	911 GT3 R	71	Robin Donovan (GB)/Terry Lingner (US)/Chris MacAllister (US)	Racing Engineering	LM GT		44	Accident

2002

June 15–16

Only seven Porsches competed in the 2002 Le Mans, and all were entered by as many different teams. The race car of choice in the GT class was the Type 996 911 GT3 RS, a 3,598cc traditional flat six Porsche engine developing 420 horsepower.

An unknown team—unknown to the European racing scene, that is—arrived with a brand-new GT3 RS that they had just picked up from Stuttgart in time for the May test session. The California-based team, known as the Racer's Group, just happened to be fresh from their class victory in Daytona earlier in the year, and were justifiably optimistic about their chances. It was the American team's first trip to the French classic, however, and they were under no illusions as to how challenging the race would be.

Seikel Motorsport was also justifiably buoyant about their chances of class honors, as that title had been theirs in 2001. As a privateer race team, Seikel could also claim the unique record of having competed in all the major twenty-four-hour races around the world, including Le Mans, Spa, Daytona, Nürburgring, and Bathurst in Australia. The team also participated at Sebring on five occasions, so endurance racing was indeed in their blood.

The Racer's Group and Seikel would have their work cut out for them, though, as they sought to stamp their authority on the GT class: they were up against the likes of Freisinger, Luc Alphand, Orbit Racing, PK Sport, and Team Taisan, all of whom had their own lines of pedigree in European or Asian GT racing. Seikel and Freisinger boasted factory support, however, which meant that these two teams included Porsche factory drivers in their lineup.

Dave Warnock/Robin Liddell/Piers Masarati ran their No. 78 911 GT3 RS under Mike Pickup's PK Sport banner but were forced to retire with engine overheating trouble at around 9:00 p.m. on Saturday after eighty-three laps. Warnock recalls, "Robin was a fairly accomplished, up-and-coming swift driver, and Piers, that was his first time as a driver at Le Mans, but he had obviously been involved with Pickup for many years. We were running well, so we were actually expecting a good result. I had had three years of experience at Le Mans, and both Robin and Piers were very fast from the get-go, so we had some major expectations, to be honest. But when it is not your year, it is not your year, and things just didn't happen for us."
John Brooks

Retiring before half distance was the No. 75 Orbit Racing 911 GT3 RS of Americans Leo Hindery/Peter Baron/Tony Kester. Transmission trouble was the car's downfall on lap 165. *Porsche-Werkfoto*

In twenty-fourth place was the No. 72 Luc Alphand Aventures 911 GT3 RS of Luc Alphand/Christophe Lavielle/Olivier Thevenin. *Corporate Archives Porsche AG*

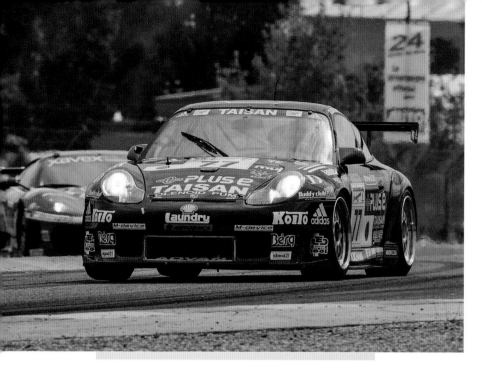

With overall honors for the Le Mans crown a foregone conclusion, the most exciting action was to be found in the GT class. This class was the scene of two battles, one between the Racer's Group and Freisinger for the top two slots and the other between the No. 77 Team Taisan Advan car and the No. 82 Seikel Motorsport car. The winner of the first battle was the Racer's Group. Of the second battle, it was the No. 77 911 GT3 RS driven by the Japanese trio of Akira Iida/Atsushi Yogo/Kazuyuki Nishizawa that finished twenty-first overall and third in class. *John Brooks*

The Seikel Motorsport No. 82 911 GT3 RS, driven by Italians Gabrio Rosa/Luca Drudi/Luca Riccitelli, was beaten into fourth place in the GT class after an epic racelong duel with Team Taisan Advan. Completing 315 laps, the car finished twenty-second overall. *John Brooks*

A racelong duel between the No. 80 Freisinger Motorsport 911 GT3 RS, piloted by Romain Dumas/Sascha Maassen/Jörg Bergmeister, and the No. 81 Racer's Group car never saw these two contestants separated by more than a lap throughout the twenty-four hours. The Freisinger car was the subject of a stop/go penalty, which cost the team about a minute, the precise gap that separated the two GT cars at the final flag. The No. 80 car finished seventeenth and second in class. *John Brooks*

Kevin Buckler, owner of the Racer's Group, outlined the 2002 team strategy: "The plan was, 'go to Le Mans and don't get caught up in anything except the competition.' We were like the 'Dirty Dozen,' we were tough and I got all the guys together every morning and had a team meeting, and I told them, 'guys, we can do this,' and we put our heads down and we didn't let any of the pomp and circumstance get in the way, we just fought the whole time and really executed on our plan." Winning on the first time out at Le Mans is not something that many teams can claim, but the Racer's Group did just that. The No. 81 car thrilled the crowds as it battled the Freisinger car for

class honors. In the end, though, it was the No. 81 car of Kevin Buckler/Lucas Lühr/Timo Bernhard that prevailed, finishing sixteenth overall and top of class. How much did their recent Daytona victory influence their approach at Le Mans? "It was really big, very big," Buckler replied, "because we'd just won it, we felt confident and, you know, Daytona is a really tough race. In many ways it is tougher than Le Mans because you are racing people sometimes in every corner. Le Mans is different, there you have a different strategy, but we had the same crew, same pit stops, same people, same equipment, so it helped tremendously." *Corporate Archives Porsche AG*

2002 Race Results

Pos.	Car/Model	No.	Driver(s)	Entered	Class	Cl. Pos	Laps	Reason
16	911 GT3 RS	81	Kevin Buckler (US)/Lucas Lühr (DE)/Timo Bernhard (DE)	The Racers Group	GT	1	322	
17	911 GT3 RS	80	Romain Dumas (FR)/Sascha Maassen (DE)/Jörg Bergmeister (DE)	Freisinger Motorsport	GT	2	321	
21	911 GT3 RS	77	Akira Iida (JP)/Atsushi Yogo (JP)/Kazuyuki Nishizawa (JP)	Team Taisan Advan	GT	3	316	
22	911 GT3 RS	82	Gabrio Rosa (IT)/Luca Drudi (IT)/Luca Riccitelli (IT)	Seikel Motorsport	GT	4	315	
24	911 GT3 RS	72	Luc Alphand (FR)/Christophe Lavielle (FR)/Olivier Thevenin (FR)	Luc Alphand Aventure	GT	5	299	
DNF	911 GT3 RS	75	Leo Hindery (US)/Peter Baron (US)/Tony Kester (US)	Orbit Racing	GT		165	Transmission
DNF	911 GT3 RS	78	Robin Liddell (GB)/Dave Warnock (GB)/Piers Masarati (GB)	PK Sport	GT		83	Engine

2003

June 14–15

The LM GT class in 2003 consisted of fifteen entries made up of eight Porsche 911 GT3 RSs, three Ferrari 360 Modenas, a single Spyker C8 Double 12R, a pair of TVR T400Rs, and one Ferrari 550 Maranello. This represented one of the most varied grids in this class for many years, but it was the Stuttgart manufacturer's products that claimed the top six class positions.

Another visitor making its presence felt in European GT racing was the Florida-based Alex Job Racing team. It seemed that quite a number of Porsche Carrera Cup and Supercup drivers were making their way into Le Mans teams, and the spectacle of close and competitive racing was to the benefit of the paying public. Also, several Porsche-contracted drivers involved in the ALMS series were able to juggle their schedules and join those teams best able to exploit their considerable skills, all in Porsche's favor.

For a change, the event enjoyed hot, dry weather conditions. The year 2003 marked the eightieth anniversary of the 24 Hours of Le Mans, but it was in fact the seventy-first running of the great race because of a nine-year interruption during World War II.

In uncharacteristic fashion, the No. 83 Seikel Motorsport 911 GT3 RS of Tony Burgess/Andrew Bagnall/David Shep retired after 134 laps with a broken driveshaft. David Shep was at the wheel when the problem occurred on the straight between Mulsanne and Indianapolis. *Corporate Archives Porsche AG*

The No. 84 T2M Motorsport 911 GT3 RS of Frenchmen Patrick Bourdais and Roland Bervillé, along with Vanina Ickx (daughter of "Mr. Le Mans," Jacky Ickx), finished twenty-seventh place overall and ninth in class. *John Brooks*

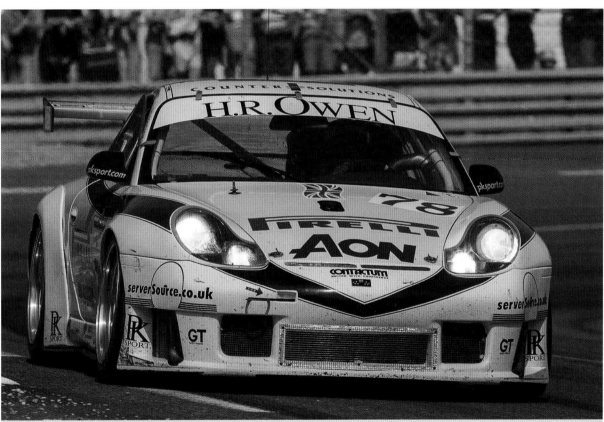

In 2003 Dave Warnock teamed up with the same partners from the preceding year (Robin Liddell/Piers Masarati), once again driving the No. 78 PK Sports 911 GT3 RS. The team were running in the top four in class when Warnock had a blowout down the Mulsanne, which tore the front right corner apart. He recounts the incident: "That was the middle of the night, it was pretty scary, but ironically the first thing you do is think of how to get back to the pits. We also had a radio malfunction as it must have torn one of the leads, and while I could hear them, they couldn't hear me, so they had no idea what was going on. I had obviously lost the front right rad[iator], so I really had to creep round as slowly as possible. We patched it up again and got back out and started climbing back up the order again, but Porsche came to us at about seven in the morning and ran a diagnostic on the engine. They told us we were, basically, limited to about 6,000 revs, which made it very difficult from that point on. So we had to throttle back." The familiar yellow Porsche finished twenty-third and sixth in class. *John Brooks*

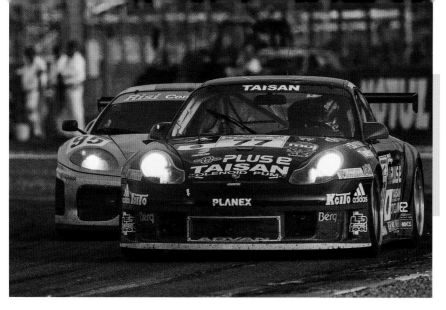

Finishing in 19th place was the No. 77 Team Taisan Advan GT3 RS of Atsushi Yogo/Kazuyuki Nishizawa/Akira Iida. As dusk set in, the all-Japanese team was running as high as second in class, but was later delayed with a damaged radiator early in the morning. Lying in third place in the final hour of the race, the car was again beset with cooling problems, putting it back to fourth in class at the finish. *John Brooks*

Having driven a steady, untroubled race throughout Saturday and most of Sunday, the No. 75 Perspective Racing GT3 RS was lying in third place in class. Le Mans has a way of leveling most players, however, and the Michel Neugarten/Nigel Smith/Ian Khan Porsche succumbed to a brake replacement and driveshaft failure in the penultimate hour (one-and-a-half hours to go), dropping the car back to fourth in class before retaking third spot in the final hour and eighteenth place overall. *Corporate Archives Porsche AG*

The lead car in this photograph is the No. 87 Orbit Racing GT3 RS of Marc Lieb/Leo Hindery/Peter Baron. The only real trouble that the car faced was a radiator change, and its eventual second place in class was established as early as midrace, earning it seventeenth place overall. As darkness fell, a one-and-a-half-hour clutch replacement cost the No. 81 Racer's Group 2002 class winners dearly, as the team dropped down to forty-second place overall. Kevin Buckler recalls, "We were leading the race handily by half a lap and we had some sort of small mechanical [problem]. It turned out that when Porsche gave us the engine it had the wrong throwout bearing, so the clutch started slipping after about six hours and we ended up having to come in and change that part, which took us several hours. It was really a shame because we didn't have one single problem after that." The highly talented trio of Timo Bernhard/Jörg Bergmeister/Kevin Buckler fought back to twentieth place overall and fifth in class. *John Brooks*

Formed in 1988, Alex Job Racing teamed up with Petersen Motorsports for the 2003 race. The driver lineup of Sascha Maassen, Lucas Lühr, and Emmanuel Collard saw the No. 93 Porsche leading their class, but a radiator change shortly after midnight dropped the team back to fifth in class. A spirited performance saw them rocket up the order once again to take class honors at the finish by a margin of six laps, in the process securing fourteenth place overall. *Corporate Archives Porsche AG*

2003 Race Results

Pos.	Car/Model	No.	Driver(s)	Entered	Class	Cl. Pos	Laps	Reason
14	911 GT3 RS	93	Lucas Lühr (DE)/Sascha Maassen (DE)/Emmanuel Collard (FR)	Alex Job Racing/Petersen Motorsports	LM GT	1	320	
17	911 GT3 RS	87	Marc Lieb (DE)/Leo Hindery (US)/Peter Baron (US)	Orbit Racing	LM GT	2	314	
18	911 GT3 RS	75	Michel Neugarten (BE)/Nigel Smith (GB)/Ian Khan (GB)	Perspective Racing	LM GT	3	305	
19	911 GT3 RS	77	Atsushi Yogo (JP)/Kazuyuki Nishizawa (JP)/Akira Iida (JP)	Team Taisan Advan	LM GT	4	304	
20	911 GT3 RS	81	Timo Bernhard (DE)/Jörg Bergmeister (DE)/Kevin Buckler (US)	The Racers Group	LM GT	5	304	
23	911 GT3 RS	78	Robin Liddell (GB)/David Warnock (GB)/Piers Masarati (GB)	PK Sport	LM GT	6	285	
27	911 GT3 RS	84	Vanina Ickx (BE)/Patrick Bourdais (FR)/Roland Bervillé (FR)	T2M Motorsport	LM GT	9	264	
DNF	911 GT3 RS	83	Tony Burgess (CA)/David Shep (CA)/Andrew Bagnall (NZ)	Seikel Motorsport	LM GT		134	Gearbox

2004
June 12–13

While the weather was warm and dry for the race, it was decidedly hot for the Audis who once again made the race their own, taking the top three places on the podium, a piece of real estate that they seemed determined to keep.

Down in the GT class, Porsche were well represented by no fewer than eleven 911s, comprising a mix of five GT3 RSs and six RSRs. While the GT class consisted of four manufacturers—Porsche, Ferrari, TVR, and Morgan—the GTS class was dominated by Ferrari and a couple of works Corvettes.

Such a strong representation by Porsche cars ensured a good result, but six out of six in class is about as impressive as it could get. Although the new GT3 RSR still used the same 3.6-liter Porsche engine, power was boosted significantly from 415 horsepower up to 450 horsepower, which didn't do much to the top-end capability, but it improved acceleration notably.

The No. 85 Freisinger Motorsport 911 GT3 RSR of Stéphane Ortelli/Romain Dumas/Ralf Kelleners undergoes scrutineering ahead of the 2004 race. Kelleners took the class lead briefly at around the halfway mark when the class-leading car at the time (No. 90) pitted for repairs, but despite several stops for electrical repairs themselves, the No. 85 GT3 RSR was driven to thirteenth overall and third in the GT class. *Corporate Archives Porsche AG*

Dave Warnock had first run at Le Mans in 1997 in a Saleen Mustang, but the following year returned with a Porsche GT2. As he explains, "I wanted to go with a car that was capable of finishing, and I think it was the view of most people back then that if you wanted to finish an endurance race, you went with Porsche." In 2004, however, the No. 78 PK Sport GT3 RS, driven by David Warnock/ Jim Matthews/Paul Daniels, was the first Porsche to retire after just twenty-seven laps due to electrical problems. Warnock recounts the incident: "I started the race and

did the first hour or so, then handed over to Jim, and I think he did about four or five laps before something happened with the engine and it started chucking fluid out. That was the reason why the Audi went off when Allan McNish crashed. It was because of us, and that wasn't very good. So Jim brought the car back into the pits and we tried to fix it, and Porsche was there plugging in all their computers, and then Paul went out to do three or four more laps, and it just became apparent in the end that unfortunately we would have to park it." *John Brooks*

Following a crash at the Ford Chicane by team owner Leo Hindery, the No. 87 BAM/ Orbit Racing GT3 RSR, codriven by Marc Lieb and Mike Rockenfeller, fought its way back up the order once again, but the Porsche finally retired with gearbox trouble after 223 laps. *John Brooks*

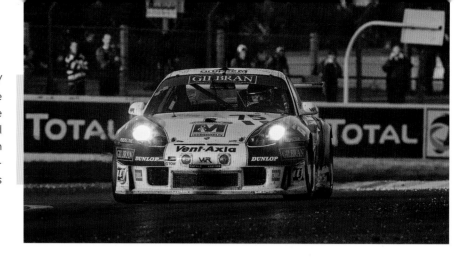

The No. 75 Thierry Perrier/ Perspective Racing Porsche 911 GT3 RS, piloted by the British trio of Tim Sugden/Nigel Smith/Ian Khan, finished tenth in the GT class and twenty-third overall. *John Brooks*

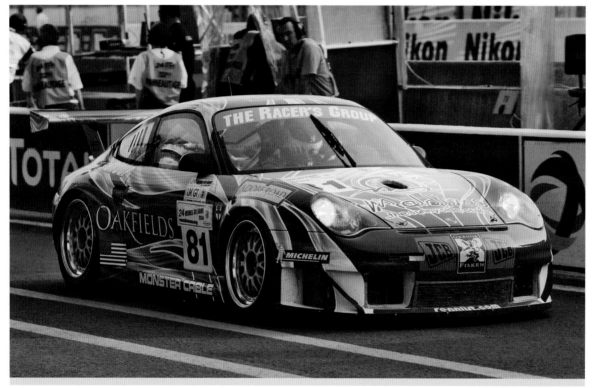

Kevin Buckler's Racer's Group arrived at Le Mans in 2004 with a brand-new GT3 RSR under their wing. Without a sponsor, and therefore unable to drive himself, Buckler put together a program whereby he managed the No. 81 car, which was owned by Lars-Erik Nielsen, the Danish Porsche importer. The Racer's Group had quickly built up a reputation in Europe for running a slick operation, and Buckler filled the available seats with Nielsen and Britons Ian Donaldson and Gregor Fisken. The Porsche's livery, a colorful shrink-wrap coating, was sponsored by the Maldives Islands PR operation with the slogan "The Sunny Side of Life," and their entry became known as the Maldives car. Apart from an early, unscheduled stop for a nonexistent puncture, the Porsche ran faultlessly, as Fisken pointed out: "The car ran like a top, it was fantastic, it was as strong in the twenty-fourth hour as it was in the first hour. We were probably the last car that ever ran with a manual H-pattern gearbox." At one point, as Fisken was coming out of a chicane, he was squeezed by a prototype on one side, so he moved over to give that car some space and found another prototype on his other side, the slight coming together that resulted in some minor

damage. A further unscheduled pit stop allowed the team to duct-tape the front bumper in place, but otherwise the car recorded the shortest pit time of any car that year, amounting to a remarkable thirty-eight minutes over the full twenty-four hours. Fisken recalls that, on the Sunday afternoon, "when you really go racing," he had a personal battle with the No. 92 Cirtek Ferrari 360 Modena in the next-door pit garage. He picks up the story: "I remember coming around Tertre Rouge and Hans Hugenholtz had gone out on cold tires and he lost it there, putting it in the barriers." His radio communications with the pits that followed were a bit confusing, as the message came through, "Are you alright, what's happened?" Fisken replied, "He's off, he's off," and the concerned reply came back, "You're off, you've gone off, where have you gone off?" Fisken shouted back, "I haven't gone off, Hans has gone off, the Ferrari is off, the Ferrari is off, it's in the barriers at Tertre Rouge!" Although the car was back in forty-second place on the starting grid, the team didn't make a mistake or have any problems throughout the twenty-four hours. Such reliability earned them sixth place in class and eighteenth overall. *Corporate Archives Porsche AG*

A good run saw the No. 72 Luc Alphand Aventures 911 GT3 RS securing a solid sixteenth place overall and fifth in class in this all-French team. Both Luc Alphand and Christian Lavielle needed no introduction to the circuit, but the young Philippe Alméras had a bit of a scare in practice when his right door flew off at speed as a result of air pressure in the cabin. *Corporate Archives Porsche AG*

Having only just scraped onto the entry list, the No. 84 Seikel 911 GT3 RS gave a good account of itself. Driven by Tony Burgess/Andrew Bagnall/ Philip Collin, the older Porsche put in a faultless performance, running through the night without a hint of concern and securing fourth spot in class at 9:00 a.m. on Sunday. The team held on to that position until the end of the race, finishing fifteenth overall. In this photograph, Philip Collin is replacing Tony Burgess after his stint behind the wheel. *Seikel Motorsport*

In a race lasting twenty-four hours, a minor setback can seem like the end of a team's race in the moment. In the broader scheme of things, most teams suffer similar mishaps, and often a team can work its way back into the race as a result. This happened to the No. 77 ChoroQ Racing Team Porsche 911 GT3 RSR, driven by the all-Japanese team of Haruki Kurosawa/Kazuyuki Nishizawa/Manabu Orido, when Nishizawa had a minor off-track excursion followed by a string of electrical problems. With the electrics fixed, the team set about putting in some steady laps. They were rewarded with placing twelfth overall and second in the GT class. *John Brooks*

Despite losing seven laps with gearbox woes—Bergmeister pitted with his gear selector stuck in gear in the eleventh hour—and later throttle-linkage problems, the highly talented team of Sascha Maassen/Jörg Bergmeister/Patrick Long brought the No. 90 Petersen White Lightning Racing 911 GT3 RSR right back into contention. Tipped as the favorite to win its class before the race, the car did not disappoint, taking an impressive overall tenth place in the process. *Corporate Archives Porsche AG*

2004 Race Results

Pos.	Car/Model	No.	Driver(s)	Entered	Class	Cl. Pos	Laps	Reason
10	911 GT3 RSR	90	Sascha Maassen (DE)/Jörg Bergmeister (DE)/Patrick Long (US)	Petersen/White Lightning Racing	LM GT	1	327	
12	911 GT3 RSR	77	Haruki Kurosawa (JP)/Kazuyuki Nishizawa (JP)/Manabu Orido (JP)	ChoroQ Racing Team	LM GT	2	322	
13	911 GT3 RSR	85	Stéphane Ortelli (FR)/Romain Dumas (FR)/Ralf Kelleners (DE)	Freisinger Motorsport	LM GT	3	321	
15	911 GT3 RS	84	Tony Burgess (CA)/Philip Collin (US)/Andrew Bagnall (NZ)	Seikel Motorsport	LM GT	4	317	
16	911 GT3 RS	72	Luc Alphand (FR)/Philippe Alméras (FR)/Christian Lavielle (FR)	Luc Alphand Aventures	LM GT	5	316	
18	911 GT3 RSR	81	Ian Donaldson (GB)/Lars-Erik Nielsen (DK)/Gregor Fisken (GB)	The Racers Group	LM GT	6	314	
23	911 GT3 RS	75	Tim Sugden (GB)/Nigel Smith (GB)/Ian Khan (GB)	Thierry Perrier/Perspective Racing	LM GT	10	283	
DNF	911 GT3 RSR	87	Marc Lieb (DE)/Mike Rockenfeller (DE)/Leo Hindery (US)	BAM/Orbit Racing	LM GT		223	Gearbox
DNF	911 GT3 RS	83	Alex Caffi (IT)/Gabrio Rosa (IT)/Peter van Merksteijn (NL)	Seikel Motorsport	LM GT		148	Engine
DNF	911 GT3 RSR	86	Alex Vasiliev (RU)/Robert Nearn (GB)/Nikolaj Fomenko (RU)	Freisinger Motorsport	LM GT		65	Accident
DNF	911 GT3 RS	78	David Warnock (GB)/Jim Matthews (US)/Paul Daniels (GB)	PK Sport	LM GT		27	Electrics

2005

June 18–19

History was made at the 2005 race, when Jacky Ickx's long-standing record of six Le Mans wins was finally eclipsed by the Dane, Tom Kristensen, in an Audi R8.

A new feature, triple-stacked lights on the cars' flanks, would become regulation in later years. They had appeared on some of the cars participating in the American Le Mans Series, and represented a car's class position; for instance, one light illuminated indicates that a car is first in class, two lights for second, and three for third in class. This practice originated in the ALMS to help spectators keep track of proceedings in the multiclass series.

Only eight Type 996 Porsche 911s contested the GT2 class (six GT3 RSRs and two GT3 RSs) in the hot and humid conditions that characterized the 2005 race. The highest-placed GT2 entrant on the starting grid at 4:00 p.m. on Saturday was the No. 71 Alex Job Racing Porsche GT3 RSR, a class position it would also hold at 4:00 p.m. on Sunday.

The GT2 class was no pushover for the Stuttgart marque, with five different manufacturers present in the class, including Porsche, TVR, Ferrari, Panoz, and Spyker. Of the eight Porsche entrants, though, seven were classified as finishers, snatching the first seven places in class. This was an excellent result, even if the number of Stuttgart contenders was on the low side.

The only nonfinisher from Stuttgart was the Japanese-run No. 91 T2M Motorsport 911 GT3 RS of Xavier Pompidou/Yutaka Yamagishi/Jean-Luc Blanchemain. The car was completely mangled, with Pompidou at the wheel, in an accident at around 8:00 a.m. on Sunday, having covered 183 laps. *Corporate Archives Porsche AG*

The No. 83 Felbermayr-sponsored 911 GT3 RSR, piloted by Horst Felbermayr/David Shep/Philip Collin, was delayed in the pits because of a broken suspension arm at 2:00 a.m. on Sunday, but rejoined after one hour to put in some spirited laps to the end. From forty-seventh place on the starting grid, the car finished twenty-third overall and seventh in the GT2 class. *Seikel Motorsport*

Thorkild Thyrring/Pierre Ehret/Lars-Erik Nielsen brought the British-based Sebah Automotive No. 89 911 GT3 RSR home in nineteenth place and sixth in class. *Corporate Archives Porsche AG*

Putting in yet another solid performance was the No. 72 Luc Alphand Aventures Type 996 GT3 RS, driven by team owner Luc Alphand together with French colleagues Christopher Campbell and Jérôme Policand. The French car finished eighteenth overall and fifth in class. *Corporate Archives Porsche AG*

The No. 76 Raymond Narac–entered Porsche 911 GT3 RSR, driven by the team owner himself with Sébastien Dumez and Romain Dumas, fought a racelong duel with the No. 80 Flying Lizard Porsche. Just a lap separated the two cars at the flag, with the Narac Porsche in fifteenth place overall and fourth in class. *Corporate Archives Porsche AG*

The second visit to Le Mans for the No. 80 Flying Lizard Motorsports team took place in 2005. The all-American driver lineup of Johannes van Overbeek/Seth Neiman/ Lonnie Pechnik brought their Porsche 911 GT3 RSR home in thirteenth place overall and third in GT class, which ensured that all three podium places in the class that year were filled by American teams. *Corporate Archives Porsche AG*

Piloted by such high-caliber drivers as Jörg Bergmeister/Patrick Long/Timo Bernhard, the No. 90 Petersen White Lightning Racing Type 996 GT3 RSR was always going to be a threat in its class. From fortieth place on the starting grid, the American-entered Porsche encountered gear selection problems in the early hours of Sunday morning but recovered to finish eleventh overall and second in class, just a lap down on the GT winners. *Corporate Archives Porsche AG*

Located in the thirty-third spot on the starting grid, the No. 71 Alex Job Racing/BAM! Motorsport Porsche 911 GT3 RSR was ideally positioned as the lead GT2 contender, occupying pole position in class. Young guns Mike Rockenfeller and Marc Lieb did most of the driving, while team principal Leo Hindery directed affairs from within the pit garage, taking just one early stint and the final stint to cross the line and claim tenth place overall, first in GT2 class. Rockenfeller and Lieb both went on to successful racing careers with Audi and Porsche, respectively. *Corporate Archives Porsche AG*

2005 Race Results

Pos.	Car/Model	No.	Driver(s)	Entered	Class	Cl. Pos	Laps	Reason
10	911 GT3 RSR	71	Mike Rockenfeller (DE)/Marc Lieb (DE)/Leo Hindery (US)	Alex Job Racing/BAM!	LM GT2	1	332	
11	911 GT3 RSR	90	Jörg Bergmeister (DE)/Patrick Long (US)/Timo Bernhard (DE)	Petersen/White Lightning Racing	LM GT2	2	331	
13	911 GT3 RSR	80	Johannes van Overbeek (US)/Seth Neiman (US)/Lonnie Pechnik (US)	Flying Lizard Motorsports	LM GT2	3	323	
15	911 GT3 RSR	76	Raymond Narac (FR)/Sébastien Dumez (FR)/Romain Dumas (FR)	Raymond Narac	LM GT2	4	322	
18	911 GT3 RS	72	Luc Alphand (FR)/Christopher Campbell (FR)/Jérôme Policand (FR)	Luc Alphand Aventures	LM GT2	5	311	
19	911 GT3 RSR	89	Thorkild Thyrring (DK)/Pierre Ehret (DE)/Lars-Erik Nielsen (DK)	Sebah Automotive	LM GT2	6	307	
23	911 GT3 RSR	83	Philip Collin (US)/Horst Felbermayr (AT)/David Shep (CA)	Seikel Motorsport	LM GT2	7	274	
DNF	911 GT3 RS	91	Xavier Pompidou (FR)/Yutaka Yamagishi (JP)/Jean-Luc Blanchemain (FR)	T2M Motorsport	LM GT2		183	Accident

2006

June 17–18

Ensuring an interesting race, the hunt for GT2 honors in the seventy-fourth running of this classic endurance race was to be contested between four manufacturers, so it was not going to be plain sailing for the Stuttgart manufacturer. The entrants included Porsche, Ferrari, Spyker, and Panoz, who provided a fascinating mix of machines—one rear-engined, two mid-engined, and one front-engined manufacturer. Although the Porsche marque was well represented with nine 911s (two GT3 RS and the rest GT3 RSR), they would not win the GT2 class; that honor went to an American Panoz. Of the nine Porsches entered, only four would finish the race and, to show how closely fought the class was, three different manufacturers occupied the podium at 4:00 p.m. on Sunday—first Panoz, second Porsche, and third Ferrari.

On September 27, 2006, the motorsports world lost one of its most charismatic members with the passing of Erwin Kremer. Having been involved in motorsports since the 1960s, both as a driver and then as a team owner, Kremer had been responsible for many innovations and improvements to the Porsche cars he raced, a number of which were copied by the competition or even adopted by the factory.

The first Porsche retirement in the 2006 race was the No. 98 Del Bello Racing Porsche 911 GT3 RSR, driven by Adam Sharpe/Patrick Bourdais/Tom Cloet, having completed 115 laps before an accident forced their withdrawal. *John Brooks*

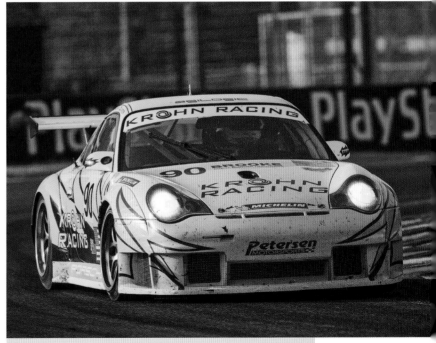

The No. 90 Petersen Racing/White Lightning Porsche 911 GT3 RSR suffered an accident at the PlayStation Chicane, with Bergmeister at the wheel at around the halfway mark, signaled the end of the car's run and the premature retirement of partners Niclas Jönsson and Tracy Krohn. *John Brooks*

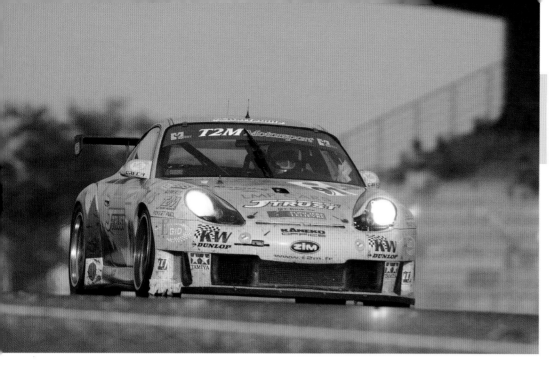

A fuel system failure resulted in the No. 91 T2M Motorsport 911 GT3 RS of Yutaka Yamagishi/Jean-René de Fournoux/Miroslav Konôpka retiring after 196 laps. *Corporate Archives Porsche AG*

With Romain Dumas having set the fastest GT2 time in qualifying in the No. 76 IMSA Performance 911 GT3 RSR, the car was then comprehensively written off by teammate Luca Riccitelli. The team was only allowed to rebuild the car using a new chassis on the condition that the car start at the back of the grid. The 3.8-liter-engined Porsche of Romain Dumas/Raymond Narac/Luca Riccitelli did not finish the race, retiring with engine failure after 211 laps. *John Brooks*

Prop shaft failure caused the retirement of Thorkild Thyrring/Xavier Pompidou/Christian Ried in their No. 89 Sebah Automotive 911 GT3 RSR after 256 laps. *John Brooks*

Finishing sixth in class and twenty-third overall was the Belgian No. 73 Ice Pol Racing Team's 911 GT3 RSR, driven by Yves Lambert/Christian Lefort/Romain Iannetta. The car was one of only two 911s fitted with the larger 3,795cc engine. *Corporate Archives Porsche AG*

A lengthy spell in the garage around 10:00 a.m. on Sunday cost the No. 93 Team Taisan Advan Porsche 911 GT3 RS of Shinichi Yamaji/Kazuyuki Nishizawa/Philip Collin dearly. One of only two GT3 RSs in the class, the team dropped from third in class to finish fifth in the GT2 class and twenty-second overall. *Corporate Archives Porsche AG*

It all started just as planned, as Patrick Long moved up from fourth place to first in the GT2 class. After just two-and-a-half hours with Seth Neiman at the wheel, the car developed a vibration, forcing an unscheduled tire change. Then, at around 9:00 p.m., Long flat-spotted the tires, requiring a new set of rubber. Later, with Neiman at the wheel again, an engine misfire turned into an hour-long trackside repair that required another visit to the pits. By 5:00 a.m. on Sunday, a little more than half distance, the No. 80 Porsche was now back in tenth in class, but running smoothly. With consistent lapping and no further problems, the rate of attrition in the GT2 class saw the Lizard car up in fourth place in class by 1:00 p.m. on Sunday. Although the car was outpacing the other class runners by 30–45 seconds per lap, there was simply too much ground to make up. Some eleven laps behind the class-leading Panoz at the flag, the No. 80 Flying Lizard Motorsports 911 GT3 RSR, driven by the American trio of Patrick Long/Johannes van Overbeek/Seth Neiman, finished fourth in the GT2 class and eighteenth overall. *Corporate Archives Porsche AG*

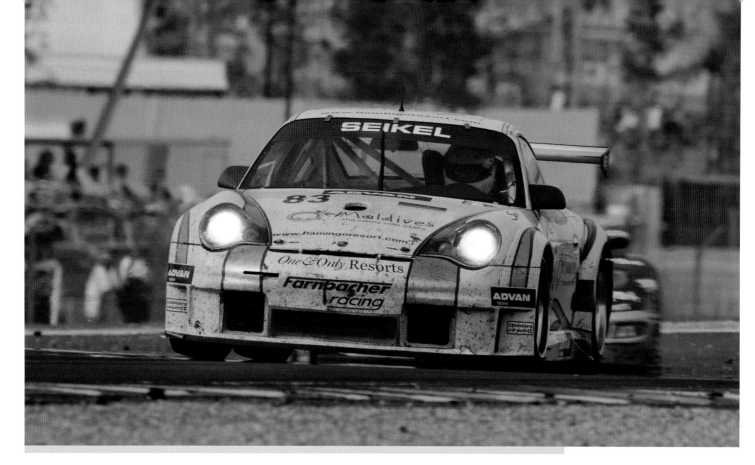

By the sixth hour (10:00 p.m.), the No. 83 Seikel/
Farnbacher 911 GT3 RSR of Lars-Erik Nielsen/Pierre
Ehret/Dominik Farnbacher had already built up
a sizable class lead (fourteenth overall), which
they held until the twenty-third hour. Then disaster
struck: while reveling in a six-lap class lead, the
gear lever broke with Farnbacher at the wheel.
Effecting a makeshift trackside repair, he limped
back to the pits where the team carried out a "more

permanent" temporary repair, only for the following
Panoz to slip by into the class lead. Farnbacher
went back out but spun at Tertre Rouge, where he
struck the wall. Extracting himself from that mess,
Farnbacher continued on to the finish, claiming
second in class to the Panoz and sixteenth overall.
Nevertheless, the team had the satisfaction of
being the first Porsche to make it home. *Corporate
Archives Porsche AG*

2006 Race Results

Pos.	Car/Model	No.	Driver(s)	Entered	Class	Cl. Pos	Laps	Reason
16	911 GT3 RSR	83	Lars-Erik Nielsen (DK)/Pierre Ehret (DE)/Dominik Farnbacher (DE)	Seikel Motorsport (Farnbacher Racing)	LM GT2	2	320	
18	911 GT3 RSR	80	Patrick Long (US)/Johannes van Overbeek (US)/Seth Neiman (US)	Flying Lizard Motorsports	LM GT2	4	309	
22	911 GT3 RS	93	Shinichi Yamaji (JP)/Kazuyuki Nishizawa (JP)/Philip Collin (US)	Team Taisan Advan	LM GT2	5	290	
23	911 GT3 RSR	73	Yves Lambert (BE)/Christian Lefort (BE)/Romain Iannetta (FR)	Ice Pol Racing Team	LM GT2	6	282	
DNF	911 GT3 RSR	89	Thorkild Thyrring (DK)/Xavier Pompidou (FR)/Christian Ried (DE)	Sebah Automotive	LM GT2		256	Propshaft
DNF	911 GT3 RSR	76	Romain Dumas (FR)/Raymond Narac (FR)/Luca Riccitelli (IT)	IMSA Performance Matmut	LM GT2		211	Engine
DNF	911 GT3 RS	91	Yutaka Yamagishi (JP)/Jean-René de Fournoux (FR)/Miroslav Konôpka (SK)	T2M Motorsport	LM GT2		196	Fuel system
DNF	911 GT3 RSR	90	Jörg Bergmeister (DE)/Niclas Jönsson (SE)/Tracy Krohn (US)	Petersen/White Lightning Racing	LM GT2		148	Accident
DNF	911 GT3 RSR	98	Adam Sharpe (GB)/Patrick Bourdais (FR)/Tom Cloet (BE)	Del Bello Racing	LM GT2		115	Accident

2007

June 16–17

Despite all the 911s now sporting the larger 3,795cc engine, one would have to go back to the years 1954, 1962, and 1963 to find previous Le Mans races that had four Porsches or fewer in the field.

The wild and changeable weather conditions at midweek set a pattern that lasted through the weekend, repeatedly lashing spectators and cars alike. But the weather did not deter the encouraging field of fifteen starters in the GT2 class, the largest of the four categories, consisting of five Ferraris, four Porsches, two Spykers, and two Panoz Esperantes—of which the Ferraris were considered the favorites.

Waved away by Roland du Luart, president of the Syndicat Mixte Circuit des 24 Heures du Mans (the Le Mans town and circuit council), the 2007 race got underway under bright, sunny and hot conditions, starting at the earlier time of 3:00 p.m. because of French legislative elections. The skies hinted at some later storm activity, however, and it was not long before the first cloudburst hit the seventy-fifth running of the legendary race. The rain fell in such sheets that visibility was significantly impaired. Several safety car periods resulted, the longest perhaps caused when Mike Rockenfeller slammed his Audi into the barriers at Tertre Rouge, necessitating repairs to the Armco barrier that seemed to take an hour or more. The last hour of the race was also run in similar conditions, as the clouds appeared to want to pour out twelve months' worth of rain in just an hour.

This year also saw the final race entry by Seikel Motorsport. The charismatic Peter Seikel announced his retirement from motorsports at the race, after leading teams that had participated in eleven Le Mans races and been classified as finishers in eight of them. Over the years, Seikel entered a variety of models, including a 968 Turbo, GT2, 911 GT3 R, 911 GT3 RS, 911 GT3 RSR, and 911 (Type 997) GT3 RSR.

The Type 997 Porsche GT3 RSR was powered by the familiar 3,795cc flat six engine, well within the 4,000cc class limit, but this year power was boosted to 465 horsepower. Despite the Porsche marque being represented only by four cars this year, though, a 911 did take the all-important class win as well as third position in the GT2 class.

As official fuel supplier for Le Mans, Shell supplied approximately 260,000 liters (57,174 gallons) of LM24 fuel to the whole grid, a blend specially prepared at their Hamburg facility according to the ACO's regulations.

The No. 71 Seikel Motorsport Porsche 911 GT3 RSR, driven by Horst Felbermayr Jr./Horst Felbermayr Sr./Philip Collin is pushed into position for the start of the race under sunny skies, although dark clouds can be seen in the background. This would be the team's final outing at Le Mans, but it was not destined to be a successful one: the car retired during the evening with engine problems, marking a disappointing end to a memorable Le Mans presence. *Seikel Motorsport*

The No. 71 Seikel Motorsport Porsche 911 GT3 RSR slides around the tricky Tertre Rouge section after one of numerous rainstorms. The strong GT2 class contender posted a DNF after just 68 laps. *Glen Smale*

Now racing in their third consecutive Le Mans, the Flying Lizard team, with their 911 GT3 RSR, driven by Johannes Van Overbeek/Seth Neiman/Jörg Bergmeister, were full of confidence, and after three hours chief engineer Craig Watkins said, "We're doing OK." That confidence didn't last: just after the six-hour mark, while lying second in class, Jörg radioed in that the passenger door had blown out. He was able to pit for a replacement door and rejoined the field without losing a position. Then a mechanical problem in the tenth hour retired the Lizard Porsche. The car's livery remains one of the most memorable in recent Le Mans history. Created by Troy Lee Designs and depicting the team's familiar Flying Lizard image emblazoned across the Porsche's curves, it was used only once on the Lizard Porsche, at this race. *Glen Smale*

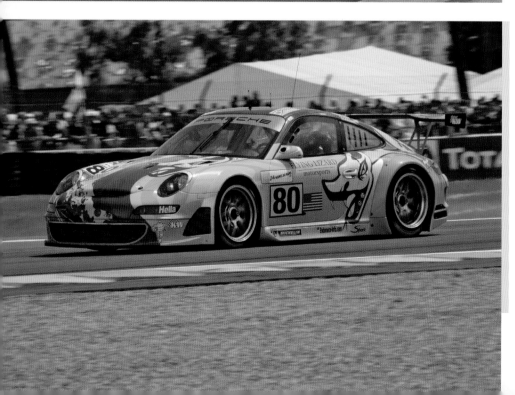

The No. 80 Flying Lizard Motorsport Porsche 911 GT3 RSR of Johannes van Overbeek/Seth Neiman/ Jörg Bergmeister ran in the top three in class during practice and qualifying. At the six-and-a-half-hour mark, however, with Bergmeister running in second position, the rear spoiler collapsed, requiring a pit stop to repair the damage; the time lost pushed the team back to sixth. Nine-and-a-half hours into the race, Johannes van Overbeek was once again moving back up the field and had made it to fifth in class when he reported the loss of sixth gear and pitted for the crew to diagnose the problem. ACO regulations stipulate that a team may not replace an entire transmission, only the transmission's internal components. After much deliberation it was determined that the problem could not be repaired and the car was retired at the ten-hour mark, after having completed 124 laps. *Glen Smale*

The Italian-run Autorlando Sport No. 93 Porsche 911 GT3 RSR of Allan Simonsen/Pierre Ehret/Lars-Erik Nielsen tiptoes through the Esses toward the Tertre Rouge during a sudden downpour. Following their start from fifth in class, Allan Simonsen brought the car up to lead the field at the end of two hours. This was the Italian team's debut at the French classic, and what a baptism it was: just getting to the finish was an achievement in itself. *Glen Smale*

An early evening pit stop for the No. 93 Autorlando Sport 911 GT3 RSR sees Simonsen/Nielsen/Ehret back in the fray in very wet conditions. Although Pierre Ehret and Lars-Erik Nielsen had driven at Le Mans before, it was Allan Simonsen's first outing there, which makes his eleven hours behind the wheel all the more remarkable. *Glen Smale*

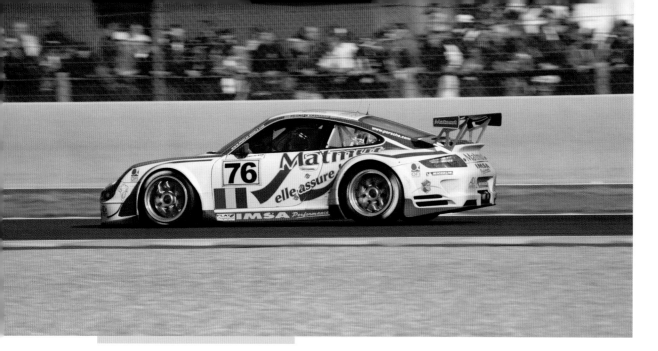

During a sunny moment, the No. 76 Porsche 911 GT3 RSR—sponsored by Matmut, a large French insurance company specializing in motoring, and driven by Raymond Narac/ Richard Lietz/Patrick Long—rounds the bend at the end of the pit straight, approaching the Dunlop Curves for the start of another lap. Only a puncture in the sixth hour blotted an otherwise clean sheet as the car put in one solid lap after the other. The driver team represented a combination of experience and new blood, as the 2007 race was the fourth Le Mans for Long, the third for Narac, and the race debut for Lietz. *Glen Smale*

The No. 76 IMSA Performance Matmut 911 GT3 RSR splashes its way down the pit straight on one of the final laps of the race. From pole position in class, and thanks to a near-faultless run, Long/ Lietz/Narac kept it all together for twenty-four long hours to post fifteenth overall (320 laps) and first in the GT2 class, a stellar showing for Lietz's debut. *Glen Smale*

2007 Race Results

Pos.	Car/Model	No.	Driver(s)	Entered	Class	Cl. Pos	Laps	Reason
15	997 GT3 RSR	76	Patrick Long (US)/Richard Lietz (AT)/Raymond Narac (FR)	IMSA Performance Matmut	LM GT2	1	320	
21	997 GT3 RSR	93	Allan Simonsen (DK)/Pierre Ehret (DE)/Lars-Erik Nielsen (DK)	Autorlando Sport	LM GT2	3	309	
DNF	997 GT3 RSR	80	Johannes van Overbeek (US)/Seth Neiman (US)/Jörg Bergmeister (DE)	Flying Lizard Motorsport	LM GT2		124	Gearbox
DNF	997 GT3 RSR	71	Horst Felbermayr, Jr. (AT)/Horst Felbermayr (AT)/Philip Collin (US)	Seikel Motorsport	LM GT2		68	Engine/electrics

2008

June 14–15

Ten years after Porsche's last factory team victory at Le Mans (the No. 26 GT1 of Laurent Aiello/Allan McNish/Stéphane Ortelli in 1998), the company introduced its latest motorsports weapon to the race-goers at the Circuit de la Sarthe. This time, however, the RS Spyder was not entered by the factory, but instead by two independent teams, one Danish and one Dutch. It was also a decade since any Le Mans had been contested by Porsche in more than one class; those multiclass works entries of the 1960s and 1970s were now nothing but a distant memory.

The GT2 class consisted of a very competitive field of three Porsche 911 GT3 RSRs, seven Ferrari F430 GTs, and two Spyker C8s. Gone were the days when Porsche had things all their own way at Le Mans, but the Stuttgart manufacturer had not been idle since the previous twenty-four-hour event, as the GT3 RSR now featured an improved and much lighter gearbox containing know-how derived from the RS Spyder. A total of only thirty-five of these RSR variants were made at Weissach.

As expected, the two RS Spyders ran away with the LMP2 class, the winning car eventually finishing seven laps ahead of its stablemate, and a whopping twenty-one laps ahead of the third-place No. 35 Pescarolo-Judd. Two full and very successful seasons with the RS Spyder in the ALMS had taught the engineers a lot about the car, and Porsche was keen to see the Spyder add another victory to the already impressive list of accomplishments.

The rate of attrition among the GT2 class contenders was high, and by midnight on Saturday four class runners had already retired. By 3:00 a.m. on Sunday, another car had withdrawn. By the end of the race, six of the initial dozen GT2 starters had fallen by the wayside.

It had become part of Le Mans lore for the Hawaiian Tropic girls to give the crowds something to whistle at. Here they pose around the No. 80 Flying Lizard 911 GT3 RSR, giving the team a bit of a lift. This obviously worked, because Bergmeister/Neiman/van Overbeek gave an excellent account of themselves in the race, despite almost overwhelming setbacks. *Corporate Archives Porsche AG*

Twenty years after Dutchman Jan Lammers' victory at Le Mans (albeit in a Jaguar), and after victories by countryman Gijs van Lennep in 1971 (Martini Porsche 917) and 1976 (Martini Porsche 936), the Dutch van Merksteijn Motorsport team was set to register another victory in the famous event. The No. 34 Porsche RS Spyder, driven by three Dutchmen, Peter van Merksteijn/Jos Verstappen/Jeroen Bleekemolen, would take home the LMP2 class title at the 2008 event. *Corporate Archives Porsche AG*

The main opposition for the van Merksteijn Porsche came from the Danish Essex team, who fielded the same spec RS Spyder. The No. 31 Team Essex RS Spyder, piloted by the experienced Danish pair of John Nielsen and Casper Elgaard, together with the talented German driver Sascha Maassen, built up an early lead over their No. 34 rivals, until their progress was checked by a puncture in the early evening. *Corporate Archives Porsche AG*

The French No. 76 IMSA Performance Matmut Porsche 997 GT3 RSR driven by Patrick Long/Richard Lietz/Raymond Narac posted a DNF as a result of losing a wheel in an accident with the Flying Lizard Porsche at Indianapolis. Long became the second GT2 driver to break the four-minute barrier when he snatched class pole from Henzler in the No. 77 Porsche; Henzler had just broken that mark earlier in the session. The feat didn't count, though, as the pole was wrested away from the French team because of an infringement. *Corporate Archives Porsche AG*

The race started well for Jörg Bergmeister, placed third on the GT2 grid in the No. 80 Flying Lizard Motorsports 911 GT3 RSR (the No. 80 had qualified fourth, but the No. 76 IMSA Performance Matmut Porsche GT2 pole-sitter was moved to the back of the grid because of a prerace infringement). A clean start by Bergmeister saw the No. 80 car move quickly up into first position. An hour and forty minutes into the race, though, Seth Neiman took the wheel for his stint when, just ten minutes later, the No. 76 IMSA Performance Matmut Porsche collided with the Flying Lizard car, putting both cars into the gravel. The No. 76 car couldn't continue the race, but, despite significant damage—including a broken wheel, broken front radiators, and damaged rear suspension—the No. 80 car was able to limp slowly back to the pits. The crew completely rebuilt the car, replacing nearly every piece of bodywork, including the undertray, two front radiators and both sides of the rear suspension; an hour later, Bergmeister took the car back out on the track. Although now down in tenth in class, he regained some lost ground. Around the sixth hour, he handed the car to Seth Neiman, who proceeded to spin on an oil patch and hit the wall, leading to another slow return to the pits for a further ninety-minute rebuild. Despite the battle scars, Bergmeister continued to set the race's fastest times and, with the heavy rate of attrition in the GT2 class, by 3:00 a.m. on Sunday the car was up to seventh in class. As night turned to day, the rain began to fall heavily, requiring a switch to wet tires. Rain continued to fall intermittently throughout the remainder of the race, but the No. 80 Porsche, driven by Bergmeister/Neiman/van Overbeek, eventually crossed the line sixth in class, earning the team the coveted 2008 Prix ESCRA award for excellent team and pit work. *Corporate Archives Porsche AG*

Heavily outnumbered in the GT2 class by the larger-engined Ferrari F430s, the No. 77 Team Felbermayr-Proton Porsche 997 GT3 RSR was the highest-finishing Porsche in its class. Suffering clutch bearing problems around the ninth hour, the Felbermayr Porsche fell back and was beaten to the line by no fewer than four Ferraris. Alex Davison/Wolf Henzler/Horst Felbermayr Sr. brought their Porsche home fifth in class and twenty-seventh overall. Although the result was disappointing, Henzler did have the honor of being the first driver to break the four-minute barrier in a GT2 machine, clocking a fastest lap in qualifying of 3:59.072. *John Brooks*

The No. 31 Team Essex Porsche RS Spyder of Nielsen/Elgaard/Maassen pitted at 9:30 p.m. for a tire change due to a puncture, which handed the class lead to the No. 34 Porsche. An industry source pointed out that the Essex car was running on Dunlop tires in 2008, which caused vibrations in the car. As a result, it suffered two blowouts during the course of the race, which had a significant impact on the team's progress. The blue Team Essex Porsche was again delayed, this time for five laps, when it had to pit for repairs at 4:00 a.m. on Sunday. This enabled their opposite number to stretch their lead in the LMP2 class. *Corporate Archives Porsche AG*

Driving a relatively trouble-free race, the No. 34 van Merksteijn Porsche RS Spyder finished an impressive tenth overall, from fourteenth on the starting grid, and first in the LMP2 class. Peter van Merksteijn/Jos Verstappen/Jeroen Bleekemolen had driven a clever race, putting in multiple stints behind the wheel when the Porsche pitted to stretch their lead—and it worked. *Corporate Archives Porsche AG*

2008 Race Results

Pos.	Car/Model	No.	Driver(s)	Entered	Class	Cl. Pos	Laps	Reason
10	RS Spyder	34	Peter van Merksteijn (NL)/Jos Verstappen (NL)/Jeroen Bleekemolen (NL)	Van Merksteijn Motorsport	LM P2	1	354	
12	RS Spyder	31	John Nielsen (DK)/Casper Elgaard (DK)/Sascha Maassen (DE)	Team Essex	LM P2	2	347	
27	997 GT3 RSR	77	Alex Davison (AU)/Wolf Henzler (DE)/Horst Felbermayr, Sr. (AT)	Team Felbermayr-Proton	LM GT2	5	309	
32	997 GT3 RSR	80	Jörg Bergmeister (DE)/Seth Neiman (US)/Johannes van Overbeek (US)	Flying Lizard Motorsports	LM GT2	6	289	
DNF	997 GT3 RSR	76	Patrick Long (US)/Richard Lietz (AT)/Raymond Narac (FR)	IMSA Performance Matmut	LM GT2		27	Accident

PORSCHE RS SPYDER

At the prompting of its North American subsidiary, Porsche Cars North America (PCNA), Porsche set about designing and building a completely new sports prototype for customer racing in America's most important sports car series, the American Le Mans Series. Compliant with the technical specifications for the LMP2 class (Le Mans prototypes eligible for the ALMS, the European Le Mans Series [LMS], and the Le Mans race itself), it was the first purpose-built factory race car since the successful 911 GT1 of 1998.

Reviving an earlier partnership from the 1970s, Penske Motorsports was to race the new prototype in the final two ALMS races of the 2005 season, followed by a full program in 2006. Works drivers Lucas Luhr and Sascha Maassen shared the cockpit during an initial three-day test program under race-like conditions at the Estoril circuit in southern Portugal, which proved successful and produced some encouraging results.

In recognition of its long motorsports tradition with open sports prototypes, Porsche named the new racer the RS Spyder, linking this newcomer with the company's remarkable success story in endurance racing that began as far back as 1953 with the Spyder 550 1500 RS.

The purpose-built 3,397cc 90-degree V-8 racing engine built by Porsche for long-distance events developed 480 horsepower from its 3.4-liter displacement while fitted with an air volume restrictor as required by the regulations. With the new RS Spyder weighing in at 1,709 pounds (775 kilograms), this was exactly in line with the ACO regulations. Built around a full carbon-fiber monocoque chassis, the prototype racer was driven through a sequential six-speed dog-shift gearbox.

To say that the new racer exceeded the Stuttgart engineers' expectations in 2006 would probably have been the understatement of the year, as the RS Spyder racked up seven class wins and seven class seconds, including winning the ALMS LMP2 Championship in its debut season. In the process, the RS Spyder snatched a sensational one–two overall victory on the winding Mid-Ohio racetrack in May, beating the more powerful LMP1 prototypes to the line— much to their embarrassment.

Porsche presented the 2007 RS Spyder to the public for the first time at the Paris Motor Show between September 30 and October 15, 2006. Now featuring an upgraded chassis, an optimized rear spoiler and rear diffuser, and a more powerful engine (503 horsepower), it also appeared at the Geneva Motor Show in March 2007 before the start of that year's season. The improvements not only enhanced the aerodynamic efficiency of the car, but also extended the range of setup options for different kinds of racetracks.

If the public and racing authorities thought that 2006 had been nothing more than good luck in their first season, then 2007 would confirm the nagging suspicion in the back of their minds that Porsche was back. In 2007, the RS Spyder was the dominant vehicle in the ALMS, notching up no fewer than eleven wins in twelve races, including eight overall wins. Raised eyebrows at the end of the 2006 season had turned to feelings of déjà vu the following year, as shades of the 917's dominance in the 1970s came flooding back.

In January 2008, Porsche announced that its model RS Spyder for the year had had its weight increased by regulation to 1,764 pounds (800 kilograms) in the ALMS series and 1,819 pounds (825 kilograms) for Le Mans and the European LMS series, while the LMP1 class cars had their weight limit reduced, thus widening the performance gap between the two classes. The RS Spyder's power output had also been restricted to 476 horsepower, and the fuel tank size was reduced by 2 gallons to 20 gallons (10 liters to 80 liters), necessitating at least one extra refueling in a typical 1,000-kilometer LMS event.

Looking to improve the Spyder's performance under the new restrictions, Porsche sought to enhance the racer's aerodynamic efficiency as Martijn Meijs, race engineer for the RS Spyder customer teams in the Le Mans Series, explained, "The changes at the beginning of the season were small upgrades in the bodywork, and some aerodynamic tuning mainly based on high downforce. We modified the 'flicks' [the small upward-sloping winglets located on the lower front wings] and also the nose changed a bit, we made it a little bit bigger, and we had louvers in the rear that we didn't have in 2007."

When it came to setting the car up for Le Mans, Meijs commented, "For Le Mans we run a Le Mans kit, as most cars do, which has far less drag, based on the long straights and the faster corners. There we run a completely different front nose with very small 'flicks.' It is just to reduce the air resistance, because the straights are so long, you are focused on the speed and not on the lack of downforce."

The RS Spyder at the Geneva Motor Show on press days March 6–7, 2007. *Glen Smale*

2009

June 13–14

For the seventy-seventh running of the Le Mans in 2009, the starter of honor was none other than Luca di Montezemolo, president of Ferrari. This year's race marked the sixtieth anniversary of the first of Ferrari's nine victories at the Circuit de la Sarthe back in 1949 by a Ferrari 166MM. In recognition of the company's sporting achievements, no fewer than ten Ferrari F430s were down on the entry list, taking a leaf out of Porsche's book when the GT classes were swamped by 911s, and thereby ensuring a victory.

The GT2 class in 2009 boasted seventeen entrants, comprising ten Ferrari F430 GTCs, five Porsche 997 GT3 RSRs, a lone Spyker C8, and one Aston Martin V8 Vantage. The new GT3 RSR was fitted with a larger version of the 3,996cc flat six engine, now developing in excess of 450 horsepower. In the LMP2 class the RS Spyder was fully expected to deliver the goods, as the Porsche prototype had proved itself in the ALMS and LMS series.

Qualifying saw Porsche cars in pole position in both the LMP2 and GT2 classes, signaling a good start for the Stuttgart manufacturer. For Denmark's Essex Racing, Casper Elgaard qualified the RS Spyder on pole in the LMP2 class with a time of 3:37.720. In the GT2 class, Porsche works drivers Jörg Bergmeister (No. 80 Flying Lizard Motorsport team) and Marc Lieb (No. 77 Team Felbermayr-Proton team) were separated by just 0.03 seconds at the top of the field, with Bergmeister just taking pole position in class.

The race itself was a different matter. From a Porsche perspective, this must rank as one of the Stuttgart manufacturer's poorest years in terms of finishers and results. Only one RS Spyder crossed the line (albeit by the impressively large margin of fourteen laps) and not a single 911 was classified as a finisher. One would have to go back to 1963 to find the last Le Mans where Porsche only had one finisher, a gap of forty-six years, a result that could at best be regarded as dismal.

Despite practice being intermittently very wet, the start of the race, which was waved off by Montezemolo at 3:00 p.m., was hot and dry. Of the fifty-five starters, thirty-two were classified as finishers, of which ten (from seventeen starters) were in the GT2 class, which was perhaps predictably won by Ferrari.

"Carefully now!" The Japanese-entered No. 5 Navi Team Goh Porsche RS Spyder is wheeled away after its successful scrutineering. *Corporate Archives Porsche AG*

For the second year in a row, the French-entered No. 76 IMSA Performance Matmut Porsche 997 GT3 RSR failed to finish. Although the Patrick Long/Raymond Narac/Patrick Pilet Porsche briefly held the class lead just before the end of the first hour, setbacks dropped the car down the order, where it maintained a steady third place for two-thirds of the race. A problem with the engine restrictor on Saturday night, and power transmission problems that cropped up later, put an end to their promising run on Sunday morning. *John Brooks*

Following a late withdrawal by another team, Endurance Asia Team was given the nod to join the entry list for the 2009 event. Founded this year, they were a Hong Kong–based racing team run by Thierry Perrier's Perspective Racing squad. This marked the first-ever Chinese Le Mans entry. Sponsored by the Mediterranean Shipping Company in its distinctive orange livery, the Porsche 997 GT3 RSR was driven by Darryl O'Young/Philippe Hesnault/Plamen Kralev. It was beset by problems from the start: after just three hours, Bulgarian FIA GT3 driver Kralev (the first Bulgarian to compete at Le Mans) was brought to a standstill on the Hunaudières for more than an hour and a half with a fuel pump problem, but it later made back to the pits where O'Young took the wheel. The No. 75 Porsche would finally be retired on Sunday morning following gearbox woes that led to clutch failure. The Endurance Asia Team car was the only GT2-class Porsche on Dunlop rubber. *Corporate Archives Porsche AG*

Leading the GT2 qualifying table was the No. 77 Team Felbermayr-Proton Porsche 997 GT3 RSR, until they were beaten to the punch by Jörg Bergmeister in the No. 80 Flying Lizard Porsche. Lying in second place in the GT2 standings and thirty-ninth on the starting grid, Marc Lieb/Richard Lietz/Wolf Henzler drove a steady race and gave the team a sense of optimism. After just two hours, though, things came to an abrupt end when, only 100 meters from the entrance to the pit lane, the engine cut out and failed to restart, owing to a fault with the reserve fuel system. As the regulations do not permit a car to be retrieved outside the pit lane area, the team could not assist the stricken driver and the otherwise technically sound 911. The GT2 class leader at the time was forced to retire. *Corporate Archives Porsche AG*

Following a hard-fought race the previous year, the American No. 80 Flying Lizard Motorsport team arrived at the 2009 Le Mans event loaded with race experience and full of confidence. It would all end in tears when the Jörg Bergmeister/Seth Neiman/Darren Law Porsche 997 GT3 RSR crashed in the early morning hours. The American Porsche had been steadily moving up the tables when Darren Law collided heavily with the barriers at the PlayStation Chicane. *Corporate Archives Porsche AG*

Following an absence of a few years, Japanese Team Goh returned to Le Mans in 2009 with the No. 5 Navi Team Goh RS Spyder, driven by Seiji Ara/Keisuke Kunimoto/Sascha Maassen. Kunimoto was the only newcomer to the circuit in the team, while Sascha Maassen needed no introduction to Le Mans and Seiji Ara was the overall winner in 2004 with the No. 5 Team Goh Audi R8, which he shared with Tom Kristensen and Rinaldo Capello. With the Porsche running like clockwork, there was a momentary scare when, just before the PlayStation Chicane, the two close-running RS Spyders hit a patch of oil that caused the two to slide into each other. Kunimoto nudged the Essex car, resulting in both vehicles pitting to have various body parts replaced. The Goh car took longer than the Essex car to repair because of front-end bodywork and suspension damage. With 339 laps completed and just one hour left to go before the end of the race, the No. 5 RS Spyder was being driven hard by Seiji Ara in an effort to catch the Essex car. With a substantial ten-lap lead on the third-placed car, Ara spun on some oil dropped by another competitor just before the first chicane on the Mulsanne Straight, causing the Porsche to leave the track and collide with the barriers. Although Ara was uninjured, the DNF was a particularly hard result to swallow, especially when second place in class had seemed assured. *John Brooks*

The Team Essex crew was able to enter the 2009 Le Mans race thanks to their win in the Michelin Green X Challenge the previous year. This award is calculated on the ratio between lap times and fuel consumption, and in 2008 the RS Spyder won the energy efficiency challenge at the 24 Hours of Le Mans, the ALMS, and the European LMS. "This is a huge success for our Danish team, which only began competing in long-distance racing last year," said driver Emmanuel Collard. In recognition of this achievement, the No. 31 Team Essex Porsche RS Spyder was symbolically painted in green livery as the official ambassador of this award. The Essex Team enjoyed the support of the Porsche factory, who had supplied technical and data personnel (the mechanics were all Team Essex) and included race engineer Owen Hayes and driver Emmanuel Collard, while Bo Nielsen was the team manager. On the direction of team owner Peter Halvorsen, Casper Elgaard was given the responsibility of qualifying the car, and he promptly claimed class pole. A team source revealed, "The race

went very smoothly, we had two incidents, two collisions with other cars—one where we picked up a slow puncture in the left-hand rear tire, so we came straight in for a tire change. The other contact was with the Goh Porsche and we lost the rear wing, some bodywork, and the diffuser was damaged. It looked like it was due to be a long repair, maybe ten or twenty minutes, but a hundred-and-twenty seconds later the car was ready to go." Triple-stinting by race engineer Hayes put the Essex car ahead of Team Goh, and in the end just two laps separated the two RS Spyders before the Japanese car's retirement. The Danish team went on to win the Michelin Green X Challenge yet again at the 2009 Le Mans, a fitting tribute to the two Danes, Casper Elgaard and Kristian Poulsen (who debuted at Le Mans this year) and the experienced French driver Emmanuel Collard. After the No. 31 prototype had crossed the line in tenth overall and first in the LMP2 class, Porsche works driver Collard added, "We didn't have the slightest technical problem." *John Brooks*

2009 Race Results

Pos.	Car/Model	No.	Driver(s)	Entered	Class	Cl. Pos	Laps	Reason
10	RS Spyder	31	Emmanuel Collard (FR)/Casper Elgaard (DK)/Kristian Poulsen (DK)	Team Essex	LM P2	1	357	
DNF	RS Spyder	5	Seiji Ara (JP)/Keisuke Kunimoto (JP)/Sascha Maassen (DE)	Navi Team Goh	LM P2		339	Accident
DNF	997 GT3 RSR	76	Patrick Long (US)/Raymond Narac (FR)/Patrick Pilet (FR)	IMSA Performance Matmut	LM GT2		265	Gearbox
NC	997 GT3 RSR	75	Darryl O'Young (HK)/Philippe Hesnault (FR)/Plamen Kralev (BG)	Endurance Asia Team	LM GT2		196	Retired
DNF	997 GT3 RSR	80	Jörg Bergmeister (DE)/Seth Neiman (US)/Darren Law (US)	Flying Lizard Motorsport	LM GT2		194	Accident
DNF	997 GT3 RSR	70	Horst Felbermayr, Jr. (AT)/Horst Felbermayr, Sr. (AT)/Michel Lecourt (FR)	IMSA Performance Matmut	LM GT2		102	Engine
DNF	997 GT3 RSR	77	Marc Lieb (DE)/Richard Lietz (AT)/Wolf Henzler (DR)	Team Felbermayr-Proton	LM GT2		24	Out of fuel

CHAPTER 7

2010s
... and Beyond

Having set the fastest qualifying time, the Swiss driver, Neel Jani, was given the privilege of starting the race. During the race, the No. 2 Porsche driven by Marc Lieb/Romain Dumas/Neel Jani performed like clockwork, pitting only for tires, fuel, or a driver change. Although the racing up front had been agonizingly close for much of the race, in the closing stages the order looked set, with the No. 5 Toyota in first place followed home by the No. 2 Porsche. As the clock ticked towards the 3:00 p.m. finish on Sunday afternoon, the No. 5 Toyota slowed noticeably on the penultimate lap and then crawled to a stop after crossing the start/finish line. Coming up behind the stricken Toyota was the No. 2 Porsche, but as the Toyota limped away, the No. 2 Porsche passed the Toyota and took the checkered flag. This dramatic end handed Porsche its 18th Le Mans victory, much to the delight of Porsche enthusiasts around the world. *Glen Smale*

World Championship Status

While the decade of the aughts did not see Porsche represented in large numbers at Le Mans, there was a whisper on the breeze in the early 2010s that the factory might be returning to Le Mans with a works team. But there are questions a manufacturer must ask before considering whether to participate in a series: What budget is required to develop a car that can compete and win? How significant is the series? Will it bring a return on our investment?

In the early 2010s, manufacturers and private teams could compete on the international stage in the FIA GT1 World Championship or the Intercontinental Le Mans Cup (ILMC). The FIA GT1 World Championship featured multiple grand tourer race cars based on production road cars conforming to GT1 (2010–2011) and GT3 (2012) regulations. Although these races were held on multiple continents, the races were only a single hour in duration, and they weren't endurance races. The ILMC, on the other hand, commenced in 2010 with three events on three continents, expanding to seven events in 2011.

For 2012, the ACO and the FIA announced the creation of a new FIA World Endurance Championship (WEC) to replace the ILMC. Using similar rules to the ILMC, the FIA WEC was the first endurance series of world championship status since the World Sportscar Championship ceased in 1992, bringing to an end the ever-popular Group C era.

The WEC effectively brought the 24 Hours of Le Mans into the World Championship, with double points for the winners of this classic endurance race. In 2013, Porsche announced that it would enter the WEC with a pair of 911 RSRs, the first time the manufacturer had officially participated on the international stage since its win at Le Mans back in 1998.

While the factory GT cars certainly raised some interest among the enthusiastic Porsche supporters around the world, the dedicated *Porschephiles* were really waiting for the arrival of new Porsche prototypes, which were slated to appear in 2014. These prototype hybrids, or LMP1-Hs, became the top category for the factory prototype teams in 2014, effectively splitting the LMP1 category into two separate categories: hybrid and non-hybrid.

It was certainly a testing year for the Porsche LMP1-H, as the team only scored one victory—at the last race in São Paulo, Brazil—in the WEC in its debut season. Although Audi won at Le Mans in 2014, the World Championship went to Toyota that year. In the Le Mans race, the No. 14 Porsche 919 finished in eleventh place and the No. 20 Porsche was marked as "did not complete" (NC). But in Porsche's second year with the 919 Hybrid, they began to show their true colors, winning the World Manufacturers' Championship in 2015, 2016, and 2017.

Although Porsche's GTE entries did not shine throughout the 2013 season, they did win the big one in June, finishing 1–2 in the Pro class that year. The following season saw them on the podium at Le Mans (third place), while 2015 and 2016 were quite disastrous by comparison. In 2017 they managed a fourth place at Le Mans, but in 2018 they were back with a vengeance, finishing 1–2 in the GTE Pro class once again. In the 2019 race, the Porsche 911 RSRs finished second and third behind a Ferrari 488 GTE Evo. The 2020 race was not a glorious one for Porsche, as their two works GTE Pro cars were outclassed.

The factory cars were well supported by the privateer teams during these years, so Porsche can look back at the decade with a sense of satisfaction for a job well done, with numerous victories in the LMP1, GTE Pro, and GTE Am classes.

2010

June 12–13

There was no question that there was going to be an almighty battle between the works Peugeots and Audis, and the rest of the field was just going to have to stay out of their way. More of an uncertainty, however, was the weather, and, if Friday night was anything to go by, then rain looked like it was going to play a part in the seventy-eighth running of the race.

This year marked an important double milestone for Porsche, as it was the fortieth anniversary of Porsche's first win at Le Mans with the No. 23 Herrmann/Attwood victory in 1970 with the Salzburg 917. This year also represented the sixtieth year of competition at Le Mans for the Stuttgart manufacturer, since the 356 made its first tentative appearance in the twenty-four hour classic endurance race back in 1951 in which it won the 1,100cc class.

It was from such humble beginnings that Porsche's motorsports heritage grew, and Ferry Porsche had been quick to realize the publicity value of winning races. The story of the company's rise to the top of the sport in the ensuing years is charted in these pages, but the resultant boom in sales and brand popularity exceeded the wildest expectations of even the most forward-thinking Porsche employees all those years ago. The 2010 race saw just half-a-dozen privately entered GT3 RSRs in the race, however, which was a far cry from the heady days of the 1970s when upwards of thirty race cars (such as in 1971, with 34 entries across three classes) belonging to the Stuttgart brand appeared on the entry list.

Comparisons with the 2010 race show how things had changed. The highest-placed Porsche on the starting grid in 2010 was the No. 77 GT3 RSR of Marc Lieb/Richard Lietz/Wolf Henzler in a fourth-class position, but this was itself a promotion from fifth place after the Risi Ferrari was sent to the back of the grid because of an aerodynamic infringement. Worryingly for Porsche, though, as the 2010 race got underway, was the fact that their cars were just not on the pace, as the early battle for class honors saw the works Corvettes and the Ferraris out in front.

Of the six Stuttgart entrants this year, five would cross the finish line. A good result, especially as, importantly, a Porsche would take class honors. But the rate of attrition (only nine out of seventeen GT2 cars finished) among the Corvettes and Ferraris played its part in the outcome. While Audi claimed all the big headlines on Sunday following their ninth Le Mans victory, Porsche GT3 RSRs filled positions 1–3–5–7–8 in the GT2 class, which speaks volumes for the car's reliability, making this the Stuttgart manufacturer's first class victory since 2007, and only their second in the last five years.

In stark contrast with the torrential rainstorm during Friday night of this year's race, the Saturday 3:00 p.m. start took place in warm and dry conditions, even if the track was still a bit damp in places.

On their sixth visit to Le Mans, the American-entered No. 80 Flying Lizard Motorsport 997 GT3 RSR, driven by Seth Neiman, Darren Law, and Jörg Bergmeister, bowed out after just sixty-one laps with a damaged radiator and other mechanical woes. Having started ninth in class, all three drivers put in reliable stints until midway through the fourth hour, when radiator and front undertray damage required an unscheduled pit stop. On the car's out lap, however, just before 8:00 p.m. and now lying back fourteenth in class, further mechanical damage ruled the No. 80 Porsche out of the race, a disappointing withdrawal for the team as much as for the fans. It was the only Porsche retirement in 2010. *Glen Smale*

At the end of the second hour, the No. 88 Team Felbermayr-Proton Porsche 997 GT3 RSR, driven by the elder and younger Felbermayr and Slovakian Miro Konôpka, was lying fourteenth in class and forty-ninth overall. At the twenty-two-hour mark, the car was eighth in the vastly diminished GT2 class, in which only nine cars were left running. It finished in that place, making it the last Porsche finisher. *Glen Smale*

The No. 75 Belgian-entered Prospeed Competition Porsche GT3 RSR, driven by Paul van Splunteren/ Niek Hommerson/Louis Machiels, crests the brow under the Dunlop Bridge at 8:45 p.m. on Saturday while tenth in class. At around 8:00 a.m. on Sunday, the No. 75 Prospeed Porsche spun just before Tertre Rouge, smacking backwards into the barriers. It recovered, but performed another spin an hour later, this time at the Mulsanne Corner, and the marshals immediately set about getting it back on the track. While seventh in class at around noon on Sunday (18 hours), the blue-and-white Porsche came into the pits with its left rear tire shredded, having picked up some debris on the track. The car held on to its seventh place in class until the end of the race. *Glen Smale*

In fifth place on the starting grid, the No. 76 French-entered IMSA Performance Matmut Porsche GT3 RSR was driven by Raymond Narac/Patrick Pilet/Patrick Long. At quarter distance (six hours), the car was lying sixth in class, the second of the Porsches. At the halfway mark (twelve hours), it was up to fourth in class, a lap down on its nearest Stuttgart rival, the No. 77 Porsche. *Glen Smale*

At the end of the first ninety minutes, the Italian-entered No. 97 BMS Scuderia Italia SPA Porsche, driven by three Le Mans first-timers, Marco Holzer/Richard Westbrook/Timo Scheider, was lying fifth in class behind a pair of Corvettes and a pair of Ferraris. At 7:30 a.m. on Sunday, while still fifth, the No. 97 Porsche limped into the pits with a shredded tire, but by 9:00 a.m. it was back up and into fourth in class. The car had its fair share of mishaps, including a broken damper as well as clutch and steering problems. It overcame these setbacks, and the red Porsche finished well, even though it was only running on five cylinders at the end. Here the car enters Arnage just after noon on Sunday on its way to third in class, making it the second Porsche across the finish line, securing a fourteenth place overall. *Glen Smale*

Starting from fourth in class, No. 77 Team Felbermayr-Proton 997 GT3 RSR, driven by Porsche works drivers Marc Lieb, Richard Lietz, and Wolf Henzler, stuck to their race strategy while the Corvettes and Ferraris fought each other for class leadership. Although the Porsche didn't have the pace of the works Corvettes or the Ferraris, it was blessed with rock-solid reliability. At 10:00 p.m. on Saturday, the car had maintained its fourth place in class, but at the halfway mark the leading Porsche was up to third in class behind the two works Corvettes and just one lap down on the leading No. 64 Corvette. When the No. 63 Corvette retired after seventeen hours, Lieb moved

up to second in class behind the No. 64 Corvette. An hour later, the No. 77 Porsche took over the class lead following the attack on the No. 64 Corvette by Anthony Davidson in No. 1 LMP1 Peugeot. At three-quarter distance, the Porsche was also three laps ahead of the leading No. 50 GT1 Saleen, and by 1:00 p.m. the Porsche was two laps clear of the second-place No. 89 Hankook Ferrari, also in the GT2 class. After an almost trouble-free run, the No. 77 Felbermayr Porsche took class honors and finished eleventh overall, ending a barren run at Le Mans for the Stuttgart manufacturer since their GT2 class win there back in 2007. *Glen Smale*

2010 Race Results

Pos.	Car/Model	No.	Driver(s)	Entered	Class	Cl. Pos	Laps	Reason
11	997 GT3 RSR	77	Marc Lieb (DE)/Richard Lietz (AT)/Wolf Henzler (DE)	Team Felbermayr-Proton	LM GT2	1	338	
14	997 GT3 RSR	97	Marco Holzer (DE)/Richard Westbrook (GB)/Timo Scheider (DE)	BMS Scuderia Italia SPA	LM GT2	3	327	
17	997 GT3 RSR	76	Raymond Narac (FR)/Patrick Pilet (FR)/Patrick Long (US)	IMSA Performance Matmut	LM GT2	5	321	
21	997 GT3 RSR	75	Paul van Splunteren (NL)/Niek Hommerson (NL)/Louis Machiels (BE)	Prospeed Competition	LM GT2	7	317	
24	997 GT3 RSR	88	Horst Felbermayr, Sr. (AT)/Horst Felbermayr, Jr. (AT)/Miro Konôpka (SK)	Team Felbermayr-Proton	LM GT2	8	304	
DNF	997 GT3 RSR	80	Seth Neiman (US)/Darren Law (US)/Jörg Bergmeister (DE)	Flying Lizard Motorsport	LM GT2		61	Radiator

2011

June 11–12

The seventy-ninth Grand Prix of Endurance was also the third round of the 2011 Intercontinental Le Mans Cup. This year's race saw one of the most varied and interesting grids, with eighteen entries in the GTE Pro class alone. This was made up of six different manufacturers, comprising twelve teams, and included six Ferrari 458 Italia GT2 and five Porsche 997 GT3 RSR. In the GTE Am class, the variation was similar, with ten entries spread across five manufacturers. Of the nine teams, four entered Ferrari F430 GTEs and three teams with Porsche 997 GT3 RSRs. Such a variety of manufacturers, teams, and mechanical platforms could only ensure an entertaining twenty-four hours of racing.

The race got underway under warm and sunny skies and, as expected up front, the Audis shot off into the distance followed closely by the Peugeots. But within the first hour, one of the biggest accidents seen at Le Mans in recent years took place. Allan McNish in the No. 3 Audi attempted an overtaking maneuver on the inside of the No. 58 Ferrari 458 Italia GT2 just after the Dunlop Bridge. But with the door closing as the two cars drew level, the result was going to be unpleasant. The impact as the Audi thumped into the barriers was substantial. Although, fortunately, both drivers were unhurt, the barrier repair took forty-five minutes.

It was only in the seventh hour of racing that a Porsche rose to the top of its class, and this was the No. 70 Larbre Compétition Porsche 997 GT3 RSR, a position it held for the next three hours. It took the lead again in the thirteenth hour for another three hours, but remained right on the tail of the class-leading Corvette. While the GTE Pro didn't see a Porsche at the top throughout the race, it was the No. 75 Porsche that rose to third place after six hours where it remained in that position for the next five hours. The No. 80 Flying Lizard Porsche carried the flag for a couple of hours before the No. 77 Team Felbermayr-Proton Porsche moved into third position with five hours left to run, slipping to fourth place at the finish.

The start of the 2011 race sees the No. 75 Porsche lead away a group of GTE cars. The fourth car is the No. 80 Flying Lizard Porsche, while the No. 77 Felbermayr car can be seen just pulling away from the wall. At this stage the cars embark on a formation lap before twenty-four hours of hard racing commences.
Glen Smale

The Austrian pair, Horst Felbermayr Sr. and Jr. (father and son), was behind the wheel of the 4-liter No. 63 Proton Competition Porsche 997 GT3 RSR with Christian Ried of Germany. Their race in the LMGTE Am class was not a happy one, and they retired after 199 laps. *Glen Smale*

A regular at Le Mans was the ever-colorful No. 81 Flying Lizard Motorsports Porsche 997 GT3 RSR driven by the all-American trio of Seth Neiman/Darren Law/Spencer Pumpelly. Their race this year came to an end after just 211 laps. This photograph was taken on the Saturday afternoon of the race weekend. *Glen Smale*

Marc Goossens/Marco Holzer/Jaap van Lagen drove the Belgian-entered No. 75 Prospeed Competition Porsche 997 GT3 RSR, completing 293 laps and finishing twenty-third overall and ninth in the LMGTE Pro class. *Glen Smale*

The all-French trio of Christophe Bourret, Pascal Gibon, and Jean-Philippe Belloc was behind the wheel of the French-entered No. 70 Larbre Compétition Porsche 997 GT3 RSR. The car finished twenty-first overall and an excellent second in the GTE Am class, having completed 301 laps. *Glen Smale*

The No. 80 Flying Lizard Motorsports Porsche 997 GT3 RSR is shown here in full flight on Sunday morning exiting the Tertre Rouge. Jörg Bergmeister, Lucas Luhr, and Patrick Long completed 310 laps, finishing eighteenth overall and sixth in the LMGTE Pro class. *Glen Smale*

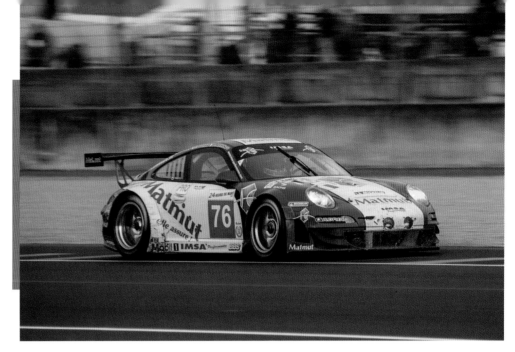

The all-French trio and Le Mans regulars, Raymond Narac/Patrick Pilet/Nicolas Armindo, brought their No. 76 IMSA Performance Matmut Porsche 997 GT3 RSR home in seventeenth place overall and fifth in the LMGTE Pro class, having completed 311 laps. This photograph was taken early on Sunday morning as the Porsche negotiated the Dunlop Curve at top speed just before the uphill section to the bridge. *Glen Smale*

Porsche works drivers, Marc Lieb/Wolf Henzler/Richard Lietz, drove a solid race to bring their No. 77 Team Felbermayr-Proton Porsche 997 GT3 RSR home in sixteenth place overall and fourth in the LMGTE Pro class. In this photograph, the car lifts a wheel as it jumps the baguettes in the Ford Chicane. Completing 312 laps, they were the highest-placed Porsche finisher this year. *Glen Smale*

2011 Race Results

Pos.	Car/Model	No.	Driver(s)	Entered	Class	Cl. Pos	Laps	Reason
16	997 GT3 RSR	77	Marc Lieb (DE)/Richard Lietz (AT)/Wolf Henzler (DE)	Team Felbermayr-Proton	GTE Pro	4	312	
17	997 GT3 RSR	76	Raymond Narac (FR)/Patrick Pilet (FR)/Nicolas Armindo (FR)	IMSA Performance Matmut	GTE Pro	5	311	
18	997 GT3 RSR	80	Jörg Bergmeister (DE)/Lucas Luhr (DE)/Patrick Long (US)	Flying Lizard Motorsport	GTE Pro	6	310	
21	997 GT3 RSR	70	Christophe Bourret (FR)/Pascal Gibon (FR)/Jean-Philippe Belloc (FR)	Larbre Compétition	GTE Am	2	301	
23	997 GT3 RSR	75	Marc Goossens (BE)/Marco Holzer (DE)/Jaap van Lagen (NL)	Prospeed Competition	GTE Pro	8	293	
DNF	997 GT3 RSR	81	Seth Neiman (US)/Darren Law (US)/Spencer Pumpelly (US)	Flying Lizard Motorsports	GTE Am		211	Engine failure
DNF	997 GT3 RSR	63	Horst Felbermayr, Sr. (AT)/Horst Felbermayr, Jr. (AT)/Christian Ried (DE)	Proton Competition	GTE Am		199	Retired
DNF	997 GT3 RSR	88	Nick Tandy (UK)/Abdulaziz Al Faisal (SA)/Bryce Miller (US)	Team Felbermayr-Proton	GTE Pro		169	Retired

2012

June 16–17

Although Porsche had not fielded a full works team in any class of motorsports for many years, they had obviously remained deeply involved in the Grand Touring classes through their Supercup, Carrera Cup, and Le Mans customer teams. Nevertheless, many racing fans were united in feeling that there was something missing from the sport, and that was a Porsche factory team. Thankfully, this would be the last time in the decade that they would have to endure a Le Mans race without an official Porsche works team.

The GTE Pro class included only two Porsche 911 RSRs (997) among the significantly depleted number of just nine entries, half that of the previous year. Ferrari fielded double the number of Porsches this year, entering four cars. In the GTE Am class, the number of Porsche entries was more numerous, with five cars listed, compared with three the previous year. It should be remembered that the GTE Pro and Am classes are structured so that the Am cars in the current year are actually the Pro cars from the previous year, meaning that a well-populated Am class in any year relies on a healthy Pro entry from the year before.

The Porsches in the GTE Am class gave an excellent account of themselves in qualifying, as the No. 79 Flying Lizard Porsche was in first place, followed by the No. 75 Prospeed Competition car in second place in class. In fact, sandwiched in between these two GTE Am Porsches was the No. 80 Flying Lizard GTE Pro Porsche. The No. 77 Porsche was the fastest Porsche back in sixth place in the GTE Pro class, with the No. 80 car one position back in seventh place in the Pro class.

Neither of the two GTE Pro Porsches finished the race this year, but in the GTE Am class it was a different matter, with the No. 67 IMSA Performance Matmut car finishing second in class and the No. 79 Flying Lizard Porsche crossing the line in fourth place.

On the grid—the drivers and crew line up next to their cars before the start while the French national anthem is played. Standing next to the No. 67 IMSA Performance Matmut Porsche 911 RSR (997) is Raymond Narac *nearest the camera*, Nicolas Armindo *obscured*, and Anthony Pons. *Glen Smale*

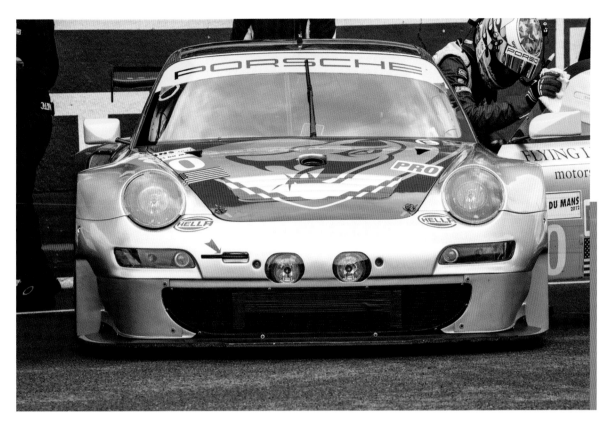

Jörg Bergmeister climbs aboard the American-entered No. 80 Flying Lizard Motorsports Porsche 911 RSR (997). Driven by Jörg Bergmeister/Patrick Long/Marco Holzer, No. 80 retired with just 114 laps completed. Long slid on gravel, which another vehicle had just spread on the track at the first chicane, then smashed into a stack of tires. He couldn't make it back to the pits. *Glen Smale*

The only remaining Porsche in the GTE Pro class was the No. 77 Team Felbermayr-Proton Porsche 911 RSR (997), driven by Richard Lietz/Marc Lieb/Wolf Henzler. They weren't destined to finish: their car came to a standstill on the Hunaudières straight with Marc Lieb behind the wheel, having completed 184 laps. The car retired with gearbox damage while running in fourth place. *Glen Smale*

Driving the Belgian-entered No. 75 Prospeed Competition Porsche 911 RSR (997) were Abdulaziz Al Faisal/Bret Curtis/Sean Edwards. Their race was cut short following an accident after 180 laps. *Glen Smale*

German team owner Christian Ried and his Italian teammates Gianluca Roda and Paolo Ruberti, class winners in the season opening round at Sebring, were running a promising fourth in the race in the No. 88 Team Felbermayr-Proton Porsche 911 RSR (997). But after 222 laps, Gianluca Roda had to park the 911 trackside without any drive. *Glen Smale*

Driving a steady race in the British-entered No. 55 JWA-AVILA Porsche 911 RSR (997) were Paul Daniels/Markus Palttala/Joël Camathias. This team finished thirty-third overall and eighth in the GTE Am class. *Glen Smale*

Posting a blistering qualifying time ahead of the two GTE Pro Porsches was the No. 79 Flying Lizard Motorsports Porsche 911 GT3 RSR, driven by Porsche works driver, Patrick Pilet with Americans Seth Neiman and Spencer Pumpelly. Starting the race as pole-sitters in their class, they defended their top position in the early phase of the race, only to be temporarily thrown out of the top ten after a quick tour into the gravel. They recovered from this mishap to finish twenty-seventh overall and fourth in the GTE Am class. *Glen Smale*

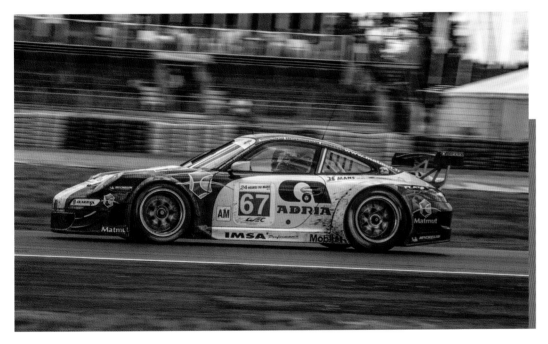

Starting from eighth place in class on the grid, the all-French team of Raymond Narac, Nicolas Armindo, and Anthony Pons held the highest position at the end of twenty-four hours in their No. 67 IMSA Performance Matmut Porsche 911 RSR (997). They were robbed of class victory by tire damage in the final minutes, having led the field until just a few laps before the flag came down at the end of the race. *Glen Smale*

2012 Race Results

Pos.	Car/Model	No.	Driver(s)	Entered	Class	Cl. Pos	Laps	Reason
21	911 RSR	67	Anthony Pons (FR)/Raymond Narac (FR)/Nicolas Armindo (FR)	IMSA Performance Matmut	GTE Am	2	328	
27	911 RSR	79	Seth Neiman (US)/Patrick Pilet (FR)/Spencer Pumpelly (US)	Flying Lizard Motorsport	GTE Am	4	313	
33	911 RSR	55	Paul Daniels (GB)/Markus Palttala (FI)/Joël Camathias (CH)	JWA-AVILA	GTE Am	8	290	
DNF	911 RSR	88	Christian Ried (DE)/Gianluca Roda (IT)/Paolo Ruberti (IT)	Team Felbermayr-Proton	GTE Am		222	Retired
DNF	911 RSR	77	Richard Lietz (AT)/Marc Lieb (DE)/Wolf Henzler (DE)	Team Felbermayr-Proton	GTE Pro		184	Retired
DNF	911 RSR	75	Abdulaziz Al Faisal (SA)/Bret Curtis (US)/Sean Edwards (GB)	Prospeed Competition	GTE Am		180	Accident
DNF	911 RSR	80	Jörg Bergmeister (DE)/Patrick Long (US)/Marco Holzer (DE)	Flying Lizard Motorsports	GTE Pro		114	Accident

2013

June 22–23

This was the first full season for Porsche's all-new 911 RSR, a race car homologated on the 911 Carrera 4 because, as Hartmut Kristen put it in 2013, "The GT3 was not in production at that stage, so we couldn't use the GT3 as a platform for homologation."

Porsche was granted a waiver for the Le Mans race, which gave the Porsche RSR a slightly larger 29.6mm air restrictor, up from the 29.3mm as used at Silverstone and Spa. Several of the drivers commented that, with a longer body and the RSR's Le Mans aero package in place, the handling and aerodynamics were much improved. Team manager Olaf Manthey added, "The Porsche is the fastest GTE car at Le Mans in a straight line thanks to an improved aero package resulting in less drag, and it is also faster than before in the medium and fast corners due to the longer wheelbase. This is despite having the smallest engine in class."

Historically, Le Mans has long been a happy hunting ground for the Stuttgart manufacturer, but Porsche arrived for the French race, the third round in the 2013 WEC, without having scored a podium finish so far in the season. As a works team, this level of nonachievement was not familiar territory for Porsche.

Wolfgang Hatz shared with the author, "It's an in-house team, the cars are built in Weissach and Olaf Manthey is a part of our works team. The mechanics are from Weissach but some mechanics are from the Manthey operation at the Nürburgring, but this is a full works team."

Race day arrived and the weather looked no more settled than it had for the whole week as Bergmeister was nominated to start the race in the No. 91 car and Lieb in the No. 92 car. The race was a story of changeable weather, with heavy rain at times that turned into a deluge at one point. During the course of the race, Porsche's main battle was with the Aston Martins, but the British cars were plagued by a variety of maladies while the Porsches kept going reliably.

The last couple of hours made for some tense moments as the heavens opened at regular intervals, dumping huge amounts of water on the circuit that resulted in numerous offs and spins. Fortunately, the Porsches came through this period unscathed. There was a heart-stopping moment on Sunday around midday when Lietz's Porsche was tapped by a GTE Am Ferrari going into the Dunlop Curves, resulting in a 180-degree spin. No following cars made contact with the stranded Porsche, which continued on its way.

As the 3:00 p.m. finish approached, it could not have been expected that, after twenty-four hours of tense racing, the two Porsches would finish on the same lap with just two minutes separating them. It is also worth mentioning that, with a win in both the GTE Pro and Am classes in 2013, Porsche secured its hundredth class victory at Le Mans, which sat very well with the fiftieth anniversary celebrations for the 911!

Discussing tactics for the race on the grid before the start are, *at left*, Olaf Manthey, team manager, and, *at right*, Porsche CEO Matthias Müller. *Glen Smale*

Ready and waiting to go! Saturday morning, the No. 91 and No. 92 Porsches wait for the signal to move onto the grid for the start of the race. *Glen Smale*

The No. 75 Prospeed Competition Porsche 911 GT3 RSR of Emmanuel Collard/ François Perrodo/Sebastien Crubilé negotiates the Porsche Curves on Sunday morning. The all-French trio finished thirty-sixth overall and ninth in the LMGTE Am class. *Glen Smale*

Christian Ried/Gianluca Roda/Paolo Ruberti brought the 4-liter No. 88 Proton Competition Porsche 911 GT3 RSR home in thirty-fifth overall and eighth in the LMGTE Am class. Here the Porsche crests the Dunlop rise on its way to a solid finish. *Glen Smale*

Porsche factory driver Wolf Henzler joined the two French drivers Pascal Gibon and Patrice Milesi in the No. 67 IMSA Performance Matmut 911 GT3 RSR, enjoying a fine run to finish thirty-third overall and seventh in the LMGTE Am class. Here the car approaches the Porsche Curves on Sunday morning. *Glen Smale*

The No. 77 Dempsey Del Piero-Proton 911 GT3 RSR approaches the Porsche Curves on Sunday morning. The all-American driver lineup of actor Patrick Dempsey/Patrick Long/ Joe Foster drove a steady race to bring their car home twenty-eighth overall and fourth in the LMGTE Am, just one lap away from a podium place. *Glen Smale*

The No. 76 IMSA Performance Matmut Porsche 911 GT3 RSR was the LMGTE Am class winner, giving Porsche its ninety-ninth class win at Le Mans. Driven by the all-French trio of Le Mans stalwart Raymond Narac with Christophe Bourret and Jean-Karl Vernay, the team completed 306 laps on its way to finish twenty-fifth overall, just nine laps off the factory Porsches—an excellent effort! *Glen Smale*

The No. 91 Porsche 911 RSR, driven by Jörg Bergmeister/ Timo Bernhard/Patrick Pilet, approaches the Dunlop Chicane during the early part of the race. The No. 91 factory team completed 315 laps to finish sixteenth overall and second in the LMGTE Pro class. *Glen Smale*

Winners on debut! The No. 92 factory Porsche AG Team Manthey 911 RSR, driven by Marc Lieb/Richard Lietz/ Romain Dumas, gave the new car its first win in the 24 Hours of Le Mans, much to the delight of the whole team. The suits in the marketing department back in Stuttgart must have been particularly pleased, as this was the 911's fiftieth anniversary year. This win would have given them an ideal opportunity to promote the model's victory. The car's fifteenth overall placing was every bit as impressive as its LMGTE Pro class win, which earned the marque its hundredth class victory at Le Mans. *Glen Smale*

2013 Race Results

Pos.	Car/Model	No.	Driver(s)	Entered	Class	Cl. Pos	Laps	Reason
16	911 RSR	92	Marc Lieb (DE)/Richard Lietz (AT)/Romain Dumas (FR)	Porsche AG Team Manthey	GTE Pro	1	315	
17	911 RSR	91	Jörg Bergmeister (DE)/Timo Bernhard (DE)/Patrick Pilet (FR)	Porsche AG Team Manthey	GTE Pro	2	315	
26	911 GT3 RSR	76	Raymond Narac (FR)/Christophe Bourret (FR)/Jean-Karl Vernay (FR)	IMSA Performance Matmut	GTE Am	1	306	
29	911 GT3 RSR	77	Patrick Dempsey (US)/Patrick Long (US)/Joe Foster (US)	Dempsey Del Piero-Proton	GTE Am	4	305	
34	911 GT3 RSR	67	Pascal Gibon (FR)/Patrice Milesi (FR)/Wolf Henzler (DE)	IMSA Performance Matmut	GTE Am	7	300	
36	911 GT3 RSR	88	Christian Ried (DE)/Gianluca Roda (IT)/Paolo Ruberti (IT)	Proton Competition	GTE Am	8	300	
37	911 GT3 RSR	75	Emmanuel Collard (FR)/François Perrodo (FR)/Sebastien Crubilé (FR)	Prospeed Competition	GTE Am	9	298	

2014

June 14–15

Porsche's return to Le Mans brought to an end a fifteen-year hiatus, during which time the Stuttgart manufacturer did not compete for overall victory at Le Mans. All around the circuit at the 2013 race, the Porsche signage shouted out, "Mission 2014. Our return"—and what an excellent buildup that campaign provided in announcing Porsche's return to the big league.

When it was decided in late 2011 that Porsche would be returning to the top class of the sport, the motor racing world breathed a global sigh of relief, as one could almost hear it blowing on the wind: "About time!" And so it was with a sense of heightened expectation that many spectators came to watch the fifty-five gladiators battle it out for honors in the eighty-second running of the Le Mans twenty-four-hour race, leading to an attendance of 263,300 people, the highest in two decades.

In 2014, the Porsche 919 boasted the most innovative drivetrain concept on the grid, consisting of a turbocharged, direct-injection, 2-liter, four-cylinder gasoline engine driving the rear axle, an exhaust energy recovery system, lithium-ion battery technology for energy storage (6 megajoules) to serve the electric motor on the front axle, and a complex hybrid management. With this, Porsche established a technological advantage in that their engine was not only the most efficient combustion engine the company had ever built, but it was also the lightest in the class. The engine and the hybrid system was said to produce around 500 horsepower each, for a total of approximately 1,000 horsepower.

That expectation was heightened when the No. 14 Porsche 919 occupied the second spot on the starting grid with its stablemate, the No. 20 car in fourth spot. In first and third places were the two Toyotas, with the Audis in fifth, sixth, and seventh places. Any one of the three manufacturers could realistically have won the race as Toyota had won the first two races of the WEC season, Silverstone, and Spa, but Audi had monopolized Le Mans in recent years. The times, they were certainly interesting!

In the GTE Pro stakes, the 911 RSRs were further back in the pack, in sixth and seventh places. It was a similar situation in the GTE Am class, with the top Porsche in sixth place. Porsche teams usually tell you that grid positions aren't that important in such a long race, as they are testing their race setup.

The French/Finnish combination of François Perrodo/Emmanuel Collard/Markus Palttala were nonfinishers in the No. 75 Prospeed Competition Porsche 997 GT3-RSR. *Glen Smale*

The No. 67 IMSA Performance Matmut Porsche 997 GT3 RSR 4-liter calls in to the pits during the night hours. The all-French team of Erik Maris/Jean-Marc Merlin/Éric Hélary finished twelfth in the LMGTE Am class. *Glen Smale*

A two-driver pair, Jeroen Bleekemolen and Cooper MacNeil drove a fine race to bring their No. 79 Prospeed Competition Porsche 997 GT3 RSR 4-liter home in fifth place in the LMGTE Pro class, completing 319 laps. The only GT3 RSR in the field, it was entered in the Pro class and finished two positions behind the lead factory 911 and two laps ahead of the second of the factory 911s. *Glen Smale*

A regular at Le Mans has been the No. 76 IMSA Performance Matmut Porsche 997 GT3 RSR 4-liter, this time driven by the French trio of Raymond Narac/Nicolas Armindo/David Hallyday. This car finished eleventh in the LMGTE Am class. *Glen Smale*

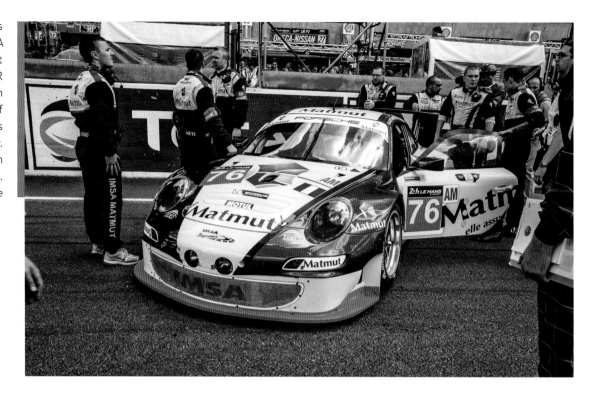

Starting from seventh on the grid, the No. 77 Dempsey Racing-Proton Porsche 911 RSR 4-liter put in a solid performance, driven by the all-American trio of Patrick Dempsey, Joe Foster, and works driver Patrick Long. As Long commented, "We certainly could have done more this year. Still, I'm satisfied with our performance as a team. Our car didn't have the slightest technical problem and Patrick improved constantly and posted super times. Not everyone can climb the podium at Le Mans. If it was that easy then everyone would have a Le Mans trophy at home." They finished fifth in the LMGTE Am class. *Glen Smale*

The duo of Christian Ried and Khaled Al Qubaisi was joined by Porsche junior driver Klaus Bachler on his debut in the French race. All three asserted themselves well, bringing the No. 88 Proton Competition Porsche 911 RSR 4-liter home in second place in the LMGTE Am class. *Glen Smale*

The two factory Porsche 911 RSRs run by Team Manthey were initially running in first and second places in the LMGTE Pro class. Patrick Pilet/Nick Tandy/Jörg Bergmeister in the No. 91 Porsche 911 RSR saw their lead evaporate as they were pushed back during the night by a fuel pressure problem. The extra pit stop lasted forty-one minutes, throwing them into seventh place in class after a strong performance. They completed 309 laps, finishing seventh in class and thirty-sixth place overall. *Glen Smale*

The pair of factory RSRs got off to a good start, each making up a position within the first hour. Two heavy rain showers left parts of the track underwater several hours after the race began, a situation that played into the 911's hands. The No. 92 Porsche 911 RSR, driven by Marco Holzer/Frédéric Makowiecki/Richard Lietz continued on its way strongly: with three hours to the flag, they had moved up the order to lie in second place. But the 2013

winning car was unable to maintain this position, losing out in the dramatic final phase. Le Mans is never kind, exposing any weakness in either car or driver, but a third-place and podium finish in the GTE Pro class was a well-deserved reward for a strong performance. Olaf Manthey, while clearly disappointed, added, "Both cars reached the finish line and third place is good. You win some, you lose some. You just have to make it through." *Glen Smale*

Le Mans stalwart Timo Bernhard started the race from fourth place on the grid in the No. 20 Porsche. A suspected puncture delayed the car at around the 7:30 p.m. mark, but through the night hours the No. 20 car began to make up time on the field during Webber's quadruple stint. Hartley made contact with a slower car and pitted around 4:30 a.m. for a checkup. As the morning hours unfolded, the Bernhard/Webber/Hartley Porsche continued to run strongly in second position. In the second-to-last hour of the race, when Mark Webber climbed aboard the No. 20 Porsche, everything looked set for a thrilling finale, but he

ground to a halt twenty minutes later. Webber eventually made it back to the pits using electric power, heading straight for the garage, from where it did not reemerge. As he puts it, "I think we never expected to be in such a great position toward the end of the race. Few people know how hard it is to get the cars to this point in the race. I'm really sorry for the guys, because there is never ever a good retirement in Le Mans, but today is one of the best you could probably have in a way, because we went so far and we learned so much." Having completed 346 laps, the car was listed as not classified (NC). *Glen Smale*

Neel Jani started the race from second place on the grid in the No. 14 car. After thirty minutes of racing, Jani came in for an unscheduled stop. The team found a problem with the fuel flow. After nine minutes he was able to rejoin the race down in fifty-first position. At 6:20 p.m., he had brought the car back up to fifteenth place overall and pitted, letting Marc Lieb take the wheel. Two hours later, when Dumas took over, the car was up in sixth place. Lieb needed to replace his door at 3:13 a.m., but Jani had another unscheduled stop for recurrent fuel pressure problems, rejoining the race again in sixth place. The No. 14 Porsche continued reliably through the remainder of the night and into the morning, but, with two hours left to run, the car was pushed into the garage while lying in fourth place. The No. 14 Porsche 919 Hybrid, driven by Lieb/ Dumas/Jani, was wheeled out of the garage just before the end of the race so it could finish under its own power. This it did, but it too was declared NC. *Glen Smale*

2014 Race Results

Pos.	Car/Model	No.	Driver(s)	Entered	Class	Cl. Pos	Laps	Reason
11	919 Hybrid	14	Marc Lieb (DE)/Romain Dumas (FR)/Neel Jani (CH)	Porsche Team	LMP1	5	348	
NC	919 Hybrid	20	Timo Bernhard (DE)/Brendon Hartley (NZ)/Mark Webber (AU)	Porsche Team	LMP1	NC	346	
17	911 RSR	92	Marco Holzer (DE)/Frédéric Makowiecki (FR)/Richard Lietz (AT)	Porsche Team Manthey	GTE Pro	3	337	
21	911 RSR	88	Christian Ried (DE)/Klaus Bachler (AT)/Khaled Al Qubaisi (AE)	Proton Competition	GTE Am	2	332	
24	911 RSR	77	Patrick Dempsey (US)/Joe Foster (US)/Patrick Long (US)	Dempsey Racing-Proton	GTE Am	5	329	
31	911 RSR	76	Raymond Narac (FR)/Nicolas Armindo (FR)/David Hallyday (FR)	IMSA Performance Matmut	GTE Am	11	323	
33	997 GT3-RSR	79	Jeroen Bleekemolen (NL)/Cooper MacNeil (US)	Prospeed Competition	GTE Pro	5	319	
34	997 GT3-RSR	67	Erik Maris (FR)/Jean-Marc Merlin (FR)/Éric Hélary (FR)	IMSA Performance Matmut	GTE Am	13	317	
36	911 RSR	91	Patrick Pilet (FR)/Nick Tandy (UK)/Jörg Bergmeister (DE)	Porsche Team Manthey	GTE Pro	7	309	
DNF	997 GT3-RSR	75	François Perrodo (FR)/Emmanuel Collard (FR)/Markus Palttala (FI)	Prospeed Competition	GTE Am		194	Lost wheel

2015

June 13–14

This was only the second year of competition for the Porsche 919 Hybrid. In the previous season, the Porsche had recorded just one victory in the last race in Brazil. For 2015, Porsche upped its recoverable energy to 8 megajoules per lap at Le Mans. This kept the total combined system output at approximately 1,000 horsepower, while only burning 4.76 liters of fuel per lap.

For Le Mans, Porsche entered three 919s each liveried in a single color: red, white and black. Porsche were clearly in a much better place than they had been the previous year. The 31-year-old Swiss driver, Neel Jani, set a target time in the first qualifying session on the Wednesday evening in the No. 18 Porsche, a result that wasn't topped in either of the two remaining qualifying sessions. His time of 3:16.887 minutes was a new qualifying lap record on the current circuit layout, beating the time set by the Peugeot 908 in 2008 of 3:18.513 minutes. The second-place No. 17 Porsche also beat the old record while the third Porsche on the grid, the No. 19 car, secured Porsche's ninth lockout of the top three grid places since 1968. Jani was the starting driver in the No. 18 pole car, with Timo Bernhard in the second-place No. 17 car and Nico Hülkenberg taking the wheel of the No. 19 Porsche.

The GTE contingent consisted of a pair of works 911 RSRs (Nos. 91 and 92) in the Pro Class, with a pair of Team AAI 911s (Nos. 67 and 68), Dempsey-Proton Racing (No. 77), and Abu Dhabi-Proton Racing (No. 88) in the Am class. In the GTE Pro cars, Richard Lietz piloted the No. 91 car off the start line while Patrick Pilet was in the No. 92 car.

Pictured on the starting grid before the race are, *from left to right*: No. 18, driven by Marc Lieb/Romain Dumas/Neel Jani; No. 17, driven by Timo Bernhard/Brendon Hartley/Mark Webber; and No. 19, driven by Earl Bamber/Nick Tandy/Nico Hülkenberg. *Glen Smale*

The first Porsche to drop out of the race was the works No. 92 Porsche 911 RSR driven by Patrick Pilet. Having completed just fourteen laps, the Porsche caught fire with no warning on the Mulsanne Straight. The author caught up with Olaf Manthey a few weeks later at the Goodwood Festival of Speed to ask what went wrong. Manthey explained, "A con rod broke, which came through the crankcase wall, and the oil obviously came out all over the exhaust system and as a result we had the fire." Patrick Pilet abandoned ship without injury, but it was a disappointing end for him and colleagues Frédéric Makowiecki and Wolf Henzler. *Glen Smale*

The second Porsche to retire was the No. 88 Abu Dhabi-Proton Racing 911 RSR driven by Christian Ried/Klaus Bachler/Khalid Al Qubaisi. This LMGTE Am class car suffered as a result of a fire after just forty-four laps. *Glen Smale*

The only Porsche 911 GT3 RSR in the field, the No. 67 Team AAI, was driven by Jun-San Chen/Xavier Maassen/Alex Kapadia. This car finished thirty-seventh overall and eighth in the LMGTE Am class. *Glen Smale*

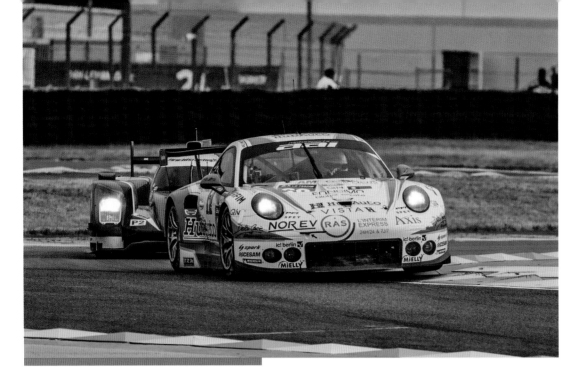

The No. 68 Team AAI Porsche 911 RSR, driven by Han-Chen Chen/Gilles Vannelet/Mike Parisy, drove a solid race to finish sixth in LMGTE Am class after completing 320 laps. *John Mountney*

After five hours, the No. 91 works Porsche of Richard Lietz/Michael Christensen/Jörg Bergmeister was up to fourth place. Around 10:00 p.m., the car pitted due to a flat left rear tire, but fourth position was retained and, by midnight, it was up to third in class. An hour later the car had moved up to second place and the car yo-yoed between the second, third, and fourth places until almost midday on Sunday. But two pit stops for repairs lost the team a total of thirty minutes, which saw them cross the line fifth in class. *Glen Smale*

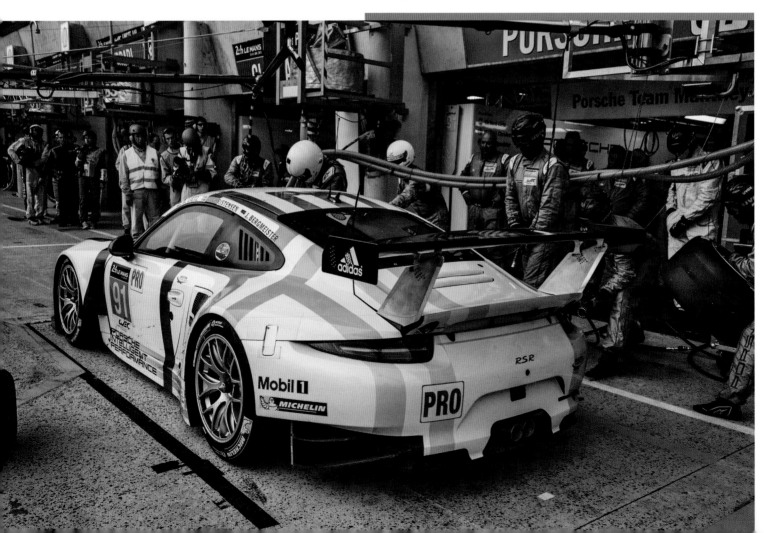

Ecstatic was the only way to describe Patrick Dempsey's reaction when the No. 77 Dempsey-Proton Racing Porsche 911 RSR crossed the finish line in second place in class on Sunday afternoon. Dempsey shared the wheel with works drivers Patrick Long and Marco Seefried. *Glen Smale*

At 10:00 p.m., the No. 18 Porsche 919 Hybrid driven by Marc Lieb/Romain Dumas/Neel Jani pitted for a regulation fuel and tire stop, but the car also received a new nosepiece. At around 1:15 a.m. on Sunday morning, the car pitted again for a new nose, this time the result of an accident. Apart from those two components, no other repairs were required during the race, and the No. 18 Porsche ran reliably to the finish. The black-liveried car completed 391 laps and finished fifth overall. *John Mountney*

Starting from second place on the grid, the No. 17 Porsche 919 Hybrid enjoyed a trouble-free run in the hands of Timo Bernhard/Brendon Hartley/Mark Webber. It was the Australian Mark Webber who clocked the highest top speed by a Porsche on the Mulsanne Straight at 340.2 kilometers per hour on Saturday at 4:40 p.m. The No. 17 Porsche, which finished second overall, one lap short of the winning car, required no repairs or replacement components and needed only one liter of oil to be replenished during the race. *Glen Smale*

Earl Bamber had only recently signed on as a Porsche works driver, and Nico Hülkenberg was borrowed from Formula One for the Le Mans race; Nick Tandy had driven as a Porsche works driver in the 911 RSR. None of them had driven a Porsche prototype. When compared with the collective experience of the drivers in the No. 17 and No. 18 Porsches, the No. 19 trio had to be considered prototype rookies. Yet it was the No. 19 Porsche that ran an almost faultless race, apart from having its rear wing and engine cover panel replaced at 8:00 a.m. on Sunday. Completing 395 laps (one more than the No. 17 sister car), they finished first, just two laps short of the record set in 2010 on this course. *Glen Smale*

2015 Race Results

Pos.	Car/Model	No.	Driver(s)	Entered	Class	Cl. Pos	Laps	Reason
1	919 Hybrid	19	Earl Bamber (NZ)/Nick Tandy (UK)/Nico Hülkenberg (DE)	Porsche Team	LMP1	1	395	
2	919 Hybrid	17	Timo Bernhard (DE)/Brendon Hartley (NZ)/Mark Webber (AU)	Porsche Team	LMP1	2	394	
5	919 Hybrid	18	Marc Lieb (DE)/Romain Dumas (FR)/Neel Jani (CH)	Porsche Team	LMP1	5	391	
22	911 RSR	77	Patrick Dempsey (US)/Patrick Long (US)/Marco Seefried (DE)	Dempsey-Proton Racing	GTE Am	2	331	
30	911 RSR	91	Richard Lietz (AT)/Michael Christensen (DK)/Jörg Bergmeister (DE)	Porsche Team Manthey	GTE Pro	5	327	
35	911 RSR	68	Han-Chen Chen (TW)/Gilles Vannelet (FR)/Mike Parisy (FR)	Team AAI	GTE Am	6	320	
37	911 RSR	67	Jun-San Chen (TW)/Xavier Maassen (NL)/Alex Kapadia (UK)	Team AAI	GTE Am	8	316	
DNF	911 RSR	88	Christian Ried (DE)/Klaus Bachler (AT)/Khalid Al Qubaisi (AE)	Abu Dhabi-Proton Racing	GTE Am		44	Fire
DNF	911 RSR	92	Patrick Pilet (FR)/Frédéric Makowiecki (FR)/Wolf Henzler (DE)	Porsche Team Manthey	GTE Pro		14	Engine/fire

2016

June 18–19

Drawing on two years of development and racing data, Porsche was able to fine-tune the 919 Hybrid to an even higher level of efficiency in 2016. The regulations this year required a lower amount of energy from the fuel used per lap and thus the fuel flow for all the prototypes had to be reduced. For the Porsche 919 Hybrid, this resulted in an 8 percent loss of fuel, which translated into an output of less than 500 horsepower being produced by the gasoline engine. The electrical energy from the two recovery systems (brake energy from the front axle and exhaust turbo energy) served the engine generator unit (EGU) on the front axle, which meant the overall power system of the Porsche 919 Hybrid developed 900 horsepower. In order to boost performance, the Porsche engineers worked some magic on the car's aerodynamics for the new season, while energy recovery was increased from 6 to 8 megajoules.

As in 2015, Jani set the fastest time of the week in the first qualifying session, which was just as well, as the following two qualifying sessions on Thursday were affected by rain. In fact, the final Thursday night session was red-flagged, with a torrential downpour that caused such wide rivers across the track that the safety car almost spun off.

The results sheet shows that the No. 2 Porsche was on pole for the start of the race, and the same car, with the same driver at the wheel, took the checkered flag twenty-four hours later. We might think that the No. 2 Porsche led from flag to flag, but this would ignore twenty-four hours' worth of nail-biting, nose-to-tail racing that wound up in one of the most dramatic finishes in years.

The prolonged safety car period at the start had a profound effect on the race for the whole field, because by the time the race went green, the rain had abated and the track had dried. This meant that the cars were now all on the wrong tires, with most having to pit for slicks. For the Porsche RSRs this was a double blow: not only were they also on the wrong tires, but the 911s are better in the wet and the period of potential advantage had been taken out of the equation for them.

In fact, the 911s faced odds that precluded any chance for victory, as their new car was not yet ready for the track; this was the only race of the 2016 WEC season in which the factory team would compete, using an upgraded 2015 RSR. With an unfavorable balance of performance (BoP) index, this left the Porsches with an even bigger performance deficit. The team had only one option: to go flat out for as long as the cars lasted.

The start of the 2016 race will be remembered for one image: the train of race cars being led around by the safety car for fifty-two minutes. As the end of the first hour approached, the spectators in the grandstands on the start/finish straight became audibly dissatisfied, as they had paid to watch motor racing, not a procession. *Glen Smale*

The No. 89 WeatherTech Proton Racing 911 RSR was hit unexpectedly with the late withdrawal of Cooper MacNeil, who had become too ill to drive. Reserve driver Gunnar Jeannette was ready to step in, but this was disallowed by the ACO. This meant that Keen and Miller faced the task of sharing the whole twenty-four-hour drive between them. Miller explains how their race unfolded: "We faced the challenge of driving this race with only two drivers. It was great to be in the lead temporarily at the beginning, we were consistently fast. Then a car lost coolant in front of me, in the fast Turn 1, and I reached it in fifth gear and didn't have any chance." After just fifty laps, the No. 89 was the first Porsche retiree. *Glen Smale*

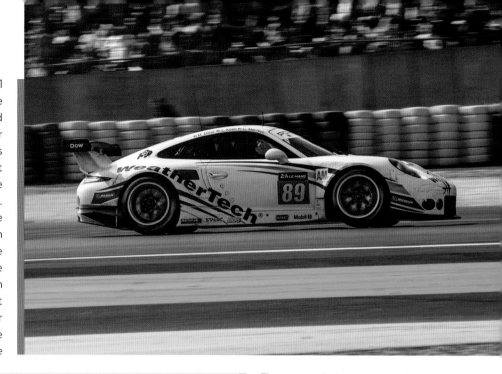

The race ended prematurely for the works No. 91 911 RSR driven by Patrick Pilet/Kévin Estre/Nick Tandy. At thirty-eight minutes past midnight, Tandy pitted and handed the car over to Estre. At twelve minutes past 1:00 a.m., a little more than a half hour later, an engine fire forced the retirement of the No. 91 Porsche with 135 laps completed. *Glen Smale*

It was known before the start that the works Porsche 911s were going to have a battle on their hands just to stay with the opposition. Pushing the cars harder than normal would have consequences, as Jörg Bergmeister explained: "During my stint the left rear wheel peg sheared and I had to pit for repairs. To keep up with our opponents we had to drive over the curbs much harder and more often, but everything was running pretty well up until then." The No. 92 Porsche that Bergmeister shared with Frédéric Makowiecki and Earl Bamber retired at 2:36 a.m. after 140 laps. *John Mountney*

KCMG's No. 78 Porsche 911 RSR, shared by Wolf Henzler, Christian Ried, and Joël Camathias, finished tenth in the GTE AM class. They were set back by a technical issue, with their car garaged twice for repairs, pushing them down the field. *Glen Smale*

Starting from eleventh place in the GTE AM class, the No. 86 Gulf Racing Porsche RSR, driven by Michael Wainwright/Ben Barker/Adam Carroll, enjoyed an almost faultless race, with drivers Barker and Carroll double-stinting through the night. It was Ben Barker who brought the car home in fifth place at 3:00 p.m. on Sunday afternoon, having completed 328 laps. *Glen Smale*

Contending the whole 2016 WEC season in the GTE PRO class was the works-supported No. 77 Dempsey-Proton Racing 911 RSR. Driven by Richard Lietz/Philipp Eng/Michael Christensen, the three experienced drivers finished eighth in the LMGTE Pro class, having completed 329 laps. Lietz said after the race, "This was a typical Le Mans with rain, a drying track, and wonderful sunshine. It's an amazing challenge to drive here, and our 911 RSR ran really perfectly most of the time. Unfortunately, we had a minor problem with the driveshaft at night." *Glen Smale*

Finishing third in the GTE Am class was the No. 88 Abu Dhabi Proton Racing 911 RSR driven by Patrick Long/Khaled Al Qubaisi/David Heinemeier Hansson. The familiar checkered 911 was the top-finishing 911, completing 330 laps. After the race, Long was full of praise for the team's performance: "We drove a strong race, and the car performed well. I'm incredibly proud of my team, which didn't only work in an extremely professional way, but also kept cool when it didn't go that well." *John Mountney*

Apart from the slow start behind the safety car for the first fifty-two minutes, the No. 1 Porsche 919 Hybrid, driven by Timo Bernhard/Brendon Hartley/Mark Webber, ran reliably up until 11:12 p.m. With Hartley driving, the car made an unscheduled pit stop due to an abnormally high engine temperature. The crew replaced the water pump and the car returned to the track, only to pit again after one lap for further repairs. The total time spent in the pits amounted to a crippling two-and-a-half hours, setting the car back thirty-nine laps. Around 2:00 a.m. and now down to fifty-third place, the No. 1 Porsche was sent on its way again with Hartley behind the wheel. As the morning wore on, the No. 1 Porsche continued its run, circulating lap after lap without requiring anything other than tires, fuel, or a driver change. The No. 1 Porsche crossed the finish line in thirteenth place having completed 346 laps. *John Mountney*

2016 Race Results

Pos.	Car/Model	No.	Driver(s)	Entered	Class	Cl. Pos	Laps	Reason
1	919 Hybrid	2	Marc Lieb (DE)/Romain Dumas (FR)/Neel Jani (CH)	Porsche Team	LMP1	1	384	
13	919 Hybrid	1	Timo Bernhard (DE)/Brendon Hartley (NZ)/Mark Webber (AU)	Porsche Team	LMP1	5	346	
28	911 RSR	88	Khaled Al Qubaisi (AE)/Patrick Long (US)/David Heinemeier Hansson (DK)	Abu Dhabi-Proton Racing	GTE Am	3	330	
31	911 RSR	77	Richard Lietz (AT)/Philipp Eng (AT)/Michael Christensen (DK)	Dempsey-Proton Racing	GTE Pro	8	329	
33	911 RSR	86	Mike Wainwright (UK)/Adam Carroll (UK)/Ben Barker (UK)	Gulf Racing	GTE Am	5	328	
41	911 RSR	78	Christian Ried (DE), Wolf Henzler (DE), Joël Camathias (CH)	KCMG	GTE Am	10	300	
DNF	911 RSR	92	Frédéric Makowiecki (FR)/Jörg Bergmeister (DE)/Earl Bamber (NZ)	Porsche Motorsport	GTE Pro		140	Suspension
DNF	911 RSR	91	Patrick Pilet (FR)/Kévin Estre (FR)/Nick Tandy (UK)	Porsche Motorsport	GTE Pro		135	Engine
DNF	911 RSR	89	Lehman Keen (US)/Marc Miller (US)/Cooper MacNeil (US)	Proton Competition	GTE Am		50	Accident

2017

June 17–18

On July 28, 2017, Porsche announced that it would withdraw its LMP1 919 Hybrids at the end of the 2017 season. This came after the company had recently confirmed its participation in the LMP1-H class of the FIA World Endurance Championship as a manufacturer up to the end of the 2018 season. It was a blow to Porsche enthusiasts around the world, to say nothing of the racing fraternity, considering Audi's withdrawal at the end of the 2016 season.

The rumor mill was rife with speculation about Porsche's departure, but it was thought that the complexity of the LMP1-H cars was one issue, as the 2017 Le Mans race showed. The cost of maintaining and transporting these cars around the world to different WEC venues possibly played a part, as did the fact that Porsche already had two WEC crowns under its belt. Their decision came a little more than a month after the company had secured its nineteenth Le Mans title, and Porsche was on track for a possible third consecutive WEC crown.

But perhaps of greater interest to Porsche enthusiasts was the fact that this was the first Le Mans race to see the new mid-engined 911. Some will argue that the 911 GT1 of 1996–1998 was the first mid-engined 911, but the new 2017 model was based on a traditional production 911 model. By rotating the engine and gearbox 180 degrees, this allowed the engineers to give the 911 a truly effective rear diffuser, resulting in much better handling.

Although the total number of cars on track for the start of the 2017 race was at a new high with sixty vehicles, the race saw the lowest number of Porsches in recent years. Seven Porsches took to the track: the two works 919 Hybrids and five 911s consisting of the two new works GTE Pro cars, with just three GTE Am cars. With no new 2016 GTE Pro car available for the private teams in 2017, the private Porsche teams in GTE had to be content with upgraded 2015 cars. To blame, so it would appear, was the current Pro and Am setup in the GTE class of the WEC.

A Guards Red 1989 Porsche 911 Turbo 3.3 Cabriolet delivers the Le Mans trophy to be handed over to the ACO before the start of the 2017 race. *Glen Smale*

The first Porsche incident involved the No. 92 Porsche 911 RSR driven by Michael Christensen/Kévin Estre/Dirk Werner. Rear-ended by a Corvette in the Dunlop Curves, the car returned to the pits for repairs just after 7:00 p.m. and was soon out racing again. Making excellent time with occasional periods in the lead, Christensen lost control of the car during the night while curb-hopping in the Ford Chicane and crashed into the barriers with the rear of his car. Thus after 179 laps, the No. 92 Porsche was retired. *John Mountney*

Having started the race from third position on the grid, the No.1 Porsche 919 Hybrid of Neel Jani/Nick Tandy/André Lotterer maintained a strong position in the lead group, shadowed by its No. 2 sister car. The extremely hot conditions caused problems for all of the competitors and numerous "slow zones" played havoc with the drivers' rhythm. Toyota lost their race leader when the clutch failed on the No. 7 car, but this was followed just fifteen minutes later by the retirement of the No. 9 car, which was hit by an LMP2 car. This promoted the No. 1 Porsche into the lead, which widened massively to twenty-nine laps over the sole remaining Toyota. For more than ten hours, the No. 1 Porsche led the race, until just after 11:00 a.m. on Sunday, when the car stopped on track. Lotterer, who was at the wheel, was unable to restart the car using the gasoline engine, and with the battery level too low to get back to the pits, the car was retired at the track side with 318 laps completed. The No. 1 Porsche held a thirteen-lap lead over the now second-place car, the No. 38 Jackie Chan Oreca 07. The race lead was now taken over by an LMP2 car! *Glen Smale*

The No. 86 Gulf Racing UK Porsche 911 RSR, driven by Michael Wainwright/Ben Barker/Nick Foster, drove a smooth, untroubled race to complete 328 laps, finishing in thirty-eighth place overall and tenth in the LMGTE Am class. *John Mountney*

The No. 93 Proton Competition Porsche 911 RSR was driven by Patrick Long/Mike Hedlund/ Abdulaziz Al Faisal. At the start, Long complained about a lack of front-end grip and straightline speed, but eventually the handling improved over the remainder of the race. Long commented after the race: "The only place we couldn't match the pace of our opponents was on the straights. We put pressure on right to the end and the team gave their utmost. We can be proud of our effort. We've all enjoyed the unique atmosphere of this race." The team drove a clean race to finish ninth in the LMGTE Am class. *Glen Smale*

Driving the No. 77 Dempsey-Proton Racing Porsche 911 RSR was veteran campaigner Christian Ried, who was partnered with two Le Mans rookies, Matteo Cairoli and Marvin Dienst. With Ried's experience and the youthful exuberance of Cairoli and Dienst, the team drove a steady race despite early tire problems and a technical issue during the night, finishing sixth in the LMGTE Am class. *John Mountney*

Frédéric Makowiecki started the race in the No. 91 Porsche 911 RSR, which he shared with Richard Lietz and Patrick Pilet. Both Pilet and Lietz complained about the slow straightline speed, as Lietz confirmed: "We're lacking top speed on the straights, the competition can overtake us there as they please." At the nine-hour mark the No. 91 Porsche was running in third place, and in the early morning hours the car was regularly up in the lead. Lietz again: "The car is running flawlessly in almost all respects, and the car's balance is excellent." On Sunday morning all three of the drivers had turns leading the race. With an hour and a half to go, Frédéric Makowiecki was running in third place. A puncture one hour before the end forced the vehicle back for an unscheduled pit stop, resulting in a fourth-place finish in the LMGTE Pro class. *Glen Smale*

TImo Bernhard qualified the No. 2 Porsche 919 Hybrid in fourth place on the starting grid, the veteran Porsche factory driver sharing the car with the two New Zealanders, Brendon Hartley and Earl Bamber. Three hours into the race, the No. 2 car was still running in fourth place, but at 6:30 p.m. the car spent an hour in the pits with no drive to the front axles. The Porsche had to fight its way back through the field; by 6:00 a.m. the car was back in tenth place overall and second in class, having made steady progress during the night. By 10:15 a.m., Brendon Hartley had moved up into seventh place overall—at this stage the calculators were going crazy: were there enough laps left for the No. 2 Porsche to catch and overtake the leading LMP2 car?

At just before 1:00 p.m., Bernhard took the wheel from Hartley with the car lying in fourth place overall, but importantly on the same lap as the lead car. By this stage most folks had worked out that, barring any further incidents, the Porsche would move into the lead, and this it did: after 367 event-filled laps, the No. 2 Porsche took the checkered flag as the winner. This gave Porsche its nineteenth overall victory at Le Mans! For Bernhard and Bamber it was their second overall win each, but it was Hartley's first Le Mans win. A remarkable race in which three LMP1 cars were eliminated (two Toyotas and one Porsche). For far too many laps for comfort, the race was led by an LMP2 car. *Glen Smale*

2017 Race Results

Pos.	Car/Model	No.	Driver(s)	Entered	Class	Cl. Pos	Laps	Reason
1	919 Hybrid	2	Timo Bernhard (DE)/Brendon Hartley (NZ)/Earl Bamber (NZ)	Porsche LMP Team	LMP1	1	367	
20	911 RSR	91	Richard Lietz (AT)/Frédéric Makowiecki (FR)/Patrick Pilet (FR)	Porsche GT Team	GTE Pro	4	339	
34	911 RSR	77	Christian Ried (DE)/Marvin Dienst (DE)/Matteo Cairoli (IT)	Dempsey-Proton Racing	GTE Am	6	329	
37	911 RSR	93	Patrick Long (US)/Mike Hedlund (US)/Abdulaziz Al Faisal (SB)	Proton Competition	GTE Am	9	329	
38	911 RSR	86	Michael Wainwright (UK)/Ben Barker (UK)/Nick Foster (AU)	Gulf Racing UK	GTE Am	10	328	
DNF	919 Hybrid	1	Neel Jani (CH)/Nick Tandy (UK)/André Lotterer (DE)	Porsche LMP Team	LMP1		318	Mechanical
DNF	911 RSR	92	Michael Christensen (DK)/Kévin Estre (FR)/Dirk Werner (DE)	Porsche GT Team	GTE Pro		179	Accident
DNF	911 RSR	88	Klaus Bachler (AT)/Stéphane Lémeret (BE)/Khalid Al Qubaisi (AE)	Proton Competition	GTE Am		18	Accident

2018

June 16–17

Spectators and members of the media agreed that the real battle in eighty-sixth edition of Le Mans was going to be among the ranks of the GTE Pro and Am cars. To be honest, it really was, and even though the eventual winners were those cars that had run at the front of the pack for most of the race, the laurels could have gone to a number of contenders.

With Porsche having abandoned the LMP1 class battle, the fight for overall honors was between the two Toyotas. What Porsche lacked in the LMP1 stakes, though, it made up for in the two GTE classes. In the GTE Pro class, Porsche fielded four works 911 RSRs, while no less than six of the 2017 RSRs filled the Am class, all of which featured the mid-engined layout. Another factor present was the fact that 2018 was the seventieth anniversary since Porsche's founding in 1948.

Throughout the year, Porsche made much of this milestone. Putting ten 911s on the track certainly was a statement in support of that achievement.

Of the sixty starters, forty-three cars were classified finishers, with sixteen cars dropping out and one additional car being unclassified, resulting in a very low rate of retirement. Out of the ten 911s on track, all but two crossed the finish line, with one car in each of the Pro and Am classes retiring. This made for an intense level of competition across the board.

On all four factory cars, the end plates of the 911 RSR's rear wing were adorned with the "70 Years 1948–2018" logo, in support of the company's milestone anniversary. *Glen Smale*

Following Müller's accident at Indianapolis in qualifying, the No. 94 works Porsche 911 RSR was ready for the race and started from eighth position in class. Despite finding their rhythm early in the race, the car was retired during the seventh hour (ninety-two laps) as a result of suspension damage on the left rear. All three drivers were understandably disappointed, but after a lengthy attempt to repair the damaged suspension, the car was eventually withdrawn. *John Mountney*

The No. 88 Dempsey-Proton Racing Porsche 911 RSR, driven by Khaled Al Qubaisi/Matteo Cairoli/Giorgio Roda, was in pole position in class for the start of the race, even ahead of two GTE Pro cars. The young Italian, Cairoli, started the race and the car ran strongly at first but then started to fall back down the order. The trio then made their way back up the class and ran in the top half of the class for many hours before a suspension failure forced the car's retirement in the seventeenth hour after 225 laps. *Glen Smale*

The No. 86 Gulf Racing (UK) Porsche 911 RSR, driven by Michael Wainwright/Ben Barker/Alex Davison, is pushed to its excellent second place in class on the starting grid ahead of the race. After the end of the first hour, the No. 86 Porsche was leading the class, but then it dropped right down to last in class by the end of the second hour. Barker revealed to the author, "I had a slow puncture at the end of my stint, so I had to pit early and we therefore lost positions. Our car also had a crash at Indianapolis which cost us a lot of time." The team persisted, finishing the race in tenth place in the LMGTE Am class. *Glen Smale*

Having qualified in fifth place in class, the No. 56 Team Project 1 Porsche 911 RSR ran a solid race. In the hands of Jörg Bergmeister/Patrick Lindsey/Egidio Perfetti, the car climbed to second in class by the end of the sixth hour. For the subsequent ten hours, the car occupied positions that varied between third and sixth. Starting in the seventeenth hour, they once again moved up to fourth place. A podium result was looking like a realistic possibility, but in the twenty-second hour Patrick Lindsey experienced brake failure at the first chicane. He was able to nurse the car home and the team replaced both rear brakes, but this mishap had ruined any chance of a top spot and the team finished seventh. *Glen Smale*

Established in 1998, Ebimotors was no newcomer to the sport, this year marking their twentieth year of racing Porsche GT cars. But this was their first time at Le Mans. In the pit garage, the No. 80 Ebimotors Porsche 911 RSR team was run by the capable and amiable Alice Menin. Behind the wheel of the No. 80 Porsche was veteran Fabio Babini, supported by Christina Nielsen and Erik Maris, both of whom had driven at Le Mans several times before. The Ebimotors Porsche ran well throughout the twenty-four hours, with only minor issues such as brakes and an unexpected puncture. The team did well to bring their car home midclass without any major issues on their first attempt in this great race. *John Mountney*

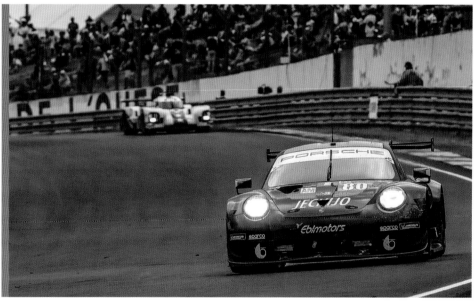

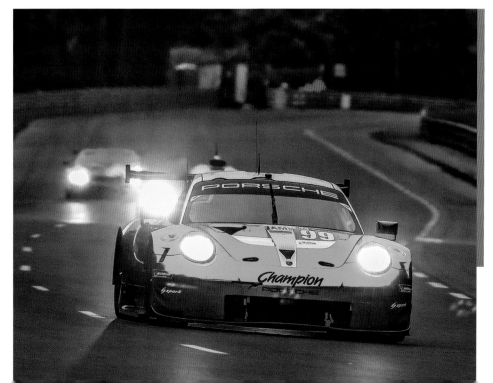

Crossing the finish line in the fourth spot was the bright green No. 99 Proton Competition Porsche 911 RSR driven by the all-American team of Patrick Long/Tim Pappas/Spencer Pumpelly. The team survived some challenges during practice and didn't look that strong up until race day, when it really counted, as Patrick Long confirmed. "Wednesday was a difficult day for us, but now things are improving. We decided not to attack with a couple of fast laps. Instead we used the time to help get my teammates more familiar with the car. The baseline setup now fits, everyone is focused and we look forward to contesting this unique race. This is my fifteenth time in a row here." A fourth-place finish was an excellent result for the team. *John Mountney*

For much of the race it was the No. 88 Porsche RSR that led the class, followed by the No. 77 Dempsey-Proton Racing 911 RSR driven by Matt Campbell/Christian Ried/Julien Andlauer. Porsche's young professional, Andlauer put in a sterling effort through the hours of darkness, driving around four hours and keeping the team in close touch with the lead car. Then Cairoli spun out early on Sunday morning while leading in the No. 88 car, which promoted the No. 77 car into a lead that held to the end of the race. Andlauer commented after the race, "At 18 years of age I was given the chance to contest Le Mans for the first time and we won. I'm very proud of the whole team and I can't really believe it yet. Now I'm the youngest Le Mans winner, incredible." *Glen Smale*

Driving the works No. 93 Porsche 911 RSR were Patrick Pilet/Nick Tandy/Earl Bamber. They qualified the car sixth in class, a place they held for several hours, even improving to second place by the end of the sixth hour. But during the evening, the No. 93 Porsche pitted and was wheeled into the pit garage, suffering from a failed alternator. The replacement took around twenty-five minutes to fit, setting the car well back down the field, a situation from which it never recovered. Patrick Pilet had this to say: "It was a difficult race. At times we were running with the leaders and had a very fast car. But a technical problem then threw us down the field. We were determined to finish the race and we finished eleventh, that's how it is at Le Mans." *Glen Smale*

Behind the wheel of the No. 91 Porsche 911 RSR were works drivers Richard Lietz/Gianmaria Bruni/Frédéric Makowiecki. It was evident during the race that this car was delivering peak performance. At one time on Sunday, Makowiecki fought off the attentions of one of the Ford GTs for an hour. Speaking to the Porsche staff after the race, they confirmed that the No. 91 Porsche never missed a beat for the full duration of the race. Drivers and tires were changed on schedule and fuel was added, but no repairs or additional attention was given to this car throughout the twenty-four hours. When the flag came down at just after 3:00 p.m. on Sunday, the No. 91 Porsche crossed the line in second place in the GTE Pro class, just one lap down on its stablemate, the No. 92 Porsche. Gianmaria Bruni said, "This double victory is fantastic—for Porsche and our team. We had a great race and a great fight with our No. 92 sister car. We tried everything but our team colleagues didn't make any mistakes and they deserve this win." *John Mountney*

Starting from second place on the grid (in class), the No. 92 Porsche 911 RSR of Michael Christensen/Kévin Estre/Laurens Vanthoor looked resplendent in its Pink Pig livery, reminiscent of the 1971 Porsche 917/20 Sau. Many fans, and certainly most of the media, warmed to the retrospective livery of the No. 91 and No. 92 Porsches, as it brought to mind those favorite racing memories of yesteryear. Posing both from trackside and in the pit lane, the No. 92 Porsche looked and sounded as healthy at the end of

twenty-four hours as it did at the beginning. As with its No. 91 sister car, the No. 92 Porsche did not require any repairs or attention throughout the duration of the race. Kévin Estre was ecstatic after it was all over: "It's simply unbelievable. I just can't describe my feelings. Today is the best day of my life. We have won the world's most difficult and wonderful race. That can't be put into words." This was certainly the best that Porsche could have wished for in the year of the company's seventieth anniversary. *Glen Smale*

2018 Race Results

Pos.	Car/Model	No.	Driver(s)	Entered	Class	Cl. Pos	Laps	Reason
15	911 RSR	92	Michael Christensen (DK)/Kévin Estre (FR)/Laurens Vanthoor (BE)	Porsche GT Team	GTE Pro	1	344	
16	911 RSR	91	Richard Lietz (AT)/Gianmaria Bruni (IT)/Frédéric Makowiecki (FR)	Porsche GT Team	GTE Pro	2	343	
25	911 RSR	77	Matt Campbell (AU)/Christian Ried (DE)/Julien Andlauer (FR)	Dempsey-Proton Racing	GTE Am	1	335	
27	911 RSR	93	Patrick Pilet (FR)/Nick Tandy (UK)/Earl Bamber (NZ)	Porsche GT Team (US)	GTE Pro	10	334	
29	911 RSR	99	Patrick Long (US)/Tim Pappas (US)/Spencer Pumpelly (US)	Proton Competition	GTE Am	4	334	
31	911 RSR	80	Fabio Babini (IT)/Christina Nielsen (DK)/Erik Maris (FR)	Ebimotors	GTE Am	6	332	
34	911 RSR	56	Jörg Bergmeister (DE)/Patrick Lindsey (US)/Egidio Perfetti (NO)	Team Project 1	GTE Am	7	332	
40	911 RSR	86	Michael Wainwright (UK)/Ben Barker (UK)/Alex Davison (AU)	Gulf Racing (UK)	GTE Am	10	283	
DNF	911 RSR	88	Khaled Al Qubaisi (AE)/Matteo Cairoli (IT)/Giorgio Roda (IT)	Dempsey-Proton Racing	GTE Am		225	Suspension
DNF	911 RSR	94	Romain Dumas (FR)/Timo Bernhard (DE), Sven Müller (DE)	Porsche GT Team (US)	GTE Pro		92	Suspension

2019

June 15–16

This year saw the conclusion of the WEC's first Super Season, with the final round of the 2018–2019 sequence being the jewel in the crown: the eighty-seventh running of the Le Mans. The Super Season ran from the first race after the 2018 Le Mans race and finished with the 2019 Le Mans as the final "big one."

On the afternoon of June 15, 2019, sixty-two vehicles took to the track at Le Mans across the four classes, which represented a record starting field. Once again, Porsche fielded four works 911 RSRs with six cars entered by private teams in the GTE Am class. At the end of twenty-four hours of hard racing, just twelve of the original sixty-two starters were nonfinishers, the winning Toyotas having completed a total of 385 laps.

A seasoned endurance racing driver with many Le Mans races under his belt once said that, to be successful at Le Mans, you needed to stay out of trouble, drive consistent laps, and aim to have smooth pit stops. You needed to ensure that you made it through the night hours, then survive the morning hours of Sunday without any hiccups, and only at noon on Sunday

did you go racing for the remaining three hours. But the latest generation of drivers call this a lot of baloney—you can't do that anymore, because if you drive well, do everything right, and stay out of trouble, you'll be lucky to make it into the top five or six in your class. Today, the racing in a twenty-four-hour race begins when the lights go green, and lasts for the duration of the race.

A lap of Le Mans will typically see cars running flat out for 80 percent of the lap, which is why the circuit is regarded as a low-downforce, high-speed circuit. With car reliability having increased across the field, it would take an unforced error or some mishap to interrupt a driver's progress, so the pace and pressure are relentless.

Porsche was in the fortunate position of arriving at Le Mans having claimed the 2018–2019 WEC Manufacturers' title at the previous Circuit de Spa-Francorchamps. With that title in the bag, the one title still up for grabs was the Drivers' Championship, and here Michael Christensen and Kévin Estre were very much in the frame.

The first Free Practice session on Wednesday afternoon was red-flagged early on when the No. 99 Porsche 911 RSR GTE Am car driven by Tracy Krohn collided with an LMP car. The incident took place between the first and second chicane on the Mulsanne Straight, and it resulted in a write-off for the Porsche. Krohn was taken to the hospital where he was kept overnight on Wednesday for observation; although he felt fine on Thursday, he was not allowed to drive for a week, which ruled out his participation in the weekend's race. His codrivers, Patrick Long and Niclas Jönsson, didn't even get a chance behind the wheel. *Glen Smale*

Having qualified the No. 88 Dempsey-Proton Porsche on pole in class, the expectations of Matteo Cairoli/Giorgio Roda/Satoshi Hoshino were no doubt running high. The No. 88 Dempsey-Proton Porsche and the No. 64 Corvette made contact in the Porsche Curves on lap 79. The result of the collision was that the Corvette, driven by Marcel Fässler, hit the tire wall heavily and the car was so badly damaged that it was retired. The undamaged Porsche, after being checked over, continued on its way. But a few laps later, a spin ended in the No. 88's retirement and a DNF. *Glen Smale*

Showing great promise, the No. 86 Gulf Racing (UK) Porsche 911 RSR qualified third for the start. The car was driven by Michael Wainwright/Ben Barker/Thomas Preining. At the end of the first hour, the No. 86 Gulf Racing Porsche was still running in third place in class, but as the hours slipped by, it moved steadily down the order and spent much of the race in the middle of the class. With a little more than four hours to run, the No. 86 Gulf Racing Porsche in tenth place, a position they improved on by finishing eighth in the LMGTE Am class. *Glen Smale*

The Italian father-and-son team, Philippe and Louis Prette, joined by the Frenchman Vincent Abril, competed in the No. 78 Proton Competition Porsche 911 RSR. Having qualified fifth in class for the start, Louis Prette said, "We three drivers in the No. 78 car are all Le Mans rookies. Because we lack experience, our expectations for the race are not too high." As morning dawned on Sunday, the No. 78 Porsche was running in the top ten, and by 11:00 a.m. the car was up in eighth place. When the checkered flag came down at 3:00 p.m., the No. 78 Porsche crossed the line in sixth place in class! An ecstatic Louis Prette exclaimed, "We came here as greenhorns, so my dad and I and our teammate Vincent tackled this mighty race as rookies. We didn't care about where we placed, we just wanted to reach the finish line. But in the end we finished sixth, it's crazy!" *Glen Smale*

Starting from second place on the grid in the No. 77 Dempsey-Proton Porsche 911 RSR were Matt Campbell/Christian Ried/Julien Andlauer. In the second, third, and fourth hours, the team led the field, but the car slipped down to sixth in class around the sixth hour before starting the climb back up the ladder. Michael Ried, Christian's brother, explained that there had been some problems with the underfloor during the night, where some "bolts had come loose." As Campbell admitted, "We wanted to win and we came fourth. It's not ideal, but that's just the way it is at Le Mans. The competition is intense, the rivals are incredibly strong, and the race is very demanding." *Glen Smale*

Team Project 1 lined up on the grid in sixth place with the No. 56 Porsche 911 RSR, boasting an interesting livery created by American pop artist Richard Phillips. Driven by Jörg Bergmeister/Patrick Lindsey/Egidio Perfetti, the team hovered around their starting position for the first five hours of racing before climbing to third place in the sixth hour and second place in the tenth hour. They were the leading Porsche customer team to make it through the Le Mans night, maintaining their second place in class. With exactly an hour to go, the No. 85 Ford GT leader in Am had to call in to the pits for a stop/go penalty immediately after having carried out a regular pit stop. This allowed the No. 56 car, driven by Bergmeister, to close the gap between himself and the class leader to just over five seconds. As the laps unfolded, Bergmeister continued to eat into this gap, but he couldn't catch the Ford GT and had to settle for second place. The class-winning No. 85 Ford GT was later disqualified, thus promoting the No. 56 Project 1 team into first place as GTE Am class winners. *Glen Smale*

Having started from seventh place on the grid, the No. 92 works Porsche 911 RSR, driven by Michael Christensen/Kévin Estre/Laurens Vanthoor, was up in second place at the end of the first hour. From the fifth hour to the twelfth hour (apart from pit stops), the No. 92 Porsche led the class, but a faulty exhaust manifold and the subsequent twenty-minute repair at 3:47 a.m. cost them five laps, pushing the car well down the class order. Estre commented, "The first half of the race was sensational. Our Porsche 911 RSR was incredibly fast, we were very clearly the favorites to win. After the setback during the night, all that mattered was to bring the car home and win the drivers' title." The No. 92 works Porsche finished the race ninth in class. *Glen Smale*

Works driver Sven Müller and two of Porsche's young professionals, Mathieu Jaminet and Dennis Olsen, shared driving duties for the No. 94 Porsche GT Team (US) 911 RSR. During the qualifying rounds, Jaminet said, "I couldn't get the best out of the first set of tires. I simply lack Le Mans experience, especially in the dark, but it went much better on the second set. The car feels fantastic." Fifteenth position on the starting grid in their class was not where they wanted to be, but Jaminet was realistic about it: "Still, we just have to deal with it. Our car is definitely better than it might seem at first glance. In the race we'll be able to set a good pace. And that's all that matters." During the race, the squad of drivers improved their position consistently, but a steering issue hampered them during the night. The car finished seventh in the GTE Pro class. *Glen Smale*

Proudly wearing the livery reminiscent of the Brumos Porsches of yesteryear, the No. 93 Porsche GT Team (US) 911 RSR was driven by Patrick Pilet/Nick Tandy/Earl Bamber. Starting from fourth place on the grid, the No. 93 car was the highest-qualifying Porsche. By the end of the first hour, the team had gained another place. Apart from a short spell around the sixth and seventh hours, when the car dropped to sixth place, the No. 93 Porsche spent the rest of the race in the top four, putting in a consistent effort throughout. After the race, Pilet had this to say: "To finish second and third with two cars is a very good result for the team and for Porsche. Not everything ran well, we made too many mistakes to win the race. But a podium result is still a wonderful success that we aim to enjoy." The No. 93 Porsche finished third in the LMGTE Pro class. *Glen Smale*

Wearing a gold band in recognition of winning the 2018/2019 WEC Manufacturer's Championship, the No. 91 works Porsche 911 RSR was driven by Richard Lietz/Gianmaria Bruni/Frédéric Makowiecki. Having qualified down in thirteenth place in class, it just proves that pole position is not that important in a twenty-four-hour endurance race. The No. 91 Porsche spent the first ten hours in a midfield position, and in the eleventh hour they moved into fourth place in class, then into third place three-tenths of a second behind its No. 93 stablemate. After sixteen hours, the No. 91 Porsche took the class lead briefly, but then fell in behind the lead Ferrari. Bruni had this to say after the race: "Like last year, we were very unlucky with the safety car phases. Because of these, we lost more than a minute to the top on two occasions, much more than our gap to the winners at the flag. This shows that we could've won." After an eventful twenty-four hours of racing, the No. 91 Porsche crossed the line in second place in the LMGTE Pro class. *Glen Smale*

2019 Race Results

Pos.	Car/Model	No.	Driver(s)	Entered	Class	Cl. Pos	Laps	Reason
21	911 RSR	91	Richard Lietz (AT)/Gianmaria Bruni (IT)/Frédéric Makowiecki (FR)	Porsche GT Team	GTE Pro	2	342	
22	911 RSR	93	Patrick Pilet (FR)/Nick Tandy (UK)/Earl Bamber (NZ)	Porsche GT Team (US)	GTE Pro	3	342	
27	911 RSR	94	Sven Müller (DE)/Mathieu Jaminet (FR)/Dennis Olsen (NO)	Porsche GT Team (US)	GTE Pro	7	339	
29	911 RSR	92	Michael Christensen (DK)/Kévin Estre (FR)/Laurens Vanthoor (BE)	Porsche GT Team	GTE Pro	9	337	
31	911 RSR	56	Jörg Bergmeister (DE)/Patrick Lindsey (US)/Egidio Perfetti (NO)	Team Project 1	GTE Am	1	334	
34	911 RSR	77	Matt Campbell (AU)/Christian Ried (DE)/Julien Andlauer (FR)	Dempsey-Proton Racing	GTE Am	4	332	
36	911 RSR	78	Louis Prette (MC)/Philippe Prette (MC)/Vincent Abril (MC)	Proton Competition	GTE Am	6	332	
38	911 RSR	86	Michael Wainwright (UK)/Ben Barker (UK)/Thomas Preining (AT)	Gulf Racing (UK)	GTE Am	8	331	
DNF	911 RSR	88	Matteo Cairoli (IT)/Giorgio Roda (IT)/Satoshi Hoshino (JP)	Dempsey-Proton Racing	GTE Am		79	DQ
DNS	911 RSR	99	Patrick Long (US)/Tracy Krohn (US)/Niclas Jönsson (SE)	Dempsey-Proton Racing	GTE Am		-	Accident in practice

2020

September 19–20

The 2020 season was really thrown into a state of chaos and uncertainty, with the presence of the global COVID-19 pandemic. Around the world, major events were canceled, from football to Wimbledon, from the Olympics to motorsports, as well as major musical concerts—everything was put on hold. It was hoped that the eighty-eighth running of the Le Mans could still be held on the original date June 13–14, but as the months passed by, it became obvious that this was not going to happen, and the ACO announced a date later in the year, September 19–20.

Then there was the question of whether spectators would be allowed to attend. As the date approached, the ACO announced that the race would be held without spectators—a first for this great event! This wasn't the first time that the Le Mans race has been held in September (this had happened back in 1968), but it would require some strategy changes for the teams, as almost half the race was run during the hours of darkness.

The revised entry list included just two works Porsche 911 RSR-19s in the GTE Pro class, with eight 911 RSRs in the GTE Am class. This year, though, the Porsches would be up against four Ferraris in the Pro class and no less than twelve Ferraris in the Am class, with just a pair of Aston Martins in each of the Pro and Am classes.

Introduced at the Goodwood Festival of Speed in July 2019, the all-new 911 RSR featured a larger, 4.2-liter engine, the largest capacity for an engine ever to power the 911. Although power output was quoted as being similar to the previous model's, torque was increased, allowing the new 911 to power out of corners quicker and reach its terminal speed quicker. Due to the global COVID-19 pandemic, the event was shortened from its traditional week of activities, condensed into just four days. The final grid order was decided by means of a Hyperpole shootout on the Friday before the race. In this contest, the No. 91 Porsche secured pole position in the GTE Pro class.

The bigger engine helped the factory team secure two wins in the 2019-2020 World Endurance Championship season, but at the most important race of year, the 24 Hours of Le Mans, all they could manage was fifth (No. 91) and seventh (No. 92) in their class. This result was due in large part to the that old Porsche nemesis, BoP, which had plagued these great race cars for years. Porsche does not comment officially on BoP matters, but this year they stated quite openly in their press releases that they could not keep pace with their class rivals on the Mulsanne Straight. This revelation showed that the BoP handed down to the Porsches affected the straight-line performance of the 911s so negatively that they were relegated to the back of the field.

The prerace grid was a busy place despite the COVID-19 pandemic. Note the empty main grandstand. *Glen Smale*

The No. 88 Dempsey-Proton Racing 911 RSR was involved in an early accident. It was eventually recovered to the pit garage, repaired, and sent back out again. Although the car was well down the field, drivers Dominique Bastien/Adrien De Leener/Thomas Preining finished the race but were not classified, as they had not completed the required number of laps. Here the car speeds through the early hours of Sunday morning. *Glen Smale*

The No. 89 Team Project 1 Porsche 911 RSR of Steve Brooks/Andreas Laskaratos/ Julien Piguet approaches the Dunlop Bridge. This Porsche finished sixteenth in the GTE Am class. *Glen Smale*

The No. 57 Team Project 1 Porsche 911 RSR GTE Am, driven by Jeroen Bleekemolen/Felipe Fraga/Ben Keating, would have finished better than its eventual fourteenth in the GTE Am class had it not been for an accident and various technical problems. *Glen Smale*

A favorite at Le Mans from some years back was the No. 78 Proton Competition Felbermayr Porsche 911 RSR driven by Michele Beretta/ Horst Felbermayr Jr./Max van Splunteren. This car finished twelfth in the GTE Am class. *Glen Smale*

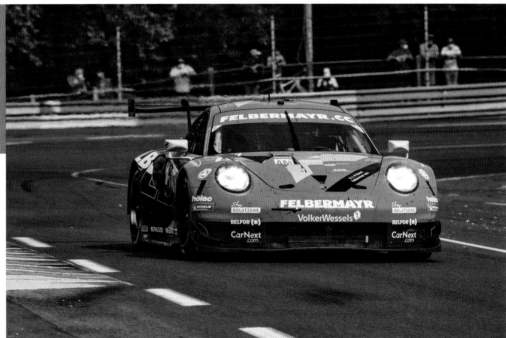

The No. 99 Dempsey-Proton Racing Porsche 911 RSR, driven by Julien Andlauer/Vutthikorn Inthraphuvasak/ Lucas Legeret, passes under the Dunlop Bridge early on Sunday morning. This car would finish tenth in the GTE AM class. *Glen Smale*

Michael Christensen, Kévin Estre, and Laurens Vanthoor start another lap of Le Mans just before the finish of the race in the No. 92 works Porsche 911 RSR. They would finish sixth and last in the GTE Pro class. *Glen Smale*

The No. 91 works Porsche 911 RSR is seen here in the hands of Gianmaria Bruni exiting Tertre Rouge on the Friday during the Hyperpole shootout in which the Italian set the fastest qualifying time in the GTE Pro class. *Glen Smale*

A regular at Le Mans was the No. 86 Gulf Racing Porsche 911 RSR GTE Am driven by Ben Barker/Michael Wainwright/Andrew Watson. The Gulf Porsche finished fifth in the GTE Am class. *Glen Smale*

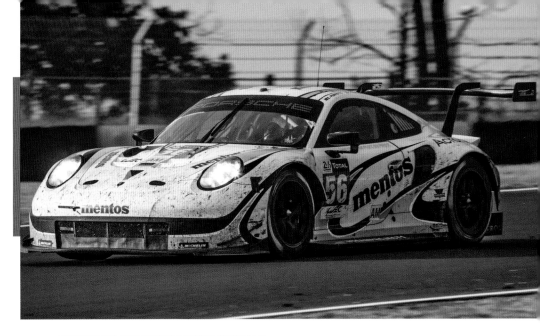

The No. 56 Team Project 1 Porsche 911 RSR, driven by Matteo Cairoli/Egidio Perfetti/Larry ten Voorde, ran a spirited race, but their efforts were thwarted in the closing laps by a disadvantageous safety car phase. Here the car passes under the Dunlop Bridge early on Sunday morning on its way to a fourth-place finish in the GTE Am class. *Glen Smale*

Matt Campbell, Riccardo Pera, and Christian Ried drove a steady and competitive race in the No. 77 Dempsey-Proton Racing 911 RSR. The top four cars in the GTE Am class all finished on the same lap (339 laps), which illustrates how close the racing was. Here the car exits Indianapolis on its way to a fine second-place finish in the GTE Am class. *Glen Smale*

2020 Race Results

Pos.	Car/Model	No.	Driver(s)	Entered	Class	Cl. Pos	Laps	Reason
25	911 RSR	77	Matt Campbell (AU)/Christian Ried (DE)/Riccardo Pera (IT)	Dempsey-Proton Racing	GTE Am	2	339	
27	911 RSR	56	Matteo Cairoli (IT)/Larry ten Voorde (NL)/Egidio Perfetti (NO)	Team Project 1	GTE Am	4	339	
29	911 RSR	86	Michael Wainwright (UK)/Ben Barker (UK)/Andrew Watson (UK)	Gulf Racing (UK)	GTE Am	5	337	
31	911 RSR	91	Richard Lietz (AT)/Gianmaria Bruni (IT)/Frédéric Makowiecki (FR)	Porsche GT Team	GTE Pro	5	335	
35	911 RSR	92	Michael Christensen (DK)/Kévin Estre (FR)/Laurens Vanthoor (BE)	Porsche GT Team	GTE Pro	6	331	
36	911 RSR	99	Julien Andlauer (FR)/Vutthikorn Inthraphuvasak (TH)/Lucas Légeret (CH)	Dempsey-Proton Racing	GTE Am	10	331	
38	911 RSR	78	Michele Beretta (IT)/Horst Felbermayr, Jr. (AT)/Max van Splunteren (NL)	Proton Competition	GTE Am	12	330	
40	911 RSR	57	Jeroen Bleekemolen NL)/Felipe Fraga (BR)/Ben Keating (US)	Team Project 1	GTE Am	14	326	
43	911 RSR	89	"Steve Brooks" (FR)/Andreas Laskaratos (GR)/Julien Piguet (FR)	Team Project 1	GTE Am	16	313	
NC	911 RSR	88	Dominique Bastien (US)/Adrien de Leener (BE)/Thomas Preining (AT)	Dempsey-Proton Racing	GTE Am		238	

Acknowledgments

An unbroken run of seventy years competing in the most challenging endurance race in the world, the 24 Hours of Le Mans, is a magnificent achievement for any motor manufacturer. For Porsche, though, which by the time of their first attempt at Le Mans in 1951 had only been producing the diminutive 356 model for three years, just finishing the race was a big deal. Winning the 1,100cc class in the process was monumental. Through perseverance and ingenuity, Porsche today can boast of nineteen overall victories in this great race, which is a fantastic milestone worth celebrating.

Undertaking the challenge of recording these achievements by Porsche over seven decades in a book was indeed a humbling experience requiring the support, cooperation, and help of a number of people who all helped in different ways. Some assisted with photos, some with race information, others by agreeing to be interviewed, and still others by simply helping with a contact.

My good friend, Jens Torner at the Porsche Archives in Stuttgart, was once again a huge help with this project, providing numerous photographs and information for captions. Jens's subject knowledge and willingness to help were a great encouragement, and without these, my project would have been infinitely more difficult.

I must also mention my long-suffering friend, John Brooks, who shared his vast experience covering this fantastic race for so many years. John also provided many images (including the front dustjacket image), for which I am most grateful. Also possessing almost endless knowledge of sports car racing was Malcolm Cracknell, who was a tremendous help.

A special note of thanks must also go to Joest Racing stalwarts Ralf and Sigrun Jüttner, who were once again a great help with race car information and images. Lucian Sonea at Seikel Motorsport provided fascinating accounts of the exploits of the Seikel team and made available many photos—a big thank you for your time and swift responses to my many "urgent" questions.

Jennifer Hart at Flying Lizards Motorsport in the US was very helpful with information and team accounts of the Lizards' achievements at Le Mans. Such team insights were extremely helpful. I also would like to thank Peter Cook at the Porsche Club Great Britain for his time and knowledge and for allowing me to dig through the club's photographic records for those gems. Fellow snapper John Mountney also contributed a selection of images and I would like to thank him for this and for the hours spent "comparing notes" trackside—it was great working with you.

Then there were all the racing drivers, team principals and owners, PR managers, race engineers, and photographers who spent time responding to my many questions—a huge thank you to all of you. Some requested not to be named, but they know who they are. Finally, a huge thank you to my editor, Dennis Pernu of Motorbooks, for persuading me in a most gracious manner to consider writing the update to my earlier edition from a decade ago.

And then there is the team at home who have patiently put up with a sometimes frustrated author and supplied endless cups of coffee and encouraging words. In this respect, I would like to thank my wife Elke for always taking the pressure off just when it was needed and for believing in my ability to finish the task even when I was desperate. *Vielen Dank für deine Unterstützung und Geduld!*

Glen Smale
Carmarthenshire, Wales
March 2021

Index